LET THERE BE CLOTHES

40,000 YEARS OF FASHION

LET THERE BE CLOTHES

LYNN SCHNURNBERGER

WORKMAN PUBLISHING • NEW YORK

**To mon amour, Yves Chauffaille
and in memory of Douglas Eric Fuchs,
who dressed up the lives of everyone he knew.**

Copyright © 1991 by Lynn Schnurnberger

Library of Congress Cataloging-in-Publication Data

Schnurnberger, Lynn Edelman.
   Let there be clothes: a fashion timeline/Lynn Schnurnberger.
      p. cm.
   ISBN 0-89480-833-8 : $19.95
   1. Costume—History. 2. Fashion—History.
      I. Title.
   GT520.S38 1991
   391'.009—dc20   91-315
                                         CIP

**Workman Publishing
708 Broadway
New York, New York 10003**

Printed in the United States of America

First Printing February 1991
10 9 8 7 6 5 4 3 2 1

"Shoes Stole My Heart Away" and
"Trivial Hairsuit" first appeared
in the *Village Voice*.

Cover photo: Josephine
Baker, 1920s, George Hoy-
ningen-Huené photograph,
Frederick R. Koch
collection, Harvard
Theatre Collection.

ACKNOWLEDGMENTS

Writing about forty thousand years of fashion history took me from the '80s into the '90s, and would have been impossible without the help of the following people:

Peter Workman and Sally Kovalchick share an eye for detail that set high standards for the production of this book. Elysa Petrini's editorial guidance shaped the early chapters; Shawna McCarthy took over the latter half; Lois Adams copyedited the manuscript. I came to this book with a lot of visual ideas and had the opportunity to work closely with the art department. Barbara Reichart conceived the design which was embellished upon by Lisa Hollander, Francine Kass, Regina Dalton-Fischel, Kathy Herlihy-Paoli, and Zoe Brotman of Icon Design with wit and style. Lori S. Malkin smoothly coordinated all of this activity with assistance from Stefan Sadowski. Susan Reinhardt designed the cover. Sheilah Scully brought a sense of fun and a tireless supply of energy to finding exactly the pictures I asked for, and pictures that I hadn't asked for, which were exactly the ones we needed. When all else failed, Sheilah, a skillful photographer, took the pictures herself. Marianne Butler made finding obscure caption material seem effortless.

My thanks to Jane Gelfman, my agent, and her associate, Deborah Schneider. Karla Dougherty was my research assistant for the first year of this project. Karla is a talented writer who contributed "The Agrafe and the Lady" and "The Case Study of Elizabeth I" to this text. Tom McDonough provided solace, some of my best lines, and even his computer.

During the writing of this book, Richard Stolley, Jim Seymore, and Judy Daniels at (then) Time Inc. let me come in from the cold with writing jobs that offered much needed paychecks and the companionship of fellow staff members.

To those who provided work space and library resources: Gordon Stone at the Metropolitan Museum of Art; the Fashion Institute of Technology; the Lake Placid Center for the Arts; the Writers Room, my fellow early-morning roommates, and the Room's unflappable director, Renata Rizzo-Harvi.

To the friends, family and associates who generously shared their ideas, good humor and support, thank you: Len Blavatnik, Nancy Burson, Jim Calio, Peter Cortes, David Ehrlich, John Gabree, H.B. Gilmour, Lois Gould, Donna Harkavy, Felicia Hirsch, Joanne Kaufman, Janet King, David Kramlich, Harry Maurer, Nicholas Politis, Jim Ridgeway, Ron Rosenbaum, Ruth Rosenbaum, Susan Seliger, Martha Smilgis, Stuart Tepper, Hugh Thomas, Dina Von Zweck, Gerry Wallman, Anne Watson, Seymour Wishman, Chuck Young.

And to my parents, Marian and Jerry Edelman, who have always been there for me, and my mother—who during my formative years tooled around town in a two-toned Ford Fairlane and matching leather jacket—for encouraging my interest in fashion.

CONTENTS

INTRODUCTION
The World According to Garb

1

REVIVAL OF THE FITTEST

6

PREHISTORY
Skin and Bones

9

MESOPOTAMIA
In the Biblical Sense

21

EGYPT
Mummy Dearest

41

GREECE AND ROME
Clash of the Chitons

61

BYZANTIUM AND THE DARK AGES
Long Day's Journey Into Light

97

THE MIDDLE AGES 121
Crusader Habits

THE RENAISSANCE 153
As the World Turns

THE SEVENTEENTH CENTURY 181
Louie, Louie

THE EIGHTEENTH CENTURY 207
Rococo Motion

THE NINETEENTH CENTURY 249
Industrial Strength

THE TWENTIETH CENTURY 321
Back to the Future

RE-REVIVAL OF THE FITTEST 413

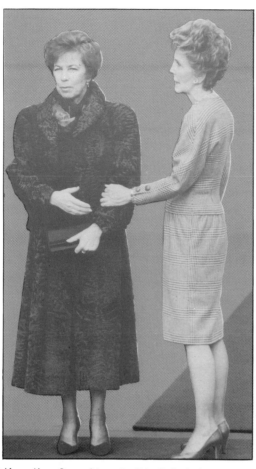

Above: Nancy Reagan interrupting Raisa Gorbachev's conversation with the press outside the White House, December 9, 1987. **Left:** Mother and Child, Mary Cassatt, ca. 1905; **Below:** Lady Diana Spencer arriving at St. Paul's Cathedral for her wedding to Prince Charles, July 29, 1981.

THE WORLD ACCORDING TO GARB

"**P**eople don't talk to me," a priest once confided. "They talk to the collar." What people wear sets a scene, creates a mood, establishes an image. We trust people, we like or steer clear of them, and we even think we know who they are based on how they are dressed.

Would Di have been "shy" if she'd swaggered down the aisle wearing a black leather jacket? (And would anyone have believed she was a virgin?) Imagine if Raisa had shown up in the U.S. wearing a graffito micro-mini. (Remember what a sensation she created by appearing in stylish clothes? Aha—maybe there's more to these Russians than babushkas.) And what would have happened if Marie Antoinette had stuck to gingham? Would France still be a monarchy?

▌**Top:** *Advertisement for clerical rabats, 1952.* **Right:** *Punks in Dallas, 1984.*

1

From time immemorial, there has been one habit that mankind has passed down from generation to generation: Everyone gets dressed. And everyone makes some sort of statement by how they get dressed (even if that statement is that they're not going to get dressed). Whoever first decreed "Let There Be Clothes!" created a complete cultural language. We look. We see. We hear volumes about customs, sex, politics, ego, status, and even the local weather based upon what people are wearing.

MAN MAKES THE CLOTHES

Why do people wear what they wear? Sometimes to send an intentional message: A heavy-metal fan wears leather and studs to communicate his affiliation. To show the depth of their commitment to McCarthy's 1968 presidential campaign, young supporters cut their hair and went "Clean for Gene." Often the message is unintentional: When social climber Stella Dallas showed up at an upper-crust country club dressed in frills and furbelows, she gave away her lower-class origins without saying a word.

Social historians have long debated the reason man gets dressed at all. But whether it's to keep warm, keep up appearances, or to keep your significant other interested, superstition, economics, politics, physical environment, and the cross-pollination of cultures that results from exploration all influ-

This page, clockwise from top right: Generations of women in a family photo, 1905; Barbara Stanwyck in Stella Dallas, 1937; heavy-metal band Motley Crue, 1983; MIT student volunteer working for Senator Eugene McCarthy, 1968; couple in front of their teepee at a California commune, 1971; happy yuppie couple, 1987. Opposite page: clockwise from top right: Fort Worth National Bank's tower in Texas, 1975; Paco Rabanne's mini-dress made of linked plastic triangles, 1967; Chinese civilians and soldiers in Shanghai, 1969; French advertisement for a hoop, 1862; Crystal Palace, 1851.

2

ence what's "in fashion."

Because the medieval church taught that the ear is a sexual organ, women of the time always kept their ears covered. Because the harsh climate of the New World was more severe than they'd dreamed, the first European settlers had to learn quickly from Native Americans how to tan buckskin and weave cotton. (In return, the colonists introduced the local tribes to breeches—a dubious achievement at best.)

What would you do if you wanted the citizens of your country to conform to a unified cultural mold? Force them to wear identical clothes, as the Communist Chinese did. And when a society created something really spectacular, as the Victorians did with the dome-shaped Crystal Palace or the Americans did with the modular, mirrored skyscrapers of the 1960s, it was echoed in their clothing with Victorian crinolines and trapezoidal mirrored dresses.

CLOTHES MAKE THE MAN

But fashion is not merely window dressing. Montezuma handed over an entire kingdom to Cortés because the conquistador wore a small black hat that Montezuma had dreamt about: the very hat that Quetzalcoatl would be wearing when he came to reclaim the Aztec throne. Fashion affects its era as much as it is affected by the times—what people wear has impact on their customs, economics, politics, and physical environment.

Although the Berlin Wall probably didn't come down because hemlines went up, there is an indisputable link between fashion and the "big picture." The sixteenth-century meeting between Francis I and Henry VIII on the Field of the Cloth of Gold saw each ruler hoping to overwhelm the other through the sheer magnificence of his dress. The production of fashion and textiles is directly related to the rise of guilds and towns in the Middle Ages and sweatshops in the twentieth century. And you could say that the British lost the war and the Colonies because the Red Coats stood out like a sore thumb. Fifteenth-century doorways were redesigned to accommodate toppling hats, the long-handled spoon was invented so people could eat over their ruffs, and the Victorian woman caged in a crinoline redefined the century's sense of personal space (only three women wearing crinolines could possibly stand in a room at the same time). And Pat Nixon's "cloth coat" saved her husband's political career (well, it worked *once*).

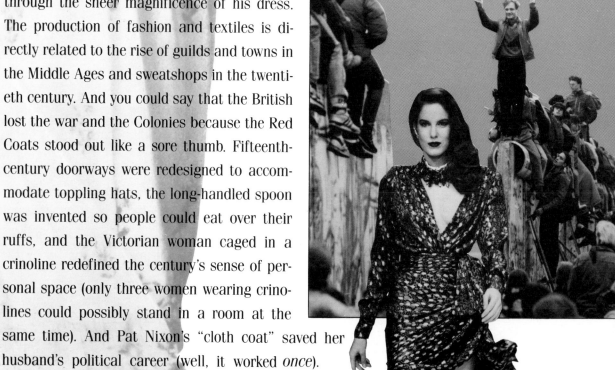

TOGETHER, THEY MAKE HISTORY

Taking a century-by-century romp through civilization's wardrobes, we'll see how fashion reveals (at least some of) the naked truth about history. Are you beautiful? If you have varicose veins, Cleopatra would have thought so. The Mayans, however, were dazzled by crossed eyes. A generation of baby boomers has been raised to believe that thin is in, but just sixty or seventy years ago the ideal Edwardian beauty had forty-inch hips.

Philosophers and theologians tell us that Homo sapiens differs from other animals in that we're the only species afflicted with the knowledge that we're going to die—in other words, that human beings have consciousness. Maybe so. But whatever the imponderables, this much we know for sure: We are the only species that gets dressed up.

Opposite page, clockwise from top right: Contemporary painting of Aztec emissaries meeting with Cortes; East Germans flooding into West Berlin through a passage opened in the Berlin Wall, November 12, 1989; Givenchy mini-dress, 1990; Lillian Russell, 1894. This page: Gown by Pierre Balmain, 1952.

REVIVAL OF THE FITTEST

Proving that history repeats itself, everything old is new again, and you should never throw anything away.

The fashion for slashing on the dashing 16th-century poet and celebrated member of Queen Elizabeth's court, Sir Philip Sidney, updated in denim, ca. 1988, here worn by New York teen Lori Edelman.

Was it the codpiece-inspired jeans worn by Richie Sambora of the rock group Bon Jovi that won Cher's, er, heart? It worked for the likes of Henry VIII, and (above right)Antonio Navagero in 1565.

Linked: Paco Rabanne's metal dress and headdress from the 1960s, and medieval chainmail, donned by Robert Taylor (right) for his title role in Ivanhoe.

Above: The "belle curve" plotted from the 1860s crinoline to the 1950s crinoline.

Too cloche for comfort?: the helmeted Roman legionary soldier, 1st c. A.D. and the flapper in the popular 20s chapeau.

England's most popular "Gibson Girl," Camille Clifford, (inset: photograph by Bassano) and her possible great-great-granddaughter, decked out in Yves St. Laurent's 1986 black silk jersey tube dress, both go for the s-curved look.

Who could have guessed that the "pumpkin breeches" and hose worn by 17th-century dandies (far right: George Villier, Duke of Buckingham, 1616), would be resurrected as a bubble-shaped mini-skirt by French designer Thierry Mugler in 1990? The only question is why. . . .

PREHISTORY

PREHISTORY

SKIN AND BONES

What would life be like if you were the first person on earth? What kind of house would you build? Would you think to invent windows and the septic tank? Would wood-burning fireplaces and an antenna for cable be part of the original design? Would you be satisfied to eat milk, bread, and eggs, or would you whip them together to make french toast? And what *would* you wear? Would it be enough just to keep warm? Or is this the dawn of the eternal question that has plagued man throughout his existence: Should I dress for myself, for my peers, or to snag a member of the opposite sex?

Whether the earth begins with a bang or with the Garden of Eden, geologists have determined that there are a series of Ice Ages when the climate over much of the earth is extremely frosty. So the Old Stone Age Paleolithic Man needs some clothes that will keep him *warm*. He may not have more than one way to skin a bear (which he does with a chipped flint), but he has more than one use for it—not only is it tasty, but the skin can be wrapped around his body. His earliest garment is probably a hide, worn like a poncho, with a hole cut in the center.

Of course, changes are taking place at different rates in different parts of the world, but in Europe, it isn't until after the last Ice Age (100,000 B.C. to 10,000 B.C.) that the sun shines, the ice melts, and gardens are in bloom. Now Neolithic Man smiles and takes up farming and sheep herding. He begins to weave material from his crops (cotton, flax, and hemp) and wool from his flocks (vicuna, llama, and alpaca) into cloth to be used for clothes—and the first loomed fabrics are born.

It is 10,000 B.C. Man is a hunter and gatherer. He has fire, the bow and arrow, picks made from the antlers of red deer, ox-shoulder-blade shovels; and he paddles down the river in a canoe to catch fish. He has been doodling on the walls of his cave for twenty thousand years, and he has a dog for a pet. Probably the most famous ragtrade legend is the First Fruit theory—the story of clothes based on the combination of a forbidden apple and an available fig leaf. Since no one has come up with a better explanation, let's say that . . .

IN THE BEGINNING, THERE IS THE FIG LEAF.

Adam faces the first ready-to-wear decision.

PREFAB: Man learns how to weave by watching the animals: a spider spinning his web; a bird building a nest. In his first attempts, he probably simply crisscrosses twigs, grasses, and leaves into "cloth." Human hair could also be used for weaving, or to make a handsome fringed trim.

CHEWING THE FAT

Early cavemen sport fur, but it's "ready to wear," not custom-designed. They strip skins off big-horned bison, sabertooths, and mammoths—and, in time, the pelts of reindeer, gorillas, and wolves as well—and simply drape them around their bodies.

Animal skins become hard (and unwearable) when their natural moisture evaporates. Today "tanning," or soaking hides in tannic acid, takes care of the problem. But before tanning, people soak hides in water, beat them with mallets, or employ the practice still used by Eskimos today—they chew the entire skin thoroughly to get it pliable enough to make garments.

Left: *It is not until 1966 that Raquel Welch wears the world's first (and probably only) fur bikini in* One Million Years B.C.

DYE, DYE MY DARLING: The first dyes emerge around **30,000** B.C. Blue dye is squeezed out of bloodwort berries, lilac color is extracted from myrtle, and yellow comes from an artichokelike plant called reseda. But in the belief that it will ruin the process, hot-blooded cavemen are forbidden from gazing on their womenfolk while they are actually dyeing fabric.

FIRST BORN

The oldest, most complete skeleton of any erect-walking human ancestor ever is discovered in Ethiopia in 1974. Lucy—named after the Beatles' song, "Lucy in the Sky with Diamonds"—is three feet tall, sixty pounds light, and 3.5 million years old.

How she improves on the fig leaf, we don't know.

MUDSLINGERS

From earliest times, cavemen in South America and Africa cover their bodies with mud, applied in decorative swirl and circle patterns. This first fashion effort is protective as well as attractive—the mud helps repel insects.

Above: *Lucy (not quite) in the flesh, but a beauty at three and a half million years old.*

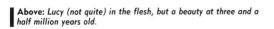

S T E P P I N G   O U T

In 25,000 B.C., the caveman wraps strips of hide around his feet and invents the first shoe. From there it's only a short step to moccasins and, in the chill of the Ice Age, the first boots.

Below: *Cave makeup provides a cover for Darryl Hannah in Clan of the Cave Bear, 1986.*

FIRST BLUSH: Cave-dwellers of 25,000 B.C. believe that they can transfer energy from nature to themselves. They dye their skin red to strengthen their lifeblood, yellow to gain power from the sun, and white to remind fearful enemies of bleached bones and evil spirits. And while latter-day lovelies use rouge to attract, prehistoric people use makeup, elaborately spiraled and crisscrossed over their faces, to repel lurking enemies. From there, it's just a stone's throw to cultivating sex appeal. Soon cavemen are rubbing red-ochre-colored earth on their cheeks to make them rosy. In fact, early man may have discovered copper while searching for its ores malachite and azurite in the quest to satisfy his need for dramatic eyeshadow.

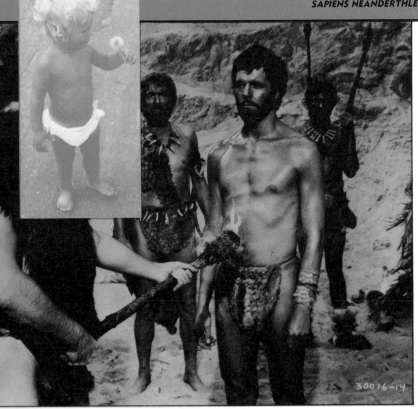

HAZARDOUS TO
WARNING
YOUR HEALTH

To avoid capture by enemy tribes, primitive lovelies elongate their necks, mouths, earlobes, and noses with brass and leather rings to make themselves look like ugly ducklings. It works. They are, however, followed around by flocks of birds.

THE SHORT AND THE LOIN OF IT

A Brief History

Before the Ice Age and the invention of woven cloth, people are happy to walk around naked, covered with red ochre, or sometimes wrapped in a cloak of hide or fur called a loinskin.

But thanks to weavers, cloth begins to replace hides, and after 10,000 B.C. in the temperate Near East, farmers discover that light linen is a lot more comfortable than sweaty loinskins. At first the primitive *pagne* looks like fake animal skin—unable to forget the old ways of animal magic, early men tuft the cloth to make it look like fleece. They wear their new fleeced cloth draped around their shoulders, but the heat of the sun and the need to free their shoulders for work forces them to drop the *pagne* to their waist, in what becomes the first loin*cloth*.

A loincloth by any other name is a *breech clout* (old English), *waistcloth*, *dhoti* (India), *moocha* (South Africa), or *hipping* (Scottish). In the Middle Ages they were called *slops*; the French called them *cache sexe*—hidden sex.

It's a fashion that has endured for 20,000 years, right up to the present day, most popular in India, where it's been around since 2000 B.C. in natty cotton; and under the name of *diaper*, among infants under two years old—also available in a disposable version called *Pampers*.

BARKING UP THE RIGHT TREE? While primitive man elsewhere experiments with weaving, Oceanic peoples of 10,000 B.C. still think clothes grow on trees. And they do—aborigines strip the layers from spongy fig trees and hammer them together to make fabric. Although bark cloth can be decorated, the stiff, scratchy fabric is not very easily cut and so most often is simply wrapped around the body.

Above left: When Dinosaurs Ruled the Earth, 1969. Inset: *Twentieth-century boy in Pampers*.

BATTLE OF THE BULGE: Beauties in 10,000 B.C. find bulging buttocks, thighs, arms, and bellies sexy. To achieve the fashionable bulge, cavemen (and women) tie tight bands just above the area they want to accentuate.

Above, left to right: Prehistoric fertility figures: "Venus of Laussel," Cro-Magnon period; "Willendorf Venus," Upper Paleolithic period; and "Venus of Lespugue," Upper Paleolithic period.

THE SHELL GAME: To celebrate their sex, men and women alike tie a cowrie shell around their waists. From the shape of this shell, men develop a codpiece made of cloth and fur, while women don an apron that's open in the back to expose a prehistoric turn-on: the buttocks.

17

REASON ENOUGH: Besides cowrie shells, prehistoric pinups wear ferocious-looking necklaces of lion and bear teeth (attached with leather strips), and carve mammoth tusks into beads. Anthropologists say that it probably took up to a hundred hours just to carve a string of fifty beads—and they ponder whether the effort was made to ward off evil spirits or attract a cave mate.

BY A THREAD: The eyed needle emerges around 10,000 B.C., made of mammoth ivory, the bones of birds, fish, and reindeer, the tusks of walrus, or even bamboo. Paired with animal-tendon thread, its possibilities are "seamingly" endless, as sewing allows for more intricate and flexible clothing. It doesn't take long for cavewomen to catch on, and so they soon sport shawls and skirts made from stitched animal hides.

Top: *Elk-tooth necklace, ca. 10,000 B.C.* **Above:** *Prehistoric bone needles from British Columbia.*

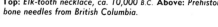

c. 7000 BC

AS THE STONE AGE DRAWS TO A CLOSE, THE HUNTER/GATHERERS ARE TURNING TO FARMING, SETTING THE STAGE FOR THE NEXT CHAPTER OF HUMAN HISTORY.

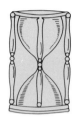

COLD COMFORT: The Ice Ages last nearly 90,000 years—from about 100,000 to 10,000 B.C., when the glaciers finally retreat. The people of the Ice Age are the Cro-Magnons. Although we call them "cavemen," the Cro-Magnons actually live in huts made from mammoth bones, covered with animal skins, or even wood. Huts are snug and warm, equipped with cozy hearths and stone floors.

The Cro-Magnons live on raspberries, wild grasses, and nuts, as well as meat, which they "refrigerate" in icy caves and cook in skin-lined pits. Apparently, their diet is healthy, for they may live to be sixty years old—long enough to transmit their knowledge to future generations (fully two decades longer than their Neanderthal forebears, who are lucky to make forty). And their nutritional habits give them other benefits, too—in these days before toothpaste, Cro-Magnon teeth are all cavity-free.

Naturally, only a few remnants of Cro-Magnon clothes survive. But anthropologists believe that they wore parkas to keep warm, tunics with sewn leggings, and rather classy shirts, with collars and cuffed sleeves.

LOOMING POWER

The first true fabrics are made from flax and sheep's hair twisted and pulled into individual strands and then crisscrossed by hand. This primitive cloth is flexible and tough, but it's not until the loom is invented, around 10,000 B.C., that the garment business really takes off. Since the first looms are very small, early weavers probably have to make tiny pieces of fabric and sew them all together.

The first fruits of the loom? Nubby fabrics in the "potholder weave" still practiced by kindergarten children today. These precious pieces are so valuable that they are bent but never mutilated—and besides, they fray easily. So early man drapes, folds, wraps, or knots cloth onto his body—anything to keep from cutting it.

Bottom left: *Pig painted by Andy Warhol for an RCA advertisement.*

DRESSED TO KILL

PREY FOR ME: The leaders of the pack (and other prehistoric huntsmen) don animal skins, so they look like the prey they stalk. Wearing lion skins gives them the force of the king of the jungle, and elephant tusk amulets bolster their endurance.

But since animal heads (to give them animal instincts?) are hard to come by, they carve wooden replicas of boar and beast heads, add a touch of red terra cotta for some color.

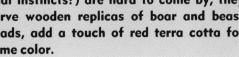

MESOPOTAMIA

MESOPOTAMIA

IN THE BIBLICAL SENSE

t's often asked how two children in the same family can turn out so differently. With Egypt and Mesopotamia we have the case of sister civilizations coming into their own around the same time (circa 3000 B.C.), which almost appear to have sprung up in totally separate universes.

Mesopotamia is the land between the Tigris and the Euphrates rivers—the area that is now eastern Syria, southeastern Turkey, and most of Iraq.

Unlike Egypt, which maintains a tranquil stability for three millennia, Mesopotamia is constantly being conquered by tribe after tribe of barbarians, with new warlike gods, odd customs, and strange clothes. Understandably, Mesopotamians are gloomy and pessimistic and, unlike the Egyptians, never talk of a glorious afterlife. They don't have much in the way of earthly pleasures, either, and consider their more fun-loving Egyptian neighbors shameful. Let's face it: Even when the Egyptians *are* dressed, it's scantily. But through any number of plagues, burning bushes, flash floods, mountain scalings, sea partings, and long-term desert wanderings, the Mesopotamians swelter in thick, heavy wools.

Overleaf: *Engraving of the Euphrates and Tigris valleys showing Nineveh, Babylon, and the Tower of Babel, 17th c.* Above: *Assyrian wall painting, 722–705 B.C.* Left: *Boundary-stone of Nebuchadnezzar I, 12th c. B.C.* Opposite: top left: *Assyrian dwelling, bas-relief.* Opposite: bottom right: *Alexander the Great, Persian miniature.*

The Sumerians are the first tribe to populate Mesopotamia, around 3000 B.C. They invent the world's first writing system, a set of word-pictures called *cuneiform* symbols, made by pressing a thin wedge into wet clay tablets that are then dried in the sun. From the cuneiform tablets that survive today we find records of Sumerian laws, military victories, medical prescriptions—and their basic, straight wool tunics.

Around 2000 B.C. the Babylonians come to power, creating the 360-degree circle, the 60-minute hour, and a prototypical legal system, the Code of Hammurabi. They also understand fractions, square roots, and the eclipses of the sun and the moon; they build a beautiful capital in Babylon. Understandably, they're bored by the simple Sumerian tunic and embellish it with fringe, decorative patterns and elaborate shawls.

When the militaristic Assyrians swoop down on them around 1500 B.C., they're wearing the first armor—leather tunics plated with small, overlapping pieces of iron, which look like the scales of a fish. Like the Babylonians and Sumerians before them, many Assyrians are farmers, and they continue to wear coatlike fringed tunics and sandals. Craftspeople make pottery, as well as decorative objects from gold, silver, bronze, ivory, and wood. They collect the books of their times, huge stone tablets, into great libraries—but the Assyrians will best be remembered as movers, not thinkers: Their talents lie in conquest. They also begin the custom that prevails in Islamic nations today of swathing their women, despite the desert heat, in veils from head to toe.

They lose, however, to the Persians, who gallop into the valley around 600 B.C. wearing—of all things—pants. Yes; this is big news, but let's keep it in perspective: It's simply more comfortable to sit astride a horse in a pair of pants than it is in a skirt. After all, the Persians are great horsemen who develop a "pony express" system of mail, among other innovations, such as using coins for money and standardizing weights and measures. And since they have access to silk, which they bring from China by the long caravan route, they can indulge a taste for luxury that even extends to dousings of perfume and curled hair and beards.

So do things finally settle down into the humdrum rhythm of daily living in this fertile valley? Hardly. Look out for Alexander the Great, who shows a decided flair for manifest destiny. In the end, Egypt and Mesopotamia have something in common: In 330 B.C. the zealous Alexander conquers the Persian empire, acquiring tens of thousands of new subjects—who will all soon be dressing like the Greeks.

3000 BC THE CITY OF TROY IS FOUNDED.

2700 BC THE FIRST 365-DAY CALENDAR IS INTRODUCED IN EGYPT.

ARK OUTERWEAR: The elephants and the giraffes might prefer the bare look, but around 3000 B.C., Noah comes aboard the ark in a plain, loose, ankle-length tunic paired with a draped headdress for protection against the rain. This primitive foul-weather gear is surely no match for the deluge that sweeps the valley—the great flood leaves mud deposits eleven feet deep, confounding efforts to trace Mesopotamian civilizations for several thousand years.

Right: *John Huston in* The Bible, *1966.* **Below:** *The star of* Joseph and the Amazing Technicolor Dreamcoat, *by Andrew Lloyd Webber and Tim Rice, 1972.*

A COAT TALE: "Now Israel loved Joseph more than all his children because he was the son of his old age: and he made him a coat of *many* colors."

Genesis 37:3

ON THE FRINGE

Like the Egyptians, the earliest Sumerians probably wear little more than the primitive loincloth—a strip of fabric tied around the waist or passed between the legs. By 3000 B.C., men appear in wraparound skirts that may be knee- to ankle-length, patterned, or trimmed in the style Mesopotamians love best—with fringe. Indeed, fringe is so popular in the Tigris–Euphrates Valley each succeeding group in power—Sumerians, Babylonians, and Assyrians—will adapt it to their clothing. Fringe will stay in style for more than two thousand years.

FUR-ST: Around 2500 B.C., the Sumerians thread strands of wool through a coarsely woven panel and brush the strands of wool into tufts. The result: a shaggy wool garment called a *kaunakes*, the world's first fake fur. The kaunakes might have four, five, or six tiers of tufts and be worn like a sheepskin, draped about the loins or passed over the shoulder to look like a shirt-and-stole ensemble. Soon, however, the bulky kaunakes becomes more of a skirt, and the upper body gains mobility under a less cumbersome shawl.

Clockwise from bottom left: A Sumerian stone figure (ca. 2200 B.C.), a Sumerian alabaster worshipping figure (ca. 2500 B.C.), and a cowgirl from NBC-TV's Midwest Hayride, (1951–1959) all share fringe benefits.

> "You shall not wear clothes woven with two kinds of yarn, wool and flax together."
>
> Deuteronomy 22:11
> *The New English Bible*

MOPTOPS: Sumerian men generally wear their hair long, parted in the center, although they may be shorn to participate in religious rites and have to compensate with wigs. And in these early days, though beards are common, mustaches are rare—they're removed with copper razors.

Sumerian women, by contrast, love complicated hairdos, and may separate their tresses into four to six braids, which are then combined into one huge plait to wrap around the head. Other women—perhaps less patient—prefer to conceal their hair, usually under intricate turbans that are masterpieces of draping. By 2500 B.C., good sense prevails, and Sumerian women abandon complex styles for simple chignons at the back of the neck, with headbands to keep the hair out of their faces.

AND IN EVERY OVER-NIGHT CASE: Believing in a neat appearance, meticulous Sumerians invent tweezers to get rid of unwanted hair, toothpicks for cleaning teeth, ear scoops, and even a flat bone for pushing back unruly cuticles.

IN FOR THE LONG SHAWL: Mesopotamians are simply mad for shawls By 2250 B.C., both men and women wear fringed shawls of varying dimensions, often topping the four-, five-, or six-tiered skirts that have become the Sumerian's signature. Shawls become a virtual uniform for both sexes over the next century. Men's shawls are smaller than women's by the nineteenth century B.C., but the Babylonian king's shawl is so large that it spirals around his body like a barber's pole, completely hiding the tunic underneath.

*Top left: A whimsical "polos" head-dress on a Sumerian noblewoman, ca. 2700–2300 B.C. **Left:** Ivory figurine, from the palace of Megiddo in ancient Palestine, ca. 1350–1150 B.C. **Right:** A diagonally draped fringed shawl adds pizazz to a 5,000-year-old Sumerian statue.*

BAND OF GOLD: To complement their simple robes, Sumerian women like their gems. They wear lapis lazuli necklaces, gold bangles, bracelets of alabaster, carnelian earrings, and rock crystal pendants. Necklaces are gold balls or dog collars of gold set with precious stones; and earrings, judging from those found in the Royal Tomb of Ur, dating to 2400 B.C., are giant golden hoops. There are even capes made of strands of beads, for a queen to clatter around in; and hair is entwined with gold ribbons, leaves, rosettes, and thin mesh made of gold. Miniature animals are among the favorite motifs, exquisitely crafted in gold, dangling as whimsical pendants or gracing a regal diadem.

Above and below: *Chaplet of gold beech leaves with beads of carnelian and lapis lazuli; a gold choker, found at Ur, ca. 2700 B.C.*

"**L**ike apples of gold set in silver filigree is a word spoken in season. Like a golden earring or a necklace of Nubian gold is a wise man whose reproof finds attentive ears."

Proverbs 25:11–12
The New English Bible

27

They used violet, purple, and scarlet yarn in making the sacred vestments for Aaron, as the Lord commanded Moses.

They made the ephod [outer garment] of gold, with violet, purple, and scarlet yarn, and finely woven linen. The gold was beaten into thin plates, cut and twisted into braid to be worked in by a seamster.

They made the breastpiece square, folded, a span long and a span wide. They set in it four rows of precious stones: the first row, sardin, chrysolite, and green feldspar; the second row, purple garnet, lapis lazuli, and jade; the third row, turquoise, agate, and jasper; the fourth row, topaz, carnelian, and green jasper, all set in gold rosettes. The stones corresponded to the twelve sons of Israel, name by name.

They made the mantle of the ephod a single piece of woven violet stuff, with a hole in the middle of it, which had a hem round it, with an oversewn edge so it could not be torn. All round its skirts they made pomegranates of violet, purple, and scarlet stuff, and finely woven linen. They made bells of pure gold and put them all round the skirts of the mantle between the pomegranates, a bell and a pomegranate alternately the whole way round the skirts of the mantle, to be worn while ministering, as the Lord commanded Moses.

—Exodus 39:2–26
The New English Bible

BY DESIGN: There are guilds for linen and wool weavers, and the art of embroidery is revered. The most popular patterns are simple circles or rosettes. The colors of the day are blue, extracted from indigo; yellow, from saffron; and "Sardinian red," a dye made from the blossoms of the sandix tree.

And from 2000 B.C. on, Semitic merchants do a brisk business in Canaan, selling the color that gives the town the nickname "Land of Purple." The dye, called Tyrian purple, comes from the glands of an ancient mollusk found *solely* in this single spot on the Mediterranean. It takes 240,000 glands to make one drop of dye. Expensive and rare, the use of Tyrian purple is reserved for royalty only.

Above: *Bronze statue of Napir Azu, Mesopotamian, ca. 1250 B.C.* **Right:** *Sandstone stele, Mesopotamian, ca. 2500 B.C.*

2100 BC ABRAHAM LEAVES UR IN CHALDEA, AND A NEW RELIGION IS BORN.

2100 BC PAINTED AND BLACK POTTERY IS BEING PRODUCED IN CHINA, ALONG WITH MUSIC ON A FIVE-TONE SCALE.

DRESSED TO KILL

The Tigris—Euphrates Valley, with its rich land, is a natural target for invaders. So early on, the Sumerians are armed for battle. They carry leather shields that stretch from neck to ankle and, when carried by an army, look like an impenetrable wall of turtle shells. Helmets protect their heads and are probably made of leather. The king wears a special one featuring a false chignon, attached to the helmet by a headband, and it may be made of gold.

In 2350 B.C., Sargon the Great challenges the ruling Sumerian authorities and establishes his Akkadians in power. Not only does he wear the first sandals ever depicted in Mesopotamian art, he dresses his soldiers in huge gold headpieces, fringed capes, and menacing-looking leather bands across their chests—the first military uniforms in history.

Above: *Wall painting of a sacrificial scene, Babylonian, ca. 1900 B.C.* Below: *Silver statue of a man wearing a candys, Persian, 559–330 B.C.*

SWEET INSPIRATION: Around 2100 B.C., the Babylonians take over. They still like loinskirts, but with a difference—as the civilization grows wealthier, decorations grow wilder. Soon clothing is arrayed with staggered patterns of multicolored fringe. More venturesome fashionplates begin to appear in *candys*: straight, round-necked, short-sleeved tunics that may be edged with fringe, knee-length or ankle-length (for ranking nobles). Both sexes adopt the candys over the next millennium, but hers are for his eyes only. Low-status Babylonian, and later, Assyrian women rarely leave the house.

29

1800 BC

YOU CAN NOW GET YOUR HOROSCOPE CAST IN BABYLONIA—THEY'VE DISCOVERED THE ZODIAC.

PRIEST FOR A DAY: Babylonians wear hats with high crowns and turned-up brims, something like modern-day sailor hats. Their priests wear spiraling caps that look like tiaras. Adopted by high dignitaries, the spirals eventually *do* become tiaras, adorned and elaborate; and kings wear cone-shaped leather or felt crowns for important state occasions. Women like to wear diadems, or headbands, around their heads, decorated with assorted gemstones, gold, lapis lazuli, and delicate leaves and flowers.

Statue of a kneeling god, Mesopotamian, ca. 2500–2000 B.C.

GOLD RUSH: Babylonian men powder their hair with gold dust. Since both gold and flowing tresses are associated with power, they might as well combine them for even more strength. And, as an added plus, it looks good, too.

Above: *Golden boy Stephen Boyd as King Nimrod, in The Bible, 1966.* **Below:** *Engraving of Delilah, 18th c. A.D.*

HEADSHRINKING

Samson is an Israelite, a judge, and so strong, legend has it, that he can cause a building to crumble by standing between its two pillars and pushing them down. His Achilles' heel is his hair; and to retain his strength, his long, flowing tresses must be left untouched. Enter Delilah. Wearing gold hoop earrings, necklaces and bracelets, a loose tunic with three-quarter-length sleeves, a long embroidered fringed shawl of many colors, and fluttering a seductive fan, she sets her cap (actually a gold headband) on the poor lug—and he doesn't stand a chance. In a snip, her infamy is secured. Samson becomes the first person in history to lose by a hair.

> "You shall not round off your hair from side to side, and you shall not shave the edge of your beards. You shall not tattoo yourself."
>
> Leviticus 10:27–28
> *The New English Bible*

IF YOU HAVE IT, FLAUNT IT: When you're conquering heroes, the sky's the limit, and the Assyrians shoot the moon in jewelry—the heavier the better—gold and silver bracelets for wrists, upper arms, and ankles; as well as medallions, crowns, lots of rings, and heavy earrings. While traditionally, men have been the ones to buy the jewelry, the Assyrian male is the one who usually wears it, too. After all, what use does a woman really have for a tiara under all those veils? Besides, bulky, gaudy jewelry not only shows their wealth, it enhances their husky, warlike, masculine physiques.

PROMISE HIM ANYTHING: Oil and perfumes are so highly valued in Mesopotamian circles that salaried soldiers of 1500 B.C. receive bottles of scent instead of cash.

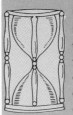

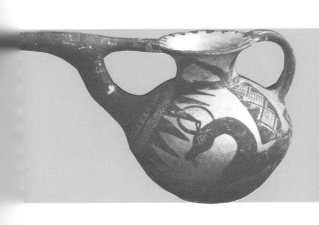

UNDER THE INFLUENCE: Around the fifteenth century B.C., the Assyrians swoop down on the valley and over the next few centuries build a vast empire. Fierce warriors, they loot and pillage—and they appropriate the fashions of the conquered. They love color and ostentation, so they embellish the Babylonians' tunics with elaborate patterns; embroidered geometrics, palms, and rosettes; or weave in gold and silver threads or painted leather. And of course, they festoon everything with fringe, fringe, fringe, and finish off with that all-important shawl. Typical shawls are small squares or rectangles placed on the back and attached to the belt by long cords, or larger semicircles held in place by two belts—a broad linen one and a narrower one of brightly colored leather—tossed over one shoulder with a victor's panache.

And that's just the men. Since women are kept indoors, under wraps, they rarely have a chance to pose for sculptures or friezes, leaving modern-day historians guessing about what they wore.

Top left: *Wall relief, Assyrian, ca. 722–705 B.C.* **Bottom, left to right:** *Ancient Mesopotamian ivory perfume flask; Persian flask, ca. 1000 B.C.; Assyrian charioteers.*

1400 BC THE OBELISK CALLED "CLEOPATRA'S NEEDLE" IS ERECTED BY THUTMOSE III IN EGYPT—LONG BEFORE CLEO HERSELF IS BORN.

1300 BC HORSE-DRAWN CHARIOTS GET SIX-SPOKED WHEELS.

THE KICK OFF: In Biblical times, removing a sandal is a sign of swearing an oath.

Then Moses takes off his shoes before the burning bush, and the custom of removing your shoes before entering a holy place is born.

Moses in a Byzantine mosaic from the Church of San Vitale, Ravenna, ca. A.D. 550.

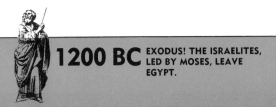

1200 BC IN MEXICO, THE OLMECS ARE CARVING HUGE, 40-TON STONE HEADS.

1200 BC EXODUS! THE ISRAELITES, LED BY MOSES, LEAVE EGYPT.

VEILED THREAT

Engraving of a modest Japanese woman from Arnoldus Montanus's Ambassades Mémorables.

In 1200 B.C., the Assyrians decree that, in public, respectable women must wear veils. Since their men already treat them like chattel, confined to quarters, this is the next logical step. Rebels who go out barefaced can be flogged and sent to labor camps. And in an unusual example of sexual equality, men who recognize ladies through their veils and don't report them to the authorities are whipped into shape as well.

The only women exempt from the law are prostitutes and slaves—and if a prostitute does don a veil, pretending to be a lady, she too gets a hundred lashes.

VEIL! VEIL! VEIL!

Purdah, the custom of veiling women, has been practiced in many cultures right up to the present day; it is even echoed in our modern bridal veil.

• In the Old Testament, when Jacob wants to marry pretty Rachel, he has to work for her strict father for seven years. But at the altar, Rachel's father pulls a fast one and sticks her ugly older sister, Leah, under the wedding veil. All is not lost, however, as in those days men are allowed to have more than one wife. So, in exchange for another seven years' work, Jacob finally gets to marry Rachel.

• Some say that the Christian custom of a veiled, blushing bride dates from the Middle Ages, when the wimple is worn to hide "sinful" hair. (Hair is believed to be the "devil's work," and women who flaunt their long tresses are considered wanton.)

Gloria Swanson by Edward Steichen, 1924.

Others hold that the veil represents the wedding canopy, which in turn represents heaven, which in turn represents God.

• In seventeenth-century Armenia, women unveil only in the dark, in bed, and then make sure to wake up earlier than their husbands to don their veils again. A husband might never actually see his wife's face and would sometimes have trouble recognizing her out of groping distance.

• In 1925, when Turkish women are finally emancipated, the veil, which for years has been a symbol of their inferiority, is lifted. Still, in other countries as recently as 1930, Moslem women who unveil are burned at the stake.

• On the other hand, in the twentieth-century Tuareg tribe of the Western Sahara, it's the *men* who hide their faces behind dark blue cotton veils while the women bare all.

HEAVY LEATHER:

EAVY LEATHER: Assyrian women pad around the house barefoot or wear soft moccasins. Real Assyrian men, however, like leather. For war, they put on buskins, which lace from top to instep, and protect their knees and calves with molded plates of bronze or brass. For everyday wear, they choose low-heeled shoes and sandals with leather soles and a ring for the large toe, painted red, yellow, or pale blue and embroidered with gold threads and gems.

However glorious they sound, according to one Greek author—who, possibly fearing retribution from the warmongering Assyrians, remains anonymous—Assyrian sandals are "second-rate."

BEAUTY HINTS FROM THE FIELD

Like the Babylonians before them, while pillaging and plundering their enemies, Assyrian men know the secret of success: the well-groomed look. What foe can resist the charms of a curly-haired man, with a full, fluffy beard, sporting eyeshadow and some rouge? Assyrians braid their locks and beards to wave them, or fashion them into Shirley Temple corkscrews. They augment their tresses with false hair; oil them and douse them with perfume; and even touch up with a little black dye if they need to improve on nature.

To set off their coifs, Assyrian men wear headbands or hats shaped like inverted flowerpots. For kings, the pots are taller, topped with decorative upside-down cones, with long streamers trailing down the back.

Right: Head of Sargon II of Assyria, from Khorsabad on the Tigris River.

800 BC OVER IN GREECE, THE FIRST RECORDED OLYMPIC GAMES ARE UNDER WAY.

MIXED MEDIA

In the seventh century B.C., the Persians overrun the Assyrian empire, thanks to maneuvering of Cyrus the Great. The next three hundred years see a succession of famous leaders: Darius I, who wins the Battle of Marathon; Xerxes (Ahasuerus of the Bible, husband of Queen Esther); and Darius III, who finally loses out to Alexander the Great. The Persians treat defeated nations better than the Assyrians, but they too are quick to recognize chic. Ancient friezes show them dressed in kimono-style robes with narrow, knotted sashes, and snappy fluted caps—just like their conquered subjects.

Left: *Relief of a Persian and a Mede, found in Persepolis, ca. 500–350 B.C.*

HORSE CLOTHES

COSMETIC CHANGES: In the ninth century B.C., the wife of the King of Israel adorns her face with cosmetics, dramatizing her flirtatious eyes with kohl. Sultry seductresses (and a Bette Davis movie) get a new name—Jezebel.

Makeup has been around for a long time, but Hebrew women are forbidden to wear it. But that doesn't stop the feisty Jezebel who also wears racy jewel-encrusted tunics, a sultry shawl that slips off her shoulder, and a jeweled diadem in her elaborately curled hair. Let's face it: Jezebel has already done so many nasty things—having her husband steal vineyards, go to war, and kill people—that wearing make-up (and sexy clothes) is simply the tip of the iceberg.

Right: *Modern Jezebel Bette Davis, 1938.*

600 BC CONSTRUCTION ON THE ACROPOLIS IS BEGUN.

500 BC A SURGEON IN INDIA PERFORMS THE FIRST CATARACT OPERATION.

TAILOR MADE

Long before Coco Chanel, the Persians wear tailored clothes that are actually cut and sewn to measure, rather than simply draped, including tunics and shirts with set-in sleeves. One wall carving from the fifth century B.C. shows a Persian wearing history's first real coat—a dignified ankle-length topper with a natural shoulder and a smart tuxedo collar—that would be welcome in the checkrooms of New York's best restaurants today.

Women, too, adopt these tailoring technologies in a new, fitted silhouette—a relief after centuries of swathing. Their classic long skirts, trimmed with deep fringe and sequins, are now topped with well-fitted bodices. And to offset the waistline, a sash or girdle becomes the hot fashion accessory, while doubling as a place to stash cash. In the sixth century B.C., it's not unusual for a Persian queen to carry revenues her husband collects from a whole city in a "tightwad": a bag dangling from her golden girdle.

BEAUTY IS AS BEAUTY DOES: In the seventh century B.C., the Babylonians enjoy a brief resurgence under King Nebuchadnezzar, who is also famous for building the Tower of Babel and seeing the handwriting on the wall. Amid all this activity, he still maintains his appearance, and so makeup and lavish costumes are a must for upstanding citizens throughout the valley. But Parsondes, an ambitious warrior, is disgusted with paint and perfume and complains to the king about the governor of Nanarus' emphasis on beauty instead of affairs of state.

Word gets back to the governor, and to teach Parsondes a lesson, he orders the warrior to shave off all his hair and to apply makeup and perfumed oils. He also insists that he take music lessons and develop his singing voice. So remarkable is the transformation that when Nebuchadnezzar sends an emissary to choose a wife from the governor's harem, Parsondes is selected—singled out as the most beautiful woman in all Babylon.

The Tower of Babel in The Bible, *1966.*

500 BC A JOURNEYMAN ACTOR NAMED THESPIS RUNS A ONE-MAN THEATER IN ATHENS.

400 BC THE PENTATEUCH, OR THE FIVE BOOKS OF MOSES, RECEIVE THEIR DEFINITE FORM.

MAKING WAVES: Persian soldiers of the fifth century B.C. want fashionably curly beards and hair. So in those days before marcelling and permanent waves, they courageously frizz up their hair with a pair of hot tongs.

Below: *Floor mosaic of Alexander the Great and his friend Krateros on a lion hunt, ca. 300 B.C.* **Below left:** *Portrait of Doge Giovanni Mocenigo, Gentile Bellini, ca. 1475.* **Below right:** *Allegorical figure of Liberty.*

GIVE ME LIBERTY!

THE BIRTH OF A NEW HAT STYLE

Hats off to the Persians for adopting the soft cap of the Phrygians in the sixth century B.C. Not only does it strike an impressive chord in the hearts of tribes they conquer, it inspires the headdress of the doges of Venice and, two thousand years later, the French revolutionaries' "red cap of liberty." It is worn by representations of the Goddess Liberty in the fledgling United States, as well as by prototypes of the famous statue now standing in New York Harbor (though in the final version, it is replaced by a crown). Throughout the early twentieth century, it appears on the head of the goddess pictured on the American Liberty dime.

Ironically, though the word *Phrygian* means "free" in Greece, the first Phrygians come to Greece as slaves. The most famous Phrygian is the legendary king Midas, ruling about 700 B.C., who turned all he touched into gold.

SAM, YOU MADE
THE PANTS TOO LONG

For all their borrowings, Persian conquerors prove to be true fashion crusaders. Although their Central Asian ancestors and some tribes in Northern Europe claim credit for the invention, it is the Persians who bring the modern world its first pair of trousers. Persian pants are baggy, with narrow cuffs tucked into their shoe tops. And in some early friezes Persians have trousers with built-in feet—the first Dr. Dentons?

For rough riding—the Persians hail from mountainous country and are the region's best horsemen—leather pants made of several animal hides stitched together are *de rigueur.*

Top left: *Little 20th c. warriors in footed sleepwear.* Top right: *Assyrian God-fish, ca. 9th c. B.C.* Bottom right: *"God the Father" in a detail of Disputa dei Sacramento, Raphael, 1509–1511.*

You must make tassels like flowers on the corners of your garments. Into this tassel you shall work a violet thread, and whenever you see this in the tassel, you shall remember all the Lord's commands and obey them.

Numbers 15:37–38
The New English Bible

DID GOD WEAR?

Clockwise from top left: Holy Trinity, *Black Prince's tomb, Canterbury Cathedral,* A.D. *1376; Assyrian winged genie, 9th c.* B.C.*; bronze statue of the demon Pazuzu, Assyrian, 900–700* B.C.*; Sun god emerging from the Gates of the East, Persian, ca. 200* B.C.

EGYPT

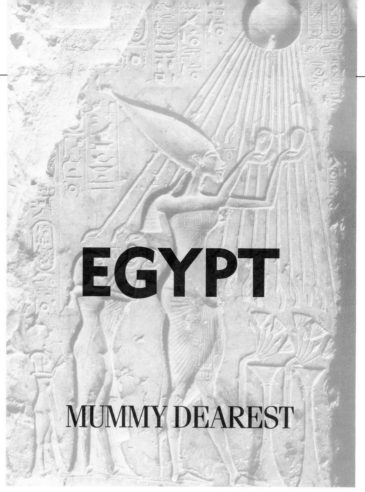

EGYPT

MUMMY DEAREST

Ancient Egypt is the world's first great civilization, born on the banks of the River Nile around 4000 B.C. Life ebbs and flows with the behavior of the river and its rich silt deposits, which allow the cultivation of food in an otherwise arid land. The Egyptians yoke oxen to plow their fields and dig sophisticated channels for irrigation. Master builders, they enslave their neighbors to aid in construction projects, including the monumental pyramids, which are one of the seven Wonders of the World.

The people who inhabit the Nile Valley believe in many gods and the divinity of one human leader—the pharaoh. From the time of the Old Kingdom (2686 to 2181 B.C.) through 30 B.C., Cleopatra's rout by Rome, the story of the pharaohs unfolds more like a season of, well, *Dynasty*—murders, marriages, mayhem, struggles for power—than any divine plan. But the Egyptian religion with its animal deities (the pharaoh represents Horus, the falcon god) endures until the Christian era. Egyptians are conservative and like to maintain the past, the good old days, when the gods ruled Egypt.

A mainstay of the Egyptian faith is a belief in the afterlife that has indeed preserved their world for us today. They mummify their dead; and to enhance their new state, pack them off with a survival-kit's worth of earthly comforts: jewels, clay makeup jars, polished silver mirrors, papyrus sandals, fans, and long-handled umbrellas. These artifacts and paintings on the walls of tombs, surviving through the millennia, help us reconstruct a detailed picture of Egyptian daily life.

The men wear loincloths; the women, simple sheaths. And the basic style of Egyptian clothing hardly varies for more than three thousand years. Of course,

any civilization that can construct the Great Pyramid at Giza—made of 2.3 million blocks at two and one-half tons each—can certainly manage to design a new dress every couple of centuries. But these loincloths and sheaths are well suited to the climate (they're lightweight cottons and linens, draped around the body to allow air circulation)—and more importantly, their ancestors wore them. The Egyptians believe when you have a good thing going, why change it?

But if the Egyptians are not particularly clothes-conscious, they are body-conscious: chests are bared; well-turned calves and sturdy thighs catch a maiden's eye; a breast or two peek out from a gown that may be teasingly transparent. Egyptians exercise and put their doctors to work on the problems of balding, aging, and sagging breasts. Toenails and fingernails are

Page 41: *Relief sculpture from the tomb of Kamose, ca. 1580 B.C.* **Opposite:** *Limestone carving of King Akhnaten and Queen Nefertiti, making an offering to the sungod Aten, ca. 1370 B.C.* **Above:** *Wall from the tomb of Khum-Hotpe, ca. 1900 B.C.*

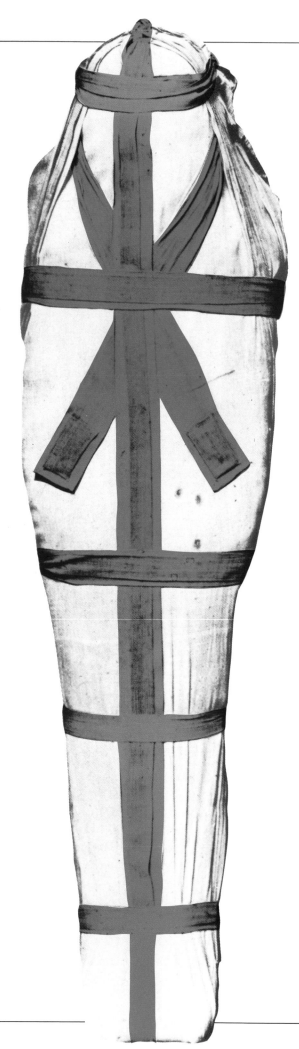

hennaed for sex appeal; oils, pastes, potions, lotions, and perfumes are slathered on lavishly; and both sexes pumice their bodies to make them smooth and hairless.

To offset the simplicity of their clothing, Egyptians don magnificent jewelry. Egypt has more gold than any other country in the ancient world. The soft precious metal is easy to work with, and its shiny color never dulls; the Egyptians call it "the flesh of the gods." With tools much cruder than any modern craftsman's, Egyptian goldsmiths fashion pendants, amulets, bracelets, and anklets; and for the pharaoh and his queen, an assortment of glorious crowns to wear on special occasions.

The Egyptian lives isolated, by choice, in his own universe—even his hieroglyphs can be used only to translate his own tongue. Over the centuries Egypt stalwartly resists the influence of foreigners; but outsiders see the prosperous valley as a prize to be conquered. When the Romans finally overcome the Egyptians at the brutal sea battle of Actium, the sultry, mysterious evenings of Egyptian white linen cease. And the Egyptian empire expires, not with a roar but, finally, with a gasp.

Previous page, right: *Cedar lid of the inner coffin of Sheben-Wen, musician of Amen-Ra, 1570–1320 B.C.* **Left:** *Wrapped for eternity in simple linen, the mummy of Queen Esemkhebe.*

THE BALD TRUTH

Both men and women shave their heads bare. The rich wear wigs of sheep's wool or slaves' hair, generally small and curled during the Old Kingdom but growing larger and more elaborate over the centuries. In the Middle Kingdom they are bushy and long, with the sides pulled forward in two ponytails to form a roll covering each breast. Later wigs feature masses of braids, sometimes interspersed with gold tubes, aglitter with gold powder, or bedecked with golden beads. And in the thir-teenth century B.C., Queen Nefretiri, wife of Ramses II, decides to eschew ostentation for a more tasteful, elegant wig—in a rich, vibrant blue.

More than mere vanity, the long, tightly crimped wigs serve a practical purpose as well—protecting their wearers from the blazing Sahara sun—and they're easier than hair to keep clean.

The poor are stuck with their own hair or sometimes a small felt skullcap. They need the caps to prevent sunburn— since, male or female, they all have crewcuts.

Top right: *painting of a gardener drawing water, ca. 1250 B.C.*
Right: *Alabaster lid of a canopic jar, 1570—1320 B.C.*
Below: *Painting of Nefretiri kneeling in adoration, 1320—1200 B.C.* **Inset:** *glass inlay of a Ptolemaic king, 305 B.C.*

A HAT TO MATCH

Early Egyptians are proud of their wigs and don't like to muss them with headdresses. The most they attempt is a tasteful gold headband, tied around the brow, sometimes inlaid with amethysts or bearing the uraeus, the sacred asp, as a symbol of royal power.

In time, though, headdresses grow more ornate, adorned with plumes and horns, or metal and wool creations shaped like bundles of papyrus that look like candelabra perched on the head. Early kings wear double crowns, signifying the unification of Upper and Lower Egypt in 3100 B.C.; or in the Old Kingdom they might add other symbols of the gods— the two upright feathers of Amon, the ostrich feathers of Osiris, the ram's horns of Khnum, or the sun disk of Ra. And in 1180 B.C., there's the portable crown, a veritable Rubik's cube—a huge, solid gold headpiece adorned with filigree and studded with gems, that comes apart into hundreds of small pieces for easy transport down the Nile.

For every day, there is the *khat*, a square of heavy, striped linen tied back like a babushka, framing the face like stylized hair, trailing down like a ponytail, or squared off in the pyramid shape that Egyptians just adore. Tut, the boy king, goes in for maximum coverage—he encloses his wig entirely, in a snood.

In the fourteenth century B.C., Queen Nefertiti and her husband/brother Akhenaton introduce the wide-topped crown. Queen Nefertiti, however, comes to a bad end—she bears six daughters and no sons, then disappears off the face of the earth—so the style doesn't really catch on. Instead, queens continue to prefer smooth vulture headdresses— the vulture is the Egyptian hieroglyph for mother—with wings skimming their cheeks and with the sacred asp, the uraeus, rising from the top. The vulture headdress stays in fashion until the fall of Egypt in 30 B.C., when it's worn by the nation's last great queen, Cleopatra.

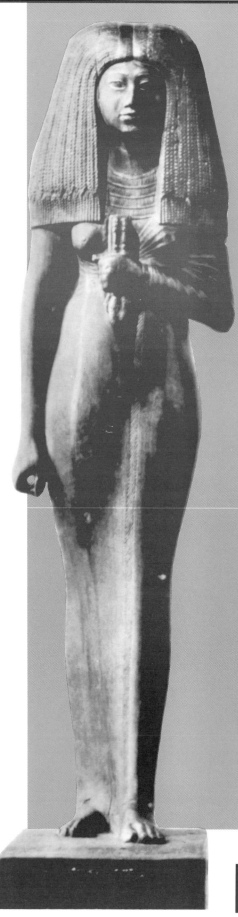

STATUESQUE

Based on an exhaustive study of Egyptian statues, historians have concluded the following about the ideal Egyptian woman. She's:

Five feet, three inches tall

•

Seven inches from head to neck

•

Thirty-seven inches from her shoulders to tops of her kneecaps

•

Nineteen inches from kneecaps to soles of feet

•

Small headed, with a slight, upturned nose and full, sensuous lips

•

Long-armed with no muscles

•

Broad-shouldered, with a handsome stance (No one ever slouches in an Egyptian statue)

•

Slender through the waist

•

Long-legged, with large, squat feet

•

Breasts are available in one of four styles: bowl-shaped, hemispherical, conical, and elongated. Most Egyptian breasts are bowl-shaped. Cleopatra's are conical.

OIL'S WELL: The Egyptians of 3,000 B.C. are fastidious about hygiene and bathe twice a day. To ward off dry skin, they slather on one of thirty different moisturizers, made from animal fat, olive oil, seeds and flowers. These oils are so much a part of their daily life that they're distributed to workers and farmers along with their food.

Left: Wooden statue of the Lady Thuya, 1570–1320 B.C. **Top right:** *Alabaster perfume container, ca. 1375 B.C.* **Right:** *Jugging along: a perfume carrier, 1570–1085 B.C.*

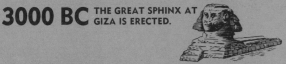

3000 BC THE GREAT SPHINX AT GIZA IS ERECTED.

3000 BC THE SUMERIANS INVENT POETRY, CREATING THE FIRST EPIC TALES OF GILGAMESH.

THE CASWELL MASK-Y CATALOGUE

No sultry Egyptian beauty would ever get caught dead barefaced. So whether you want to stock your tomb or your fore-life personal pharmacy, come to Caswell Mask-y for all your makeup needs:

- **Egg-white facials**
- **Quince complexion cream and rosewater**
- **Perfumed oils, especially frankincense, myrrh, thyme, marjoram, almond, and sesame.**
- **Yellow-red henna for nails, and lipstick in alluring shades of orange**
- **Powdered kohl, or if you prefer, crushed ants' eggs to outline eyes**
- **Plant stems filled with red and green paint for eyeshadow**
- **Stone palettes and pestles to grind eyeshadows and kohl**
- **Cosmetics spoons of ivory, faience, alabaster, and bronze face-cream jars**
- **Mirrors, especially ones inlaid with precious stones**
- **Yellow dye makeup base and dish for mixing with water**
- **Slippers to wear during your long hours at the makeup table**
- **Wooden makeup chests**
  - **Linen for applying makeup**
  - **Razors for shaving eyebrows**
  - **Ivory combs**
  - **Pumice stones**
  - **Rouge pots**

Top left: *Cedar and ebony toilet box of Kemen, 2040–1786 B.C.* **Above:** *Ointment jar in the shape of a Nubian servant girl carrying a pot, ca. 1400 B.C.* **Far left:** *Mirror of reflector silver, with a wood handle sheathed in gold, from the reign of Thutmose III.* **Left:** *Golden finger and toe guards from the reign of Thutmose III.*

JUST THE FLAX

In 3000 B.C. most Asians wear wool, but the Egyptians consider it impure and prefer to make their clothing from linen. But what is linen? All most of us know about linen is that it rumples easily, so you can look like an unmade bed in a chic, expensive dress. Linen is light and cool for hot desert days. It is also naturally white—a color sacred to the Egyptians. The Egyptians manufacture linen from the abundant flax plants on the banks of the Nile, which are dried, combed, soaked, beaten, washed, dressed, spun, and woven on wide looms. And while our impression is that linen is always fine and costly—as in linen tablecloths and Irish linen hankies—woven in different textures, linen becomes "duck," or sailcloth material, and in its coarsest variety, burlap, which is often used to clothe large quantities of potatoes.

Background: *Linen found in a tomb, 2890–2686 B.C.* **Below:** *Wall painting from the tomb of Djeserkaraseneb, ca. 1570–1320 B.C.*

BARE ESSENCE

Throughout Egyptian history, fashions are body revealing—transparent gowns and loinskirts—for men and women alike. But the flimsiness of these costumes has nothing to do with sex; they're simply status symbols: Poor people wear coarse linen, so the more transparent and fine your gown, the higher your social standing.

DAYLIGHT: For everyday, men wear the *schenti*, a long loincloth-like scarf wrapped around their hips and fastened in the front by a tied belt or jeweled girdle. Long or short, pleated (to represent the rays of the sun) or unpleated, the loincloth remains the uniform of the well-dressed, semiclad man.

▍*Priestly costume, 1570–1320 B.C.*

AM I BLUE?

The answer for millions of American women distressed by varicose veins is yes. But they were merely born too late. Egyptian beauties of 3000 B.C. covet those veiny blue lines, and when they're lucky enough to have them on their legs and breasts, carefully outline them with blue dye.

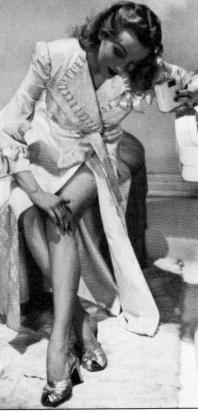

REIGN WEAR (*THE EARLY DYNASTIES*, 2900 to 2700 B.C.): Egyptian history proper begins about 3100 B.C. when Upper and Lower Egypt are united by the Pharaoh Menes. This achievement gives him the right to wear two crowns—the white conehead crown of the upper Nile and the flatter one, rising to a point in the back, of the south—soon to be combined into a single, cumbersome headdress, the *pschent*. Royal clothing in the early dynasties is a new wrinkle on the loincloth: a strip of fabric looped around the body as a skirt, then draped over the left shoulder, leaving the right one bare. In these days before buttons and zippers, the outfit is held in place by an elaborate girdle decorated with a lion's tail—a symbol of prowess that kings love to affect throughout the Egyptian civilization.

▍**Above:** *Relief sculpture of King Sesostris III, 1878 B.C.* **Left:** *Leg make-up advertisements, 1940s.*

49

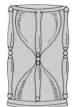

CLASSMATES (*THE OLD AND MIDDLE KINGDOMS, DYNASTIES III TO VI, 2686–2181 B.C., AND DYNASTIES XI AND XII, 2133–1786 B.C.*):

By the time the Old Kingdom rolls around, dress is an index of social class, as well as royal privilege. The lower classes go virtually naked, wearing only loincloths—the old caveman standby—now available in three basic styles. The narrow look, favored by boatmen and fishermen, is tied around the waist, with streamers hanging down in front, barely veiling the genitals. Land workers choose an even skimpier style, with only one broad flap in front; while prudes stick to the modest, reliable diaper—a triangle of cloth passed between the legs.

Upper classes sport the more refined knee-length loinskirt, which over time develops a strange projecting front, almost like a nose cone. By the end of the Middle Kingdom, loinskirt hemlines have fallen to midcalf or even to the ankle, and the bizarre front bustle has disappeared.

Loinskirts are often patterned—with leopard skin, including simulated head and claws, being very popular with the nobility—and a skilled tradesman might wear the tools of his profession to accessorize. The sign of a butcher, for instance, is a whetstone at his waist, tied to one of the tucked-up ends of his loinskirt.

SEEING RED

The Egyptians love to wear brightly colored gowns and *schentis*, though we always imagine them in white— that's because, today, the colors have worn off the artworks that depict them. But the one color they *never* wear is red. To the Egyptians, red is magical, so they ban its use. Redheads are considered freaks; lipsticks prudently tend toward orange and magenta shades. The judicious use of red ink, however, *is* allowed when scribes want to write an evil curse.

INVESTMENT DRESSING: Very early in Egyptian history, women take to the sheath, a straight, narrow gown draped from the breasts to the ankles. Sheaths might have beaded straps, pleats, or herringbone designs; and they probably come in vivid shades of blue-green, blue, and yellow—though since it's hard to dye linen colorfast, white's the most popular, and in the hot desert sun, comfortable hue.

And talk about timeless classics! If Nefertiti went to a party at Cleopatra's in the dress of her own era, she would have been the height of fashion—over a thousand years later.

Top right: *Limestone sculpture of a seated scribe, ca. 2500 B.C.* Right: *Fresco of Bedouin captives from a rock tomb in Egypt, ca. 1890 B.C.*

ANIMAL MAGNETISM: Long before Sheena of the Jungle first whoops, Egyptian fashionplates drape leopardskins over their shoulders to lend a regal air to their loincloths. It may be a bit warm, but that's the price one pays for fashion.

W R A P U P

For those chilly desert nights, from the time of the early dynasties, Egyptian men probably wear enveloping cloaks, though they are rarely depicted in art. During the Old Kingdom, women sometimes top off their sheaths with light shawls, a fashion even he-men come to favor around 2000 B.C. These wraps are adorned with elegant embroidered borders and trimmed with semiprecious stones, clay beads, enamels, or silver and gold. And a king might affect a *haik* — a large rectangular piece of very thin cloth, knotted around the body. Its draping might be so complex that Kings appear to be wearing three garments—a short skirt, a tunic with flaring sleeves, and a cloak.

GO DOWN MOSES:

By 2000 B.C., the first laundrymen are working down by the riverside. Poor people wash their own clothes, but the rich send them to the washerman, who beats them clean with palm sticks and flat stones. There's no soap or bleach yet, to get those linens white. Instead the Egyptians use fine sand.

Above: Procession with animal skins from Beir el-Weli, 1290–1223 *B.C.* **Right:** Laundry women still bank on the river some 3,800 years later.

SUN STROKE: In 2000 B.C., miners cause the first recorded "kohl" strike in history when they fail to deliver the goods on time. Foremen refuse to let workers continue building the pyramids until makeup supplies like kohl, green malachite, and galena—to protect the eyes and skin from the blazing sun—arrive.

"Your right eye is the night bark [of the sun god], your left eye is the day bark, your eyebrows are [those of] the Ennead of the Gods, your forehead is [that of] Anubis, the nape of your neck is [that of] Ptah-Soker."
—A compliment from *The Book of the Dead*

Above: *A powerful Egyptian eye dominates a painting of a king, 1320–1085 B.C.*
Right: *The Steward Memy-Sabu and his wife, ca. 2360 B.C.*

UPKEEP

Cosmetic surgery for pendulous breasts, among other physical defects, is practiced as early as 2000 B.C. Egyptian women are so concerned about the body beautiful that, when they die, they have their sagging breasts plumped out with wax and sawdust so their mummies can face eternity in good shape.

THE GOLDEN RULE

Those simple, all-white dresses are just crying out for some flash, and jewelers happily come to the rescue. Early jewelry is fairly simple—just a stack of bangles or maybe a narrow collar—but from 2000 B.C. on, restraint is thrown to the winds. The last two thousand years of Egyptian civilization see an explosion of ornamentation—a veritable riot of dazzling decorations in gold, enamel, and stones.

Favorite adornments are:

• BROAD BEAD COLLARS. The hieroglyph for gold is a bead, probably the most common feature seen in Egyptian jewelry. Beads strung on gold wires are arranged in parallel rows to form deep, semicircular bibs, tied at the back of the neck, that are worn by both men and women. Since Egyptians don't have precious stones as we know them (sorry, no rubies or diamonds), they intersperse turquoise, carnelian, faience, and feldspar with gold beads in the collars. Sometimes collars get so elaborate and heavy that a queen will need a counterweight, hanging down her back, to keep her collar from throwing her off balance.

• PECTORALS. These fancy golden breastplates are inlaid with gleaming stones or worked with symbols of might and divinity. A pectoral can jazz up an outfit, ward off evil spirits or bring good luck.

• EARRINGS, ANKLETS, AND BRACELETS. These are worn by both sexes. Young boys, however, have to stop wearing earrings when they become men.

• RINGS. Some have pictures of the gods on them, to bring the wearers luck, but others are kept on chains and used as money. If you want to know how wealthy (or poor) your date is, just check out the length of his chain.

Popular jewelry motifs are birds, especially the falcon, sacred to the god Horus; a serpent coming out of a mouth, a sign of power; and the *ankh*, a cross with a loop at the top, which is the Egyptian symbol for life. Another favorite is the *udjat* eye, a representation of a human eye and brow that stands for filial piety. Added benefits: It protects the wearer against illness and can even revive the dead. Not bad!

But most of all, Egyptians love the scarab, a carved beetle that symbolizes the sun god for a rather surprising reason: One day someone sees a beetle pushing a piece of dung and realizes that, every day, some invisible power is rolling the sun across the sky. Then, too, the sun god seems to have created himself—just as beetles seem to be born from dung.

Above: Gold collar inlaid with turquoise and lapis lazuli, 332–330 B.C. **Left and right:** Scarab decoration on a gold bracelet, and a gold collar in the form of a vulture-goddess, found in the tomb of Tutankhamen, 1352 B.C.

BEAUTY SECRETS
OF THE ANCIENTS

Egyptian innovations in astronomy and architecture continue to dazzle us today. The civilization that builds the pyramids surely knows a thing or two—how *do* they lift those two-ton blocks without bulldozers and cranes? No doubt they can give us some beauty tips as well. You might want to try out a few ancient Egyptian recipes:

TO CLEAR AN UNRULY COMPLEXION:

- bullock's bile
- oil
- whipped ostrich eggs
- dough
- refined natron
- hautet resin
- milk

Then apply the concoction to your face.

TO ELIMINATE TELL-TALE WRINKLES, ADD TO THE ABOVE:

- incense
- olive oil
- cyperus (crushed)
- wax

Leave on face for six full days.

And don't neglect your hair: For extra body, add the womb of a cat that's been heated in oil, and pray to Isis.

▌ *Wall painting from a tomb in Thebes, 1320–1200 B.C.*

VANITY, THY NAME IS EGYPT

The best-selling papyrus in 2000 B.C. is "How to Turn a Man into a Youth," which details formulas for removing wrinkles, pimples, age spots, and other blemishes. Even earlier, Queen Nitocris emerges as the Jane Fonda of her day, advocating a rigorous beauty regimen. She recommends taking a daily bath and then, before and after each meal, washing your hands, arms, and neck with a mixture of water and calcium cabonate, using a cleansing detergent made from clay and ashes. Your knees and elbows should be pumiced daily to prevent unqueenly roughness. You'll also need to pumice all that unsightly hair off your body. And to maintain a sylphlike figure you'll want to reveal in sheer linens, she promotes a daily program of vigorous massage and strenuous physical exercise.

Above: Egyptian women literally bend over backwards to keep in shape: dancer etched on limestone flint, ca. 1580–1085 B.C. Below left: Statuette of the god Amun from his temple at Karnak, ca. 900 B.C. Below right: Painting and gilded headpiece from a mummy, 2nd c. A.D.

KINGS HAVE MORE FUN: In the Old Kingdom, for festive occasions, pharaohs don the *gala* skirt which boasts a flounce of descending pleats at one side. The flounce—or sometimes the entire skirt—is woven with gold thread or simply overlaid with gold leaf.

For more casual wear, a king might wear a *shendot*, a loinskirt pleated all around, with a long flap extending down from the girdle. By the time of the Middle Kingdom, upper-class men win the privilege of donning the shendot; and by the sixteenth century B.C., it loses all its social distinction: anyone can wear one.

HAZARDOUS TO

WARNING

YOUR HEALTH

Egyptian women paint their face lily white with deadly powder made from lead carbonate and water.

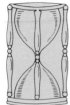

PINCHED PLEATS (THE EMPIRE PERIOD, DYNASTIES XVIII TO XX, 1567 TO 1080 B.C. . . . AND BEYOND:
Around the 16th century B.C., the Egyptians go on an imperialistic spree and steal some fashion ideas from conquered peoples. Not too many—they're too old-fogeyish for that—but a few. For example, the working class now sometimes wears *leather* loincloths, cut into airy latticework to ventilate their thighs.

But in the Empire Period, styles *really* change—by Egyptian standards, that is. Fashionable men cover their upper bodies with the kimono, which is often sheer, pleated, and slit up the front. To keep their robes closed, they add those old indispensables, elaborate girdles, which sometimes get so long and wide that they start to look like loincloths.

Another variation in menswear is the layered look—a short opaque loinskirt topped by a longer sheer one, perhaps with a gaily decorated end hanging down in front like an apron. It might be paired with a short kimono for a snappy skirt-and-blouse combination.

Women take to the kimono too, but with a high, long sash, rather than a girdle, hanging down below their knees. For the unabashed, the top-off is a sari-like shawl that bares the right arm and exposes one beautiful breast.

AFTER-DINNER MELTS: The thoughtful Egyptian host provides his guests with cones of perfumed ointments. The guests turn the cones upside down on top of their heads to allow cooling, sweet-smelling myrrh and cinnamon to drench their wigs and run down their faces. No one worries about which fork to use.

Above: *Egyptian women head for relief with perfumed cones: stone carving, ca. 1365–1348 B.C.* **Below left:** *Wall painting of Isis leading Nefretiri, 1320–1200 B.C.* **Below right:** *Red granite statue of kneeling Queen Hatshepsut, 1570–1320 B.C.*

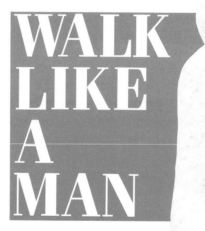

WALK LIKE A MAN

Think of Queen Elizabeth I or Golda Meir and you just might see Queen Hatshepsut of the Eighteenth Dynasty. Her name might not come as easily on the tongue, but in her day she is a household word. In order to seize power when her half-brother/husband dies, she knows she has to look like a warrior. So, for twenty-two years, whenever she appears in public, she conceals her breasts and adopts the ceremonial false beard. Soon she is being hailed as the "Son of the Sun" and "Lord of Two Lands," with obelisks and temples built in her honor. And, as legend has it, it is she who finds the baby Moses in the bulrushes while having her daily bath.

She is the third pharaoh to reside in the Valley of the Kings. When she dies, to show that Hatshepsut is no longer powerful, the new pharaoh has all the beards chopped off her statues.

Strangely enough, even male pharaohs continue to use false beards as a sign of distinction, rather than grow their own. There are three major styles: short and stubby for high-ranking men; larger and thick for kings; and slender and curved for gods. Men use copper razors to maintain the cleanshaven look that is de rigueur.

1490 BC INTERNATIONAL TRADE BEGINS AS THE PHOENICIANS IMPORT TIN FROM ENGLAND.

1400 BC THE WHEEL IS USED AS A PULLEY TO DRAW WATER.

TUT-STUFF

In these days before hostelry health clubs and cable-in-every-room, Tut knows travel in the afterlife can be boring. So he makes sure to pack some board games to do a little gambling just to while away the afterlife. And to ensure a good night's sleep he brings along his own pillow—a full-sized headrest made of ivory, carved with two protective lions to ward off nightmares during his long sleep.

Of course, Tut's too famous to need prestigious credit cards—the boy king is recognized everywhere. But since every traveler risks trouble, he's careful about insurance: To guard against the robbers who pillage the pyramids, he seals up his tomb—with the deadly Mummy's Curse.

Ancient Egyptian game, "Hounds and Jackals," ivory and ebony veneer board and pieces, ca. 1801–1792 B.C.

HORSE
CLOTHES

DRESSED TO RESURRECT

Tut may be just a boy-king, but he sure knows how to dress. Just look at the smart wardrobe King Tutankhamen assembles for his journey through the afterlife.

He packs a fine linen miniskirt with a knee-length, wedge-shaped tab with very tight pleats to keep it crisp all day. A decorated belt completes the ensemble. And because it's trimmed with gold beads (the forerunners of sequins) and topped with a smashing overskirt, his outfit goes straight into evening—for cocktails, dinner, or templehopping—with only change of accessories, adding a luxurious girdle.

Travel is tough on the complexion, so to light up his small eyes and fleshy lips, and to hide his elongated skull (and because he *is* the king), Tut takes his red crown, the symbol of upper Egypt. In case he needs divine protection against shipboard food, churlish slaves, or cancelled meetings, he wears a huge gold collar inlaid with glass, in the shape of a vulture, symbol of the goddess Nekhbet. Since he's young enough to swing it, he wears earrings, too, but only one at a time. Tut's earrings are made of glass in translucent blue inlaid with red, green and white, with just a touch of faience; shaped like hybrid birds (a duck/falcon blend.) You just can't trust the pursers with your real gems anymore, not even in the best hotels. Tut, tut.

Right: *Sculpture of King Tut atop a lioness. 1352 B.C.*

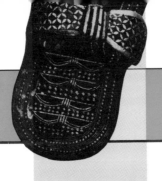

WALK SOFTLY: A coveted palace job? Sandalbearer. Sandals, with a thong between the big and second toes, are made from plaited papyrus, wood, or leather. The sandalbearer handles them with great care, cradling them in his hands. In the early days, only the rich wear sandals, which they remove before entering a house or the pharaoh's court, while others go barefoot all the time. By the thirteenth century B.C., everyone finally takes to sandals, sometimes ones with the upturned points of the Eastern Mediterranean. Tutankhamen, the boy king, has sandals encrusted with gold.

NOSED OUT

Cleopatra VII, the last great queen of Egypt, is famed for her learning and her command of at least five languages. The Talmud records that she debates Hebrew leaders on their differing views of the afterlife, especially wondering whether a resurrected soul, according to Jewish teaching, would wear clothes.

She forms a military alliance with Julius Caesar and a personal one as well, even bearing him a son. But she is remembered best for her doomed passion for Marc Antony, who controls Rome with Octavian after Caesar's death. Hopelessly in love, Antony leaves his wife, Octavian's sister, to marry Cleopatra, and in revenge, Octavian declares war. After losing the battle of Actium in 31 B.C.—hounded by Rome and haunted by the fall of Egypt—Antony and Cleopatra die in a tragic double suicide.

Octavian is left to rule Rome alone, assuming the name Caesar Augustus. As emperor, he finally brings peace to the Roman empire that prompts a great flowering of the arts. His reign sees the masterworks of Horace and Virgil, as well as the birth of Christ. But as philosopher Blaise Pascal says in the seventeenth century, commenting on her aquiline beauty, "If Cleopatra's nose had been shorter, the destiny of the world would have been otherwise."

WHAT A HEEL

During the reign of Thotmes II in 1485, Egyptians paint pictures of their enemies inside their sandals. Later pharaohs have hated faces painted on their footstools so they can give them a good, swift kick whenever they sit down.

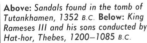

Above: *Sandals found in the tomb of Tutankhamen, 1352 B.C.* Below: *King Rameses III and his sons conducted by Hat-hor, Thebes, 1200–1085 B.C.*

Opposite: *The two Cleopatras: Elizabeth Taylor in* Cleopatra, *1963, and a stone relief.*

THE STAFF OF FIEFS: By the thirteenth century B.C., since everyone's wearing the shendot, kings need other symbols of authority. Now as scepters, they carry crooks, symbol of their dominion over shepherds; and flails, to signify that the farmers follow them, too. Around this same time they adopt the "royal apron"; but, in this case, it's not to show their power over cooks. The apron is closely related to the shendot—a burst of gold or decorated fabric dangling from the waist, often inset with glass and jewels.

200 BC THE ROSETTA STONE IS ENGRAVED WITH ITS FAMOUS INSCRIPTION.

30 BC MARK ANTONY AND CLEOPATRA ARE OUTWITTED BY OCTAVIAN. THEY COMMIT SUICIDE. EGYPT BECOMES A ROMAN PROVINCE.

CLEOPATRA EYES

On the off chance you missed movie queen Elizabeth Taylor enter Rome on a giant sphinx in the 1963 extravaganza *Cleopatra*, here's the answer to the riddle that has troubled womankind since the real queen rode down the Nile: What kind of eye makeup did Cleopatra really use? With these easy, step-by-step directions, you too can have Cleopatra eyes.

1. Get yourself a "see face." (That's a mirror, to you.)

2. Gather together black, green, and gray eyeliners; green, aqua, terra cotta, black, turquoise, and brown powder eyeshadows, along with green malachite to crush by hand; as well as burnt almonds, and the ores of antimony, manganese, and lead for grind-your-own kohl.

3. Experiment with different combinations. For example, you might want a deep Nile green on your eyelids and a blue-black eyeshadow for the area between your upper eyelid and your eyebrow.

4. Have your servant girl prepare a pot of kohl and use it to draw thick lines around and extending past the corners of your eyes.

5. If you really want to go all the way, shave off your eyebrows. Then use kohl to pencil in thick, undulating lines slightly above where your natural brows used to be. If you're less daring, just draw over your own brows.

6. Add a little rouge to your lips and cheeks, and henna your nails.

There. You're ready to dazzle a Caesar, a Marc Antony, or a Richard Burton (twice)*, anytime.

*Or a Conrad Hilton, Jr., a Michael Wilding, a Michael Todd, an Eddie Fisher, or a John Warner.

GREECE AND ROME

GREECE AND ROME

CLASH OF THE CHITONS

Before Greece is in its Golden Age and Zeus and Aphrodite play with lovers atop Mount Olympus, the seat of Greek power is on the tiny island of Crete, sixty miles off the mainland. From about 3000 to 1400 B.C., Crete is ruled by the Minoans (named after their legendary King Minos, keeper of the Minotaur, a monster that is half man and half bull). The Minoans are skilled artisans, who build the Palace of Knossos, a thirteen-hundred-room complex with running water and flushing toilets. They love to dress flamboyantly, and it is here that we see a fashion phenomenon that there is simply no accounting for—women cinch their waists for an hourglass figure, and let their breasts spill entirely out of their cutaway bodices. When the palace is mysteriously destroyed around 1400 B.C., mainland Greeks get their chance to dominate the Mediterranean.

First come the Mycenaeans (*Mycenae* means "rich in gold"), who migrate from the north and stay around to create some exciting history: Free associate on Homer, the *Iliad* and the *Odyssey*, the launching face of Helen of Troy, and the Trojan horse to conjure up a picture of the times. By the fifth century B.C., Greece enters its Golden Age, with the nation organized into numerous city-states, each with its own laws and traditions. One of these, Sparta, is known for its army, while in Athens, the government provides the model for all future democracies. Athens also has the Greek Broadway—home to Aeschylus, Euripides, Sophocles, and Aristophanes—and is the think tank producing the major philosophers: Socrates, Plato, and Aristotle.

Life in Greece can be fun, provided you're not a wife or a slave. While the aristocratic men sit around exalting the human body, the personal search for happiness, and the rational powers of man, slaves do the work and wives stay at home. Only *heterae*, or prostitutes, get to pal around with the boys.

So what are these mainland Greeks wearing while they build the Acropolis, create theater, and consider the meaning of life? Unlike the luxury-loving Cretan, the typical Golden Ager wears simple, draped garments, principally a belted robe called the *chiton*. And while the Cretan female was tightly corseted, these Greeks wear loose clothes that require no sewing and little cutting—kind of "instant costumes." Rather than worry about his dress, the Greek concentrates on his muscles, and likes to display his physique: Athenian gentlemen while away many an hour at the gymnasia, and proudly compete in the Olympics, sans team colors—in the buff.

After the conquests of Alexander the Great, the Greek Empire starts to crumble, and our attention shifts to Rome. The story of ancient Rome is a tale of how a small community of shepherds in central Italy grows to become one of the most powerful empires in the world. At its peak, Rome rules 50 to 70 million people in an area that covers almost half of Europe, much of the Middle East, and the north coast of Africa.

Above: *The warrior from Cagli, bronze, Etruscan, 4th c. B.C.*

From Rome will come Latin, the basis for all the Romance languages; a legal system that provides the model for most countries in Western Europe; the arch and concrete, as well as roads, bridges, and aqueducts—some of which are still used today. The Roman era is also one of the most decadent periods of history—there are so many holidays that the emperor Marcus Aurelius has to cut back the number of celebrations to 135 a year; and fifty thousand spectators a week watch the bloody fights at the Colosseum. Midway through the time when Rome holds sway, Christ is born.

Page 61: *Marble frieze from the Parthenon, designed by Pheidias, 447–432 B.C.* **Opposite:** *Aphrodite, Pan, and Eros, ca. 100 B.C.* **Above:** *The Chimeara of Arezzo, Etruscan, 4th c. B.C.*

The city of Rome is founded in the eighth century B.C. Etruscan kings dominate Italy in the fifth century, when the Roman

republic begins its first incredible spurt of growth. The Etruscans, who have a sophisticated, extravagant culture, seem to have sprung up out of nowhere—historians even to this day remain uncertain where they came from. But the contributions are recorded—roads, temples, and public buildings; the idea of a citizen assembly; the first gladiator battles; and the practice of fortune-telling by (among other things) studying the flight of birds. Etruscan dress seems to be influenced by the Orient, suggesting some ties with the East. Women wear long, close-fitting embroidered dresses made of linen, while men wear cloaks and tunics. Finally exhausted by wars with the Gauls and local tribes, the Etruscans are vanquished by the Romans during the third century B.C. and their culture all but disappears.

Rather than adopt Etruscan ways, the Romans opt to emulate another conquered people, the Greeks. Roman art and architecture develop along Hellenistic lines, and in dress they adopt the *toga*, a simple, all-purpose wrap that bears a striking resemblance to the chiton. But the Roman toga is heavier and more complexly draped than the chiton, sometimes requiring the employment of a servant whose sole job is to help his master dress. And as the Republic expands, so does the toga, until Romans turn wrapping a sheet into a fine art.

In the early days a Roman woman's fate is not much better than her Greek counterpart's, but by the second century B.C., the climate improves, and women hold salons, go to the public baths, attend dinner parties, and root for their favorite arena gladiators. Roman women, too, copy Greek styles of dress and wear the *stola* (also like a chiton, but unlike the toga, it never becomes unwieldy to drape) and the *palla*, a himation-like robe.

Shoes are a status symbol in ancient Rome. Romans don't remove their sandals before entering the house, as the Greeks do, but they do kick them off before the start of a meal. Like the Greeks, they rarely wear hats, preferring not to mess the elaborate coiffures they've spent hours concocting, or to cast a shadow on a heavily pasted and powdered face. But after all is said and done, it's the toga that will be remembered: Trudging up and down those seven hills, all *sheets* lead to Rome.

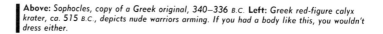

Above: Sophocles, copy of a Greek original, 340–336 B.C. **Left:** Greek red-figure calyx krater, ca. 515 B.C., depicts nude warriors arming. If you had a body like this, you wouldn't dress either.

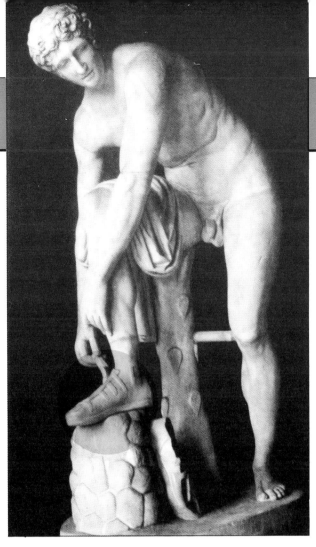

IN HONOR OF THE TWO MOST CELEBRATED BODY PARTS IN GREEK HISTORY:
The heel of Achilles and the face of Helen of Troy

RINGTIME FOR LOVERS

For stealing fire from heaven for mortal men, around 15,000 B.C. Prometheus is doomed by Zeus to be chained to a rock (where vultures feed on his liver, no less) for 3,000 years. The sentence is commuted, but Zeus insists that Prometheus wear one link of the chain around his finger as a reminder of his bondage. Thus, rather inauspiciously, as legend would have it, the first ring is born.

Did Neanderthal man whack his main squeeze over the head and haul her away he-man style, or did he drink a pterodactyl juice toast and slip a band of gold on her finger? We'll never know (although if there was a ring involved, it was probably simple iron). The first recorded wedding rings seem to have been used in the Third Dynasty of the Old Kingdom of Egypt, around 2700 B.C. To the Egyptians, a circle, having no beginning or end, signified eternity; and gold was their most precious commodity.

There's also a romantic theory that the ring was placed on the fourth finger of the left hand (what we today commonly call the "ring finger"), in the belief that the vein of this finger ran directly to the heart. Of course there's a more cynical view: Egyptian texts also suggest that the left is the hand of subjugation. In either case, it's probably wisest to demand a double-ring ceremony.

Top: Ancient Greek statue of Achilles tending to his heel, and the famous face of Helen of Troy, Frederick Leighton, ca. 1880. **Bottom:** Gold rings with pagan religious symbols found in a hoard of jewelry from Roman Britain, 4th c. A.D.

CRETAN CREATION

The ankle-length flared skirt is all the rage. It is fitted at the hips, with several rows of pleated flounces, and worn with a breast-revealing, well-tailored jacket; or for the timid, a blouse in transparent linen—recalling the days (before 1750 B.C.) when all women went topless. And to complete the drop-dead feminine effect, waists are cinched in with metal or leather belts, sometimes with the help of the first metal corsets to hit Europe. In fact, the Cretans are so silhouette-conscious that they solder boys and girls into metal corsets during early childhood.

We can only surmise that Cretan men are too busy gawking to worry about clothes. They stick to the classic loincloth, sometimes jazzed up with fringe or even fur trim, or gaily patterned loinskirts, with a beaded tassel in front to give them a honky-tonk flair. Men do, however, work hard to maintain slim and elegant masculine physiques.

Left: *Throwing a curve into styles which up to now have been straight laced: Snake Goddess faience statuette found in the central sanctuary crypt of the Palace of Knossos, Crete, 1600–1580 B.C.*

Above: "Priest King" wearing a loincloth and a crown of lilies and peacock feathers, from the Palace of Knossos, ca. 1500 B.C. **Right:** Gold necklace, Cretan, ca. 1400 B.C.

EXTRAS, EXTRAS, READ ALL ABOUT IT: The Cretans adore color and have an unquenchable thirst for trimmings. Women's skirts are brilliant red, purple, blue, and yellow—all used in the same garment—fringed, pleated, banded, or inset with panels of contrasting colors, black and gold, and even shining metal plates. And as if these embellishments aren't enough, they embroider everything lavishly with spirals, lozenges, and trellises, for added panache.

Still, both Cretan men and women feel naked without jewelry—stacks of bracelets, finely crafted belts, rows of necklaces, gaudy rings, and dangling earrings. Their favorite gems are amethyst, jasper, porphyry, and agate, as well as the old standbys lapis lazuli and carnelian, arrayed in gold, silver, and bronze. Considering the Cretans' love of display, it's not surprising that cutting and polishing gems develops into a fine art. Settings are ornate and glorious, with lily, rosette, and papyrus motifs; and like their Mesopotamian neighbors, Cretans adore animals—tiny bull's heads or winsome ducks and lions—dangling from a necklace or nipping a shapely ankle.

CROWNING GLORY

Cretans go heads over heels for curly hair. Both men and women wear their locks very long, with masses of corkscrews and ringlets tumbling down their chests; in back the hair is piled high and anchored with golden ribbons, flowers, or exquisite gem-strewn pins. Their hats are just as lavish—jeweled berets and turbans; huge, towering fezzes, worn at a jaunty tilt; decorated fillets; or tall, candle-shaped crowns plopped onto wide, flat brims.

The stylish Cretan's worst fear: meeting a sudden shower or a strong gust of wind.

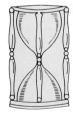

EPICRITIC: By 1600 B.C., Greek-speaking pirates start making waves around the Aegean, settling in mainland Greece. They establish a number of cities, including Mycenae, Argos, Tiryns, and Ithaca; and it is their rulers whom King Agamemnon summons when Trojan raiders kidnap the beautiful Helen and start the ten-year Trojan War. Troy finally falls in 1184 B.C., but when Homer tells the story some four centuries later, he fudges a bit on the fashions. The truth is, the simple garb of Homer's Greece had not yet been invented. The heroes and heroines, gods and goddesses of the *Iliad* and the *Odyssey* more likely wore the loinskirts, flounces and barebreasted jackets so loved by the dominant Cretans.

Dancers in a Minoan fresco, ca. 1500 B.C.

FIRST FOUNDATIONS: The first bra is seen around 1500 B.C. on a young Greek's "maiden form," although it is hardly form-fitting. Worn over her robes, the ribbons that make up the *bandolette* are loosely wrapped across the shoulders and underneath the breasts. But when a Greek woman puts on her *zone*, a band of linen tightly wrapped around her waist and lower torso, it flattens her stomach in a zip.

Women do continue to worry about their bustlines, however. In 400 B.C., the Greek physician Hippocrates, famed for his code of medical ethics, is moved to offer advice to women who want to develop their breasts: Sing at the top of your lungs, he recommends. Since his method is less than sure-fire, Greek women often resort to a more time-honored solution—the padded bra, formed by crinkling their robes around their bodices.

Right: *Bound for glory? Marble sculpture of a wounded Amazon, Roman copy of an original by Polykleitos, 440–430 B.C.* **Far right:** *Bronze statue of Artemis, 340–330 B.C.* **Below:** *Athena, possibly by Antenor, ca. 525 B.C.*

HOW DOES A GODDESS GET DRESSED?

Her chamber then she sought, by Vulcan built . . .

And with ambrosia first her lovely skin

She purified, with fragrant oil anointing . . .

Combed out her flaming locks, and with her hand

Wreathed the thick masses of the glossy hair,

Immortal, bright, that crowned the imperial head,

A robe ambrosial thin, by Pallas wrought,

She donned, with many a curious pattern traced,

With golden brooch beneath her breast confined.

Her gown, from which a hundred tassels hung,

She girt about her; in three bright drops,

Her glittering gems suspended from her ears . . .

Then o'er her head the imperial Goddess threw

A beauteous veil, new-wrought, as sunlight white;

And on her well-turned feet her sandals bound.

—Homer, *The Iliad*

THE SHIELD OF ACHILLES

There were five folds composing the shield itself, and upon it he elaborated many things in his skill and craftsmanship.

He made the earth upon it, and the sky, and the sea's water, and the tireless sun, and the moon waxing into her fullness, and on it all the constellations that festoon the heavens . . .

On it he wrought in all their beauty two cities of mortal men. And there were marriages in one, and festivals. They were leading the brides along the city from their maiden chambers under the flaring of torches, and the loud bride song was arising . . .

But around the other city were lying two forces of armed men shining in their war gear. . . . Their beloved wives and their little children stood on the rampart to hold it, and with them the men with age upon them, but meanwhile the others went out. And Ares led them, and Pallas Athena. These were gold, both, and golden raiment upon them, and they were beautiful and huge in their armour, being divinities . . .

He made upon it a soft field, the pride of the tilled land, wide and triple-ploughed, with many ploughmen upon it who wheeled their teams at the turn and drove them in either direction. . . . The earth darkened behind them and looked like earth that has been ploughed though it was gold. Such was the wonder of the shield's forging . . .

And the renowned smith of the strong arms made elaborate on it a dancing floor . . . there were young men on it and young girls sought for their beauty with gifts of oxen, dancing, and holding hands at the wrist. These wore, the maidens long light robes, but the men wore tunics of fines-pun work and shining softly, touched with olive oil. And the girls wore fair garlands on their heads, while the young men carried golden knives that hung from sword-belts of silver . . .

Then after he had wrought this shield, which was huge and heavy, he wrought for him a corselet brighter than fire in its shining, and wrought him a helmet, massive and fitting close to his temples, lovely and intricate work, and laid a gold top-ridge along it, and out of pliable tin wrought him leg-armour. Thereafter when the renowned smith of the strong arms had finished the armour he lifted it and laid it before the mother of Achilles. And she like a hawk came sweeping down from the snows of Olympus and carried with her the shining armour, the gift of Hephaestus.

—Homer, The *Iliad*

D R E S S E D   T O **K I L L** Mycenaean soldiers wear mini-length tunics edged (naturally) with fringe, but with a surprisingly modest feature—long sleeves. For a touch of cavalier pizzazz, they decorate their helmets with polka dots, crests, and ferocious-looking horns. Major heroes, however, get special, one-of-a-kind ensembles often designed by the gods. For example, Achilles, thanks to his goddess mother, Thetis, has Hephaestus, god of the forge, create his shield. Understandably, this divine couture seems to give him an unfair advantage, prompting bitter complaints from less-privileged, underdressed mortals.

Battle between the Greeks and the Trojans on a frieze from the island of Siphnos, ca. 525 B.C.

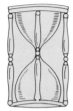

DOR-TO-DOR: In the upheaval following the Trojan war, Greece comes to be dominated by the Dorians, who take over Sparta, Messenia, Argos, and other cities. Since these more primitive Northerners wear simple, woolen robes, their forays rock the fashion world as well, especially for women. Now wasp waists and party skirts give way to the *peplos*—the beginnings of a national dress in Greece—a narrow, ankle-length tunic, doubled over at the top to create a blouson bodice, fastened at the shoulders with long hatpin-like *fibulae*. While accepting the new, simplified style, Greek women still long for their old Cretan and Mycenaean finery. So the peplos is vividly colored, adorned with elaborate patterns, and trimmed with fancifully designated borders.

The shawl is a fashion that dies hard, too. Men wear the Dorian *chlamys*, a simple wrap of dark wool pinned at the throat or the shoulder; and both sexes adopt the *himation*, a large square wrapper or its rectangular version, the *diplax*. Over the years, the ability to drape the cumbersome himation gracefully becomes a sign of good breeding and social status.

Right: *Bone fibula decorated with a figure of Fortuna holding a cornucopia and a steering oar, found in Roman-Britain, 2nd c. A.D.* **Top right:** *Athenian pitcher, 5th c. B.C.*

KEEPING TRACK: In 1194 B.C., Achilles goes to war in a backless sandal. The rest, as they say, is history. Other warriors wear more sensible ankle-high boots, with socks brightly patterned in the Cretan style; or *greaves*—leg protectors linked with silver fastenings. (Later Greek boots will lace, either through eyelets or around double rows of buttons.) And while many soldiers sport latticework or fur-trimmed boots, Hermes, messenger of the gods, gets an extra lift—his boots have built-in wings.

After the war, the Greeks will make leather sandals, with double soles for height and jeweled ones to strap around a feminine ankle. The Greeks will even distinguish left from right shoes. But don't grow up to be a sandalmaker if you want to buy a palatial estate in the country—the job promises only limited earning potential. Greeks do wear sandals on trips abroad, but they prefer to walk barefoot when they can.

Of course, if he *is* wearing sandals, you can find out if that young Adonis of 1000 B.C. is free to fool around—Greek husbands carve the names of their wives on the bottoms of the soles of their shoes, leaving witness to their devotion wherever they tread.

SHOES STOLE MY HEART AWAY

It is popularly thought that primitive man invented the first shoes to protect his feet. This is only partly true. In fact, shoes were invented because they are the one item of clothing that everyone is always willing to shop for—you never feel too old, too ugly, or too fat to buy shoes. And so, for many of us, shoes have taken on very special meanings.

Shoes may have magical powers:

• If an actor's shoes squeak before a performance, he'll be well received;

• For jockeys, it's bad luck to place their shoes on the floor before a big race;

• Witches are presumed powerless against those who wear shoes with the points turned upward;

• Wellington attributes his military success to the fact that his soldiers were the best shod in all Europe;

• Creaking shoes are said to mean that the shoemaker has not been paid.

• An old Egyptian cure for headaches was to inhale the smoke from a burning sandal.

• Three clicks of the heels of the ruby shoes get Dorothy back to Kansas.

Shoes play a role in rituals such as marriage in many cultures:

• Shoes are thrown at a bridal couple and tied to the bumper of their honeymoon getaway car as a reminder of the days when a father gave the man one of his daughter's shoes as a symbol of the transfer of authority;

• In China, a bride's red shoe is gaily tossed from the roof to ensure happiness;

• In Hungary, a groom drinks a toast to his bride out of her slipper;

• An old Anglo-Saxon toast to a groom has the wellwisher raise a shoe and proclaim, "May you fit her as this old shoe has fit me";

• It is the custom at English weddings for a groom to untie the bride's shoe at the ceremony, a ritual suggesting his "opening up" of his new wife.

• And in Arab countries a man can terminate his marriage by exclaiming, "She was my slipper—I have cast her off."

Some American shoe facts:

• Presidential candidate John F. Kennedy, who owned 35 pairs of shoes, understood the politics of clothing. He confided what he described as a "helluva dilemma" to a Massachusetts shoe manufacturer: "I like sexy shoes," Kennedy said, "but in my position, I have to wear shoes that are semiconservative, which conflicts with my natural style. No wonder," he concluded, "they say politics is a Jekyll-and-Hyde game."

• In 1872, a pair of front-laced polished shoes made from bronze kid with patent leather straps won the silver medal at the Grand Industrial Exposition of Manufacturing. The shoes, made by Stribley and Co. of Cincinnati, were sewn together with a record 287,816 stitches.

• Charles Goodyear, who would later give us the blimp, invented vulcanization in the mid-19th century and shoes got a rubber sole.

• The Sandusky Public Library today proudly houses the shoes of one of its most illustrious women—circus performer Fanny Mills, who, wearing a size 22, was billed as having "the world's largest foot".

• But, in fact, the largest shoe ever recorded was worn by giant Harley Davidson of Florida—a whopping 42. (That's five size 8½ espadrilles laid heel to toe);

• The United States President who made the biggest impression on wet beaches was Abraham Lincoln. He wore a size 14.

▌ **Top left:** *Woman's shoe, ca. 1700* A.D. **Left:** *Judy Garland in* The Wizard of Oz, *1939.*

71

DIARY OF A GREEK HOUSEWIFE:

7:05 Rises.

7:08 Eats small piece of bread soaked in wine. Is still hungry, but must be careful about her figure.

7:09 Pecks husband on cheek and sends him off to the agora. Sighs. Looks at the four bare (slightly tinted) walls. Rarely allowed out of house, she prepares for another day at home.

7:15 Summons handmaiden to cool her with huge peacock feather.

7:20 Two slaves massage her from head to foot, before placing her in a scented bath.

7:30 They dry her off with swan's feathers, rub her with perfumed oils, and carefully apply a depilatory.

7:40 While her maid holds a mirror, yet another attendant washes, perfumes, and braids her hair with gold and silver ribbons.

8:00 Her eyes are widened with lines of kohl.

8:05 Sixth servant brings jewelry box from which she selects rings, earrings, armlets, neck and hair chains, and brooches she will wear today.

8:15 Maid drapes and pins chiton around her body.

8:30 All dressed up with no place to go, wanders into kitchen, eyeing a piece of honey cake. Resists.

9:27 Hears argument in courtyard between two servants—delightedly rushes out to mediate.

10:30 Wonders about the meaning of life.

11:15 Wanders into courtyard near flowerbed where slavegirls are spinning and giggling. Asks to join them. Is reminded this is improper behavior—they suggest she ready herself for lunch.

11:25 Summons handmaiden who helps rearrange her hair and freshens perfume.

11:47 Calls for servant to bring jewelry box. Changes brooch.

12:15 Husband arrives, chiding her about the foolishness of makeup. Pretends to agree.

12:17 They sit down to lunch: bread, oil, wine, a few figs. Is still hungry, but must be careful about figure.

12:22 Husband leaves.

12:23 Walks from *andron* (dining room) to *thalamos* (master bedroom) where she surveys her best possessions and thinks about taking nap on four-poster bed.

12:30 Wonders about the meaning of life.

1:00 Wonders about snatching a piece of honey cake.

1:30 Wonders if her hands and feet are still beautiful. Calls handmaiden to ask her opinion.

2:00 Listens futilely for the sound of another squabble.

3:00 Summons daughter to instruct her in duties of being a wife.

3:03 Wanders back to the thalamos for that nap.

5:05 Summons handmaiden to cool her with huge, peacock feather while maid arranges her hair and third attendant holds metallic mirror.

6:00 Fidgets.

6:30 Waits for husband.

7:00 Wonders about the meaning of life.

8:00 Wonders whether hands and feet are still beautiful. Before she has a chance to call handmaiden to ask her opinion, husband arrives home.

8:05 They sit down at low table to dinner: bread, oil, wine, a few figs, small portion of fish (only 320 calories) and beans. She hears about his day. He tells her she should not bother about the affairs of men. Pretends to agree. She is too hungry to argue.

9:00 Despite extreme longing, forgoes piece of cake.

9:05 Summons handmaiden to cool her with huge, peacock feather while maid disarranges her hair.

9:25 Servant brings jewelry box. She takes off finger rings, earrings, gold amulets, chains for neck and hair and brooches, which are put away.

9:30 Maid unpins her himation.

9:45 Wonders about the meaning of life.

10:00 Wonders whether hands and feet are still beautiful.

10:05 Wonders if tomorrow, for some excitement, she shouldn't dye her hair auburn or bleach her husband's hair blond.

10:10 Falls asleep. Does not dream of tomorrow.

Top left: *Greek terra-cotta, 4th ca. B.C.*

STONE AGE

The Greeks of 700 B.C. believe that gems have magical properties and so invent birthstones, much to the relief of bewildered gift-buyers of future generations. In Grecian times the gems of the months changed constantly, depending on the superstitions (or maybe just the taste) of those in power, though by now we've pretty much agreed on who gets what. Since no one ever remembers any stone but their own, here's the list:

- January—garnet
- February—amethyst
- March—aquamarine
- April—diamond
- May—emerald
- June—pearl
- July—ruby
- August—peridot
- September—sapphire
- October—opal
- November—topaz
- December—turquoise

THE SWEET SMELL OF SUCCESS: Like the Egyptians and Mesopotamians, the Greeks use scent as a way to beat the heat. At the games at Daphne in the ninth century B.C., over two hundred women sprinkle the air with perfume; small boys march around with aromatic golden plates filled with myrrh, saffron, and frankincense; and young ushers hold perfume for arriving guests to sample. After the runners, throwers, and fighters have finished, the victorious Syrians give everyone in the audience his very own crown of frankincense.

SERPENTINE: Medusa has one of the wildest hairdos around, but it isn't her idea. A lovely young girl, famed for her luxuriant hair, she is raped by the god Neptune in the temple of Minerva. Outraged, Minerva tansforms Medusa's locks into a writhing mass of serpents to repel future advances; and just to be on the safe side, makes any man who looks at Medusa turn instantly to stone.

HALFTRACKS: The punk look comes to Greece in 500 B.C. when male fashionplates take to the half boot, imported from their Asian neighbors. The leather boots lace up the front and are lined with fur—clawing its way to the top, an animal paw hangs down the front for decoration.

Front of a two-headed aryballus, a vase used to hold perfumed unguents, Attic, ca. 525 B.C.

Above: *Grecian hair designs.* **Left:** *Nike kicks up her heels. Terra-cotta statuette, Greek, 3rd c. B.C.*

IT'S FRENCH TO ME

If they get bored with their hairdos, by the sixth century B.C., women do have a nice range of hat styles to choose from: the *sphendome*, a sort of scarf; the *sakkos*, which looks like a ski hat, complete with tasseled tip; or snoods of various kinds to hide their hair completely. Queens and goddesses get to wear golden coronets or—most regal of all—a crescent-shaped diadem, the *stephane*.

Unlike their Cretan ancestors, who love elaborate coiffures, Greek women prefer simple styles. Hair might be tied up in back through a fillet, a band across the brow; or, by the fifth century B.C., parted in the center and drawn back in a bun-like *chignon*.

BLUNT CUT: Baldness is unknown in ancient Greece; virtually all the men are blessed with thick, luxuriant heads of hair. But flowing tresses can easily be grabbed by an opponent in battle; and by 1000 B.C., wars with Persia become so frequent that Greek men adopt a cropped "army" cut that remains in vogue for almost 130 years. By the seventh century B.C., long hair comes back at last, hanging loose from a fillet around the brow or looped up in a club-shaped ponytail for masculine appeal. And by the fifth century B.C., men's hair has gotten *so* long that they have to plait it up and wrap it around "Heidi" style, or else tuck up all the ends in a halo-like roll.

As hair grows, however, beards begin to shrink. Early beards are long and pointed, but by the fifth century B.C., a clean-shaven chin is the rule. Until 600 B.C., no one wears a hat in Greece except on long journeys for protection against the sun. Then the *pilos*—a round or pointed fez, sometimes with a narrow brim—and the *petasos*, the first cowboy hat, are born. Made of felt or straw, with a very broad brim, the petasos has a flat or pointed crown, and as an added benefit, a neck cord so that city strollers can leave it resting on their shoulders, Annie Oakley style. It is later adopted not only by bronco busters but also for everyday wear by Roman Catholic cardinals.

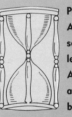

POSITIVE IONS: Around 900 B.C., the sophisticated Hellenes, who settle in Asia Minor and adjacent islands, begin to make their presence felt. The most important of these groups are the Ionians, who introduce the elegant drapery that we think of as "classical" dress. Perfect complement to the individualist philosophies of the coming Golden Age, the *chiton* is a simple piece of cloth that looks different on everyone, depending on how it is folded, pinned, and girdled.

Not to be outdone, the Dorians quickly widen the peplos into their own version of the chiton. To give it a little more style, they expand its blouson top, the *apotygma*, into a baggy fold (called the *kolpos*) that might reach as far as the hips. Unfortunately—except for, a brief stretch in fifth century B.C., when it is revived in a flurry of reactionary patriotism—even with these innovations, the Doric chiton continues to be seen as dowdy, worn only by yokels in the unfashionable hinterlands.

Top right: *Bas-relief of Hermes, from Thasos, ca. 480 B.C.* Left top: *Red-figure dish, 5th c. B.C.;* Left, bottom: *The Rampin Head, found on the Acropolis of Athens, ca. 550 B.C.*

75

550 BC SIDDHARTHA, THE FOUN- DER OF BUDDHISM IS BORN.

550 BC NEBUCHADNEZZAR II BUILDS THE HANGING GARDENS OF BABYLON.

PINSTRIKE: After a disastrous battle in the sixth century B.C., only one soldier returns alive to Athens. The newly widowed wives and girlfriends are so upset that they pull off their long golden fibulae and stab the survivor to death. Fibulae are outlawed from that day on, and so the next bearer of bad tidings must be stoned.

Worse yet, the killers are sentenced to abandon their Doric dress and wear the new Ionic chitons as punishment for their crime. But the style catches on in Athens and soon sweeps the country, becoming the standard costume for men and women alike. Over time it grows more complicated, with shirred sleeve and shoulder seams; a complex of crisscrossed belts and an "empire" waistline—and for a while even takes on the droopy Doric *apotygma*. Despite all its fussiness, it remains the ultimate in chic for more than four hundred years and, after the decline of Greece, is copied by the Romans.

ANATOMY OF A GREEK

The Greeks idealize the human form, especially the male body; and not surprisingly, they spend a lot of time working out its most harmonious proportions. Greek statues show us that:

• The Greek neck should be long. A powerful neck is supposed to promise long life.

• The second toe should be as long as the first—a definite improvement on reality. The Greeks have a special word just for "beautiful ankles"; and Aspasia, the mistress of the Golden Age ruler Pericles, is renowned for the shapeliness of her feet.

• A man should be six times as long as his foot, a woman eight times as long. Apollo (in a statue, anyway), stands seven and one-half times the size of his head. The width of his neck should be half that of his head and of his shoulders, twice the length of his head.

Fortunately, though, if you flunk the test for harmony, you can work on achieving the other ideals: rhythm and balance.

Above: Engraved gold fibulae, Greek, 8th c. B.C.; bottom, Greek, 7th c. B.C. Right: Apollo Sauroctonous, Praxiteles, ca. 330 B.C.

Above: *Hollywood's idea of a well-scrubbed hetaera.* **Right:** Charioteer of Delphi, ca. 475 *B.C.*

DRESSED TO THRILL

FREE ASSOCIATION

Girls just want to have fun, but the *hetaerae* make it a business—and a way of life. These glorious-looking ladies daub heavy white lead paint on their faces and rouge their lips. Like Eastern geishas they know music, poetry, philosophy; and they can dance. Most of the time they go naked to please their clientele, but on occasion they wear vibrant purple chitons with carefully placed bandages to make waists small and bosoms large. Cleanliness may be next to godliness, but it's also good for business—the hetaerae always have neat, clean nails, and well-curled hair.

Unlike Greek wives, hetaerae enjoy the respect of men, move about freely, and may even own property. But that doesn't mean they don't need their feminine wiles. Once, Phryne, a famous Greek courtesan, is involved in a trial in which her attorney fears the verdict will go against her. Resorting to extreme measures, he pulls away her gown—revealing his client in all her naked beauty. The judges dismiss the case, believing that such a perfect body could not house anything less than a perfect soul.

HAZARDOUS TO YOUR HEALTH

WARNING

It's not enough to win the race, it's how you play the game. Though most Greek men wear their chitons short, charioteers traditionally wear ankle-length robes that add a measure of danger to their job—they have to keep their chitons from getting caught in the whirling chariot wheels.

77

500 BC A GREEK ANATOMIST DISCOVERS THE DIFFERENCE BETWEEN VEINS AND ARTERIES, AND THE CONNECTION BETWEEN SENSES AND THE BRAIN.

497 BC PYTHAGORAS, HE OF THE THEOREM, DIES.

SPINNING YARNS

The Greeks and Romans develop a sophisticated textile industry, and consequently, fashion and clothing technology find their way into mythology and literature.

As part of his plan to punish mankind for Prometheus's theft of fire, Zeus commissions the creation of Pandora. Made by Hephaestus, god of the forge, Pandora is exquisitely beautiful, but right away, she needs some clothes. So Athena gives her a white robe and a flowing veil for her face, as well as a crown of fresh flowers. Her tresses are bound with a fillet of gold wire adorned with animal shapes. It's a fairly lavish wardrobe—the first recorded coutureware—especially compared to the Biblical Eve's.

Like Eve, Pandora gets many gifts—including language from the god Hermes and charm from Aphrodite—but lacking good sense, she too succumbs to temptation. When Zeus gives her a box that she's forbidden to open, she sneaks a quick peek—and releases a flood of calamities on the world. Fortunately, though, she slams down the lid before all the contents escape and so preserves for mankind one last thing—hope.

Hercules, the great hero, has met every kind of danger, but he is finally undone by his wife, Deianira. Despite her pleas, he allows a centaur, Nessus, to carry her over a river, and on the opposite bank, Nessus tries to rape her. Hercules stops him by wounding him with an arrow, but Nessus continues to chase Deianira, sending her his bloody robe as a reminder of his ardor. Later, when Hercules starts cheating on Deianira, she plots his death in revenge. The murder weapon? The bloody robe, which she sends to Hercules; it poisons him as soon as he puts it on.

While Ulysses is off fighting the Trojan War, his neighbors begin to covet his sumptuous house and rich lands. So they begin to

pressure his wife, Penelope, to remarry. Penelope believes that Ulysses is alive, but fearing that the suitors will take the house by force, pretends to go along with the plan. She claims that she will choose a new husband as soon as she finishes weaving a shroud for Ulysses's father Laertes; but each day she weaves a section of the shroud, then each night unravels what she's done, keeping the suitors at bay until Ulysses finally comes home to defend her—twenty years later!

After hearing about the skills of a mortal, Arachne, the goddess Minerva challenges her to a contest of spinning and weaving. Minerva creates a tapestry showing the twelve gods of Greece enthroned on Mount Olympus, with warnings about their power. The word *Danger* is woven into the four corners of the tapestry, and Minerva depicts herself in a warrior's helmet, armed with a spear. Arachne, however, overlooks these signs and weaves a picture of the gods' seductions of mortal girls. The work is so fine that Minerva is filled with jealousy and punishes Arachne by turning her into a spider, fated to spin webs forever.

Both the Greeks and the Romans hold that there are three fates—Clotho, Lachesis, and Atropos—who control human destiny. Clotho is the one who spins a thread to represent each person's life. Lachesis determines the length of each thread, the measure of longevity. And death comes in a snip, when Atropos cuts the strand.

CLOTHES PRESS:

In *Lysistrata*, Aristophanes's play of 411 B.C., normally powerless Greek wives unite to stop a war. Deciding that withholding sex is their only strategy, they plot to turn up the heat:

> *Why, they're the very things I*
> *hope will save us.*
> *Your saffron dresses and your*
> *finical shoes.*
> *Your paints, and perfumes,*
> *and your robes of gauze.*

Style saves the day. In the critical scene, the husbands appear onstage with long poles under their robes and uncomfortably contract to make peace.

Opposite, top: An epinetron, a ceramic cover for a woman's thigh while she spins wool. This one decorated with a red-figure scene of Alcestis in her bridal chamber, ca. 425 B.C. **Left:** *Greek women spin cloth and tales of yore, Attic black-figure vase, ca. 560 B.C.* **Above:** *Illustration for "Lysistrata," Beardsley, ca. 1896 A.D.*

470 BC SOCRATES IS BORN.

451 BC ROME SENDS THREE SENATORS TO ATHENS TO STUDY THE LAWS OF SOLON.

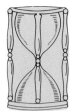

METALMORPHOSIS: With Greece in decline, the Etruscans overrun the Mediterranean. Master metalworkers, they quickly discover lapis lazuli, and the brilliant blue stone soon becomes so popular that they all but exhaust the supply. So an enterprising jeweler tries taking azurite or malachite and baking it on soapstone to form a bright blue glaze. The result is faience, well-known in nearby Mesopotamia and Egypt, but passed off by the Etruscans as lapis, thus producing the world's first fake jewelry.

While the Etruscans are famed for their magnificent bronze artifacts, many of which survive today, they also adore gold. Around 500 B.C., they invent granulation—a sophisticated process of melting down the metal into tiny globules, which are then soldered onto breastplates, robes, and tunics in patterns so elaborate that they look like embroidery. The Etruscans also fashion gold into necklaces, disk earrings, spiral bracelets, coronets, and fancy fibulae, as well as *bulla*—beautifully decorated lockets worn by men and women alike. Later, the Romans adopt the *bulla* as a symbol of citizenship, giving it at birth to each aristocrat's sons. The boys can only wear them until they reach sixteen, when with great ceremony, they dedicate them to the household golds.

Above left: Ornamental gold disk containing amulets, worn as a pendant, here depicts Venus between Adonis and Eros, Etruscan, 4th c. B.C. Right: "Cowboy from Murlo," Etruscan terra-cotta, ca. 575 B.C.

BRONZE STARS: The Etruscans put their metallurgic expertise to a wide range of uses, including protection from puddles. In the fifth century B.C., long before the first rubbers, they invent the rainboot—in bronze. Presumably the Etruscans have very strong legs.

Their sunny-day shoes, however, are just as uncomfortable, with the crunching pointed toes of the Near East. The backs might rise in a peak to midcalf, attached with straps to a shin-high tongue. But being expert cobblers, they make sensible shoes, too, from sexy sandals to boots that lace. Favorite footwear colors are blue, black, and especially red—though often the gaily colored pairs don't match.

❚ *Drinking cup in the shape of a shoe.*

M I X O L O G Y

Like their culture, Etruscan dress draws on sources as mysterious as their origins—a mix of Cretan, Greek, and Near Eastern influences. Etruscan men wear tunics resembling the Greek *chiton*; while women show more Eastern flash, in sexier sewn and fitted, body-hugging gowns, with flounces or pleats at the hem. Female dancers depicted in wall paintings of tombs often wear sheer skirts and blouses, while males perform nude or draped in the *tebenna*—a half-circular wrap like the squared-off Greek *himation* that becomes the standard outerwear for both sexes.

Like the Cretans before them, Etruscans revel in vivid colors and array themselves in polka dots, exotic prints, or even plaids. Their tunics and tebennas are trimmed with *clavi*, or decorative borders, which the Romans will later adopt on their tunics and togas. Another Cretan influence is the Etruscans' flair with hair, which they pin and curl into elaborate coiffures. Women's tresses are often styled in one or more braids and extended with hairpieces to reach the ankle.

To protect their coifs from the weather, Etruscan men wear the Greek *petasos*, while women huddle under their tebennas; though either sex might affect a *tutulus*—a uniquely Etruscan creation—a curious pointed hat with an upturned brim, sometimes adorned with a coronet.

ROME

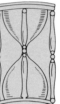

GOLDEN ANNIVERSARIES

In 450 B.C., the Romans have little gold, and unlike the Etruscans, cannot afford to buy it. So, rather than flaunt their deficit, they ban gold altogether—only high government officials and plutocrats (those wealthy enough to own horses) can wear golden rings. Others must content themselves with iron ones for sealing letters and documents; as must Roman brides, whose rings are often engraved with portraits of the wedding couple as some small consolation.

The gold ban does not extend to royalty, of course. Early Roman rulers wear diadems shaped like wreaths of laurel leaves, exquisitely rendered in gold. In the first century A.D., Nero will drop the simple, pastoral wreath for a grander crown, the *corona radiata*, with golden points like the rings of the sun.

A SOLDIER'S STORY: In 392 B.C., the Romans defeat the Etruscans and begin to consolidate an empire that eventually embraces Northern Africa, Western Europe extending to Britain, and the Near East as far as Mesopotamia. Naturally stories about the Roman foot soldier are, well, legion. Since he has a vast area to conquer, his armor has to come in a portable easy-to-pack design; it folds neatly, and weighs only about twelve pounds. His hinged metal tunic, the *cuirass*, is molded to his body and his domed iron helmet, with wide cheeks to save his face, projects down the back to protect his neck and shoulders. It comes with a hinged handle for easy carrying. His thick leather, iron-nail-studded sandals, are secured by thongs tied to his shins; and he carries a tall, rectangular shield that is curved horizontally to fully protect his body.

For cold-weather battles, he wears calf-length trousers, following the example of the Gauls, though in Rome this alien garb is disdained. And around 400 B.C., he learns to tie one on—Roman soldiers sport the first recorded scarves in history, for protection on frigid forays.

Top: *The Roman Colosseum,* **Left:** *Gold diadem of oak leaves, Etruscan, 4th c. B.C.*

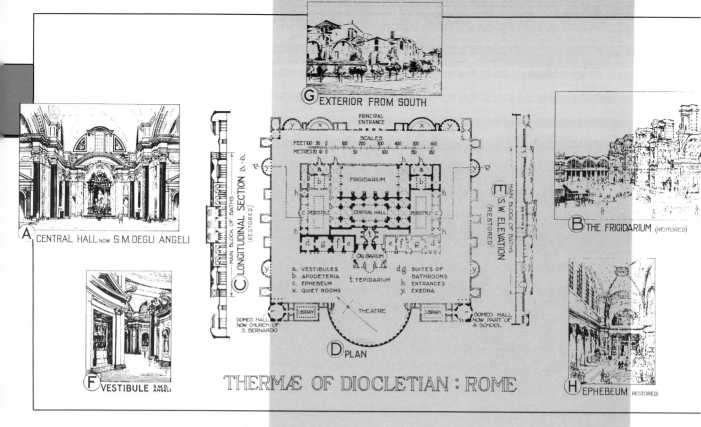

G EXTERIOR FROM SOUTH

A CENTRAL HALL NOW S.M. DEGLI ANGELI

C LONGITUDINAL SECTION a-a (RESTORED)

MAIN BLOCK OF BATHS

PRINCIPAL ENTRANCE

SCALES
FEET 100 50 0   100   200   300   400   500   600
METRES 20 10 0   50   100   150   180

FRIGIDARIUM

C PERISTYLE   CENTRAL HALL   PERISTYLE C

a. VESTIBULES
b. APODETERIA
c. EPHEBEUM
x. QUIET ROOMS
d.g. SUITES OF BATHROOMS
h. ENTRANCES
y. EXEDRA
t. TEPIDARIUM

CALIDARIUM

E S.W. ELEVATION (RESTORED)
MAIN BLOCK OF BATHS

B THE FRIGIDARIUM (RESTORED)

DOMED HALL NOW CHURCH OF S. BERNARDO

LIBRARY   THEATRE   LIBRARY

DOMED HALL NOW PART OF A SCHOOL

D PLAN

F VESTIBULE S.M.D. ANGELI

THERMÆ OF DIOCLETIAN : ROME

H EPHEBEUM RESTORED

SPLISH, SPLASH

The first bathhouses open in Rome around 300 B.C. One of the most famous, the Baths of Diocletian, covers more than five hectares and can comfortably accommodate thirty-two thousand people. These establishments offer both hot and cold swimming pools, and for the shy, individual bathing boxes. No one washes with soap at this point, but, happily, perfume is liberally applied.

And there's even a special servant called an "unctor," who has only one task—to anoint the body of his mistress with olive oil mixed with floral perfumes after her bath. It's a tough job, but somebody has to do it.

Bathing for the Romans is not only hygienic but fun—the baths have all the amenities of modern health spas and then some. There are gardens, museums, and libraries on the premises, as well as private massage rooms, a gymnasium, steam rooms, dry heat saunas, and sunning parlors. And like the health clubs of today, the baths are a lively singles scene, since in the early days they're coed. By the time of Hadrian, however, (the beginning of the second century A.D.) the baths are getting crowded—and worse, so many scandals occur that the authorities decide to segregate the sexes to preserve the morals of the public. Now women can bathe only from the first through the seventh hour of the day, with the rest of the time reserved for men.

TUNE UPS: From 500 B.C. on, Roman men and women both wear tunics—two squares of cloth simply stitched together, with holes left for their heads and arms. Women's tunics are ankle-length, while men's end just below the knee, lengthening into the shin-covering *tunica talaris* by the third century A.D. Over time, tunics grow wider, too, stretching from elbow to elbow, to create longer sleeves. As late as the second century A.D., however, Commodus creates a flap when he has the audacity to appear in a wrist-length tunic.

Above: *Architectural drawing, Thermae of Diocletian, Rome, A.D. 302.* Left: *Roman emperor Commodus, A.D. 180–192.*

CLAVICHORDS: For the Romans, the *clavi*, or decorative borders, so loved by Etruscans become status symbols. Every citizen has the right to wear these bands on his tunic, with the widest ones reserved for highest classes. The *latus clavus*, worn by men of senatorial rank or better, can be three or four inches wide and is probably purple—or at least the Roman conception of purple, which spans a range of shades including ones we'd call red. At retirement, a Roman senator takes on the narrower *angusti clavi* as a sign of his return to private life.

As time goes on, however, the clavi lose their meaning and become mere ornamentation. By the third or fourth century A.D., they feature whimsical designs—twining foliage, charging lions, and sprinting antelope and rabbits. Christian clavi are more decorous, often showing the grapevine, long the symbol of the Greek god Bacchus, that now represents the wine they believe becomes the blood of Christ.

Above: *Wall painting of a Roman wearing tunic with widest clavi and toga praetexta, Pompeii, 1st c. A.D.*

TOGGLE SWITCH

The real revolution in Roman dress comes with the rise of the *toga*, which rich and powerful men adopt around 300 B.C. Although inspired by the Greek *himation*, the toga is a semicircle, rather than a rectangle, and it is a much larger piece of fabric—up to eighteen feet long. With its extreme size and weight—early versions are heavy wool—the toga becomes an engineering marvel, achieving its shape through precision draping.

Obviously, the toga is too cumbersome to work in, so it remains an upper-class affectation. Plebeians and slaves still appear in the same old loincloths they've been wearing for millennia, sometimes topped with a cape.

Right and next page: *Relief from the Ara Pacis depicting members of Augustus's family, 13–9 B.C. The toga lives!* **Inset, left to right:** *Isadora Duncan and dancers at the Erectheion, 1920; Breast-baring dress from Yves St. Laurent's Rive Gauche Spring/Summer 1990 collection; Zero Mostel in A Funny Thing Happened on the Way to the Forum, 1966.*

THE TELL-TALE TOGA

The *toga* is the mark of the Roman citizen, though eventually freed slaves are allowed to wear them, too. They help Romans tell the rich from the poor, the powerful from the weak, the men from the boys. How much do you know about them? Test your toga-ese:

Inset, left to right: *John Belushi in* Animal House, *1978;* Liberty Enlightening the World, *a.k.a. the Statue of Liberty, Frédéric Auguste Bartholdi, 1885.*

1. There are eight different styles of toga, worn:
  a. According to rank, and only by citizens with voting rights
  b. On different days of the week
  c. Until you get tired of the last one

2. An all-white *toga pura* or *toga virilis* is worn by:
  a. A young boy coming of age at sixteen
  b. Nero's henchmen
  c. Crucified Christians

3. The white *toga praetexta*, with its purple border, is worn by:
  a. Prepubescent boys
  b. Algebra teachers
  c. Jane Fonda workout students

4. A Roman may reassume his *toga praetexta* if:
  a. He earns it back later in life by becoming a senator or a senior magistrate
  b. He claps his hands and says the magic words, "Veni, vidi, vici"
  c. He remembers where he put his checkroom ticket

5. The purple-and-gold-embroidered *toga picta* is worn by:
  a. The emperor and high-ranking officers at public games
  b. George Clinton fans
  c. Calvin Klein jeans models

6. What else is the color purple used for?
  a. It is the trimming of the *toga trabea*, a short robe
  b. It is the color worn by Mercy High's marching band
  c. It is the title of a movie produced by Steven Spielberg

7. Togas are dyed a dark color when:
  a. The owner is in mourning or disgrace
  b. The laundromat is closed
  c. Last night's orgy was much too much

8. The *toga gabiana* has:
  a. One fold thrown over the head
  b. A picture of the Colosseum embroidered on the back
  c. Mink trim, and is worn by vamps

Roman mosaic depicting philosophers wearing beards in tribute to their Greek predecessors. Insets: Beards, 100 generations later.

9. By the end of the first century B.C., the toga has grown so huge that:

    a. Its layers must be sewn or pinned to form the *banded toga*, encircling the body several times, with one end thrown over an arm

    b. It doubles as a tablecloth for feasts and banquets

    c. It can be worn by two Roman citizens at once

10. The *consular toga* of the early centuries A.D.:

    a. Has its underlayers cut away, leaving only a front panel

    b. Has visa stamps all over it

    c. Comes with two pairs of pants

11. By the time people are muttering "Et tu, Brute" in 44 B.C. togas are:

    a. Tacky, embellished with garish circles, stars and lots of gold trim

    b. Passé

    c. Selling for $14.95 apiece

ESSENCE BARE

Unlike the Greeks, the Romans abhor nudity; the Latin *nudus* means "crude" or "uncouth." Worse yet, nudity leads to trouble, as Actaeon learns when he spies the goddess Diana bathing. Ashamed at having been caught naked, Diana splashes him with water to turn him into a stag. His own friends, not recognizing him in this form, hunt him down and kill him.

CHIN UPS: The Cretans used it, the Etruscans shunned it, and by 600 B.C., the Romans, too, reject the razor as effeminate. It will take another few centuries for soldiers to realize that opponents can grab their beards and for shaving to gain popularity.

Not everyone adopts the shaving fad, however. Dionysius, the tyrant of Syracuse around 390 B.C., lives in constant fear of being assassinated and refuses to go to the barber. Instead, he has his daughter trim his beard—but since he won't trust a razor in her hand either, she must perform the task using a heated nutshell.

But it's an idea whose time has come. The first barbershop or *tonsores* opens in Rome around 303 A.D. Its hours are dawn till 8 P.M.; and since it's always crowded, clients wait seated on benches, gossiping. Iron scissors are used to cut hair, dye is available to touch up a graying temple, and there is always makeup on hand to repair a blotch or pimple. Real men are never too embarrassed to ask for a permanent wave, and everyone's head is doused with pungent perfume.

Soon barbers gain such reverence in Rome that a statue is erected in honor of the city's first one, Ticinius Mena. It becomes a state duty to shave. Senators with five o'clock shadow are refused their seats until they've seen their barber, and a boy's first haircut is actually recorded in city hall.

The clean-shaven look remains in vogue until the reign of Emperor Hadrian (117 to 138 A.D.). Hadrian grows a beard to disguise his wart-covered chin, and "when in Rome," as they say, the emperor's loyal subjects quickly sprout beards, too.

A SHAGGY STORY: A talkative barber is trimming the beard of King Archelaus. "How shall I cut it?" he asks the king. "In silence," his majesty replies.

250 BC GREEK GEOGRAPHER ERATOSTHENES ESTIMATES THE CIRCUMFERENCE OF THE EARTH.

239 BC EGYPT INTRODUCES THE LEAP YEAR TO ITS CALENDAR.

SEMPER UBI SUB UBI*: The old Latin class pun in fact reflects the truth about Roman undergarments. Noblemen wear *feminalia*. (No, they're not secret fetishists. The name refers to their brief pants—the first boxer shorts?) For lower classes, the loincloth, called the *subligaculum*, affords a measure of modesty and is often paired with the *subucula*, an undertunic. The Emperor Augustus of 27 B.C. must have been very cold—or very prudish—for he layers four tunics, plus his subucula, under his toga.

Women wear these undertunics, too, with a linen chemise called *supparum*, over briefs and a linen or woolen breastband called the *mamillare*. Others prefer the *strophium*, an early foundation garment that is a single piece of cloth wound around the torso; while statelier matrons opt for a wide, tight girdle, to rein in errant derrieres and stomachs.

*"Always wear underwear."

■ Above: *Sicilian mosaic*, A.D. 200–400.

WHO STOLA WHAT?

For all their other innovations, the Romans are simple magpies when it comes to art and culture. They happily co-opt the Greek roster of gods, assigning them Roman names; follow Greek models for the visual arts, crafts, and architecture; and adopt Greek styles of dress. Roman women wear the *stola*, which is almost identical to the *chiton*—an ankle-length tunic gathered at the waist. Stolas come in Doric, Ionic, or combination versions, with the Ionic style featuring brooches or buttons down the arms to create sleeves of lengths that vary with the season. Just to add a little style, Romans dress up their stolas with blue, red, yellow, or golden fringe or adorn them with a band of gold embroidery called the *segmentum*. High-ranking women wear very long stolas, with the hems sweeping behind them like trains, or very full ones to give a pleated or ruffled effect at the bottom.

In the early days, stolas are usually made of wool, but over time they grow more sumptuous; made of vividly colored linens, cottons, or even seductively see-through silks. These revealing silk stolas are described by one disapproving observer as being "light as a lady's reputation."

■ Left: *Sculpture of Agrippina the Elder, 14 B.C.–A.D. 33, mother of Caligula.*

CONSTRUCTION WORKERS

Dentistry may seem like a "medieval torture," but the art of dentistry actually begins thousands of years before that with the Egyptians, who use gold wire to hold loose teeth in place. It is not until 100 B.C., though, that the Romans develop gold crowns to secure false teeth carved from bone and ivory. Who else but the builders of the famous aqueducts would you expect to build the first bridge?

Above: *The Pont du Gard, a Roman aqueduct near Nîmes, France, 27 B.C.–A.D. 14.*

PALLA BY COMPARISON: Over their stolas, Roman women wear the *palla,* an imitation of the Greek *himation.* No respectable matron can appear in public without one, but still, Romans never develop the Greeks' grace and precision in controlling these voluminous wrappers. Pallas are often made of fine, brightly colored wool, decorated with embroidery; or fastened at the shoulders with handsome *fibulae.* As finishing touches, high-class women accessorize their pallas with shoulder capes, scarves, or elegant handkerchiefs.

Left: *Roman matron and her sons, ca. A.D. 188.*

87

GEMOLOGY

Left: Gold necklace set with garnets with a butterfly-shaped pendant, Roman, 1st c. A.D. **Far left:** Earring of gold and engraved stones, Roman, 3rd c. A.D. **Background:** Roman brooch of gold filigree and precious stones. **Bottom right:** Roman earring, A.D. 1–300.

By the first century B.C., restrictions on gold are finally lifted, as Rome is rich with the spoils of conquered nations. Now gold rings and bracelets are bestowed for military prowess and proudly worn in stacks on the same finger or wrist. Many soldiers also wear special rings filled with poison in case of capture—including the illustrious Hannibal of Carthage, who, when cornered in 183 B.C., bites the dust by biting the soft gold.

Precious stones begin to flood Rome, too—emeralds, sapphires, rubies, opals, and beryls—as well as amber, which ladies stroke both because it feels good and to release its faint but pleasing musky scent. Diamonds are also prized but have limited uses, since the Romans don't know how to cut them. Pearls, imported from Ceylon, are the ultimate status symbols. The Emperor Heliogabalus wears a circlet of pearls—two or three strands attached by a gem—as his tiara; and

Diocletian develops the prototype of all royal crowns—a band of gold set with pearls.

Jewelers rise to the challenge of displaying the new gems by rehashing Greek styles and pioneering new techniques for intaglio and cameo engraving, to create *fibulae,* necklaces, bracelets, and earrings, as well as rings and even hairpins. The Empress Sabina, wife of Hadrian, commissions a diadem said to be worth more than a million dollars today. And Antonia, sister-in-law of Emperor Tiberius, adorns her pet guppies and catfish with golden collars and spends hours watching them glitter as they flit through her aquarium.

Soon, in an effort to stem the golden tide the Roman senate prohibits unmarried women from wearing jewelry on their necks, ears, or fingers. As you might guess, the decree spurs a marriage boom.

PEARLS OF WISDOM

Pearls are the first gems known to mankind. Legend has it that lightning struck a mollusk and, terrified, it spit forth the first pearl. Another legend holds that while dining with Mark Antony, Cleopatra dramatically removed one of her pearl earrings, dissolved it in a glass of vinegar, and drank it. It is no legend, however, that the seventeenth-century vogue for wearing one immense pearl earring died along with Charles I, who upon the occasion of his beheading discreetly removed his jewel and handed it over to a loyal follower.

A few pearls of wisdom:

- In early times, people think pearls come from rain—when a raindrop falls into an oyster shell, the mollusk produces a substance that causes the drop to harden. This belief is partly right; pearls are created by the secretions of mollusks that form around particles of sand, not raindrops. Pearls formed in this way are called *blister pearls* because they are usually embedded in the lining of the shell (the mother of pearl) and can be cut away to make jewelry.

- The more familiar (and valuable) spherical pearls are usually formed by parasites rather than grains of sand. When a living creature enters the shell, the mollusk cannot trap it quickly enough to cement it to the lining. Instead, the mollusk immobilizes the invader in a sac of tissue and then begins to cover it with the layers of secretions that become a pearl.

- Virtually any mollusk, whether fresh- or saltwater, can form some kind of pearl, but the finest ones come from oysters. And while pearls can be any color—green, blue, rose, yellow, bronze, gray, or black—the best ones, called rosée, are white with a faint tinge of pink.

- In the Middle Ages the Chinese discover that if they shoot a pellet of mud or a tiny piece of twig or bone into a mollusk and return it to its bed for three years, they can "culture" or coax the production of a pearl. (In later years, they use tiny metal Buddhas instead of mud and twigs.) But it is the Japanese who make pearl culture a fine art, by the early twentieth century. In Japan today, there are thousands of oyster "farms" devoted solely to pearl production.

- Imitation pearls have existed for centuries; many of the ones adorning the celebrated gowns of Elizabeth I, the sixteenth-century queen of England, are fakes. These fake or "Roman" pearls are spheres of glass filled with wax and coated with fish scale essence to make them pearly.

- If you have to cast pearls before swine you'll at least want to save the real ones for a nicer occasion. But how can you tell? Discreetly rub the pearls across your pearly whites; fake pearls feel smooth while real ones are rough.

Top left and bottom right: Gold-mesh necklace with emeralds and mother-of-pearl, Pompeiian, 1st c. B.C. Top right: Earrings from an eastern province of the Roman Empire, A.D. 1–300.

71 BC SPARTACUS LEADS A LEGENDARY RE-VOLT OF SLAVES AND GLADIATORS WHICH IS CRUSHED BY POMPEY AND CRASSUS.

51 BC VINI, VIDI, VICI . . . CAESAR CONQUERS GAUL.

IMPRIMATUR The handkerchief achieves a whole new dignity during the Roman era, thanks to St. Veronica. Seeing Jesus's pain as he is dragged through the streets en route to the Crucifixion, she takes out her handkerchief and wipes his face. Miraculously Christ's features are imprinted on the cloth—and remain visible to this day.

| Below: *Encaustic painting of a Roman-Egyptian woman, 2nd c. A.D.*

PORK BARRELING: The Romans import pork for banquets from Gaul, and soon they learn that, melted down, it's also good for making soap. Pork soap replaces alkaline earth for cleaning dingy togas.

H O U S E W A R E S

Like their sisters in earlier civilizations, Roman women love makeup and develop their own line of basics. Here's all you'll need to create the great looks of the ancestors of Sophia Loren and Gina Lollobrigida:

- Fucus—red or purplish paint to rouge cheeks and lips
- Wood ash and saffron—for black and gold eyeshadow
- Antimony—to darken lids, lashes, and brows
- Blue paint—to outline veins
- Sheep's fat—to color nails
- Depilatories—to dissolve stray hairs
- Meal paste and lemon—to bleach freckles
- Pumice stone—to whiten teeth

You'll also need the saliva of a slave to grind and mix with your cheek paint. Have your slave breathe on a metal mirror. There will be a scent on the mirror. If the saliva smells healthy and perfumed, you can use it without worry. If the mirror smells bad, do away with both the mirror and the slave.

And all this is just for your "domestic face;" remember, only your husband gets to see you!

23 BC THE FIRST WRESTLING MATCH IN JAPAN.

4 AD PROBABLE DATE OF BIRTH OF JESUS CHRIST IN BETHLEHEM.

> **"S**he gave birth to her son, wrapped him in swaddling clothes, and laid him in the manger."
>
> —Luke, 2:7

MAKEOVER TAKEOVER

Around 1 A.D., gladiators bring fair-haired barbarian damsels home from the wars. As dark-haired Roman wives watch their hubbies eyeing the slaves' golden tresses, they decide long before Madison Avenue coins the phrase that blondes have more fun. So some resort to the old hair-bleaching recipes, using pomades made from yellow flowers dried in the sun, or henna to achieve a Celtic red. Very wealthy women frost their hair with silver dust or powder it with pure gold. Others choose the more direct method of cutting the slaves' hair to make wigs—killing two birds with one stone.

By 40 A.D., laws are passed requiring Roman prostitutes to dye their hair blond. This practice, however, does not discourage the blonding craze among respectable women.

IS IT HEREDITY OR ENVIRONMENT?: Unlike the Greeks, the Romans adore shoes. The *carabatina* are simple leather sandals worn by ordinary Romans; while citizens are entitled to don the *calceus,* a sportier closed shoe that either laces or ties at the ankle. The color of the calceus denotes the rank of its wearer; senators, for example, have the right to wear the "neutrals"—basic black and white.

The *crepida* combines the best of both shoe styles— a sandal-like open toe with hightop lacing; and the *cothurnus,* a shin-high boot, can achieve real pizzazz, with decorations of lions' heads and fancy tooling, if owned by a high-placed general.

Though smart shoes are status symbols, Julius Caesar goes too far when he shows up in the senate, during the first century A.D., resplendent in red high heels. Caesar says the style comes from the ancient kings of Alba, from whom he claims to be descended. Very likely jealous, his outraged fellow senators contend that he just wants to look taller; but later they, too, will adopt red shoes as a sign of nobility.

Above: A "caliga," Roman sandal. The emperor Caligula earned his nickname by wearing "little boots" as a child. **Right:** Tanagra figurine, originally painted in bright colors, 3rd c. B.C.

STONEWEAR

If it was good enough for the Greeks, it's good enough for the Romans, only more so: The Romans ape Greek hairstyles, with just a few more curls and rolls. But by the first century A.D., hairdressers come into their own, creating a veritable hirsute revolution. Now Roman women sport high pompadours supported by pads, with curls framing the forehead, or wear turbanlike wound-up braids. Brides divide their locks into six long plaits fastened on top of their heads to form a crown. Over the crown is placed the *vitta*—three woolen cords, a sign of purity—and a huge sheer veil in orange, the color of flames.

Statues may be marble (set in stone as it were), but even *their* hairstyles change frequently. Roman ladies have their portrait busts sculpted in two pieces, so that the upper part, representing the hair, can be replaced with a more fashionable coiffure.

Above, clockwise from top right: *Bust of Octavia, 1st c. B.C.; Marble bust of a Roman woman, ca. 40 B.C.; Roman matron from Fellini's Satyricon, 1969.*

> **"I**t would be easier to count the acorns on an oak tree, the Hyblaean bees, or the wild animals that live in the Alps, than the infinite number of hairstyles and new fashions that appear every day."
>
> —OVID, a Roman poet

If you thought washing your hair would upset the spirits guarding your head, you too might heed Plutarch's heady advice: to shampoo only once a year, on August 13th, birthday of the goddess Diana.

NERO'S WIFE FIDDLES WITH NATURE

Her husband has been known to do away with the women in his life who displease him, so Nero's empress, Poppea, takes no chances: She has one hundred slaves to dress her every day in transparent *stolas* of blue, yellow, green, and pink. She makes a paste of bread softened in asses' milk, which she lets dry on her face overnight as a beauty mask. She also bathes in asses' milk to keep her skin creamy soft. Her hair is blond, and she wears it in massive curls, adorned with pearls. She wears white lead on her face and reddens her lips and cheeks. Her eyebrows meet over her nose and she usually applies lots of *splenia*—beauty marks—on her face, which she then douses with perfume.

Apparently these beauty efforts please the ferocious Nero—at her funeral, it is said that he uses up a year's supply of Arabian perfumes to scent the air.

Right: *Terme di Montecatini mud treatment developed by Princess Marcella Borghese, 1980s.* **Below:** *La toilette, Roman, 3rd c.* A.D.

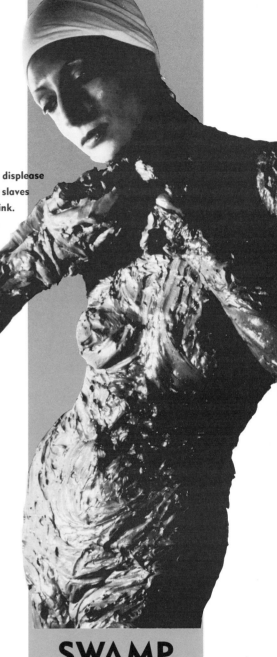

SWAMP FOX

Ovid's advice for smoothing the complexion:

Go to a swamp.

Watch where a crocodile goes after eating dinner.

Fill basket with crocodile excrement.

Spread excrement over face.

93

220 AD BARBARIANS ARE ON THE MARCH AS THE GOTHS INVADE ASIA MINOR AND THE BALKAN PENINSULA.

271 AD THE FIRST FORM OF A COMPASS MAY HAVE BEEN USED IN CHINA.

CLOTHES HORSE

THE EMPEROR'S NEW CLOTHES: In 218 Emperor Heliogabalus makes an official appearance wearing a shocking purple gown embroidered with gold suns, a many-tiered gold tiara, thirty rings—three on each finger—and to complete the look, dabs of pink and white makeup on his cheeks and black tint on his eyebrows. Somehow, somebody notices that this is the first time that anyone in the Western world is completely dressed in silk.

Though earlier Romans would have spurned him as effeminate, Heliogabalus reflects the style of his native Syria, where he had served as a priest in the Temple of the Sun. Perhaps it is his priestly robes that inspire him to bring the *dalmatic*—a long linen tunic with straight or flaring sleeves—to Rome. The dalmatic survives today as the Roman Catholic *alb*, which priests wear while saying Mass.

But Heliogabalus's other tastes are decidely unpriestly, incorporating the worst vices of East and West just as he unites their styles of dress. He loves to wield power, sinking a small fleet of ships just to show off his might. His extravagance extends to his personal effects as well—his bed is pure silver and his chamberpot solid gold, and he feeds his dogs on goose liver. He discards his shoes and linens after only a single wearing. Not surprisingly, he is assassinated four years into his reign, just after he turns eighteen.

AN EYE FOR AN EYE

How do you make mascara in the first century A.D.? Make a fine powder of:

• *Tabernamontana coronaria*

• *Costus speciosus (or arabicus)*

• *Flacourtia cataphracta*

Apply the powder to wick of lamp that's burning with blue vitriol. Take the black of lamp and apply it to your eyelashes.

▌Left: *Pop singer Boy George, 1984.*

300 AD BOWLING IS CONSIDERED A RELIGIOUS RITUAL AT CERTAIN GERMAN MONASTERIES.

331 AD THE SEAT OF THE ROMAN EMPIRE IS OFFICIALLY MOVED TO CONSTANTINOPLE.

THE TIMES THEY ARE A-CHANGIN'

Dinah Shore decked out to throw her famous kiss.

By the fourth century A.D., Rome is in decline, and its later emperors grow increasingly extravagant—Gallenius, for example, who reigns in the mid-third century, takes seven baths a day, dusts his hair with gold, and likes to build castles out of fruit. For fun he summons professional gluttons to watch them stuff themselves with food—not the sort of ruler who can manage a vast empire or rebuff barbarian incursions with any efficiency.

The Roman aristocracy happily embraces its leaders' dissipation. Now wealthy men abandon their august *togas*, badges of Roman pride, for light, gaily dyed robes called *syntheses*. Syntheses are made of linen or special silk, produced from lengths of heavy Eastern silk—too hot for the Mediterranean and literally worth their weight in gold—that are unraveled and rewoven into thin, sheer fabric to stretch the costly fibers further. Available in every color of the rainbow, syntheses are worn to fashionable dinners, where they are changed after every stage of a lavish seven-course meal.

Many centuries later, coincidentally or not, at the end of the Golden Age of Television, singer Dinah Shore goes the Romans one better: In 1962, during a single hour-long TV variety show, she changes her costume not seven but twenty-two times (that's once every three minutes) without mussing a hair!

> **"P**aint is not for the young, nor white lead, quince ointment or any other cosmetic."
>
> —Plautus

ONLY 10% INSPIRATION: To soothe his sore, blistering feet on a long hike, St. Clement lines his sandals with wool. He discovers that the constant pounding and sweat from his feet compress the wool into something new—the first felt to hit Europe. In honor of his discovery, European clothmakers make him their patron saint.

Roman carabatina.

BYZANTIUM AND THE DARK AGES

BYZANTIUM AND THE DARK AGES

THE LONG DAY'S JOURNEY INTO LIGHT

By the end of the third century, the Roman Empire is on the skids. In 330 A.D. when Emperor Constantine moves his capital to Byzantium, on the shores of the Bosporus, the empire will be forever divided into western and eastern halves. (And students of history will be forever burdened with remembering that Byzantium is first renamed Constantinople after the emperor, later dubbed "The New Rome"—to differentiate it from the old, or *other*, Rome—and today is Istanbul, Turkey.) At the dawn of the fifth century, Rome begins its final descent, succumbing to the onslaught of barbaric invaders, while Byzantium, drawn more and more into the Oriental world it borders, flourishes.

It is here, in Byzantium, the "New Rome," that the influences of Greek philosophy, Roman government and legal systems, Oriental textiles, and a newfound belief in Christianity provide the foundations of a unique society. The city of Byzantium itself becomes the seat of great power, magnificent culture, and wealth. In the sixth century, the Emperor Justinian combines the wisdom of Solomon and the building acumen of Donald Trump: he authors the famed Justinian Code, a re-vamping of Roman law that becomes the model for many countries' legal systems and he also inspires an aggressive construction program that brings Byzantium into its "Golden Age." Concerned with promoting Christianity, Byzantine art fosters magnificent religious mosaics and frescoes. Hagia Sophia, one of the most extravagant (what else?) cathedrals in the world, is erected.

Frescoes and mosaics are liberally laced with gold; and in a marble palace, silver lions guard the Byzantine emperor's gilded and jeweled throne. The twentieth-century poet William Butler Yeats paid tribute "To lords and ladies of Byzantium/ of what is past, or passing, or to come."

The Byzantines' love of show, naturally, extends to their clothing. Poised at the cross-roads of East and West, they soon come to monopolize European silk production and to fashion brilliantly colored tunics and cloaks encrusted with gold and precious stones. Headdresses are inset with glowing pearls—the gems so loved by the Romans—and feet are shod in the softest leathers in a spectrum of vibrant colors that would impress even Maud Frizon.

All this pomp doesn't come cheap, however, and soon cracks appear in Byzantium's golden veneer. By the death of Justinian in 565, the empire's coffers are empty, leaving it prey to raiders from Asia and Northern Europe. In the mid-seventh century, Arabs seize the outer territories of Byzantium, bringing with them their religion, Islam, a new source of discord. The Byzantine church has been wracked from the beginning by internal strife, as rival sects vie for control. By 1054, these disputes sever eastern Christians from Europe and, with continuing struggles as well as persistent Turkish encroachments, Byzantium capitulates completely to Islam in 1453.

Meanwhile, in the West, while Byzantium is basking in its golden triumphs, in 410 A.D. the Visigoths invade and sack the city of Rome. Roman emperors continue to rule, but only as puppets of the barbarian invaders, a sad shadow of the glory of Rome.

In 455 the city is seized again—this time by the

*Page 97: Detail from a mosaic in the ambulatory of Santa Constanza, Rome, A.D. 330. **Opposite, top:** Detail from a Byzantine costume. **Left:** Dome of the Hagia Sophia, A.D. 537. **Above:** Engraving of a fifth-century Frankish chief and warrior.*

Vandals, who, living up to their name, plunder for two straight weeks. From there on in, it's all downhill for the once-great empire. The last emperor of the western Roman empire, Romulus Augustus, is deposed in 476, and the Roman era of civilization finally comes to an end.

So what are these raiders wearing when they conquer, loot, and pillage? Since the barbarians are illiterate, little documentation exists about how they live and dress. The only view of the barbarians comes from lavishly illuminated manuscripts produced in European monasteries.

What is obvious almost immediately is that the barbarians—tall, redheaded, and physically powerful—contribute *nothing* to the world of fashion. They wear coarse woolen tunics, fur mantles, leg bandages, crude leather shoes. Men wear leather bonnets or perhaps a fur cap in the winter; women don demure kerchiefs. Oh, maybe a king has a simple crown. But just about the only jewelry of the day is the *agrafe*, a pin used to fasten a mantle around a shoulder. And it seems that all a girl can do, fashionwise, while waiting for the next invasion, is to nervously plait her hair.

As for the Romans, their economy is ruined by the Sack of Rome; morale is understandably low. The Romans now forsake their earlier costumes for simple "Christian" dress: loose unbelted wide-sleeved *dalmatics* and tunics. Fairly early on, the barbarians, too, prompted by the conversion of King Clovis, embrace Christianity. In the late fifth century Clovis unites the tribes into the so-called Merovingian Empire, and initiates the feudal system—a hierarchy of lords and serfs that will define the social fabric of Europe for the next thousand years. In the eighth century, when the Frankish king Charlemagne conquers most of the remaining recalcitrants and joins them with the papacy as the Holy Roman Empire, the barbarians finally start to get some culture. Charlemagne's reign spurs a centuries-long Carolingian renaissance—a rebirth of art and commerce that begins to shape the nations of Europe. And in 1066, after losing the Battle of Hastings to the Norman invader William the Conquerer, one of the last major holdouts—the British Isles—enters the compass of Europe.

This era of strife and migration has long been called the Dark Ages. Several years ago, a group of socially conscious historians banded together to change the name. Why, they argued, should an entire period of history have to bear such a negative monicker? But the sad fact is, they had no better solution, for in truth, the times are pretty bleak. So the Dark Ages they remain—Europe's long day's journey into light.

FOREIGN AFFAIRS: The Romans begin to encounter the barbarians — as they call the Germanic, Celtic, Asian, and other tribes who people Northern Europe — during the first millennium B.C.; in the fourth century B.C., a band of wild Gauls even succeeds in sacking Rome. Over the next several centuries, the Romans return the favor, pressing north and west into Europe. The barbarians they find there look strange to effete Roman eyes, as the historian Tacitus notes in the first century A.D.: "The dress of the women does not differ from that of the men, except that they more frequently wear linen, which they stain with purple; and do not lengthen their upper garment into sleeves but leave exposed the whole arm and part of the breast." Other tribes, he observes, tie their hair in knots on top of their heads to seem frighteningly tall to their enemies; or the warriors let their hair and beards grow, not shaving

Opposite: St. Matthew from the Book of Durrow, Irish, 7th c. **Left:** *Queen Boadicea, ca. A.D. 60.* **Bottom left:** *Hagar the Horrible, by Dik Browne looks fierce, and a bit chilly.*

until they kill their first opponent.

Julius Caesar, on encountering the Britons in the late first century B.C., mentions that they shave their bodies clean except for their upper lips; and Herodianus claims that they wear no clothes at all, but paint their skin gaily and drape it with iron chains. But by the second

century A.D., when the emperor Hadrian consolidates Roman rule in England, the barbarians are much better dressed. The British Queen, Boadicea, who leads a revolt against Roman oppression, is described as very tall, with waist-length blond hair, and as wearing a colorful plaid cloak.

Unfortunately, the uprising fails and Boadicea commits suicide, dragging the plaid down with her. Before long, the Britons have so adapted to Roman rule that they are even dressing in togas. Plaids survive in the outskirts of the British Isles, however, along with saffron-colored tunics and body painting. It's not until the fourteenth century that English kings can finally force the Irish Celts into trousers.

KILL
DRESSED TO

WHEN IN ROME

• The Visigoths, who are the second group to sack Rome, dye their hair a ferocious red. Their swords are huge and jeweled, and for extra inspiration, they tool heroic battle scenes on their leather-covered wooden shields. For good luck in war, they wear seaweed, as well as headdresses adorned with bison horns, in honor of their gods. Apparently, these strategies work, for they bring Rome to its knees in A.D. 410 • What does Attila the Hun, the "Scourge of God" wear for his vicious assault on the Roman empire in the fifth century A.D.? Legend holds that he carries a heavy, round shield and wears a scowl, as well as pants, a belted leather coat, a great, bronze horned helmet and — the pièce de résistance — a cloak of mouse skin. • The warlike Saxons often feel blue, and it's not just that they miss their wives and sweethearts. They dye their hair and their long, chest-length mustaches a vivid blue with *woad*, to frighten off their enemies. • The Gauls, too, use blue dye to scare opponents, but they go the Saxons one better. They gallop into battle with their shaggy blue mustaches, bold gold necklaces, horned helmets — and nothing else, confronting the enemy stark naked.

TALES OF THE TARTAN

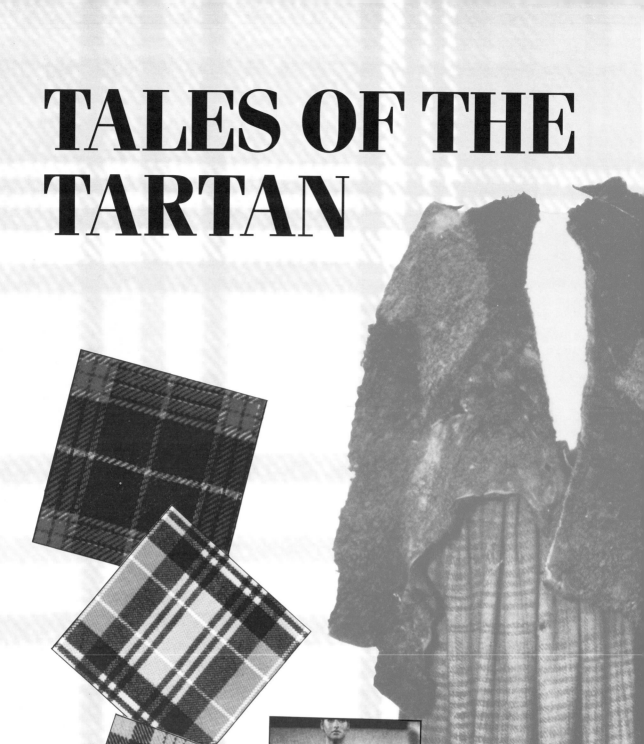

Although legend credits Queen Boadicea with wearing the first plaid, in fact patterns of stripes and checks have been with us since the dawn of history. As early as the first few millennia B.C. the Egyptians wore sheaths and schentis with plaid designs. And while many Scottish clans can trace their roots as far back as the sixth century A.D., the plaids they proudly wear are of much more recent provenance. Throughout the Dark Ages, Gaelic chieftains probably dressed just like their European cousins—in tunics, cloaks, and pants with cross-wrapped legs.

Plaid fabrics have been woven in Scotland at least since the Middle Ages. The word *plaid* means "blanket" in Gaelic and so comes to describe the patterns of the shawl blankets worn by the poor and working classes; the wealthy don them for hunting and farming. In the seventeenth century the *feile-mor* emerges—a simple six- by two-foot rectangle draped around the body and secured with a belt. Sound familiar? By the early eighteenth century the feile-mor is divided into two sections—a small shoulder plaid and a pleated skirt, the *feile-beag*, which we know as the kilt. Around 1730, Highlanders take to wearing their kilts with knee socks, topping them with shirts and jackets. And by the nineteenth century, the *sporran* (originally a simple drawstring pocketbook) becomes a major fashion accessory—a huge puff of badger or goatskin dangling down the front of a kilt.

It is only since the late eighteenth century that Scottish plaids or *tartans* (the term for the pattern and colors) have been used to distinguish clans from one another. Each clan has several tartans for different occasions—the Royal Stewarts, for example, wear an everyday tartan of large red squares, a hunting tartan of green and blue, and a dress tartan in white. And in the 1980s, upwardly mobile people of virtually any ancestry (especially monarchy-loving Americans) wear the Burberry plaid—the ubiquitous camel, red, and black plaid—on everything from scarves and raincoat linings to golf bags.

Sporting tartans: **Opposite left and above right:** patterns of the Muir, Abercromby, Buchanan, Logan, and Hay clans. **Opposite center:** Isaac Mizrahi's cashmere wool plaid dress, Fall 1989. **Opposite right:** Checked twill skirt and skin cloak, Danish, Early Iron Age. **Left:** Bay City Rollers, early 1970s.

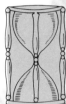

FUSION REACTORS: By the time the barbarians fall on Rome, it's no longer the empire's capital. In the mid-fourth century, the emperor Constantine establishes his capital at Byzantium, where the traditions of East and West unite in a glorious new culture with unparalleled wealth and a love of magnificent display. Not surprisingly, Byzantine dress, with its rich color and extravagance, is envied throughout the world and eventually copied by nearly every Western nation.

Major features of Byzantine dress are its Eastern-influenced patterns and exquisite embroidery, especially in Persian designs. Favorite motifs include hunters on horseback (echoes of Persian equestrian skills), images of Gilgamesh (the Babylonian hero, depicted choking a lion with each hand), and mighty animals, such as lions and eagles, as well as circles, palms, and flowers. And from the West come Christian symbols—Byzantium, after all, is the world's first Christian empire. Constantine, it is said, converted just before a battle one day after he dreamt he saw a cross in the sky, and under it the words *In hoc signo vinces:* "By this sign you shall conquer."

In these early days, Roman fashions still prevail, with all their drapes and folds, alongside such Eastern styles as stockings, tunics, and trousers. Even the Christian saints and characters from the Bible may show up in Byzantine artwork wearing pants.

103

Left: *Call of Peter and Andrew, mosaic from St. Apollinare in Ravenna, 6th c. A.D.*

IN TUNE: In the fifth and sixth centuries, most Byzantines wear tunics; men's are often knee-length and belted near the waist, while women's reach the ground. Upper-class tunics usually are made of fine wool in a riot of colors—green, yellow, purple, and red—and decorated with the *clavi* or ornamental borders so loved by the Romans. But unlike Roman tunics, they're usually long sleeved: Being Christians, Byzantines of both sexes like to keep their limbs covered.

The working class usually can't afford such compunctions: Their tunics are short, with elbow-length sleeves or even entirely sleeveless. Representations of saints Peter and Andrew, fishermen recruited by Christ, sometimes show them daringly revealing whole shoulders in short tunics resembling the Greek *exomis*. Still, Christians who can wear the *collobium*, a long-sleeved tunic that covers them from head to toe, in modest natural shades occasionally adorned with contrasting-colored clavi.

CLOAKROOM NOTES

Over their tunics, Byzantines wear the *paludamentum*, the long Roman mantle remodeled to suit their taste. Like the toga in its heyday, this cloak becomes the badge of the highly placed statesman or noble, and its color designates its wearer's social status (purple is reserved for the emperor). And the Roman *pallium*, in cut-down form, gives the Byzantines another wrapper: the *lorum*. The lorum comes in three styles: a body-length scarf that crisscrosses over the chest; a wider poncholike panel; and a straight narrow version, topped by a *maniakis*, a biblike collar adapted from Persian dress. Only royalty and dignitaries are entitled to wear the lorum and maniakis, which are often rendered in silk and gold and, like everything else, bestrewn with jewels.

PICTURE THIS: No paludamentum or tunic would be complete without decoration—embroidered or woven patterns or a *tablion*, an ornate panel on its back or front. A tablion might feature golden embroidery or be encrusted with jewels, pearls, or even insets of glass—often in the mosaic designs so beloved in Byzantium. The emperor Justinian has a tablion depicting green birds embroidered on gold.

Religious designs are perennial favorites, too: Since the Byzantines believe that glitter and glitz celebrates God's glory (as well as displaying their new treasures from the East), their tablions often show exquisitely worked Bible scenes, as well as Christian symbols. The taste for glamorous tablions even penetrates to the city of Rome itself (where one Christian senator boasts a tunic embroidered with six hundred episodes from the Scriptures)—so much so that, in the fourth century, St. Jerome has to chide pious Roman ladies for their ostentation.

LOCKET UP

Where can you keep a tooth, a piece of nail or bone, or a strand of hair from your favorite saint so everyone can see it? In the good luck charms or *relicquaries* that develop around 400 A.D. The saint's remains, or relics, are set in tiny squares of gold and placed in the middle of elaborate necklaces or jeweled crosses. Almost one thousand years later, in the court of Charles V, these relics will go secular, as lovestruck dandies take to carrying tiny paintings or wisps of their loved ones' hair in jeweled cases called *lockets*, from the French *locquet*, "to latch."

Left: *Dalmatic of Charlemagne, ca. A.D. 800; modern-day tablions for boy scouts and rock fans.* Above: *Gold reliquary cross, 10th c.*

SILK

A CAN OF WORMS

I n 552, the Byzantine emperor Justinian receives a gift of silkworms from China and, over the next few decades, develops a local silk industry. Although he keeps the best of the fabric for himself, silk becomes widely available—upper-class Byzantine men and women even have underwear made of silk. And since silk is no longer so impossibly costly, it can be used straight—in the thick, heavy form called *samite*—rather than the light, sheer, cost-conscious reweavings of the Romans.

Naturally, with such lavish fabrics to display, Byzantine styles soon begin to change: Clothing becomes stiffer and straighter, eschewing Roman draping, to show off the rich materials of which it is made.

500 AD TEA IS INTRODUCED TO CHINA FROM INDIA.

537 AD ARTHUR, KING OF THE BRITONS, IS KILLED IN THE BATTLE OF CAMLAN.

SCREEN

SILK THREADS: Like penicillin, rubber, and Cool Whip, silk is discovered by accident. In 2600 B.C., Chinese empress Xilingshi drops a silkworm cocoon into water and discovers that the thin, shimmering filament floating in the liquid is a continuous thread that can be woven: The world's first silk industry is born. The Chinese keep a jealously guarded monopoly on the secret of silk production for hundreds of years.

Then, around 1000 B.C., an enterprising Chinese princess abiding by the old adage, "Never put all your eggs in one basket," smuggles precious silkworms into India, hidden in her bridal headdress. From there, silk spreads to the rest of Asia and to Persia and eventually on into Europe. The silk importation routes are fiercely defended—people will literally kill for the priceless fabric—until the sixth century A.D., when the emperor Justinian is visited by two monks who have sneaked silkworm eggs out of China, concealed in a tube of bamboo. Byzantium then corners the European silk market until the eleventh or twelfth century, when the secret leaks to Italy. France begins raising silkworm cocoons by 1520 with worms purchased from Milan; England follows suit in the late seventeenth and early eighteenth centuries when beleaguered French Protestants settle in London, bringing silk technology with them.

The finest silks are made by moths which feed on mulberry leaves. Each moth spins a cocoon from a single, continuous thread that may be 800 to 1200 yards long—half a mile or more. Their reward for all this effort is suffocation, by steam or hot air, so that the cocoons can be unraveled to make cloth. Understandably, silkworms are quite testy. For one thing, they hate noise; so in China silk workers pad around in heavy felt slippers to avoid disturbing their charges.

In nature, moths chop their way out of their cocoons, and the threads damaged in this process are used for spun or raw silk. Over the years, there have been many attempts to replace expensive imported silkworms with other kinds of insects. Twentieth-century manufacturers try spiders but discover that, placed in the same box, the spiders eat each other. Since each spider needs its own private spinning room, the cost of this experiment proves far too dear, even for the next best Black Widow.

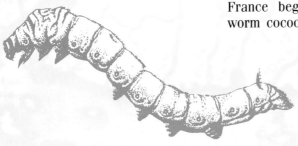

Background: Map of China, Ludovico Georgio, 1584. **Opposite inset:** Winged griffin attacking a bull, silk remnant from the tomb of St. Ursula, Cologne, 7th c.

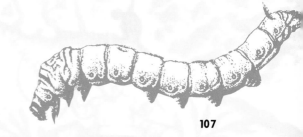

ST. SEBASTIAN

THE HOLY SEE

ST. ELIZABETH

JOHN THE BAPTIST

ST. FRANCIS OF ASSISI

JOAN OF ARC

ST. VERONICA

MARY MAGDALENE

How to spot a saint? Here's how the Catholic saints are identified in art by their fashion symbols:

St. Angela Merici: cloak
St. Bonaventure: cardinal's hat
St. Catherine Ricci: crown, ring
St. Catherine of Siena: ring
St. Cyril of Jerusalem: purse
St. Elizabeth: apron
St. Francis: rope belt
St. Gertrude: crown
St. Gregory the Great: tiara
St. Ignatius Loyola: chasuble
St. James the Less: halberd
St. Jeanne D'Arc: armor
St. John the Baptist: animal skin
St. Josaphat: crown
St. Mary Magdalene: alabaster box of ointment
St. Matilda: purse
St. Matthew: purse
St. Monica: girdle
St. Nicholas: three purses
St. Philip Neri: chasuble
St. Sebastian: loincloth
St. Simon Stock: scapular
St. Veronica: veil
St. Vincent Ferrer: cardinal's hat

And if you happen to work in the garment industry, here are the saints you might want to invoke for discounts and other special considerations:

Dyers: **Sts. Maurice and Lydia Purparia**
Goldsmiths: **St. Dunstan and St. Anastasius**
Hairdressers: **St. Martin de Porres**
Jewelers: **St. Dunstan; St. Eligius**
Hatters: **St. James the Less**
Leatherworkers: **Sts. Crispin and Crispinian**
Shoemakers: **Sts. Crispin and Crispinian**
Silversmiths: **St. Andronicus; St. Dunstan**
Tailors: **St. Homobonus**
Tanners: **Sts. Crispin and Crispinian; St. Simon**
Weavers: **St. Anastasia, St. Anastasius, Paul the Hermit**

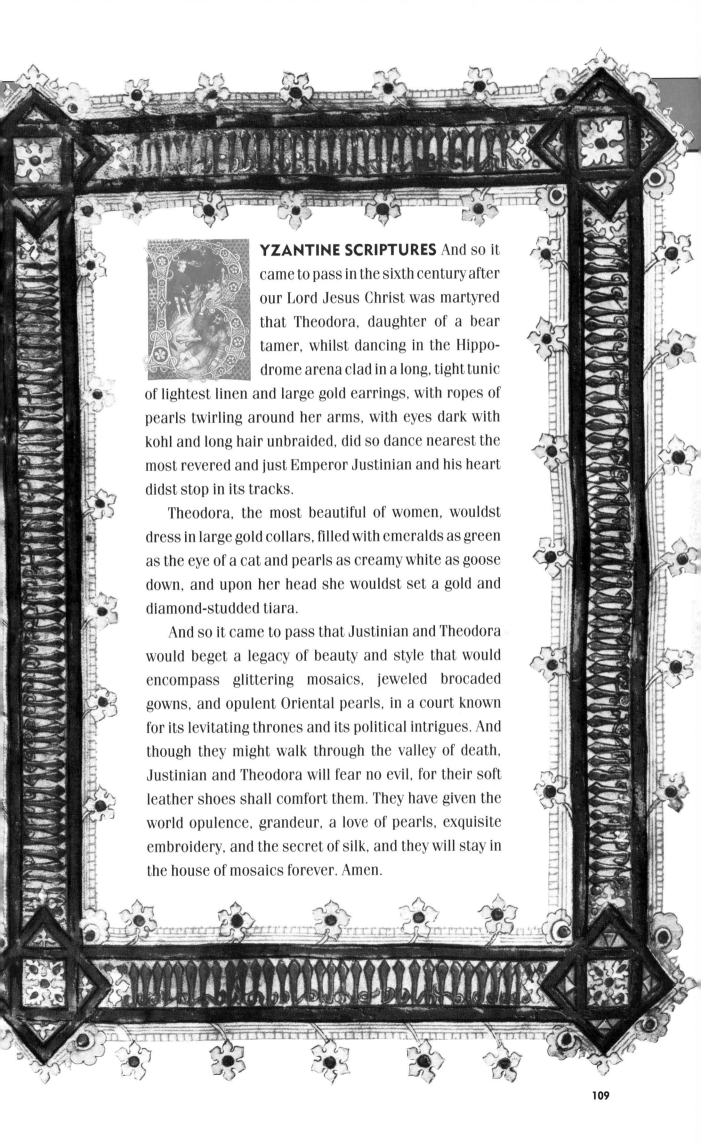

YZANTINE SCRIPTURES And so it came to pass in the sixth century after our Lord Jesus Christ was martyred that Theodora, daughter of a bear tamer, whilst dancing in the Hippodrome arena clad in a long, tight tunic of lightest linen and large gold earrings, with ropes of pearls twirling around her arms, with eyes dark with kohl and long hair unbraided, did so dance nearest the most revered and just Emperor Justinian and his heart didst stop in its tracks.

Theodora, the most beautiful of women, wouldst dress in large gold collars, filled with emeralds as green as the eye of a cat and pearls as creamy white as goose down, and upon her head she wouldst set a gold and diamond-studded tiara.

And so it came to pass that Justinian and Theodora would beget a legacy of beauty and style that would encompass glittering mosaics, jeweled brocaded gowns, and opulent Oriental pearls, in a court known for its levitating thrones and its political intrigues. And though they might walk through the valley of death, Justinian and Theodora will fear no evil, for their soft leather shoes shall comfort them. They have given the world opulence, grandeur, a love of pearls, exquisite embroidery, and the secret of silk, and they will stay in the house of mosaics forever. Amen.

TURNING INWARD: While the Byzantines in the east are embellishing their sumptuous silks, European barbarians are stuck with rough, homespun wool. (Toward the end of the Dark Ages, the wealthier classes might opt for a somewhat finer linen/wool combination called *fustian*.) And in these early days, since few can afford dyes, natural browns and grays are the favorite colors—a lucky preference since soap is unknown and garments are cleaned with ashes.

But from the sixth century on, no barbarian feels dressed without a fur. The rich wear sable, vair (the backs and bellies of squirrels sewn together in contrasting-colored stripes), or ermine, which from the time of the Greeks and Romans is thought to be a species of rat. Everyone else wears wolf or the more popular sheepskins, always warm and dependable. Even eighth-century monks, penning manuscripts with frostbitten fingers, drape themselves in sheepskin. Though furs are sometimes used as trimmings on cloaks, tunics, and gowns, their most essential purpose is warmth: and even the most splendid skins are worn fur side in.

MIRROR, MIRROR: The Egyptians saw their reflections in bronze and silver, Narcissus preferred the clarity of a still pond, and Nero learned to love himself in the green light cast by a flat emerald. Finally, in 636 A.D., the glass mirror is invented. Silver-backed and enclosed in elaborately carved ivory cases, women wear them dangling from their girdles for easy touchups, while men keep their vanity literally under their hats.

Left: *Engraving of Narcissus.* Below: *Prayer card of the Grieving Virgin on Mt. Calvary.*

HAT CHECKS: Byzantine men hate to upstage their fabulous outfits with showy hats. Most men go bareheaded, only occasionally donning a *Phrygian cap* or a hood. But for kings, the sky's the limit—Justinian sets the tone early on with his solid golden band set with pearls rimmed in precious stones, with a fringe of tear-shaped pearls dangling around the edges. Later kings opt for a wider gold band with giant gems at the front, like a miner's searchlight, backed up with smaller gleamers. By the eleventh century, Constantine IX chooses an enameled crown; and thereafter, with the Moslems firmly entrenched, crowns take on domelike splendor, with tops like the roof of an Islamic mosque.

Women, on the other hand, always appreciate smart millinery. From the fourth century on, they sport doughnut-shaped turbans entirely concealing their hair, glamorized, of course, with the usual glittering jewels. Queens anchor crowns on top of their turbans, along with bands of jewels, and loop chains of gems from the headdresses to their shoulders for a look of harem-girl seductiveness. Though saints depicted in Byzantine art often have visible hair, they too may be adorned with elegant jeweled headbands, attached, for a virginal effect, to a flowing veil.

BEAUTY TIPS

THERE'S NO PLACE LIKE HOME: When asked the secret of her good looks, Empress Zoë, considered the most beautiful woman in the Byzantine Empire, replies that she never leaves the palace. The reason? Fresh air is harmful to skin.

"**With mice fill an earthen pipkin, close the mouth with clay and let it be buried beneath the hearth-stone, but so as the fire's too great heat reach it not. So be it for one year, at the end of which take out whatever may be there. For baldness it is great. But it is urgent that whoever shall handle it have a glove on his hand, lest at his fingers ends the hair come sprouting forth.**"

HAIR RAISING: Early in the Dark Ages, barbarians wear their hair long. In fact, long hair is a fetish among the Franks, who tie up their tresses in scraggly ponytails and let their mustaches drop into their soup. By the late fifth century, the Franks, christianized by Clovis, abandon the old style for a new Merovingian look, with shoulder-length bobs or plaits bound on top of their heads. The Danes are probably the most tonsorially tidy barbarians—they believe in combing their hair every day.

Women also have long, flowing locks, worn loose, with a simple fillet to keep strays out of their faces. Merovingian women often drape their hair and bodies with floor-length veils. After the mid-eighth century, many women copy Charlemagne's mother, Bertha, who wears her hair parted in the center and tamed into two thick braids.

And to keep their hair glossy, Anglo-Saxon women apply a pomade made from a special foolproof formula—a mixture of burnt bear claws, lizard tallow, and swallow droppings.

▌ **Top left:** *Empress Zoë, mosaic from St. Sophia, ca. 1030.* **Bottom right:** *Scene from Fritz Lang's Siegfried, 1923.*

PATRON PRIMER: In 611 A.D., Mohammad has a vision and sets out to found a new religion based on one true god, Allah. Soon the new faith spreads throughout the Near East, encompassing many Christians fed up with the Byzantine orthodoxy. Over the next three centuries, Islamic invaders will capture Spain and Northern Africa, and penetrate Byzantium as well, eventually establishing traditions that will knock Byzantine culture out of step with Christian Europe.

Since the Moslems forbid realistic artistic images, a new abstract-pattern aesthetic emerges in Byzantium as early as the ninth century. As everyone knows, all patterns have meanings—so here's a key to Islamic designs:

Two wavy lines and a cluster of circles—Watch out! This is a combination of tiger stripes and leopard spots.

Arabesque—The most distinctively Islamic design, this is a succession of highly abstract leaves (as well as the name of an Audrey Hepburn/Cary Grant movie).

Calligraphy—The message is the medium. Pertinent sentences from the Koran are used as decorative elements.

Paisley—This design combines calligraphy and the arabesque, though it takes its name from the Scottish town where it was successfully reproduced.

Palm—This represents the tree of life. Europeans may have originally commissioned Islamic weavers to design it.

Geometric—This pattern uses more combinations of triangles than Euclid ever thought of.

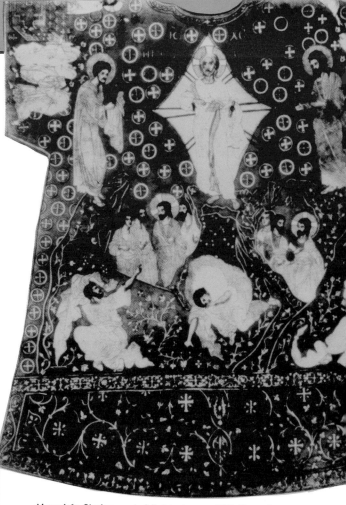

H O R S E
C L O T H E S

MY MAGNE MAN

Charlemagne uses clothes the same way he does his sword—to get his message across. A great ninth-century warrior, he unites the unruly barbarians into a vast Frankish empire and even forges an alliance with the Pope. But for all his power and wealth, he's proud of his barbarian heritage and refuses to adopt regal "foreign" dress. When he sends a gift to the Caliph of Baghdad, Harun al-Rashid, it's a simple woolen scarlet and blue cloak.

Still, he knows style when he sees it: At eleven years old, being an emperor's son, he escorts the Pope on his visit to the Franks and is awed by the pontiff's Byzantine silks and gold. Later in life, he occasionally affects such finery himself to show his support for Christianity. For his coronation in 800, he wears a silk tunic embroidered with pictures of Christ and the twelve Apostles, trimmed with golden

Above left: Charlemagne in full state dress, ca. 800. Above: Dalmatic of Charlemagne, ca. 800.

scrollwork and crosses; a brocaded silk cloak decorated with elephants; and a final, golden outfit, encrusted with rubies. On his feet are red leather shoes bedecked with gold and emeralds, and his head is graced with a magnificent jeweled crown. After all, he is being made head of the Holy Roman Empire; Pope Leo III is conducting the investiture; and it *is* Christmas Day.

His everyday wear is far more modest, tending toward the practical. Charlemagne usually dresses in a simple tunic, cross-wrapped linen breeches, and an otter coat; and he tries, sometimes in vain, to get members of his court to follow his lead. On one memorable hunt, he forces his noble companions to sleep in the clothes they're wearing. By the next morning, all the courtiers' silk and ermine finery is rumpled, tattered, and dirty; while Charlemagne's breeches and sheepskin remain pristine. This stunt makes little impact on the noblemen's tastes in dress, but it does leave Charlemagne hard-pressed for hunting partners.

He does have one sartorial passion, however: gloves. Charlemagne adores them and, in 800, lifts a deer-hunting ban to ensure himself a steady supply.

Above: Charlemagne's coronation shoe, ca. 800.

641 AD THE SCHOOL AT ALEXANDRIA, THE CENTER OF WESTERN CULTURE, IS DESTROYED.

750 AD BEDS BECOME POPULAR IN FRANCE AND GERMANY.

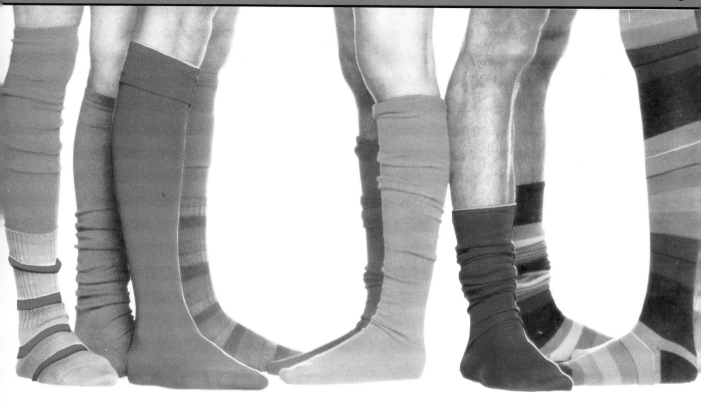

HOW TO DRESS FOR A NINTH-CENTURY COSTUME PARTY:

Ninth-century barbarian women wear long, tight gowns with wrist-length sleeves peeking out from shorter overtunics. For the upper classes, tunics and gowns come in coordinated colors and are often patterned or trimmed with embroidery, jewels, and gold. These decorations reveal the influence of far-off Byzantium—even in the hinterlands, tunics have dotted patterns that also appear in textiles from the East. But unlike their Byzantine sisters, barbarian women completely hide their hair under long flowing mantles like their men's, or else under tight kerchief-like veils.

Some lucky barbarian ladies have a little jewelry to dress up their outfits—maybe a few bracelets, or a pair of dangling earrings. But for most of the Dark Ages, there is only the *agrafe*, the simple brooch that holds a wrap together at the neck or jazzes up a girdle. Practical as well as pretty, these handy items can be found in gold or enamel, surrounded by pearls or precious stones.

WATER STORIES: The barbarians, true to their name, are careless about hygiene; although, since the Romans installed baths wherever they conquered, as long as they're there, the barbarians do take a soak from time to time. The Danes lead Europe in fastidiousness as they do in hair grooming—they bathe without fail every Saturday. Charlemagne, too, believes in hot baths and swimming and likes his men to do the same. And to prove he's committed to cleanliness, he even outlaws the practice of barefoot grape stomping.

By the tenth century, however, these reforms go, well, down the drain. King Edgar I, who unites the tribes of England, forbids his men to take warm baths or to sleep in soft beds—he claims it will make them effeminate. And one archbishop refuses to bathe at all—as a sign of his devotion to God.

Above: Benetton socks and stockings, 1989. Left: The Townley Brooch, gold enamel and pearls, German, ca. 1010; and two headdress pendants, Russian, ca. 1100.

114

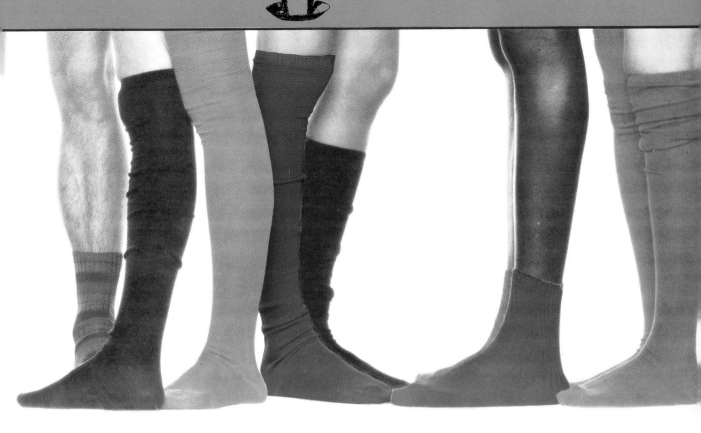

850 AD AN ARABIAN GOATHERD NAMED KALDI DISCOVERS COFFEE.

860 AD NORSE PIRATES ENTER THE MEDITERRANEAN AND SACK THE COAST AS FAR UP AS ASIA MINOR.

HOSANNAS: The barbarians are leg men, too, and they

take special pride in their hose. In the eighth century hose are brightly colored with scalloped or embroidered tops, and come in a range of lengths from socks to thigh-highs. Barbarians love hose so much that sometimes, like 1980s coeds, they double up on pairs, wearing brilliantly colored long ones with contrasting or gaily patterned anklets.

In these days before elastic, hose are held up with thongs wrapped with leg bands of linen, wool, or leather. Kings wear narrow bands, often gold, crisscrossed in open patterns up their calves. Peasants who can't afford such glamorous gartering simply have to take squares of any cloth available and tie them to their shins.

In later centuries, hose grow even more elaborate. Though cross-gartering and wrapping remain in fashion, short hose are sometimes left to droop about the shins for a rumpled, casual, cavalier effect. Thigh-high hose represent special problems, especially under skimpy tunics. Smart barbarians, however, somehow attach them to their linen underdrawers, lest they feel a breeze.

GOING THE EXTRA YARD: His legs wrapped and trussed, the barbarian dons a brightly colored tunic. Girdled or loosehanging, the longer the tunic, the higher the rank of its wearer. For ninth-century kings, tunics might even be calf-length, edged with precious stones and embroidered or woven with gold. The poorer classes, naturally, wear simple tunics, with some blousing for style.

Tunics' belts are inset with metal studs for attaching a dagger or the barbarian's trademark accessory—his sword. And because northern Europe is chilly, everyone wears a mantle, often fastened Roman-style at the shoulder with a fancy clasp.

870 AD THEY ARE USING CALIBRATED CANDLES IN ENGLAND TO MEASURE TIME.

890 AD ARABS OCCUPY THE COAST OF PROVENCE IN FRANCE.

THE AGRAFE AND THE LADY
A TELEPLAY FOR THE DARK AGES IN ONE ACT

THE SCREEN IS TOTALLY BLACK. As the voice-over commences, the screen goes to gray, filled with fog. As the voice-over ends, the screen shows a bleak landscape holding sparse, gnarled, trees; patches of brown tundra; a thick, spiraling castle on a cliff; and a solitary vulture circling the turrets in a smaller and smaller circle. . . .

ROD SERLING THE MODERN:

Voice-over

You are about to enter a world of little imagination. Of short sight and empty sound. A world of two dimensions, where what you wear means less than what you are. A hooded world, tightly laced. Your next stop—*the Dark Ages.*

DISSOLVE TO: INTERIOR OF LADY DI DIANA'S, EARLY MORNING. A cold, damp, drafty Romanesque castle room, barely lit by the sparse sun coming through the small window slits high up on the stone wall. On the right wall is a large bronze mirror and a crude wooden table holding a waist girdle made of gold and silver cord. On the left wall is a high-backed Romanesque chair, a pair of soft leather shoes underneath it. On its back is a worn, embroidered mantle. There are no pictures, but the ceiling is painted a deep blue, crudely dotted with gold-leaf stars. Lady Di Diana is pacing the room. Over a tight, long-sleeved chemise, she wears an ochre-colored tunic, tightly laced up the sides from her hips to her shoulders and over it is a long wool cloak which she clutches at her shoulder. She looks disconcerted.

LADY DI (*loudly*):

Forsooth, Rapunzel. Agrief, agrief, I've lost my agrafe! My agrafe, Rapunzel: Where is my brooch? Rapunzel, Rapunzel, come out here and help me look!

Rapunzel enters through a short wooden door on the left. She is braiding her long hair into two golden plaits. She too is wearing a tunic but, as befitting her rank, it only reaches her ankles.

RAPUNZEL (*fumbling*):

It must be here, my lady. I swear a hundred times I saw it with mine own eyes whenst I took off your jeweled girdle after last night's festivities.

LADY DI (*walking over to the table*):

Yes, but here is my girdle—and the brooch is not upon it.

RAPUNZEL:

Well, you couldn't have put it in your pocket, because they haven't been invented yet. But have you checked your leather pouch?

LADY DI:

Of course, of course I checked my leather pouch. Rapunzel, that brooch is most important to me. How can I clasp my cloak, the neck of my dresses, or decorate my waist-girdle without it?

RAPUNZEL (*biting her unpainted lip*): It must be here my lady, it must.

LADY DI (*feverishly*):

It is the only jewelry I have. The Byzantines in the East wear gold collars and pendulous headdresses. Even my husband, Long-haired Gry the Hun, has a jeweled sword. What do I, a mere woman, have? Nothing. Only one simple gold-hammered brooch with a silly name!

Lady Di strides over to the door and tries to open it. It refuses to budge. She starts to bang at the wood.

LADY DI (*hysterically*):

Do you see? I cannot leave without my agrafe! I am trapped, forever, in the dark. Do you see?

Lady Di bursts into tears as she crumples to the floor. Her voice and the castle room fade once again to the stark exterior.

ROD SERLING THE MODERN:

Voice-over

Consider the evidence: one simple gold brooch. A magic brooch? Or the rantings of a superstitious woman? Or is it simply a matter of vanity? The answer lies in the Dark Ages alone, in the days that tried men's souls.

FADE TO BLACK.

900 AD AN ARAB PHYSICIAN NAMED RHASES IS THE FIRST TO SUGGEST THAT CERTAIN DISEASES MIGHT BE INFECTIOUS.

902 AD WORK BEGINS ON THE CAMPANILE OF ST. MARK'S IN VENICE. IT WILL STAND FOR EXACTLY 1,000 YEARS.

Opposite: *Silver and translucent enamel agrafe, early 15th c.* **Above:** *Mosaic of female saints from Ravenna, ca. 560, with Betty Grable.*

HERE SHE COMES, MISS BYZANTIUM

The Byzantines are such great admirers of female pulchritude that they even stage the world's first beauty contests. One legend has it that the famed Theodora, an exotic dancer and actress in the Hippodrome, meets her royal spouse Justinian when she appears as a beauty contestant. And around 900 A.D., another empress, Theodosia, decides to play Bert Parks herself. Twelve lovelies assemble in long embroidered tunics, gold collars, headdresses, and shawls to parade in front of the royal matriarch in the hope of winning a fairy-tale prize—marriage to her son. Little is known about the new Miss Byzantium except that she is sixteen years old and wears a double strand of pearls in her hair.

ACCESSORIES TO THE FACTS: With all their blinding finery, it would hardly seem that the Byzantines need jewelry. But why not throw on a little more tinsel when it's all for the glory of God? So, in a spirit of Christian sacrifice, the Byzantines layer on bracelets, necklaces, dangling earrings (even for men), as well as combs and hairpins of ivory and gold. And from the Romans they also inherit the *fibula*, used to fasten their cloaks, and work it up in gold with three jeweled pendants to symbolize the Holy Trinity.

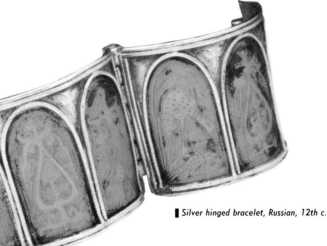

Silver hinged bracelet, Russian, 12th c.

117

NORMAN CORPSMAN:

By the eleventh or twelfth century, the restless barbarian hordes finally settle down, largely united under the banner of Christianity, and the Dark Ages draw to a close. With Europe more or less apportioned among feuding groups, arts and statecraft begin to thrive. But there are still a few wild cards left to be played, and one comes in 1066. That year, William of Normandy defeats the English at the Battle of Hastings, spreading the feudal system, the French language, and the customs of mainland Europe.

The original Normans were Vikings who gained a foothold in France in the ninth century. Given this unusual pedigree, it's not surprising that they dress quite strangely. They wear pants like the barbarians, but of a loose-legged, knee-length style—almost like modern culottes. They wrap their hose as their neighbors do, but often with horizontal bands, so their legs look like they're striped. And weirdest of all are their haircuts—the backs of the heads are entirely shaved, with the rest of their cropped hair combed to the front to create duckbill bangs. For all these oddities, they still lick the English, who are decked out in chain mail and nose-guard helmets; and from there move on to overrun most of southern Italy.

It is from Italy, in centuries to come, that they will make their other great contribution to Western culture. Bedazzled by Byzantium, they import weavers from the Bosporus and the Near East—often by force—to create a sophisticated textile industry, working in silk and gold. Sicily, especially, grows famed for its fabrics; and its weavers bring their skills to Venice, Genoa, and Florence—the great textile centers of the Renaissance.

TO BEARD OR NOT TO BEARD is a burning question in the Dark Ages, both in the east and in the west. In fact, the Byzantine emperor Constantine V is said to have set fire to his monks' beards because the beards "insulted" him. Though few other rulers go to such extremes, Byzantines generally prefer to be clean-shaven.

The barbarians by contrast, sport full beards and mustaches, with various tribes favoring round or pointed shapes. In some countries, only kings are allowed to wear beards, and for warriors, yanking off an opponent's beard is as common as scalping among American Indians. In Charlemagne's time, beards disappear briefly because he personally dislikes them; but they quickly reemerge in all their luxuriant glory, often in the Dark Ages' best-loved style—a distinguished forked version.

One major group that resists wearing beards is the Normans, who settle in France. In fact, their clean-shaven chins are part of the reason they win the Battle of Hastings. In 1066, when they land in England, sentries seeing their beardless faces believe the invaders to be priests and so fail to give warning. The rest, as they say, is history . . .

HANG LOOSE: Just when their men are taking to close, confining styles, tenth-century women adopt the baggy look—loose, wide tunics; huge poncho-like wrappers; and a voluminous headdress, the *couvre-chef*, that completely envelops the head and neck. But with all the Byzantine glamour male peacocks get to enjoy, women don't want to stay swathed for long. Though in Britain sloppy styles persist through the eleventh century, continental fashionplates soon unload their bags for a new, sleeker line: tight, laced bodices and full, feminine skirts, resplendent with gold and jewels.

NO SWEAT: By the tenth century, the barbarians acquire an even stronger taste for drama as the German king Otto II, emperor of the Holy Roman Empire, marries the princess of Byzantium. His wedding tunic is made of silk, with a wide embroidered panel, almost like a tablion, and even his shoes are jeweled. Though his crown is square, its points at the front, back, and sides are set with jewels too—a good crown, if hardly as showy as the extravagant Byzantine diadems.

Other men have begun to adopt closer-fitting tunics, tight around the chest, with skirts that flare. In England, these tighter tunics have slits up the sides to make walking easier. Here, too, the Byzantine love of decoration has started to take hold: Tunics are lavishly embroidered around their hems and up open side seams. With a few variations in hem lengths, belts, and trimmings, these tight, skirted tunics will endure a few centuries until the Dark Ages end and the chivalrous Middle Ages finally tame the barbarian sensibility.

The mantles worn over these tunics incorporate a major tenth-century fashion innovation—rather than fastening them at the shoulder, as they've done with cloaks for thousands of years, men now attach them at the front, in the middle of the chest, often with enormous clasps. Some even abandon mantles altogether for a hip-length jacket simply pulled over the head—an early version of the sweatshirt.

IS SOMETHING
UP THEIR. . .

In the tenth and eleventh centuries, the big news for barbarians is sleeves—and we mean *big*. Both sexes wear their sleeves extra long; men's are tight and worn bunched up over the forearm; women's are loose, often kneelength, secured at the wrist with bracelets or doubling as muffs in the cold. But while men's sleeve-size subsides by the eleventh century, women's continues to grow until sleeves reach enormous proportions, belling out at the wrist. And judging by their trimmings—lavish embroidery, gold, and jewels—it seems that they've learned some secret way to keep sleeves out of their gruel.

Opposite: *Ivory carving of Emperor Anastasius, A.D. 516.* **Above:** *Young noblewoman from the mosaic Discovery of the Relics of St. Mark, St. Mark's Cathedral, Venice, 13th c.* **Right:** *Byzantine empress of the eleventh century.*

119

THE
MIDDLE AGES

THE MIDDLE AGES

CRUSADER HABITS

Armored knights on horseback rescue damsels in distress; fur-clad lords and ladies rule over huge baronial castles; swirling-caped sorcerers stir up boiling cauldrons of magic potions; troubadours traipse from town to town spinning enchanting tales of courtly love. We picture the Middle Ages as romantic—the era of Arthur, Guinevere, and Camelot. In reality, it is a time marked by a brutal feudal system letting the wealthy virtually enslave the lower classes,

Overleaf: *Hunt of the Unicorn (detail), wool tapestry, Franco-Flemish, late 15th c.* **Above:** *Page from a medieval manuscript.* **Below:** *"Preaching for the Second Crusade," Emile Signol (1804–1892).*

and by a tyrannical clergy that sells God's mercy—but only to the highest bidders. No one worries about trusting anyone over thirty because most people don't live that long, thanks to the sweeping plagues and the bloody Crusades. The era opens in the eleventh century with the taming of the barbarians; by its end we will witness the rise of great cities and the social, political, and cultural dawn of the Renaissance.

People of the Middle Ages suffer pestilence, stench, and, perhaps worst of all, monotony. Some say it is simply boredom that prompts a response when Pope Urban II, in 1095, calls for soldiers to recover the Middle East regions

seized by the Arabs during the Dark Ages. Others point out that there are profits to be made on a plundering mission to the East. In any case, the Crusades, stretching from 1095 to 1291, manage to reclaim only four territories from the "infidels" — but they introduce Europe to a whole new style of living.

The young soldiers who are fortunate enough to return from the Crusades bring back wealth, power, and a new knowledge of other people and their cultures. They learn about embroidery and carpet weaving in the East, as

Above: 12th-century statues of King Solomon and the Queen of Sheba in Gothic garb. **Below left:** A medieval pope.

well as about new toilet articles, such as rouge and glass mirrors (in lieu of polished plates), that are used in the Orient. They meet bearded Arabs and stop shaving. The Crusaders also encounter a new style of architecture, and the Gothic arch, high and narrow, becomes the rage in Europe. Its popularity is echoed everywhere, even in clothing styles. Silhouettes become elongated and fashionable ladies wear impossibly high headdresses to look tall and slender. Luckily, this trend of life imitating

art is quickly nipped in the bud. Who today would want to dress in the shape of the Astrodome?

Throughout the Middle Ages, clothes are fairly standardized, with each country adding its own wrinkle. Garments are passed down through the generations so you'll not only wear your big sister's hand-me-downs but also your grandma's old cape. In the early days, most costumes are based on a simple T shape (stand in front of a mirror with your arms

Illustration of a May Day Festival from the Tres Riches Heures du Duc de Berry by the Limburg brothers, ca. 1400.

stretched out straight from your shoulders to get the idea) and, over time, grow sleeves that surpass even the most ambitious excesses of the Dark Ages. And while Princess Di made a splash in 1986 when she showed up at a ball wearing mismatched gloves, Middle Ages' clothing is often particolored—with different colored stockings worn on each leg, and dresses or tunics divided into contrasting halves or quarters.

As feudalism wanes in the late Middle Ages, the old pecking order is derailed. And since there's no Social Register to keep the common people from passing as their "betters," sumptuary laws restrict what each class can wear—from the height of their hats to the length of their shoes. For now, as cities grow and commerce resurges, a new social stratum—the middle class of burghers and craftsmen—is beginning to emerge. Everyone with money to spend wants fashionable clothes. Until now, only a few wealthy people have had the time or the inclination to worry about what they're wearing—after all, peasants spend most of their time just scrambling to stay alive. But suddenly, it's just not enough to have a shirt on your back: hemlines will go up and down more rapidly, and new necklines and sleeves will make last year's clothing look passé. From now on, right up to the present day, it will be necessary to buy a new spring dress.

Clockwise from top left: *Before the bodywave, women braid, plait, coil, and curl their hair, ca. 1380; effigy of Lord Edward Le Despenser (d. 1375) in Tewkesbury Abbey, 14th c.; The Conversion of St. Hubert, Pisanello, ca. 1430.*

BEAUTY TIPS FOR MEDIEVAL MAVENS:

What's the magic formula for a perfect complexion? Here are some tips to help ensorcel that errant knight:

For that perfect white face, pat your face with white flour. And if you're terrified of freckles (the bane of medieval ladies), hide inside the castle at all times. If you must go outside, don a veil. The lack of sunshine and your poor diet are sure to give you that glamorous pasty look.

Isabeau of Bavaria advises: Keep your skin soft and white by bathing in asses' milk. And for a beauty cream that *works:* Combine boar's brains, crocodile glands, and wolf's blood. Smooth lotion on skin.

To make a do-it-yourself sauna: Wrap yourself in a wide piece of linen. Stand on hot stones, covering them with the rim of your cloth. Have your serfs douse you with water. It's fun for them and healthy for you.

Above: *1930s starlet applying beauty creme.*
Right: *The Ugly Woman, Quentin Metsys, 1520.*

HAIR TODAY, GONE TOMORROW

Men and women alike begin the Middle Ages with long, flowing hair. For men of the twelfth century, tresses are exceptionally long, and by the thirteenth century, dandies sport a large curl over the forehead or at the nape of the neck. As chivalry blooms, swains who want to look romantic and courtly go clean-shaven.

In time, however, men grow tired of shaving and—considering the quality of medieval razors, their stubble-burnt loves probably agree—and begin to cultivate beards. The church rants and raves against the new hirsute trend, calling hairiness a sign of ungodliness. But its admonitions fall on deaf ears, especially after the Crusades, when knights return from the East fully bearded. After all, who has time to shave while battling the infidel?

The Crusades do give Europeans their first notion of the unsightliness of body hair, however, as knights bring home news of the Arab custom of full-body depilation.

Women of the twelfth century wear extremely long braids, often bound with strips of leather, with metal tips encasing the ends. During the thirteenth and fourteenth centuries, the plaits are pinned up in a coil at the neck, or wound into buns covering each ear. And by the dawn of the fifteenth century, as headdresses come to push the limits of the imagination, hair vanishes entirely. High foreheads are considered so sexy that women pluck their hairlines and even remove their eyebrows for a gleaming cueball appeal.

"Blonde or brunette, this rhyme applies, Happy is he who knows them not."

—Francois Villon

HOODWINKED: Unless they're kings (who need to wear crowns), men don't wear hats in the early Middle Ages. They wear tight-fitting skullcaps that come to a point for quick pulloffs. The lower classes, however, do wear a small hooded shoulder cape that comes from the Romans by way of the Normans. Eventually hoods separate from capes—early hats resemble open paper bags and are worn mainly outdoors; they soon achieve a cachet that they haven't enjoyed before or since. Now their points become exaggerated into long *liripipes* that dangle down past their wearer's knees. And in 1346, the *roundlet* is created, a hood that looks like a padded roll, twirled around the head and kept in place with its end stuffed into girdles. By the year 1400 the roundlet is so popular that men never take them off—and numerous brides are shocked on their wedding nights to learn that their husbands are actually bald.

This headgear does have a practical side, though. In the Middle Ages, you don't have to be sly to find out whether a man is a doctor, a lawyer, a priest, or a city official—you can tell by the shape of the hood he wears. This system proves such a field day for imposters that any deceit comes to be labeled a *falsehood*.

Top left: *Medieval friar in a small hooded shoulder-cape.* **Above:** *Triptych of the Wise Kings (detail), Roger van der Weyden, ca. 1445.* **Below, far left:** *Purse of iron and leather, Northern European, late 15th c.* **Below left:** *Detail from the tapestry* The Seven Sacraments, *Franco-Flemish, ca. 1475.*

THE POWER OF THE PURSE: The Crusades establish the purse as a fashion accessory for men. Priests issue one to every crusader, along with a must-have pilgrim's staff and cross. Early purses are hung from girdles and may be trimmed with smart tassels or, for kings, may even be made of gold.

1066 WILLIAM THE CONQUEROR DOES JUST THAT TO ENGLAND.

1136 ABELARD WRITES *HISTORIA CALAMITATUM MEARUM* (STORY OF MY MISFORTUNES), AN UNDERSTATED TITLE FOR THE STORY OF HIS LOVE AFFAIR WITH HÉLOÏSE.

TEX-TALES

The Middle Ages see the dawn of a new day for textiles, as the Crusaders import exotic fabrics from the East. Soon new textile centers emerge throughout Europe. The burgeoning industry also contributes some new words and expressions to the English language:

• Everyone wants "natural" fleece, so off-color wool has little value, and herdsmen bemoan their *black sheep.*

• When Coventry housewives discover a blue dye that withstands many washings without fading, they dub it *true blue.*

• Someone discovers that color will be more permanent if, instead of dyeing cloth, stuffs are *dyed in the wool.*

• A new type of white silk produced in Byzantium around 1100 is called *diaper,* from the Greek *diapros,* or "pure white." Soon any white cloth is called diaper—from the new fourteenth-century white table linens to the cheap cotton fabric used for babies' breeches.

• In the thirteenth century, the poor-quality linen manufactured in Silesia is sold under the trade name of Sleazy Holland—and anything inferior comes to be called *sleazy.*

> **"R**ich silks of Zazamanc, as green as any grass, and of Araby, white as the snow, were now inlaid with precious stones, to make clothing of high quality."
>
> **The *Nibelungenlied***

AN ELL FOR AN ELL: By 1100, the guilds—protective and standard-setting unions of craftsmen—are coming into their own. Consumer watchdogs, they push through a bill regulating the width of cloth, the first attempt at standardization. Fabric had to be two ells wide (about ninety inches) and of the same quality in the middle as at the edges.

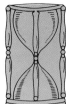

Both sexes begin the Middle Ages in *bliauts*, long overtunics with fancy embroidered borders at the hem, neck, and wrists. Noblemen's bliauts often feature slit skirts, for ease in horseback riding, while laborers favor a simpler, knee-length style for hoeing. Women's bliauts represent a major tailoring innovation—they're made of two pieces, a fitted, low-waisted bodice, sewn to a full-pleated skirt, rather than cut in the centuries-old straight T. The march of progress . . .

By the fourteenth century, however, people are tired of voluminous tunics; and the *cotehardie*, a clingier style, comes into fashion. Men's cotehardies are modestly round-necked and long-sleeved, reaching to midcalf. But trim courtly lovers keep nipping their hems until the cotehardie becomes a smooth-fitting top, attached to the briefest of flouncy miniskirts. A low-slung belt, often the most expensive item in a man's wardrobe, clinches the effect.

Women's cotehardies are more decorous, but they too get a soupçon of sex appeal. Close-cut gowns with tight flaring skirts, they have daring, low necklines for a thrilling glimpse of skin. Stylish women top them with an overgown that looks like a sleeveless jumper, with armholes open to the waist.

And to leave admirers trailing in their wakes, both sexes add *tippets*, long streamers trailing from their elbows—sometimes even reaching the floor.

Top left: *Illumination from the Luttrell Psalter, ca. 1340.* **Above:** *French costume, 1350–1375.* **Left:** *Badge of a guild of St. George, silver gilt with enamel, coral, and malachite, Hungarian, late 15th c.*

COVERATURE:

Throughout the Middle Ages, people cover up in *surcoats*. One of the hottest styles is the *cyclas*, a knee-length poncho the Crusaders adopt to cut the blinding glare of sun on chain mail. By the thirteenth century, both sexes and all social classes wear it or one of its variants—the cap-sleeved, hooded *garnache* or the long-sleeved *gardacorps*. The very wealthy continue to don mantles as a sign of distinction. Women wear huge, semicircular, fur-lined capes, which are handed down from generation to generation, for their richly embroidered material makes them extremely valu- able. Men's mantles have collars and are tossed dramatically over one shoulder. In the twelfth century, mantles are symbolic; you throw yours down as an open challenge or give it to a troubadour as payment for his songs. Often as not, the troubadour will sell it in turn to the highest bidder for some hard cash.

Left: Miracle of the Child (detail), Ghirlandaio, ca. 1434. **Above:** Costumes of the 14th c. French bourgeoisie. **Below:** Miniature of the engagement of Renaut de Montauban and Clarisse, a scene from the 12th c. French poem, "The Four Sons of Duke Aymes."

TRAIN-EES: A favorite troubadour muse, Eleanor of Aquitaine is also the first "Material Girl," wearing wide, wide sleeves and extra-long trains to flaunt her wealth. Not a great style for the klutzy (or if you're caught near a fire), the train nonetheless sweeps France and then England, when Eleanor struts it around after 1152. In the twelfth century the train is synonymous with elegance, and helps a woman achieve the elongated silhouette which apes Gothic architecture. It is worn by women of importance and rank, and naturally, sumptuary laws are soon written to regulate its length. In Italy, women are forbidden to wear trains, which of course they do anyway. By the fifteenth century trains are so long and—trimmed with fur, encrusted with jewels—so heavy, that they often must be carried by pages.

Opposite page: background: Fresco, Italian street musicians, 14th c.; **bottom left:** Painting of troubadors, 13th c.

THE WORLD'S FIRST HIPPIES

While real men go off to do battle with the Moor, troubadors dodge the draft and hit the road. These long-haired lads are the original vagabonds, travelling light, with just the shirts (or surcoats) on their backs (and some colorful hose and pointy shoes) to call their own. They spread gossip and news, paying their keep by singing songs of courtly love glorifying women. In fact, they even help the Virgin Mary regain her popularity by making her their patron saint.

Alas, they also give twentieth-century women something to yearn for: a revival of the traditions of scarf-dropping, damsel-rescuing, and—dare we say it?—chivalry.

A TROUBADOUR'S SONG

That pleasant fever
That love doth often bring
Lady, doth ever
Attune the songs I sing
Where I endeavor
To catch again your chaste
Sweet body's savor
I crave but may not taste.
　　—Gillaume de Cabestaing,
　　　　Li dous cossire

IN GLOVER

In England, mittens are de rigueur for everyone, especially for hard work in the fields, until 1175 when Henry II has gloves made with separate fingers. These gloves make for easier manipulation, whether in kissing a fair maiden's hand or hawking. By 1350, gloves are all the rage at court, made of kidskin or chamois and adorned with embroidery. The most popular color is white, though sometimes they are made in contrasting colors. To show off a fabulous jewel, the gloves are occasionally cut off at mid-finger or else a bauble peeks through a hole cut in the fabric. By the fourteenth century, Charles VI of France and, later, his sons favor violet-scented gloves for an extra sensual thrill.

Above: Gloves from the coronation ensemble of Holy Roman Emperor, ca. 1220. Below: Miniature, the murder of Becket in 1170 in Canterbury Cathedral, 13th c.

GLOVE STORY

- Before the towel, people threw in the glove.
- Before deeds, gloves are exchanged to guarantee the transfer of land.
- Knights wear the glove of their lady on their breast as a sign of devotion.
- In the Middle Ages, when a young man marries he gives the bride's father one of his gloves as a symbol that he will take care of his new wife *single-handedly.*

- In Roman times, workers use mitten-like gloves to protect themselves from thorns. These are quickly taken out of the pasture and brought into the gym, where gloves are matched on the wrestling court. But the inventive Romans soon realize that gloves are great for keeping hands *warm.* Socialites begin wearing them during meals; that way, one can eat hot meat without waiting for it to cool before beginning the orgy.
- In the 1500s, Queen Elizabeth uses her "velvet gloves" to invite flirtation, persuade, or express her pleasure. When Shakespeare finishes acting in one of his own plays the Queen is so enthused that she flings her glove at his feet.
- Jealous that Henry VIII has fallen in love with Anne Boleyn, Catherine of Aragon sets up a card game. The ruse is to trick Anne into taking off her glove, revealing her extra finger.

- In the seventeenth century, gloves are more often carried than worn. Maidens sleep with a glove under their pillow in the hope of finding a mate.
- By the nineteenth century, strict rules of etiquette dictate the color, length, and material of gloves. Black silk net mittens, for example, must be worn only indoors; and a lady's hand must be covered—always.
- The Chinese extend a gloved hand to a guest as a symbol of their anticipated pleasure of being with them. Emily Post says you should always *remove* your glove before offering it to a stranger. Which rule of thumb to follow? The customs of the place you are visiting must finally dicate your decision to glove or unglove.

Almost everyone would agree with Yogi Berra, however, with regard to the baseball glove, introduced by Al Spaulding in 1876: "When you're out in left field," says the famous Yankee, "always keep your mitt covered."

HAIR HURT: According to the Catholic Church, which has a stranglehold on the Middle Ages, humility is good and man has a need to be punished. But what can you do when such penances as walking barefoot don't provide enough pain? Don a shirt made of horsehair under your robe—with every move you'll feel a swift, unpleasant jolt to your skin. Thomas à Becket wears a hairshirt to atone for his carousing days with Henry II (and because he inwardly resents being subordinate to the king, and he wants his spiritualism back). And when Becket is assassinated by Henry's men while saying Mass, his followers rush to his side, undo his robe—and unleash a torrent of vermin. Masses of itchy insect bites apparently increase the hairshirt's devotional benefits. Later, a repentant Henry opts for the hairy punishment himself.

VIRGIN TERRITORY

The mythical unicorn has the body of a horse, beard of a goat, and the tail of the lion. The one-horned beast becomes a legendary symbol of magic and power, for it is believed that the horn can neutralize poison. He is reputed to be such a fierce animal that no one can capture him—except a *real* virgin, because the unicorn will gently lay his head in her lap. Of course, a real virgin is much easier to find than a real unicorn, but the legend persists for centuries. Caesar tells of a unicorn in his "Tall Tales," and the Greek historian Ctesias of Cnidas writes of seeing a unicorn goblet while a guest of the King of Persia in 4 B.C. A unicorn goblet is the best that Elizabeth I can find—even though she *is* a real virgin—at a cost of 10,000 pounds (about $125,000 by today's standard), which sends her financial ministers reeling.

Above: Virgin and Unicorn, *tapestry, 15th c.* **Below right:** *Errol Flynn in* The Adventures of Robin Hood, *1938.*

GROOM . . . ING: When Richard the Lion-Hearted marries in 1190, he isn't tame in his choice of wedding clothes. He dons a rose-colored satin surcoat, a long, gold-embroidered mantle, and a bonnet of scarlet and gold. How can Princess Berengaria of Navarre hold her own? We'll never know. What the bride wore, says historian Thomas B. Costain, "wasn't important enough to set down."

THE STUFF OF LEGENDS

Errol Flynn, a legend in his own time, might have sported green tights, short green doublet with dagged edges, and a neat green cap (so he'd be well camouflaged in the forest) in his portrayal of the famous folk hero, but the real Robin Hood is a mystery. He supposedly conducted guerilla warfare from his hideaway in Sherwood Forest, robbing the Norman rich and feeding the Saxon poor, for over a century. If he was real, perhaps Sherwood Forest had a hidden fountain of youth.

Slightly missing the point, when sixteenth-century King Henry VIII wonders what the simple folk do to break the monotony of everyday life, he dresses up like Robin, rounds up *his* band of merry courtiers and hides behind the doors of Catherine of Aragon's bedchamber—waiting to scare the ladies.

DRESSED TO KILL

SLENDER IS THE KNIGHT: No single figure is more identified with the Middle Ages than the noble knight—riding about the countryside on his majestic steed, performing good works, and besting opponents in jousts, all for the glory of his lady.

The "knight in shining armor" has become such a cliché that the first thing we have to do is set a little history straight—not all horses in the Middle Ages are white, and knights, at least until the end of the fifteenth century, when they are worried about gunshot wounds and willing to try anything, are not walking tin men. Originally, knights wear shirts of chain mail—made by connecting steel links with metal plates. There is much time and labor involved in making these shirts; so the knightly profession is restricted to the rich, who can afford the uniforms. As time goes on, small plates and patches of metal are applied at the knees and elbows to reinforce the mail; this seems like a good idea, so more plates are added. You get the picture—gradually we have the metal suit.

But although a full suit of armor might weigh a hefty 60–70 pounds, compared to the 98–106 pounds of baggage that nineteenth-century cavalrymen are burdened with, the knight's baggage seems pretty tolerable. Essential accessories: his *gauntlets*, leather or metal gloves; his *maritel*, a thrusting weapon; and, of course, his *lance*.

He begins his career as a page at age seven or eight by going to live on the estate of a lord. There he is expected to act as a kind of personal butler: he may carry the vegetables to table, lay out his master's clothes for the next day, or sweetly sing his mistress to sleep. He is often dressed in red and pictured carrying a white wand.

When he reaches his teens, the knight-in-waiting becomes a squire. He dresses in brown and white, which are good colors for working with horses: he oversees the stables. When he rides with his master, he changes into more elegant blue or gold and white.

Then, in preparation for knighthood, he has his hair cut in a tonsure to show his devotion to God. He is carefully bathed the night before his investiture, to insure he'll be clean when he enters Paradise. The next day, he dons three different robes—white for purity, red for the blood he is willing to shed for a worthy cause, black to show his willingness to die. Finally, he gets the swack—a hard slap to the side of his head with a sword—and as day becomes knight, so does he.

SWORDPLAY

Around 500, a young lad named Arthur pulls a sword out of a stone to become the king of England, and over the next millennium, a sword will be the badge of the well-dressed, well-heeled man. After all, swords not only look dashing, but they're also just the thing to have along if you're traipsing off to the Middle East on a Crusade.

By 1100, a tap from a king's sword turns a humble squire into a noble knight; and from then on, he'll wear his own sword proudly at all times. He'll hang it at his left side from a wide leather belt and, to balance its weight, secure it to a strap on his right. And with the same reverence with which people place their hands on the Bible to "swear to God," he'll clasp the handle of his sword to pledge an undying vow.

Other weapons become critical fashion notes, too. Throughout the Middle Ages, a nobleman will sport a decorative dagger, called a *misericorde*, stuck into his belt or through the strap of his purse. And by 1500, men will even take to wearing special dress swords, lighter and more elaborately jeweled than those used in actual battle, to give them a courtly flair.

BUTTONS ON YOUR OVERCOAT: The button is invented around 1200—but originally as a decoration, not a fastener. Why? One explanation is that buttons make it too easy to open clothes—people literally believe that they represent a "loose life." As an accessory, however, buttons are all the rage, sewn along the hems of dresses, around collars, up and down sleeves. It is not unusual for a single garment to be decorated with dozens of disks.

The button for the *most* buttons (if he can find room to pin it on), is awarded to Francis I, sixteenth century king of France, when he has his tailor decorate one posh black velvet suit with 13,600 gold buttons.

Opposite: *Italian armor, 15th c.;* **Inset:** *French armor, ca. 1450.* **Above:** *Italian sword, ca. 1490.* **Right:** *Marguerite of Provence, ca. 1390.*

> "Man's earthly interests are all hooked and buttoned together by clothes."
>
> —Thomas Carlyle

THE HERALD-RY TRIBUNE

In 10,000 B.C., creative cavemen copy buffalo drawings from their walls onto their shields when they leave home. These "totems" become the very first coats of arms.

Once armor is invented, around the eleventh century, all soldiers tend to look alike, especially after the invention of the *heaume*, a metal helmet that totally hides the face. Even a mother couldn't recognize her beloved son wearing one of these contraptions, and after allies begin killing each other off at the Battle of Hastings because they can't tell one side from the other, it's clear that something's got to be done.

Leave it to Geoffrey IV of Anjou to become the father of heraldry. After seeing how the Moslems mark their garments and livery to do battle in the Crusades, he designs a lion (a symbol of strength and beauty) to be drawn on his cap and shield. He adds a plume of yellow broom, *planta genesta*, to his helmet, and he, his son Henry II, and their descendants become known as the House of Plantagenets.

By 1270, every knight worth his armor carries a coat of arms to tell the world who he is. The Knights Templar wear a red cross emblazoned on their surcoats; the Knights of St. John the Baptist brandish a Maltese cross; and even cities and abbeys take on heraldic symbols. There's fierce competition to register particular signs first, with everyone wanting to include a good omen, such as a camel, to represent endurance, a fox for cunning, or an eagle, the most powerful bird.

If you think things got complicated in the 1980s, when married couples became "hyphenates," imagine the confusion as men and women try to combine their coats of arms. Clothes are bestrewn with symbols or, to represent two houses, divided into different colored sections—and so another fad for particolored clothing is born. By the end of the fifteenth century, men are wearing hose with one striped leg and the other a contrasting solid or with gay quadrants of bright colors.

You're not likely to see many people today wearing their family crests on their sleeves. But coats of arms are definitely still around. The most notable examples appear on state flags, designer jeans, Tudor-style family restaurants, and beer bottles.

Top right: *Coat of arms of the Vanderbilt family.* **Center left:** *Shield of Robert Washington, 1622.* **Center right:** *Standard of Romania's royal house.*

NO KIDDING: The most extreme expression of the particolor craze is the *motley* that fools or court jesters wear—outrageous combinations of patterns and colors. Not only can a fool wear any colors he wants, he can also speak his mind and get away with it. And to show it's all in good fun, he tops off his outfit with a parody of a hood—several long, floppy points, tipped with bells, that look like asses' ears.

SHOE SIZES

The Middle Ages find both noble men and women in shoes of soft leather ornamented with jewels, gold and silver medallions, and embroidery. By the twelfth century, the upper classes wear shoes of silk and velvet, some ornamented with pearls—brought back to Europe in Crusaders' pouches—which become the favorite accessory of Eleanor of Aquitaine. Shoes may be blue, green, or even pink, but red is the favorite with both sexes.

Peasant footwear is much more down to earth, sometimes just a piece of leather tied around the foot and gathered at the ankle, like a pouch. In the eleventh century French and Belgian peasants wear a wooden shoe called a *sabot*. When angry serfs trample their lord's crops, a new word is born to mean "intentional destruction" of the lord's crops: *sabotage*.

By the 1300s, men take to *poulaines* or pointed shoes, inspired by the long, stuffed toes of chain mail—though you'd think they'd have learned their lesson. In 1386, Austrian knights fighting in the Battle of Sempach are forced to break the points off their shoes before leaping from their horses and battling on the ground. Made of leather or sometimes velvet, poulaines can be fifteen inches long or more. Toes are stuffed with hay and wool; points are shaped by whalebone. The ultimate pointed shoe is the *crackow* (named for the Polish city), which is ridiculously long—up to twenty-four inches—but it's no joke. Introduced by the courtiers Isabella of France brings with her when she marries Richard II of England, the crackow grows so popular that it prompts a new sumptuary law—the wealthier a man, the longer the toes of his shoes can be.

Like men's footwear, women's shoes also get pointier during the Middle Ages, and many take to soft, inner socklike liners to protect their feet from pinching.

Outdoors, both men and women wear loose *pattens* or *galoches*, thick wooden platforms attached to the feet with buckled straps. For a while these clunkers even come indoors at the fashionable court of Burgundy. Both sexes also like loose-fitting boots made of leather that may be trimmed with lace, and stylish men often sport thigh-high, deep-cuffed models complete with cowboy spurs.

After hours (and for Christmas gift-giving) the well-heeled switch to *slippers*, which are invented in 1479 and so named because they are easy to slip on and off. Favorite colors: vermilion, purple, and scarlet.

I SPY: In 1287, Florentine Armato degli Armati makes a spectacle of himself by inventing the first eyeglass. Ground from beryl and quartz, the single lens sits in a frame with a wooden handle.

By the fifteenth century, people discover that two lenses are better than one, and so the first *pair* of glasses is born. They soon become a symbol of influence and status, as only people who can read affect them.

Fifteenth-century glasses don't sit on the nose. They're attached to handles and framed in leather, brass, nickel, or iron and, for the wealthy, silver or gold. The prominent Italian scholar and heretic, Savonarola, comes up with an even better idea—he hooks his lenses onto his hat.

▌**Top:** *Poulaine with fifteen-inch-long toe.* **Bottom right:** St. Peter and St. Dorothy *(detail), Master of Bartholomew, 1505.*

COIFUSION

During the thirteenth century, hats for men start coming back. Teachers and philosophers wear long black gowns and square-cut caps which are fitted tightly against their skulls. In an era when most people are illiterate, it becomes a widespread notion that these hats have magical powers—people talk about "putting on my thinking cap." They might not be magic, but women's pillbox-shaped caps with their attached chin straps do have the power to charm.

Then even the most august members of the clergy, as well as lawyers and academics, take to the *coif*—a close-fitting bonnet made of white linen, tied under the chin with strings. The coif survives into the sixteenth and seventeenth centuries as the emblem of the professional man and on into our own time, in wool, as a cute winter hat for a baby or a 1950s coed.

Before long, although they can't compete with women's styles, men do get some more glamorous hats—Robin Hood hats with pointed visors and high crowns; hats with ostrich plumes; turbans or *chaperons*; and tall sugarloaf hats that look like shoeboxes perched on the head. And by the fifteenth century, beaver hats, of enormous proportions, become a status symbol for the wealthy European dandy.

Clockwise from top right: Federgo da Montefeltro, *Piero della Francesca*, ca. 1465; St. Anthony and St. George, *(detail)*, Vittore Pisano, 15th c.; Money Changer with Wife, *Quentin Metsys (ca. 1466–1530)*; Resurrection of Lazarus, *(detail)*, Albert van Ouwater, mid-15th c.; The Painter's Father, *Albrecht Durer*, ca. 1497; Louis II of Anjou by *an unknown artist*, ca. 1412.

CHAILLOT, CHAILLOT, THAT TINKLING TOWN: Every thirteenth-century fashionplate who isn't covered with buttons is sewing bells, the latest fashion accessory, all over his or her gowns. The jingling makes a wonderful counterpoint to the flip-flop of their long-toed shoes.

FAIR PLAY

What do the simple folk do for recreation in the Middle Ages (and what do they wear)? Sports clothes and team uniforms haven't been invented yet, so they make do with the fashions of the times for an afternoon of ice-skating, bearbaiting, blindman's bluff (a favorite with adults as well as children), tennis, ninepins, and a lawn game with mallets that is either cricket or croquet. Indoors they may indulge in a round of cards, backgammon, chess, or dicing, although local authorities frown on gambling. In Portugal, the penalty for cheating in any game or playing with dishonest dice is death, although by the fifteenth century this penalty is reduced to flogging, exile, or payment of a fine.

COME HALF AN HOUR EARLY: By the 1300s Paris bathhouses are open twenty-four hours a day. If you're lucky enough to have a bath in your own home, it's only polite to invite dinner guests to bathe before you feed them.

Top left: Men play at an early form of curling. **Center right:** Illustration, man wearing bells, late 15th c. **Bottom right:** Medieval tailor shop.

SEW NEW

In the Middle Ages, fashionable clothes are no longer made at home. Thanks to the desire for finer, hand-crafted garments, tailoring becomes the new upscale profession. By 1292, 482 tailors are working out of Paris shops and by 1300, the figure jumps to 702.

MEDIEVAL TOOTHPASTE: Whether you bathe or not, you have to take care of your teeth. There's a medieval formula for keeping them pearly white. Combine:

3 handfuls of flowers
3 handfuls of sage, nettle, rosemary, mallow, olive, and plantain leaves
3 handfuls of walnut roots
2 handfuls each of rock rose, horehound, and bramble tops
1 pound of flour
½ pound of myrtle seed

2 handfuls of rosebuds
2 drachms each of sandalwood, coriander, and citron pips
3 drachms of cinnamon
10 drachms of cypress nuts
5 green pine cones
2 drachms of mastic and Armenian clay

Reduce the mixture to a powder, then pour in sharp black wine. Let the mixture sit for three days, then press out the wine. Distill residue on a gentle fire combined with two ounces of alum. Fill your mouth with mixture. Rub teeth with a finger wrapped in linen.

Above: *Teeth from De Humani Corporis Fabrica Libri Septem by Andreas Vesalius, physician to the Holy Roman Emperor Charles V, 1543.* **Left:** *Illustration from a medical manuscript, German, 15th c.*

ESSENCE BARE

NUDE YORK: Medieval men and women sleep naked and don't think twice about complete nudity. They often trot through the streets to the public baths wearing less than we'd dare wear on beaches today. And bosoms are often bared—pushed up and out at a population which has been decimated by the Black Plague and needs to make more babies.

QUACK, QUACK: Who is that strange, bird-like man of plague-ridden Europe? He's a doctor scurrying around the streets wearing a beak mask filled with medicines and herbs to protect him from evil vapors.

And who can blame him? As the fourteenth century unfolds, the Black Death—a form of bubonic plague—sweeps Europe, another souvenir of the Crusades. Between 1334 and 1354, nearly 75 percent of the population of Europe and Asia will die.

Left: Charity, *Lucas Cranach the Elder, ca. 1520.* **Above:** *Beak-like masks keep germs nosed out.*

IF YOU CAN STOMACH IT

Over the course of the Middle Ages, women's waistlines migrate from the hips to below the breasts, at times lodging at the natural waist. Of course, with so much attention focussed on their middles, ladies grow self-conscious about rogue bumps and bulges, so that time-honored tormentor, the corset, is revived. There's no iron-clad rule about the way a lady is corseted. Most wear a linen garment, reinforced with whalebone or metal bands, which laces up and is tightened with a wooden or whalebone busk. Damsels give their gallants their lacings as tokens of affection, which the gents display on their arms or their hats.

Not only are midriffs streamlined, but breasts are flattened too, with a "stomacher"—a rigid, decorated pasteboard that fills in the deep V openings on late-medieval gowns. Jeanne of Bourbon, the wife of Charles V of France, sports fifty buttons on her buttoned-down chest.

1334 GIOTTO, THE FATHER OF MODERN PAINTING, IS MADE ARCHITECT TO THE CITY OF FLORENCE.

1337 WILLIAM MERLEE OF OXFORD ATTEMPTS THE FIRST SCIENTIFIC WEATHER FORECASTS.

CHIN UPS

An Egyptian queen wore a false beard as a symbol of masculine power, but in the Middle Ages, swathed chins become an emblem of femininity. The English start the trend with an early form of the *wimple*—a linen cloth draped like a bib, completely encircling the face, topped off with a veil. Soon similar styles sweep Europe, beginning with the popular *barbette*, a chin band attached to a pillbox hat. A married woman might wear a *gorget*, an even more concealing bib, stretching from the chest to the ears; and widows switch to a pleated version, the *barbe*. The height of the barbe is strictly regulated by the sumptuary laws. Women of baroness rank on down wear their barbes below their chins; higher noblewomen wear them slightly above; and only a queen can wear a barbe that covers her chin completely.

Fashion becomes law in the fifteenth century when, needing some explanation for the Virgin Birth, the Catholic Church decides that Mary conceived through her ear. Consequently, it decrees the female ear a sexual organ and demands that women wear wimples at all times to keep their ears well covered.

DON'T GUILD THE LILY

By the fourteenth century guilds not only regulate the professional rights and responsibilities of workers, but they also have something to say about their dress. Merchants are advised to dress discreetly, in plain, somber clothes, to promote the confidence of their customers.

Top left: Portrait of a Woman, Albert Altdorfer, ca. 1520. Top right: Portrait head from a tomb, with stiffened linen cap and barbette, French, 13th c. Left: Miniature of merchants, Italian, early 15th c.

HAT CHAT

Like men, women shun hats in the early Middle Ages. If a maid is young, she simply wears her hair down and free. When she marries, she'll adopt a scarf or a veil. For variety she might wear a *crespine*, a band of gold or silver, occasionally embellished with jewels. And to keep stray wisps in check, she'll add a hairnet, or *caul*, of fine gold wire interwoven with pearls.

But in the late fourteenth century when Isabelle of Bavaria arrives in France to marry Charles VI, she brings with her a taste for outlandish millinery that will soon beguile all of Europe. Women of her court sport *bour-relets*—wide, padded rolls anchored on top of their hair, which is arranged in egg-shaped wads at each temple. Isabelle's greatest innovation, however, is the *hennin*—a towering, cone-shaped headdress that grows to fantastic proportions over the fifteenth century. Soon there's a horned version (two hennins in one, with a cone enclosing each twirled braid); a butterfly style, always draped with veils; and airy confections of visible wires supporting leaves of sheer fabric.

The name *hennin* has no actual meaning (though its style is an extreme version of the Turkish fez, introduced to Europe by Crusaders); rather, it's the word shouted at noblewomen as they walk down the street arrayed in the preposterous-looking hats. But whatever people think of them, hennins bolster the economy: hatmakers are kept busy; an extraordinary amount of velvet and silk, often in contrasting colors—is consumed; and architects throughout Europe have to redesign building entrances so high-hatted women can walk through them without ducking.

The hennin reaches its most extravagant heights in style-conscious France and Burgundy. Elsewhere in Europe, women opt for more compact, if equally strange, designs. The Flemish hennin is a short, blunt cone, often with a band of velvet framing the face; Italians show some hair, topped with turbanlike rolls; and Germans wear a high, padded, half-melon headdress, sheathing their foreheads with veils. The English latch on to a window theme, developing a ram's horn-shaped headpiece hung with veils, which looks like a row of curtains, complete with valance. They also construct an unusual gable hood with sharp, architectural points at the top and at the temples.

All these hat styles pose a special problem for queens: If you're wearing an outrageous hat, for fashion's sake, where do you put your crown? So throughout the Middle Ages, coronets and diadems are designed to fit an elegant queen's hat collection rather than her head.

Clockwise from top right: Portrait of a Young Princess, *Master of Moulins, 15th c.;* Portrait of a Young Lady, *Piero del Pollaiuolo, ca. 1470;* Company of court ladies from Le Livre des Trois Vertus, *Christine de Pisan, French, 15th c.;* Portrait of Isabelle of Portugal, *Flemish School, 1445.*

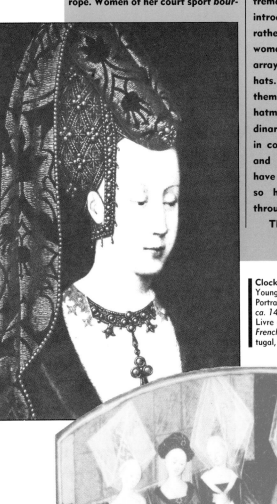

141

1350 THE SHOGUNATE OF JAPAN FORBIDS THE DRINKING OF TEA.

1352 ARAB GEOGRAPHER IBN BATTUTA EXPLORES THE SAHARA DESERT.

DOUBLET YOUR FUN

With their new, abbreviated silhouettes, fourteenth-century men need smarter coverups than long, flowing mantles. One solution is the *pourpoint* or *jupon*, which develops in the fourteenth century when plate armor replaces chain mail. Because plate armor is closely fitted, with sharp points, the pourpoint develops as a sleek, tight jacket, padded to protect the body. Better still, it makes the chest swell out and gives a girl a chance to take stock of a guy's gams.

Predictably, some moralists denounce the style as vulgar (and some claim the French lost the Battle of Crecy because their soldiers were so indecently clad). But handsome knights are loath to abandon such a sexy style, even après battle. The pourpoint and its variants—the shorter *journade* and the even sexier *courtepy*, with its pinched waist and padded shoulders (called *mahoitres*) remain in vogue until the fifteenth century, when they evolve into the *doublet*.

Top left: Charles VII of France, *Jean Fouquet, ca. 1470.* Top right: *Pourpoint of Charles of Blois, 1367.* Center left: *The Black Prince's jupon, 14th c.* Bottom right: *Silver pomander from France.* Far right: *Pomander decorated with figures of saints and a statuette of Mary, German, ca. 1470.*

FLEA FROM ME: By the mid-1300s, the hairshirt has an opposite number—the flea coat, a shaggy lounging robe, usually made out of wolfskin. Its purpose is to induce fleas to flee the wearer and make a dive for the coat.

STRONG ENOUGH FOR A MAN, BUT MADE FOR A WOMAN: Believing it wards off fevers and depressions, women of the 1350s carry a sponge soaked in perfumed vinegar in an exquisitely gilded bauble called a *pomander* that dangles from a belt or is worn as a necklace. By the 1600s, men also begin to discover the joys of pomanders, especially in Venice where a whiff can dispel ripe fumes from the canals. Later, Queen Elizabeth I of England collects pomanders along with watches, shoes, and jewels.

TRUE BLUE: As the Church strives for new heights of power in the Middle Ages, it brooks no threats to its authority. So, in 1233, Pope Gregory IX institutes the Inquisition—a system to try and to punish those suspected of heresy. These tribunals persist for some three hundred years, growing infamous for their cruelty and corruption. Then, in the late fifteenth century, Spain goes the Vatican one better by establishing a special Inquisition of its own.

Upper-crust ladies are spared the tyranny of the Spanish Inquisition. They're easily recognized by their creamy white complexions. What are the poor, swarthier Moors to do? They bleed themselves white so their blue veins stick out—to become pale, true, blue bloods.

Above: *Manuscript illustration of blood-letting, 14th c.*

FURTHERMORE

Like everything else in this era, there's a hierarchy to the hides people wear. Fourteenth-century peasants catch beavers, sheep, badgers, cats, and goats; nobles demand rarer ermines and sables. Kings and emperors opt for "vair," the designer fur of the day—a classy combination of gray and white squirrels. If you're Henry I, in the 1100s, you'll like sable in your mantle. If you're King Edward III, you'll spend 24.2% of your 1342–3 budget on furs. You'll also like black-tipped ermine so much that you'll restrict it to your personal use; and thereafter, ermine will be thought of as a symbol of royalty.

Nobleman removing his fur-lined robe before flagellation, from the Bocaccio of Duc de Berry, ca. 1390.

UNDER PINNINGS: They not only feed them to their pigs, they wear them. *Slops* are the linen underbriefs every nobleman dons under his calf-length tunic in the thirteenth century. A streamlined version of the loincloth or "diaper breeches," slops protect the skin from the harsh texture of clothes and protects clothes (at least a little) from a dirty body. Men also wear a linen undershirt.

Women still aren't wearing any underwear, although they do wear an undergown—a long-sleeved, full-skirted chemise.

1370 THE STEEL CROSSBOW IS FIRST USED AS A WEAPON OF WAR.

1375 THE CHARACTER OF "ROBIN HOOD" FIRST APPEARS IN ENGLISH LITERATURE.

PHYSICAL THERAPY

The answers to some of the great, unsolved mysteries of the fashion world can be found in the physical misfortunes of our leaders. Discover how the celebrated make lemonade when handed lemons:

Queen Nefertiti, the Nile beauty, dons a crown with a wide top, introducing a whole new look to an Egypt traditionally topped off with heavy, curled wigs, headbands, and pointed crowns. Accentuating her Audrey Hepburn cheekbones, the crown also hides her peculiar, elongated head, a trait she shares with her husband, Akenaten. Why not? He also happens to be her brother.

Emperor Hadrian grows a beard to disguise his wart-covered chin, and within two weeks, wives throughout the Empire were subject to scratchy good-morning kisses.

The rise of long skirts in the fifteenth century is attributed to the bad gams of the daughters of King Louis XI of France.

In the thirteenth century Empress Taki of China glances down at her misshappen tootsies and takes a giant step backward. She decrees that every female infant born from then on will have their feet bound. With a giant leap of faith, her subjects obey, christening their tiny club feet "little pearls."

In the 1600s, Queen Elizabeth helps to popularize the high collar by wearing one to hid her spindly neck.

The bottom buttons of vests are still left undone, because Edward VII, the corpulent son of Queen Victoria, is too fat to close his.

In the fourteenth century Count Fulk of Anjou popularizes shoes with enormous points to disguise his ugly feet.

All the women in Medieval paintings look like they're pregnant because a fat Queen Isabella makes it fashionable to be plump. Other women, embarrassed by their stick-thin figures, tie pillows to their stomachs. Years later, however, Mme. de Montespan popularizes the soft, flowing *robe de chambre* to hide her numerous pregnancies.

Crimean war hero Lord Henry Raglan appears on the scene in a slouch-shouldered jacket that is such a success that it is named after Raglan and is still worn today. No doubt the unique construction of the sleeve is due to Raglan's combat experience—in which he lost an arm.

In the late 1800s, Princess Alexandra of Wales sports a heavy parasol to support her as she walks, because a childhood illness has left her with a limp. Obviously the most influential trendsetter of all, not only is the parasol adopted as an essential accessory, so is the limp.

When Duke Phillip of Burgundy loses his hair during a severe illness, 500 loyal nobles in his Medieval court chop off their locks in sympathy.

Opposite page: left: *Limestone bust of Nefertiti, ca. 1372–1350 B.C.*; Right: *Jane Curtin as the Conehead Prymaat, on Saturday Night Live, 1976.* This page: Top: *Poulaines with pattens, known as "devil's claws," ca. 1440*; Center left: *Hadrian (A.D. 76–138)*; Center: *Hans Steininger, ca. 1565*; Center right: *Engraving by Israel Van Meckenem, ca. 1470.* Below: *Advertisement for Herpicide Hair and Scalp Remedy, 1905.*

1378 THE GREAT SCHISM BEGINS, AS TWO POPES ARE ELECTED, ONE IN ROME AND ONE IN AVIGNON.

1385 THEY HAD A BALL—THE VERY FIRST IN FRANCE—TO CELEBRATE THE MARRIAGE OF CHARLES VI AND ISABELLA OF BAVARIA.

IN THE HABIT

Considering the power of the Church in the Middle Ages, priestly attire gains a real cachet. Here are the basic garments no fashion-conscious ecclesiast could ever do without:

• **CASSOCK:** Everyday wear for priests—a long-sleeved, ankle-length, close-fitting garment with thirty-three buttons, one for each year of Christ's life.

• **AMICE:** A rectangular shawl that forms a snappy collar and protects the other sumptuous garments from sweat.

• **ALB:** A linen tunic worn under the cassock. It comes in white as a sign of chastity, and is embroidered at the hem, chest, and sleeves to signify Christ's wounds.

• **CINCTURE:** A belt that is another symbol of chastity—but how come it's tied so loosely?

• **CHASUBLE:** A poncho-style coverup made of silk and lavishly embroidered, worn while saying mass.

• **MANIPLE:** A silk handkerchief worn draped over the left arm, just like a waiter's towel.

• **STOLE:** A long scarf symbolizing ordination, worn when the priest administers the sacraments. A deacon of the church gets an extra-special privilege—he can drape his stole over one shoulder and fasten it at his hip, like a Miss America banner.

• **MITER:** a two-horned hat, worn by bishops, representing the twin rays of light that shone above Moses when he went to get the Ten Commandments; or, possibly, the mouth of a fish, the symbol of Christ.

Nuns get barely a glimmer of priestly glamour. Their costumes shape up as basically a less jazzy version of everyday medieval dress. Still, during the Middle Ages, there's a resurgence of interest in the religious life as a refuge from unchivalrous men—or simply as a source of free bed and board for those from plagued or Crusade-torn families. Women flock to convents wearing their usual huge white wimples, veils, and barbes, which then become an established part of the habit.

Aprons are added as a sign of service (although fashionable women are wearing them *to* the nunneries as well) and girdles hang from cloaks to carry the Cross of Christ. The plain white band that winds around the forehead dates from the time of Henry II (we don't know why—like it or not, there's not a reason for everything). But we *can* tell you the reason there are always nine buttons on a nun's cape— that is the exact number of letters in the word *obedience*, a nun's stock in trade.

Nuns' wear changes little throughout the centuries, though it is reported in 1593 that one order favors rouge, powder, and other makeup. This, of course, is an order of *Parisian* nuns. Does the practice last? Nun such luck. They, like their counterparts across the world, are soon clean scrubbed again.

Medieval miniature of a monk and nun conversing.

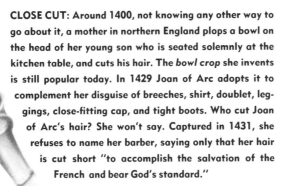

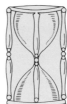

CLOSE CUT: Around 1400, not knowing any other way to go about it, a mother in northern England plops a bowl on the head of her young son who is seated solemnly at the kitchen table, and cuts his hair. The *bowl crop* she invents is still popular today. In 1429 Joan of Arc adopts it to complement her disguise of breeches, shirt, doublet, leggings, close-fitting cap, and tight boots. Who cut Joan of Arc's hair? She won't say. Captured in 1431, she refuses to name her barber, saying only that her hair is cut short "to accomplish the salvation of the French and bear God's standard."

HOOPLA: Late in the fourteenth century, the tight, confining *cotehardie* gown gives way to the flowing *houppelande*. For men, who are still reluctant to cover their shapely legs, houppelandes come in midcalf and knee-length as well as long styles. Early houppelandes have high collars, lavish draping, huge sleeves and are often made of sumptuous fabrics. At the trend-setting Burgundian court, the clotheshorse Philip the Bold wears a glamorous black houppelande adorned with twenty-two roses—in gold and precious gems—on his left sleeve.

Women's houppelandes are floor length and high waisted, belted with jeweled girdles below the breasts. Necklines start out high, but by the fifteenth century they plunge so low that bare backs and even breasts can be seen. Sometimes these low-cut, U-shaped bodices are filled in with "modesty vests"; sometimes bosoms are exposed, right to the nipple; and sometimes breasts are bound with tight, peekaboo lacing that the Catholic Church calls the "gates of hell." Well, seek and ye shall find. . . .

But overexposed or not, one thing is certain: No woman would *ever* display her bare arms. Considered indecent, arms are always covered with sleeves. In fact, the sleeves of women's gowns can grow incredibly long and wide—the ends draping down to the floor—with their edges "dagged" or cut into fantastic patterns.

"[There is] so much pouncing of chisel to make holes, so much dagging of shears, with the superfluity in length of the aforesaid gowns, trailing in the dung and in the mire, on horse and eke on foot, as well of man as of woman."

—Chaucer, "The Parson's Tale"

SOAP DISH: What to do when roast suckling pig sauce dribbles down your tunic or you're splattered with mincemeat pie? By 1450, housewives are boiling linens and wools in water and scrubbing them with the newest cleaning aid—homemade lye soap. Silk is a special problem—fuller's earth moistened with lye is applied to grease spots or, sometimes, the garment is left to soak overnight in white wine or vinegar.

In England, for washing your face, you can use soap made from candle tallow. But soap won't become a big deal or a big business until the 1500s, when Castille soap is

imported from Spain and Venetian soap is considered very elegant at a penny a pound. By the 1600s, business is really bubbling for Henry Broadstreet, who has the biggest soap store in London. He sells pounds of soap at the rate of a hundred barrels a day.

Top left: *Joan of Arc (1412–1431).* **Top right:** *"Friend of Fashion," 12th-century lace bodice on a demon guarding the gates of Hell, from the Cottonian Manuscript.* **Left:** *Female bathing attendants, Bohemian miniature, ca. 1400.*

'S WONDERFUL

The ideal fifteenth-century woman is shaped like an S—her head is inclined forward, her breast is drawn inward, and her hips and belly are pushed out. Surprisingly, though a trim waist is highly prized under a body-hugging *cotehardie* or *houppelande*, bellies are allowed to bulge free—even, if necessary, filled out with padding.

▌Above: *Portrait of a lady with a bird, Burgundian, ca. 1450.*

HORSE CLOTHES

QUE SOREL, SOREL—For all the repressiveness of the Church, courtesans achieve a new prominence during the Middle Ages. One of the most celebrated is Agnes Sorel, the eighteen-year-old chestnut-haired mistress of King Charles VII of France. Sorel's great influence over the king wins her many enemies (it is suspected that she died of poisoning); but to the French painter, Jean Fouquet, she is a Madonna, which is how he paints her. Not only is Sorel one of the most famous courtesans to come out of the closet, making royal paramours officially recognized at court, but the clothes she brings out with her expand French fashion horizons. Sorel decides that noblewomen should trim their gowns with fur, with the most important ones wearing the widest bands, and—more boldly—drops her neckline to her waist, baring her perfect breasts. She also plucks her hairline to create one of the most extreme egghead looks around. Agnes also likes a false chignon or two and, thanks to her, wigmaking becomes a huge business in France.

▌Right: *Agnes Sorel portrayed in* Virgin and Child, *Jean Fouquet, ca. 1450.* Far right: Apocalypse of St. Jean *(detail), tapestry, Nicolas Bataille, 1375–1381.*

GOOD MANNERS FOR GIRLS

Every proper young damsel knows that there's a fine line between uncouth and ladylike behavior. To keep yourself on the track, follow these tips from fifteenth-century author Jean Sulpice.

• Your dress should be clean and without filth.

• Do not let your face or hands be dirty.

• Take care that no drippings from the nose hang there like icicles that one sees hanging from the rafters and eaves of houses in winter.

• Your fingernails should not be too long or full of filth.

• Make sure that your hair is well combed and that your headdress is not full of feathers or other trash.

• Your shoes should be clean and not dirty or muddy.

• Your tongue should not be covered with filth.

• Have your teeth clean and without rust—that is to say, without the yellow matter attached to them as a result of insufficient cleansing.

• Understand that it is improper and discourteous to: scratch your head at the table, remove from your neck fleas or other vermin and kill them in front of others, scratch or pull at scabs in whatever part of the body they may be.

• If you have to blow your nose, you should not remove the excrement with the fingers, but in a handkerchief.

• If you spit or cough, you need not swallow what you have already drawn into the throat, but spit on the ground or into a handkerchief or napkin.

• If you are forced to belch, do so as quietly as possible, always averting the face.

149

THE TOP TEN MEDIEVAL PASTIMES

1. **JOUSTING**

2. **CRUSADING**

3. **WENCHING**

4. **WASTRELING**

5. **JUGGLING**

6. **FAIRING**

7. **NUNNING**

8. **CATHEDRAL BUILDING**

9. **SLEEPING IN THE NUDE**

10. **PLAYING LORD OF THE MANOR**

Clockwise from top center: *Knights jousting, Manese Manuscript, 13th c.; crusading knight, detail from an English manuscript; painting of an adulterous couple on a wood panel; Dancing minstrel, 11th c.; Anglo-Saxon gleemen of the 10th c.; engraving of everyday knightly society, Baccio Baldini, 1460; Last Judgement (detail), Giovanni di Paola, 14th c.; book illustration from Grandes Chroniques de Saint-Denis, 14th c.; Medieval depiction of the wife of Potiphar sleeping in the nude; Charles VIII entertaining Frederick III at Trier, ca. 1485.*

Below left: *Portrait medallion of Count Philip the Good of Burgundy, French, ca. 1440.* **Below center:** *Gold ring with malachite pyramid, Central European, ca. 1500.* **Right:** *St. Eligius, Petrus Christus, 1449.* **Bottom right:** *Silver-gilt brooch, Hungarian, 13th c.*

TREASURE HUNT

Medieval Anglican law decrees that a mother must bequeath land, slaves, and money to her sons—the only things you can pull a King Lear on with your daughters are rings, bracelets, and necklaces. So one of the unsung heroes of the Middle Ages is the jeweler. This painting is originally commissioned by the goldsmith's guild in 1449 to celebrate their work.

The couple in this picture are buying a wedding ring—making their purchase from none other than St. Eligius, the patron saint of goldsmiths (pictured here as just a plain old guy). Let's go on a treasure hunt. How many items of jewelry—and tools of the jeweler's trade—can you find in the painting?

WHAT YOU WIN if you spot 10 items—A badger's tooth ring, guaranteed to bring you wealth. 9 items—A toadstone, with the ability to change color in the presence of poison in food or drink (not a bad thing to have around if you have a large inheritance and don't trust your relatives, or, you frequent the Seafarer of the Aegean Coffee Shop and Reptile Museum more than four times a month). 8 items—A cameo, embossed with your portrait, suitable for sealing letters. 7 items—A wolf's tooth on a chain to act as a charm against assault. 6 items or fewer—Buy yourself a new pair of glasses.

THE ANSWERS: Filigreed gold belt buckle; string of beads; collection of unmounted rubies and other stones; cluster of seed pearls in open leather pouch; two gold brooches; a pendant embellished with rubies, pearls, and emeralds; a pair of gold-mounted fossilized shark's teeth; the wedding ring; weights; coins; the goldsmith's mirror.

THE
RENAISSANCE

THE RENAISSANCE
AS THE WORLD TURNS

The Renaissance is the Age of Discovery, and the rediscovery of Classical Aesthetics. Leonardo, who is trying to do everything well, epitomizes the "Renaissance Man." From China, Marco Polo brings back fabulous tales of golden palaces, mermaids, volcanoes, and embroidered silks and precious gems. The conquistadores (who don't care how anyone dresses) melt down most of South America and bring back extraordinary fortunes. There is a tremendous investment in the exotic. And for the first time in two centuries, both men and women abandon their loose-fitting robes.

Like a great wind, in 1300 the Renaissance begins to stir in Italy; by the fifteenth and sixteenth centuries it sweeps through Europe, blowing away customs and institutions that have dominated Europe for almost a thousand years, leaving in its wake new ideas and attitudes that still influence our lives today.

With the rise of towns that begins in the Middle Ages, the limelight shifts from feudal estates to cities. Urban life is exuberant and prosperous—and people take pleasure in being alive. It is an age of adventure and curiosity: the Renaissance man takes a new interest in the world around him. He sets out on dangerous voyages; tries daring experiments in astronomy; and most of all, devotes time to the study of himself. With the vast wealth from the freshly discovered New World pouring in, a new class of bankers and merchants emerges to lay claim to the spoils, and the fierce aristocracy of medieval times shakes loose—in the Renaissance, it's possible for an individual to rise through personal wealth and accomplishments.

This new view of the individual—kind of an early version of I'm OK, You're OK—leads to a new philosophy, humanism, centered on man rather than God. Art becomes more realistic than it was in the Middle Ages—Giotto paints figures that look like real men, and his women have strong feelings; Donatello's sculptures glorify the human form. Petrarch spearheads a revival of the classics that spurs the development of Italian literature. By the time England catches the ball in the sixteenth century, Shakespeare creates a wholly secular theater, which celebrates the whirl of human drama. Even architecture centers on man and his needs, as Renaissance designers focus their efforts on public buildings and houses as often as on majestic cathedrals. Indeed, the medieval stranglehold of the Catholic Church is itself finally broken through the Protestant Reformation.

The glorification of man and newly acquired wealth combine to create a fashion explosion. Now there are magnificent new fabrics available which, considering there are no safe-deposit boxes, are as good a place as any to store precious gems.

Styles grow bizarre. Men stuff their doublets to grow huge pot bellies, looming over tightly cinched waists, and their breeches balloon out like giant pumpkins. Women fight back with farthingales, birdcage-like constructions that puff out their hips to two feet wide and more. Even the humble collar blooms into a starched ruff, which can range from a simple frill to a choking wagon wheel, boasting status by proving that its wearer doesn't need to work—or even to turn his head.

Overleaf: *Spain's dominance portrayed in a 16th century political map.* **Opposite top:** *Ferdinand Magellan's ship, which made the first circumnavigation of the globe in 1522. Magellan died en route.* **Bottom left:** *Explorer charting journey through the wealthy Near East, Milanese woodcut, 1523.* **Bottom right:** *Mermaid decoration on a steel parade helmet commissioned by Francis I of France, Philip Negroli, 1543.* **This page, above left:** *Obsequies of St. Francis (detail), Giotto, ca. 1300.* **Above right:** *St. Peter's, entrance facade by Michelangelo, ca. 1560.*

And as if these effects aren't dramatic enough, women paint their faces with white lead and vermilion, while men spend hours trimming their beards into a variety of popular shapes. Commercial perfume-making also gets underway, as the Italian Rene, using secrets from the Orient, opens his first shop in Paris in 1500; and both men and women (and, no doubt, those they extend a hand to) enjoy perfume-scented gloves.

Since no one wants to miss out on the fun of dressing up—and since heightened trade speeds international communication—even the most extreme clothing styles disseminate quickly. Early on, thanks to New World riches, Spain becomes the fashion leader, with Italy and Switzerland (in one brief hour of glory) trailing close behind. But sheer love of clothes transcends national borders. People go nouveau-riche with all the trappings. They no longer dress as if God is punishing them.

Portrait of a noblewoman, 1569.

1500 A SWISS PIG GELDER NAMED JAKOB NUFER PERFORMS THE FIRST RECORDED CAESAREAN OPERATION ON A LIVING WOMAN.

1509 NOT A MOMENT TOO SOON: SOCIETY MAKES THE FIRST ATTEMPTS TO RESTRICT THE PRACTICE OF MEDICINE TO LICENSED AND QUALIFIED DOCTORS.

THE PAJAMA GAME

In 1497 Vasco da Gama sails around the Cape of Good Hope and discovers *pajamas* (from the Hindi for "leg clothing"). Worn for centuries by Indians, pajamas are gauzy, brightly-colored cottons twisted around the hips.

Still, no one in Europe pays much attention. Everyone who isn't still sleeping in the nude wears a silk or linen nightshift, a long-sleeved, floor-length chemise that first becomes popular in the sixteenth century. The queen of the night is Lucrezia Borgia, who includes some 200 nightshifts in her arsenal of charms.

RUB-A-DUB-DUB: When Christopher Columbus brings "caoutchouc" back from the New World, everyone thinks it's useless. A full two centuries go by before someone discovers that it's good for *rub*bing out pencil marks, and in 1798 a Monsieur Besson applies a thin layer of rubber to his coat as a water repellent. Later, Charles Macintosh, whose raincoats become synonymous with the word "waterproof," improves this process (though the first Macintosh raincoats are banned on public transportation because they smell). Did you ever wonder who got the bright idea for the reversible raincoat? The idea was born on the Mississippi with riverboat gamblers who turned their jackets inside out during a game so that Lady Luck wouldn't recognize them and change their winning streak— or keep making them lose. In 1839 Charles Goodyear, who will later give us the blimp, invents the "vulcanization of rubber" and it can now be molded. This has an incisive effect on the middle class: dental plates can be inexpensively produced from rubber, making false teeth affordable. It also helps Queen Victoria make a big splash when she daringly discards the dainty shoes of the day to become one of the first women in the world to don "rubbers."

Engraving of Columbus Before the Junta by Gebbie and Barrie, 19th c.; Goodyear's blimp and tires, rubber raincoats and galoshes, the legacy of Christopher Columbus's travels.

157

BLACK WIDOW

Lucrezia Borgia is the bad girl of the Renaissance, fabled for her treachery and lust. She has been married three times by age twenty-one, thanks to the departures of a couple of unwanted husbands: One is killed in a quarrel with her brother, and another is sent packing when the church annulment board declares Lucrezia to be a virgin. (It pays to have connections and a look-alike maid.) And just in case Number Three doesn't last—or maybe in case he *does*—she keeps a pack of lovers waiting in the wings. In keeping with her tarnished reputation, Lucrezia's favorite colors are black and gold.

Does she poison her enemies, as the legend says? No one will ever know. Many believe, in fact, it is her evil relatives who do the damsel wrong.

But there is one sin she is certainly guilty of—vanity. She is inordinately proud of her long, blond locks, which she loves to adorn with jewels. In 1500, she postpones travelling to Ferrara—where she is to meet one of her fiancés—to give herself time to wash her hair.

A MAN WHO KNOWS WHAT HE WANTS

The Renaissance introduces a new ideal of beauty, which, like anything else, can get carried to extremes. One sixteenth-century swain sets strict standards for feminine pulchritude:

"For perfect beauty the ears should be middle-sized, with the shell finely turned and of a livelier tint than the flat part; and the roll which borders all round must be transparent and of a brilliant hue like the seed of a pomegranate....

"When the mouth is closed, the lips must meet in such ways that the lower projects no more than the upper, nor the upper more than the lower; and at the corners they must diminish so as to form an obtuse angle....

"The tip of the tongue, if peradventure it should be seen, which befalls but seldom, will lend beauty while giving desire and consolation, if it be red like scarlet, but neither pointed nor square...."

Firenzuolo—"The Beauty of Women"

HOW TO BE A
BOTTICELLI BEAUTY

Everybody talks about the Botticelli woman, but few appreciate the effort it takes to become one. The artist's original model is said to have been Simonetta Cattaneo Vespucci, who died of tuberculosis at age twenty-three. You don't have to take it that far, but the Botticelli look does demand commitment and hard work. You must:

1. Appear proud and delicate and pure—even if you have to fake it.

2. Shave off your widow's peak to achieve a high brow.

3. Arrange remaining hair in massive swirls, preferably colored strawberry blond.

4. Adjust your makeup to create wide-set, dream-laden eyes.

5. Affect a long, graceful neck and small breasts (by stretching and binding, in that order). Ample thighs are also de rigueur.

Opposite top: *Lucrezia Borgia (1480–1519).* **Opposite right:** (top) *Kiss's Gene Simmons, mid-1970's, and his famous tongue with rumored surgical extension;* (bottom) *Leonard Nimoy shows off his ears as Mr. Spock in "Star Trek." Neither man meets Renaissance standards of beauty.* **Left:** *Birth of Venus (detail), Botticelli, ca. 1480.*

1515 THE CHURCH FORBIDS THE PRINTING OF BOOKS WITHOUT THE PERMISSION OF ROMAN CATHOLIC AUTHORITIES.

1517 MARTIN LUTHER TACKS UP A NOTICE WHICH CREATES QUITE A STIR—HIS 95 THESES.

Left to right: *Galileo (1564–1642); George Clifford, Earl of Cumberland, ca. 1605; John Frederick I, Elector of Saxony, Lucas Cranach, 1532.*

BULLS AND BEARDS

The trend in the Renaissance is toward dignity, and what could be more dignified than a beard? Early styles are broad and square, à la Henry VIII, but as the sixteenth century progresses, a whole range of styles crops up: the tiny, pointed *Spanish* beard; the *pencil* beard, nothing but a tuft; the *stiletto* beard, a razored strip; the *cathedral* beard, an august mass of fluff; the *spade* beard (to call it what it is); and the fetching, double-pronged *swallow's tail*. Beards are powdered, waxed, and perfumed—and, in a compliment to russet-haired Queen Elizabeth I, even dyed red. To preserve their hairy treasures overnight, men tie cloth bags around their beards or keep them clamped in iron presses.

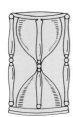

WHOLE CLOTH: The Renaissance sees an explosion of magnificent textiles—fine wools and linens from England and the Netherlands, and sumptuous tapestries from Flanders. But the heart of the textile industry is in Italy, in Lucca, Venice, Genoa, and Florence, where artisans turn out glorious silks in brilliant colors, sensuous velvets, and breathtaking brocades—even fabrics inset with gold and jewels—with a splendor that has remained unrivaled right up to the present day.

These exquisite stuffs become a cornerstone of Italy's economy. But how does Italy get the jump on the rest of Europe in textile production? Its dominance begins in the Dark Ages, when Sicily's Viking conquerors establish a center there for silk weaving. Then the Crusades answer a nation's prayer: The Fourth Crusade lets Venice simply plunder Constantinople. The foray not only brings Italians a fresh infusion of fabric ideas, but it also leaves Italy in control of the silk trade. Imagine—all these benefits and God's blessing too, for beating back the heathen hordes! No wonder the Italians never really succumb to the Protestant Reformation.

Above right: *Female Lowlanders in the early 17th c. flaunt their virtues.*

ESSENCE **BARE**

The Middle Ages found Agnes Sorel walking around bare to the waist. Most early Renaissance women take a more moderate stand on the issue, preferring wide, square necklines trimmed with jewels, framed with lacy collars, or filled with *partlets,* or filmy underblouses. Only virgins wear their necklines daringly low since a hint of nipples is considered proof of their purity. Queen Elizabeth of England flaunts her breasts well into her middle age—a declaration that she has given herself totally to her country, not a man.

160

Left to right: Mary Stuart, a.k.a. Queen of Scots (1542–1578); portrait of a young nobleman, Dutch, early 15th c.; Portrait of a Man, Benedetto Diana (1482–1525); man wearing a cap and a roundelet.

HEADY STUFF

Women begin the Renaissance with a nod to the wimple, wearing *Anne of Brittany caps*, but now pushed back on the head to show a bit of hair; or the *beguin*, a linen hood with flaps framing the face and a veil trailing down the back of the neck. Variations include the *French hood*, a crest that sits on the back of the head attached to a flowing veil; and the *Mary Queen of Scots cap*, a veil suspended from a rigid frame bowed out at the temples. But unlike their Middle Ages counterparts, these hoods are anything but demure—more often than not they're made of rich velvets, studded with precious jewels.

Before long, however, the craze for ruffs makes it more practical for women to sport hats. By the 1570s, Spanish women are sporting high-crowned toques, often trimmed with plumes; the Germans opt for jaunty toppers, perched at dramatic angles; and the Italians, who spur the neoclassical revival of the Renaissance, adorn their hair with simple, jeweled fillets.

Men's hats of the sixteenth century are varied and elegant, ranging from smart flat caps to splashy cartwheels to top hats of velvet, felt, or fur, trimmed with feathers or even narrow bands of precious gems.

In France men like small hats with large brims that dip down over one ear, while the Germans opt for the widest brims and the most luxuriant plumes. These days a knight who exhibits special gallantry is awarded a special badge of honor—a feather in his cap. And for hunting, hoods, often made of leather, are still all the rage.

With all these hat styles around, men try to abandon the flat-brimmed beret in the mid-1560s. To keep the beret industry alive, a law is passed, requiring every male over the age of six to wear a wool beret on Sundays.

HATMEN: Many of these hat styles are created by costumers from Milan who have set up shop throughout Europe. Henceforth, any hatmaker comes to be known as a "Milaner."

Right: Men's hats from 1895—fedora, engineer's cap, crusher—hang on a hall seat from 1865. Below, left to right: Philip I, ca. 1560; Portrait of a Young Man, (possibly Guidobaldo II, Duke of Urbino), Bronzino, ca. 1535–1540; etching of a young woman, English, 16th century; Portrait of a Lady in Red, Florentine School, 16th c.

Right: Henry VIII, *Hans Holbein the Younger, 1540.* Insets, left to right, last to first: Catherine Parr, *W. Scrots, 1545:* survived Henry; Catherine Howard: beheaded 1542; Anne of Cleeves, *Hans Holbein the Younger, 1540:* divorced 1540; Jane Seymour, *Hans Holbein the Younger:* died 1537; Anne Boleyn: beheaded 1536; Catherine of Aragon: divorced 1531.

THE LOOKS OF LOVE

FASHIONS WORN BY
THE WIVES OF HENRY VIII

Poor Henry VIII. Always in and out of marriages. Never sure what side of the bed his new bride will wake up on. Always afraid he'll call out the wrong name (which is probably why he marries three Catherines and two Annes). Such confusion! And pity his poor subjects, obliged to dress in the fashion of each new queen. But since he weds internationally, they're never sure what the current lady will show up wearing.

How did the wives of Henry VIII dress?

1509: CATHERINE OF ARAGON Catherine arrives at the palace with only two dresses to wear. When Henry sends her out on a shopping spree, she repays the favor by introducing a long, stiff, fur-lined cape, the *Spanish cloak*, and the waist-squelching *farthingale*. Thanks, Catherine.

1533: ANNE BOLEYN Anne Boleyn first loses her head in the bedroom—she's wild about nightgowns and introduces lingerie to Henry's court. Among her favorites: a hot black satin number trimmed in black velvet and an orange silk brocade.

The second time Anne loses her head, it's for keeps. For her date with the executioner, she dons a gray brocade with huge sleeves lined in gray squirrel and an undertunic of rose satin.

"But I have such a pretty little neck."
—Anne Boleyn, 1536

1536: JANE SEYMOUR Jane gives Henry an heir to the throne, but she dies in childbirth—having had little time to make a real impact on fashions at the court.

1540: ANNE OF CLEVES Anne directly influences her husband's style of dress: He adopts the overpadded styles and huge puffed sleeves popular in Germany. This marriage comes at a good time fashionwise, if not politically, as Henry is grossly overweight and this style minimizes his royal paunch.

1540: CATHERINE HOWARD A pretty young thing, Catherine is treated like a treasure. Henry gives her elaborate gold brooches studded with rubies, and diamond-encrusted gold collars. Catherine brings French fashions to the English court and sports a peaked, velvet headdress trimmed with brocade that makes her look like the Queen of Hearts. This is appropriate, since Henry dubs himself the King of Hearts.

1543: CATHERINE PARR Catherine Parr is frugal: The only material she buys in all of 1544 is some velvet for a hood. Since her predecessor's clothing fits her, she is content to wear hand-me-downs. She is more generous with the royal children, whom she dresses in handsome outfits of crimson velvet, and she does give in to her one true passion—shoes. In one year alone she purchases forty-seven pairs.

1520 HENRY VIII INSTALLS BOWLING LANES IN WHITEHALL. THERE'S NO MENTION OF WHICH NIGHT IS LEAGUE NIGHT.

1528 THE PLAGUE RETURNS TO ENGLAND.

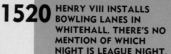

STOCK IN TRADE

Sixteenth-century men have a sense of fun about their clothes, and hose are still a means of self-expression. Hose come in all sorts of bright colors, and contrasting checked and striped patterns are playfully worn at the same time. Around 1500, *upper stocks* become popular. A kind of minibreeches, these cover the tops of the legs and are laced or fastened with *points* to the doublet. *Lower stocks*—you guessed it—cover the shins and are held up by elaborately jeweled or embroidered garters or streamers of fabric at the knee.

Early on, upper stocks look like smooth shorts and pedal pushers, but they soon become a favorite site for slashing. A dashing cavalier will make elaborate cuts in his hose to let his brightly colored underhose show through—but a daring one will forego underwear to reveal a thrilling glimpse of thigh.

But it's not till midcentury that upper hose will truly come into their own, when they blossom into fantastic *pumpkin breeches*, *Venetians*, and *gallagaskins*.

TIMELY NEWS: Around 1500, locksmiths and compassmakers pool their talents to make small, portable clocks. (Presumably they are paid by the hour for their efforts; it will be another hundred years before the minute hand is invented.) First used by civil patrols so watchmen can make their rounds on schedule, these clocks take on the peace officers' name. During the Renaissance, "watches" are encased in jeweled boxes shaped like shells, crosses, or—as a reminder that life is short?—skulls.

Because they are so costly, watches becomes status symbols: In the 1600s, they're worn on chains around the neck, as earrings, even as rings. And following the fashion, seventeenth-century Cardinal Richelieu is even able to corner "time on his side" by sewing seven three-quarter-inch gold watches along the outer seam of his waistcoat.

Top left: *Claude de Lorraine, duc de Guise (1496–1550).* **Above center:** *Gold ring incorporating a striking watch that opens to a full devotional scene, Austrian, ca. 1580.* **Above right:** *Cross-shaped watch in case of rock crystal and gold, Pierre Scheult, Paris, ca. 1630.*

WHEEDLES AND PINS!

They're so expensive that a new kind of currency is named for them. To indulge her latest passion, one of Henry VIII's Catherines wheedles so much cash out of him that he reportedly explodes in exasperation: "What—more *pin money?*"

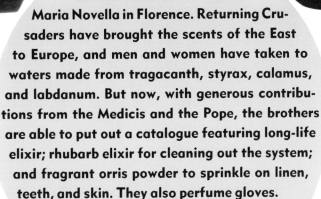

SCENTUARY

In 1508, the Dominican brotherhood establishes the world's first perfumery at the Church of Santa Maria Novella in Florence. Returning Crusaders have brought the scents of the East to Europe, and men and women have taken to waters made from tragacanth, styrax, calamus, and labdanum. But now, with generous contributions from the Medicis and the Pope, the brothers are able to put out a catalogue featuring long-life elixir; rhubarb elixir for cleaning out the system; and fragrant orris powder to sprinkle on linen, teeth, and skin. They also perfume gloves. Why are holy men involved in such a sensual pursuit? The cottage industry is ultimately an act of mercy in an era when most people never bathe.

Top to bottom: Elizabeth Taylor's "Passion." "Tabu" by Dana. "Joy" by Jean Patou.

Top to bottom: "Poison" by Christian Dior. "My Sin" by Lanvin. "Ambush" by Dana. Left: "Obsession" by Calvin Klein.

HANDS DOWN: By the Renaissance, gloves that had begun to grace European courts during the Middle Ages have become the leading fashion accessory. Every country has at least one glovemaker and perfumer to meet the demands of its nobility; Portugal has eight. Charles V of Austria has close-fitting gold gloves studded with pearls. Elizabeth I of England likes embroidered animals on her gloves, and one French duke, Jacques de Nemours, likes gloves so much he wears two pairs at the same time. Most other people just *carry* gloves, rather than wear them. And the most-dubious-achievement award for wedding presents goes to Spain's Philip III, who in 1599 presents his bride-to-be with two hundred pairs of gloves.

The ultimate luxury is perfumed gloves, a craze that lasts nearly two hundred years. But while perfume may mask unpleasant scents, it can also hide malevolent intentions: Jeanne d'Albret, mother of Henry IV of France, is murdered by a pair of poisonous perfumed gloves.

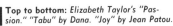

Glove reputed to have belonged to Queen Elizabeth I, 16th c.

1531 THE GREAT COMET, LATER KNOWN AS HALLEY'S, AROUSES FEAR AND SUPERSTITION.

1532 ILLITERATE SPANISH ADVENTURER FRANCISCO PIZARRO RIDES INTO PERU WITH 62 HORSES AND 106 FOOT-SOLDIERS AND CONQUERS IT.

SLASH-BUCKLING

Like buccaneers on a spree, daring dandies go slashing about—cutting slits in their outer garb to pull through and display the brightly contrasting material that lies underneath. The fad begins with the rout of the Duke of Burgundy's troops in 1477, when the Swiss got carried away; they started "slashing" at the Duke's beautiful silks, using the hacked material to mend their own battle-torn uniforms. The raid on the Duke's camp also nets the victorious Swiss his tattered banners and tents, which they make into underwear. Soon the Germans, always on the lookout for a new fad, are slashing hats, stockings, shoes, breeches, doublets, gloves, even armor.

By the sixteenth century, things have gotten out of hand. Clothing is so "slashed" it looks tattered. To put an end to the ridiculous fashion, the Protestant church decrees slashed trousers are "devils," ranking seventeenth on a list of twenty devils. Soon after, civil law follows suit with its own prohibition. One John Mischler is brought to trial on charges that he slashed his hose, but the quick-thinking defendant explains that he only did it because they were too tight and he didn't want to buy a new pair. Sympathetic to his act as an economy measure, not a vanity, the jury sets him free, perhaps to slash another innocent pair of hose.

Above: Triumphal Procession of Maximilian I (detail), woodcut, Hans Burgkmair (1473–1559). Below left: A-bedded and wedded. Below right: Two interlaced gold rings decorated with enamel, gold, and rubies, German, late 16th c.

INFANT MORALITY: In an elaborate ceremony, the Dauphin of France marries Princess Mary, daughter of Henry VIII of England, in 1518. Dressed in a gown of spun gold and wearing a jeweled black velvet cap on her head, the new bride boasts the smallest wedding band in history—she's only two years old. (Still, in some circles, she's accused of robbing the cradle—her groom is a full sixteen months younger.)

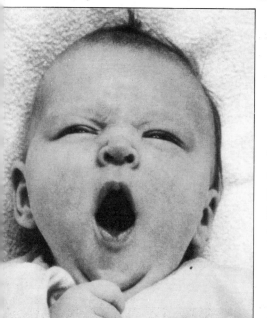

A ND BELLS ON HIS TOES: Already renowned for other excesses, Henry VIII racks up some more extraordinary numbers: He owns 234 finger rings, as many brooches as there are days of the year, and seven slim diamond sticks—which he uses to pick his teeth.

DRESSED TO KILL

JUST THE BASICS: While most Renaissance men are decked out in fancy pants, soldiers still like their skirts. And who can blame them—*bases* are apronlike wraparounds, tied over armor or sleeveless tops, and made of very glamorous fabrics with organ-pipe pleats. In 1520, Henry VIII boasts bases made of panels of silver and gold cloth, trimmed with elaborate embroidery.

And then, in 1525, those tired, old military fashions get a boost from the great Michelangelo. He pioneers a line of soldiers' uniforms still worn by the Swiss guards at the Vatican today. Sadly, Michelangelo never gets his due recognition as a fashion designer; he does, however, find other work.

I CAME, I CLOTHED, I CONQUERED: In 1519 when Hernando Cortés lands on the coast of Mexico with 550 men, Montezuma is convinced that the god Quetzalcoatl has come to reclaim his rightful throne. The Aztec king is dressed in a cotton loincloth; sandals; and huge, three-foot-long, blue-green quetzal tail feathers. What is Cortés dressed in that creates such a stir? Regular explorer garb and a small black hat the Aztecs had dreamed Quetzalcoatl would wear on his return.

Top right: *Detail of a Swiss guard from the Mass of Bolsena, Raphael, ca. 1512–1520.* **Below:** *Feather diadem of Montezuma (1466–1520);* **Left inset:** *Montezuma in the traditional dress of Aztec nobility, portrait by a native artist;* **Right inset:** *Engraving of Hernando Cortés (1485–1547).*

FRIENDLY PERSUASION: Henry VIII has long competed with his French counterpart, Francis I. When Francis gets his hair cut as a result of a head wound, Henry cuts his long locks, too. When Francis grows a beard to cover a scar, Henry also grows one. When Francis sets a style with his new beretlike hat, sporting a plume of feathers, Henry does the same in the English court. "The Field of the Cloth of the Gold" commemorates the historic meeting of the friendly rivals in 1520, in their effort to conclude a long-awaited peace. At Calais, Francis's largest golden tent is over sixty feet wide and is adorned with a six-foot statue of an angel. Not to be outdone, Henry erects a temporary palace of tents embossed with gold and velvet. But the occasion becomes a test of wills that fails, and war breaks out by 1522. So much for splendor in the grass.

1533 THE FUTURE QUEEN ELIZABETH I IS BORN.

1539 THE FIRST CHRISTMAS TREE IS ERECTED, AT STRASBOURG CATHEDRAL.

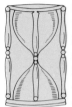

HAIR LINES: Early Renaissance men keep their locks shoulder length but, by the 1520s, adopt the short crops that they'll maintain for most of the century. The best 1530s haircuts are brushed forward to the brow, but later men comb their hair back off their faces so it sits up stiffly from their foreheads. In the 1570s, the effeminate Henry II of France sets a radical new tone: He and his followers wear their long hair in buns, or add on false chignons—and even pluck their eyebrows.

After the bald look of the Middle Ages, women are eager to show their hair—peeping teasingly out of caps; wound into spit curls at their cheeks; parted in the center and pulled back in chignons; or braided into horns. Unmarried women wear their hair long and flowing, garlanded with flowers; older, wealthier matrons try frizzing their hair, dyeing it, or adorning it with jewels. And once the ruff grows popular, a variety of styles keep hair piled high on top of the head.

By the close of the sixteenth century, women grow weary of the constant routine of braiding, frizzing, coloring, and bejeweling—and simply take to wigs.

PUTTING YOUR BEST SHOE FORWARD

Necessity being the mother of invention, Charles VIII of France wears an unusual, broad-toed shoe to hide his deformed foot. A generation later, Francis I goes him one better: His broad-toed, low-cut slippers are attached with straps across the instep. Everyone knows that when Francis I is setting a fashion trend, Henry VIII of England will not be far behind. Henry gets in step, and soon Renaissance men everywhere are wearing soft slippers of velvet, silk, leather, and brocade, the most fashionable insisting on violet cloth or leather. And to show off their beloved hose, glamorous, style-conscious courtiers even slash their shoes.

Extra bits of leather make the slippers sturdier, and over time cork soles are added for height and durability. By midcentury, the flat-foot look is dead, abandoned for more elegantly styled heeled shoes. And shoe business gains a new respectability in 1579, when Queen Elizabeth I grants shoemakers their own coat of arms.

Clockwise from top: Fit for a queen: satin shoe embroidered with silk and metal wire, worn by Queen Elizabeth I ca. 1600; leather shoe with slits and decorative edging, 16th c.; men's shoe, French, 16th c.; women's shoe, ca.1550; brocade shoe of an Elizabethan noblewoman (the buckle decorated with precious stones is now missing); silk shoe, French, 16th c.

THE SONG OF THE FARTHINGALE

In 1470, Queen Juana of Portugal invents the very first stiffened underskirt—a system of rigid hoops—to hide her pregnancy, which cannot have resulted from her marriage to the invalid Alphonso V. This is just the start of an inexplicable female desire to wear skirts that rival the expanding circumference of the earth. By 1530, linen petticoats are made with circular bands of steel or whalebone that grow wider from the waist to the hem. The voluminous skirt of a gown spreads luxuriously over the steel and linen *farthingale*, and is sometimes left open to show off an embroidered underskirt.

In France, the farthingale has no hooped inserts. Instead, a *bourrelet*, or roll of padding, usually made of felt, is stuffed around the waist to widen the skirt. In 1587, the French introduce the *drum farthingale*, in which there are hoops of the same size, giving the skirt a boxy look. As the farthingale grows in popularity, so do its dimensions—by the time it reaches England, Queen Elizabeth expands its hoops to exaggerated widths.

The farthingale makes sitting so uncomfortable that women are forced to perch, pashalike, on piles of cushions on the floor. Only a real princess could feel a pea in such a situation, but then again, only a real princess or a member of the upper class would be wearing an extremely wide farthingale—laws restrict the size of the farthingales that can be worn by the bourgeoisie. Besides, middle-class women are too busy working to worry about widening their skirts.

Below left: The Ambassadors *(detail)*, a portrait of Jean de Dinteville, French ambassador to England, Hans Holbein the Younger, 1533. **Below right:** Portrait of a Distinguished Lady, Lucas Cranach the Elder *(1472–1553)*.

Above: A hoop-de-doo under women's clothes.

NOTHING UP MY SLEEVE: Yes, they can afford the sleeves. Nevertheless, around 1520, the sleeveless fur-trimmed gown of sable, ermine, or miniver, worn with a gold chain, is *de rigueur*. Why? Because during the Renaissance, sleeves themselves become an important fashion focus, too glamorous to be kept under wraps. Men and women both wear gowns with plain sleeves that they cover with detachable, elaborate dress sleeves—pleated, sewn like wings to shoulders, adorned with slashes and/or studded with jewels. Favorite styles are the *finistrella*, two or three panels attached at intervals, to let puffs of the underchemise show through; the wicked *virago*, a full, bloused sleeve reined in at various points with bands; or the lavish *puff* of every conceivable size and design. One dress and a dozen sleeves can make any number of different outfits.

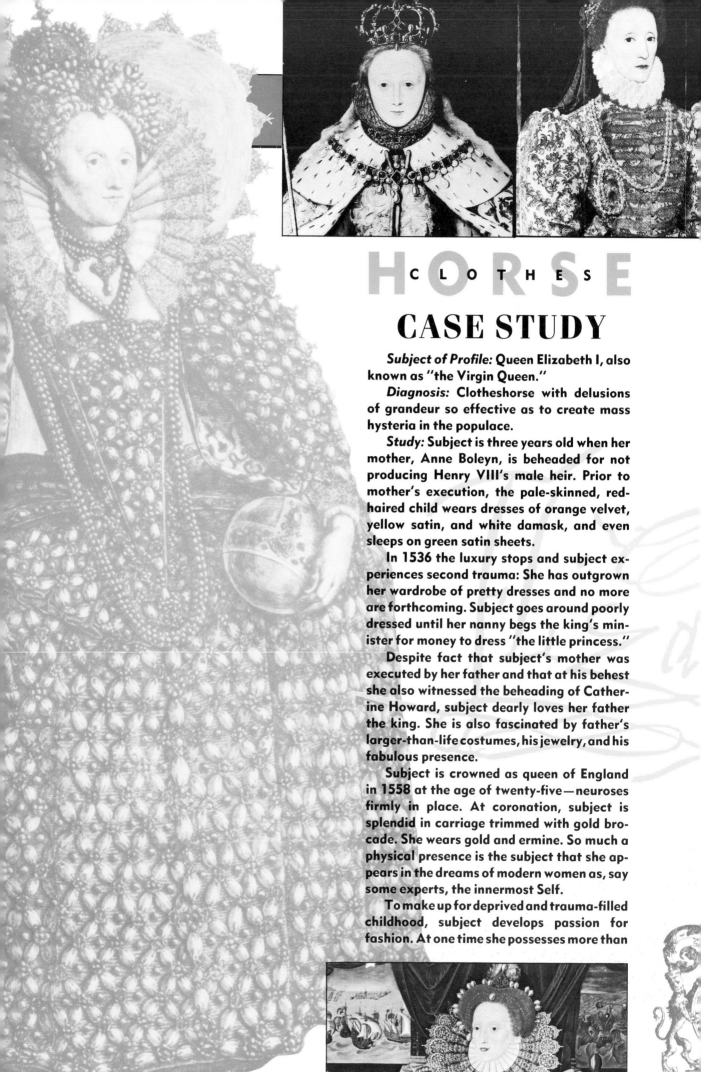

HORSE
CLOTHES

CASE STUDY

Subject of Profile: Queen Elizabeth I, also known as "the Virgin Queen."

Diagnosis: Clotheshorse with delusions of grandeur so effective as to create mass hysteria in the populace.

Study: Subject is three years old when her mother, Anne Boleyn, is beheaded for not producing Henry VIII's male heir. Prior to mother's execution, the pale-skinned, red-haired child wears dresses of orange velvet, yellow satin, and white damask, and even sleeps on green satin sheets.

In 1536 the luxury stops and subject experiences second trauma: She has outgrown her wardrobe of pretty dresses and no more are forthcoming. Subject goes around poorly dressed until her nanny begs the king's minister for money to dress "the little princess."

Despite fact that subject's mother was executed by her father and that at his behest she also witnessed the beheading of Catherine Howard, subject dearly loves her father the king. She is also fascinated by father's larger-than-life costumes, his jewelry, and his fabulous presence.

Subject is crowned as queen of England in 1558 at the age of twenty-five—neuroses firmly in place. At coronation, subject is splendid in carriage trimmed with gold brocade. She wears gold and ermine. So much a physical presence is the subject that she appears in the dreams of modern women as, say some experts, the innermost Self.

To make up for deprived and trauma-filled childhood, subject develops passion for fashion. At one time she possesses more than

eighty wigs, twenty-seven fans, and three thousand dresses. Subject favors long strands of pearls, embroidered shoes, and silk stockings; also invents a modification of the hot Spanish ruff, the "Tudor," which rises up around the sides rather than in the front and reveals the virginal royal bosom in plunging decolletage.

She makes cosmetics so valuable they are used for currency. She is a trendsetter: When she dyes her hair, plucks her eyebrows, covers her exposed breasts with white plaster and outlines her veins with blue, paints her face, or uses creams, noblewomen follow suit. Still, subject refuses to allow ladies-in-waiting to dress more nicely than she does, and she passes laws forbidding others to wear the colors and styles that favor her.

Subject hates smells, and uses spiced wine as mouthwash, along with toothpaste of honey and sugar applied with toothcloths; she also starts a fashion for toothpicks—interesting oral stage manifestations.

In old age, subject suffers third and final trauma. Unable to face reality, she refuses to look in mirror for over twenty years. When subject finally sees herself, she goes into hysterical quasi-schizophrenic manic-depressive, paranoidal hypertense repressive delusional illusional obsessive state. Fear of death quite noticeable: subject will not go to bed; lies on floor, propped up on pillows to preserve now-dirty farthingale. Refuses to change clothing. Eyes sunken. Declines to put things in her pockets. In the end, offers: "All my possessions for one moment of time."

Clockwise from far left: Engraving of the queen, Crispin Van de Passe the Elder, 1603; Elizabeth, aged 25, at the time of her coronation; Anonymous portrait of the young queen; Portrait of Elizabeth by an unknown artist; Portrait of the queen by Marc Gheerhaerts the Elder, ca. 1568–1577; Engraving of Elizabeth signing Mary Stuart's death warrant in 1587; Bette Davis in The Virgin Queen, 1955; Elizabeth's coat of arms; The Armada Portrait. Center: Signature of "Elizabeth Regina."

BEHIND CLOSED DOORS: Queen Elizabeth I has nowhere to put her three thousand dresses. But a woman as enterprising as Good Queen Bess doesn't get boxed in. She designs a special room, with a separate hook for each dress and so the closet is born.

"L'ARTE BIODEGGIANTE": By 1550 the art of blonding becomes so popular in Venice and eventually throughout Europe that, courtesy of various dyes, hennas, and bleaches, female heads are turning mellow yellow. One popular way to go blond is to streak your hair with bleach and then sit in a sun turret (a wooden hut on the castle roof) to let the afternoon rays spur a chemical change. Or you can mix honey, celandine roots, and olive madder with white wine, oil of cumin seed, box shavings, and saffron and put the solution on your head for four-and-twenty hours. Wash it off with lye of cabbage stalks and ashes of rye straw.

If you'd prefer to use magic, try combing your hair in the moonlight—your locks will turn as yellow as the moon.

Men tend to leave their hair color alone, but they keep their tresses in place with brushed-on egg whites.

Clockwise from top left: Woodcut by Christopher Chreiger from Degli Abiti e Moderni, Cesare Vecellio 1509; Blonde lovely by Bartholommeo da Venezia (1405–1461); rock and roll's original "Blondie," Debbie Harry; cutaway view of chopines, Venetian, 16th c.

THE HEIGHT OF FEMININITY: Italian women are more reluctant than their neighbors to adopt the wilder fashions of the day. Their farthingales are softer, their bodices more flexible—but they really go crazy for shoes. The trouble starts in 1533, when Catherine de' Medici comes to France in high-heeled shoes, so she'll measure up to her new husband, Henry II. The sexy new shoes create a sensation, but only the rich, who become known as "well-heeled," are allowed to wear them.

With this little boost, back in Italy the Venetians carry the idea to extremes. The *chopines* they develop are brocaded leather slippers attached to gilded wooden stilts—over two feet high. The fashion spreads, and by midcentury, it is reported that the queen of Spain needs two servants just to help her walk from room to room.

Naturally, chopine jokes abound. "Your Ladyship is nearer to Heaven than when I saw you last by the height of your chopines," a sardonic Hamlet remarks to a Venetian courtesan. "A woman wearing chopines," goes a saying of the day, "is one half woman, one half wood."

JEWELBILATION

There's no Tiffany's during the Renaissance, but who needs it, when jewelry's being designed by some of the greatest artists of the day? Botticelli and Ghirlandaio start out as goldsmiths; and if you're looking for gems, you can pick up a bauble from Holbein or Cellini.

Favorite Renaissance gems are pearls, rubies, and emeralds. Stones may be engraved—cameos are a special love—or backed with colored foil to intensify their hue. And if you can't afford the real thing, you can find some excellent fakes, or look for some of the glorious enamels perfected now.

Exhibit your jewels in:

PENDANTS: You can wear them (instead of your heart) on your sleeve, or around your neck, dangling from a chain. You might want a dragon, a sea monster, a mermaid, or a ship to celebrate the age of exploration. For more classic tastes, there are animals, birds, insects, lizards, crosses—or simply your initials.

CHAINS: Whether you wear a pendant or not, you'll certainly want some chains—long, heavy gold ones decorated with filigree or studded with—what else?—jewels. If you're a king, you might even want an entire collar of links strewn with fabulous gems.

BRACELETS, NECKLACES, AND RINGS: These old standbys of course, never go out of style, and if you have some gems left over, you can have them set in *aglets*, small brooches that you can pin all over your clothes. If your ruff gets so big that it swallows up your necklace, you can wear your strung jewels as a belt instead.

HEADGEAR: In the early sixteenth century, you'll enjoy a chaplet of pearls or a hairnet studded with gems. But as the century progresses, and hairdos grow more upswept, your jewels will look better in an elaborate diadem. For men there is the hat badge: a handsome jeweled brooch tacked boldly to an upturned brim. You might want yours to feature a picture from the Scriptures—a nice St. John writing his gospel, say, while borne on the back of an eagle—or later, a portrait of your king.

And if you still need more places to display your jewels, remember that in the Renaissance, anything goes. Just sprinkle them anywhere—sew them to your bodices, and on the edge of your robes, or even encrust them on your shoes.

Clockwise from top right: Europa and the Bull, *gold pendant, Belgian, ca. 1585; Silver brooch, German, 1580; Wooden model for a bracelet, German, ca. 1535; Cleopatra, gold sleeve ornament, German, late 16th c.*

PORTRAIT OF A LADY

Your average upper-class lady of the mid-sixteenth century is stretched to her limits:

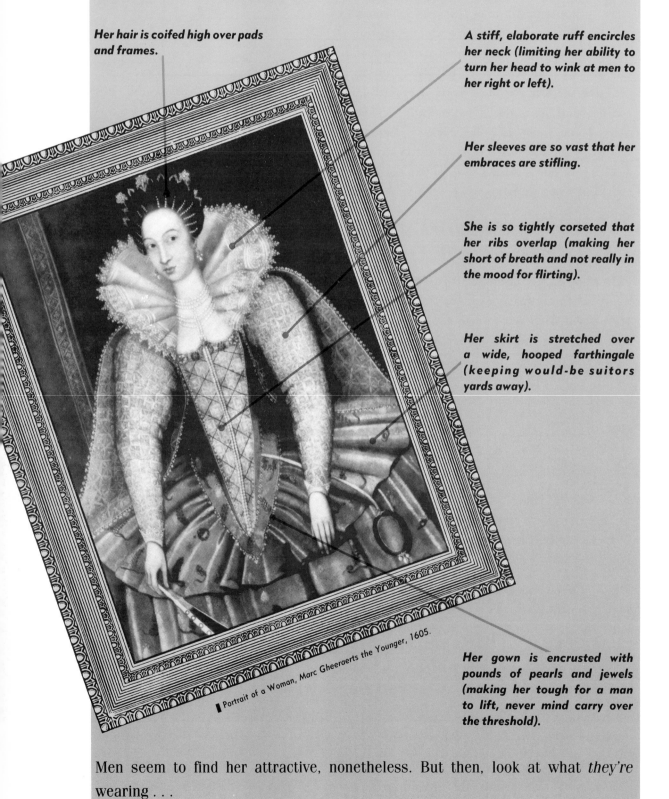

Her hair is coifed high over pads and frames.

A stiff, elaborate ruff encircles her neck (limiting her ability to turn her head to wink at men to her right or left).

Her sleeves are so vast that her embraces are stifling.

She is so tightly corseted that her ribs overlap (making her short of breath and not really in the mood for flirting).

Her skirt is stretched over a wide, hooped farthingale (keeping would-be suitors yards away).

Her gown is encrusted with pounds of pearls and jewels (making her tough for a man to lift, never mind carry over the threshold).

Portrait of a Woman, Marc Gheeraerts the Younger, 1605.

Men seem to find her attractive, nonetheless. But then, look at what *they're* wearing . . .

PURE, BUT NOT SIMPLE: In 1558 Mary Queen of Scots dons a white wedding gown to marry the Francis II of France. Though white, symbolizing purity, is becoming a popular choice for wedding dresses, at the time of the queen's marriage it's still considered a royal mourning color and Mary's subjects are upset by her choice.

▌Right: *Iron corset, ca. 1600.*

RUFF TRADE

UNDER WHERE? Get thee to a nunnery in 1559 if you don't want to be laced into a bone-crunching corset: fearing for their health, Emperor Ferdinand of Austria passes a law forbidding young girls to wear corsets in nunneries and other places of education. Like Catherine de' Medici, Queen Elizabeth at first wears an iron-winged corset, but then opts for a "softer" device made of leather or canvas, boned with wood or steel. They are lined with sheer silk and laced up the back. The corset goes on after the chemise. Then the Queen, like other noblewomen, puts on a petticoat, topped off with a farthingale. Corsets of gold and silver are only found on courtesans; until, that is, they catch Catherine de' Medici's fancy. Then Catherine de' Medici decrees that having a thick waist is "bad manners." Her ideal? A svelte thirteen inches. To achieve this end, she designs the hinged corset.

▌Below left: *Long-handled spoon with ivory decoration, 16th c.* **Below right:** Wedding celebration at the court of Henry III of France, 1581, *Herman Van der Mast, (1550–1604).*

One of the most extravagant clothing items of the sixteenth century is the *ruff*, a detachable pleated collar, supported by a wire frame, that can reach enormous proportions. The style has its roots in the East, where Indians wear collars stiffened with rice water, to protect their clothes from their hair.

In Europe, the ruff begins innocently enough as the simple, high collar of the early century, trimmed with a modest frill. But then, legend has it, in 1540 the queen of Navarre begins widening the frill to hide her ugly throat—and so the ruff is born. It soon spreads to Italy, where Catherine de' Medici, always a trendsetter, is quick to adopt it; and to England, after Mary Tudor weds Phillip II of Spain. The fad gets a boost (and the phrase "Hold the starch!" is invented), when the Dutch Madame Dingham Vander Plasse arrives in England to teach the "art of starching," using a paste made of wheat and other grains, various roots, and even pigments for a bold note of color. (Yellow is a special favorite.)

A ruff is made of linen that is *goffered* or folded with a *poking stick* while still damp. After it dries, it is stored in a *band box* (hence the term, "just stepped out of a band box," to mean impeccably turned out). The most popular styles include the large *cartwheel ruff*, the two-layer *double ruff*, and the *cabbage ruff*, with asymmetrical folds. Married women wear circular styles, while heart-shaped ones are favored by ladies who are still looking. Among the most elegant ruffs are those in the collection of Queen Elizabeth I of England—made of exquisite, intricately woven lace.

As the century progresses, wearing a stylish collar gets rough, as ruffs reach their outer limits: King Henry II sports a ruff that uses more than eighteen yards of linen and is over eleven feet deep. Two immediate products of the ruff: the chafed neck and the invention of the long-handled spoon—to help food reach people's mouths over these huge collars.

THE SARTORIAL FACTS OF LIFE

A HANDBOOK FOR MID-SIXTEENTH-CENTURY FATHERS:
Dad, by the time your son is fourteen, he will be eager to learn the secrets of dressing like a man. Remember, he's been admiring your broad, manly chest for years, hoping his will be the same. Embarrassing as it is to talk about these things, someone has to tell him about *bombast.* Before he hears on the street that you're just a stuffed shirt, he'll want to hear it from you.

So, have a stiff brandy, smooth your *pickadils* (those fancy tabs at your waistline), and give it to him straight: Bombast is composed of rags, horsehair, cotton, and bran. You stuff it in your doublet for a *peascod-bellied* look, swelling your torso to magisterial proportions. Other pluses: In these days before permanent press, it also frees your clothes from unsightly creases and it keeps the cold away. It will protect you from daggers, though often a scuffle will leave you leaking a telltale trail of cereal.

Other minuses: Bombast can add an extra five or six pounds to your daily burden and it's supported at the seams by uncomfortable strips of whalebone. The bran will also attract lice. And then there's the anxiety of doffing your doublet in the boudoir of the lady of your dreams . . . to reveal that her sturdy, virile lover is a hollow-chested, ninety-pound weakling.

Below your doublet, you'll wear *pumpkin breeches,* or trunk hose padded with bombast. These thigh- or knee-length blobs can make it hard to sit down and add another five or six pounds to your outfit. Some men favor a blousier version, called *Venetians;* or the streamlined style, called *canions,* but real sports puff right up to the waist in full-blown *gallagaskins.*

The silver lining behind this fashion cloud: Lugging all this weight makes your legs lean and muscular, sexy in tight-fitting hose. But the best payoff comes in the bedchamber—face it, *anyone* wearing these breeches is sure to look better naked.

That brings us to the most embarrassing, er, enhancement to manly appeal—the *codpiece.* When doublets grew scandalously short, the codpiece was introduced to protect a gentleman's modesty by covering the opening between his hose. So far so good, but some wags started using codpieces as pockets, and one thing led to another. By now they're so heavily padded that they're simply brazen eyecatchers. Are they sexy? Well, tell your son that Henry VIII swears by them . . .

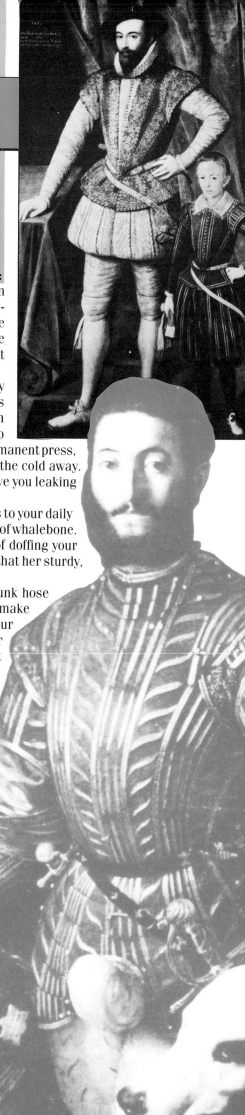

A POCKETFUL

In 1565 Charles IX of France outlaws purses because, a) they're too easy to hide daggers in, and b) a truly useful fashion advance, the pocket, is invented. Charles takes the name from the Anglo-Norman *pokete* (French: *poche*), which is already in use to signify a small pouch or purse. What Charles doesn't count on is the invention of the pocket knife!

▌ **Right:** The Old Man in Love, *Lucas Cranach the Elder, 1531.*

HANES ACROSS THE SEA: In 1561 Queen Elizabeth receives her first pair of silk stockings. Black and sexy, they are presented by her silk woman, Mistress Montague, who knits them expressly for Bess. It's not just gentlemen who prefer the new hose to the woolly knitted kind worn up till now; Liz is wild about silk and tries to wear nothing else. But when William Lee asks for funding for a machine that will do the knitting, the queen turns him down, fearing the unemployment of hand-knitters. Lee takes his invention to France, where in time it revolutionizes the hosiery trade. A week is required to hand-knit two pairs of stockings, and up to six months for one exceptionally fine pair.

BLACK SHEETS: In 1572, Margaret of Valois, the daughter of the strong-willed Catherine de' Medici and Henry II of France, marries the Protestant Henry de Bourbon, king of Navarre, while still in her teens. She waits until she leaves home, but once out of the nest, Margaret flaunts her independence by creating a promiscuous court of scandal and illicit liaisons. To show off her creamy white skin to advantage, Margaret sleeps on the world's first black satin sheets. Soon everyone's favorite bed linens are black.

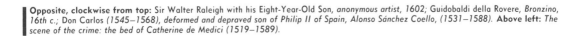

▌ **Opposite, clockwise from top:** Sir Walter Raleigh with his Eight-Year-Old Son, *anonymous artist, 1602;* Guidobaldi della Rovere, *Bronzino, 16th c.;* Don Carlos (1545–1568), *deformed and depraved son of Philip II of Spain, Alonso Sánchez Coello, (1531–1588).* **Above left:** *The scene of the crime: the bed of Catherine de Medici (1519–1589).*

1575 PARIS HAS A POPULATION OF APPROXIMATELY 300,000; LONDON 180,000; AND COLOGNE 35,000.

1577 FRANCIS DRAKE EMBARKS ON A VOYAGE AROUND THE WORLD, VIA CAPE HORN.

PROTECTIVE COATINGS: People do have to go outdoors and the fashionable Renaissance man will usually don a thigh-length cloak cut from one piece of brocaded material. In England, by the time of Elizabeth's reign, men wear lots of different kinds of cloaks: short, long, with or without sleeves. Military men wear the *mandillion*—a short tabard (like a poncho), open on both sides, and bordered with heavy braid. Horseback riders require short cloaks. Dress cloaks come in velvet and taffeta and are lined with fur for luxurious warmth.

Spanish women wear a *manto*— mantle in English—indoors and out. The length depends not on age, but on the wearer's married state: A widow's manto reaches the ground, and shrouds her completely; an unmarried woman's manto covers all of her face except her eyes. The very rich only wear small head-covering mantos of lace, because they don't ever go outside unless absolutely necessary.

In France, women in mourning wear black hooded cloaks.

In Florence, coarse wool cloaks are given to the poor.

Guild members in Germany never go outdoors without their cloaks.

Nobles, according to sumptuary laws, are allowed to wear pretty much what they want. Men's cloaks are shorter than women's (because men are wearing shorter and shorter doublets), and fur-lined cloaks and capes are fashionable: Paris alone has more than four hundred furriers filling orders in the fifteenth century. In Elizabethan England, short cloaks must be flung over one shoulder and worn that way. Fashionable Elizabethan men must have three cloaks: for morning, afternoon, and evening.

The historical dish on Little Red Riding Hood's cloak is right, but a little too much has been made of Sir Walter Raleigh's: While it is true that he gallantly spread his cloak across a muddy street so good Queen Bess could pass, it wasn't as great a sacrifice as you think. The cloak was made of leather, and easily cleaned.

FIT FOR A KING

A farthingale and a low-cut bodice draped with ropes of pearls are all the rage in the 1570s. So why do tongues wag when these fashions show up at a ball? Perhaps the French are distressed to see their new king, Henry III, wearing the *dernier cri*. Henry, it is said, is fond of feminine fashion, from his short-sleeved capes trimmed with fur to his face powder and dangling earrings. Now flowers are found in profusion all over the court: in hair, on bodices, on doublets, strewn across the floor, and even in the boudoir. He and his *mignons*, the effeminate noblemen he dallies with after the death of his one true love, Marie de Cleves, set the trends and styles throughout Europe.

Above left: *Sir Walter Raleigh (1554–1618).* Below left: *Book illustration from* Little Red Riding Hood, *Walter Crane, 1875.* Below right: *Henry III and his fair lady share a pair of earrings, tapestry detail, ca. 1580.*

1587 THE FIRST BRITISH CHILD, VIRGINIA DARE, IS BORN ON AMERICAN SOIL.

1596 GALILEO INVENTS THE THERMOMETER.

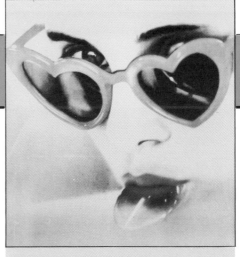

"Fashion wears out more apparel than the man."
—William Shakespeare,
Much Ado About Nothing

SHADY BUSINESS: In 1591, sunglasses are invented when lenses of amber are saturated in linseed oil for protection against the sun's rays.

Above: *Sue Lyon in her heart-shaped glasses, as Lolita, 1962.* **Bottom:** *Baths at Leula, Switzerland, Hans Bock, 1597.*

TIPS FROM THE
RENAISSANCE SPA:

Beauty is as beauty does, and in the Renaissance the doing is a complicated art that is taken quite seriously:

Herbal essence: Elder flowers improve skin tone. Rosemary restores the hair. Geranium leaves color the cheeks. Brushing with sage whitens the teeth. For that fresh breath moment, try a little spiced wine as a mouthwash.

For skin as smooth as Mary Queen of Scots', bathe daily in elderberry wine. If you're planning on getting used to this luxury, take steps to see that you're not imprisoned—pressed elderberries aren't on the dungeon menu. Want a supple, white complexion? Soak raw veal in hot milk for several hours. Then place the veal on your cheeks and watch it work its wonderful magic on your ruddy cheeks.

Secret formula of "The Earl of Oxford's Perfume," worn exclusively until now by Queen Elizabeth: Add eight grains of musk to eight spoonfuls of rose water, with three spoonfuls of damask water and a quarter ounce of sugar; boil five hours and strain.

Want to be an egghead? Wear egg whites and honey to condition your skin. To erase those wrinkles, slap on layers of white lead—and now that necklines have taken the plunge, do remember to dab some on your neck and bosom, too. For a spot of color in your cheeks, rub on some mercuric sulphide.

Better still, when in England, wash your face with your own urine to keep your complexion smooth and pale. (For the squeamish: one part rose water, one part wine.)

For a brisk, cleansing body rub, mix rosemary, cedar, and turpentine with alcohol. Dip sponges into this mixture and squeeze out into your body and hair. Stay away from an open flame unless you really want to be a hot number!

THE SEVENTEENTH CENTURY

THE SEVENTEENTH CENTURY

LOUIE, LOUIE

Galileo gazes up at the stars, Newton falls asleep under a tree and is clonked by an apple, and the world's whole view of itself is turned upside down.

With the coming of the 1600s, the spirit of exploration that characterized the Renaissance shifts toward the physical world. True, Australia is discovered in 1606 and the English penetrate India, but real seventeenth-century exploration takes place in the minds of men, leading Descartes to philosophy, Leibniz to mathematics, and Boyle to chemistry. Harvey unmasks secrets of the human body; Leeuwenhoek's microscope reveals an entire hidden universe. With the New World safely conquered, there are newer frontiers to explore. In this climate of discovery, miraculous inventions abound: the barometer, the pendulum clock, and, by the 1650s, ice cream.

The arts, too, witness an explosion of new forms. The essay and the novel are born in this century; Molière, Racine, Milton, and Bunyan emerge as literary titans. New folk tales are spun—the stories of Little Red Riding Hood, Cinderella, and Tom Thumb. And in painting, sculpture, and architecture, everyone's going Baroque, using lavish ornamentation, rich materials, and fine details. Rembrandt plays with light and shadow; Vermeer gets realistic; Rubens casts a glad eye on the ladies. While Velázquez and Van Dyck focus on the monarchy, Poussin creates the bawdy *Rape of the Sabine Women*, and Bernini shuns such earthly cares to carve his mystical *Ecstasy of St. Teresa*.

Miraculously, these accomplishments are achieved in a Europe that is wracked by war and dominated by three R's: the continuing Reformation, a midcentury Restoration, and "Roi" Louis XIV in Versailles.

In England, Charles I's uncompromising Anglicanism outrages the Puritans, who want their religion stripped of Catholic trappings. They like their clothing simple, too, and get named the Roundheads because of their close-cropped hair—in contrast to the flowing locks of Charles's Cavaliers. In the civil war that follows, Charles loses his head and the Puritan Oliver Cromwell takes control—until aristocrats recapture the throne in 1660, ushering in the Restoration.

Meanwhile, English Puritans fleeing religious persecution have already established a beachhead in the New World. Jamestown is founded in 1607, the *Mayflower* touches ground in 1620, and new settlements spring up throughout the century. They are soon joined by the Dutch, who colonize Manhattan in 1626. To the south, Spain and Portugal continue plundering and working their century-old plantations. Potatoes, tobacco, corn, and peanuts are introduced to Europe, alongside less exotic imports like cotton, sugar, and coffee. These products yield huge profits—especially since the labor used to produce them is free. From the sixteenth century on, ten million kidnapped Africans are pressed into New World slavery.

Despite its New World holdings, Spain continues to lose ground after the defeat of its invincible Armada in 1588. With Spain at bay and with the Thirty Years' War

Overleaf: *Interior dome of Sant' Ivo della Sapienza, Francesco Borromini, 1642–1660.* **Opposite page: top:** *Altar covering, Chapel of St. Sidone, Turin, ca. 1620;* **bottom left:** *Twelve-year-old Isaac Newton, H. Baude, 1881.* **This page: below left:** *The 1620 Sailing of the Mayflower,* drawing by Granville Perkins; **Below:** *Rape of the Sabine Women, Nicolas Poussin, ca. 1637.*

raging in Europe till 1648, everybody's clamoring for a piece of the action. Now a new group of nations get their day in the sun: Denmark, Sweden, and particularly Holland, which emerges as a major trading nation through its Dutch East and West India companies. But while the Scandinavians show off their newfound wealth, donning glamorous continental clothes, the Dutch frown on such frivolity. Dour Calvinists, they prefer their Puritan attire—black breeches and hose, black shoes, and white collars—which, ironically, derives from the fashions of their drama-loving enemy, Catholic Spain.

But all these small stars are outshone by France. Henry IV steers the nation steadily out of the Renaissance; and under his successor Louis XIII, the ministers Richelieu and Mazarin build the nation's military and commercial might. Lest the riches streaming in burn a hole in its pocket, Louis XIV ascends the throne in 1643 to spend them on establishing the most glorious court in history.

The seventy-two years of the Sun King's rule are called the Baroque era, a time of glittering magnificence in decoration and dress. While the 1600s bring a wave of more comfortable fashions—ruffs make barely a ripple, women are dehooped, and men lose their bombast as the silhouette returns— now everything is awash in fancy trimmings, gewgaws, ribbons, and lace. Men's wigs reach new and extravagant proportions, and for an extra lift, the 5′4″ Louis XIV has everyone teetering in high heels. As Colbert, the king's chief adviser, reasons, if subjects are enslaved by style, they will have less time for treasonous plotting. And so the most important activity at Versailles is getting dressed. Luckily for all, the eighteenth century will usher in the Age of Reason—and not a moment too soon.

1600 WILLIAM GILBERT PENS *DE MAGNETE*, A TREATISE ON MAGNETISM AND ELECTRICITY.

1601 SHAKESPEARE'S *HAMLET* IS WRITTEN.

GOLILLA MY DREAMS: As the seventeenth century opens, Spain has begun to lose its grip, not only on the rest of Europe but also on style. So in its last gasp as fashion dictator, it decides to kill off one of its most expensive contributions to the Renaissance: the ruff. Now Philip IV decrees that the *golilla* (also called the *whisk*)—a flat, embroidered collar propped on a wire frame—should supplant all other neckwear throughout the country. Strangled Spanish men are only too happy to comply with the order.

Ruffs have begun to wilt in other countries too, in favor of whisks, *falling bands* (sheer collars trimmed with lace that spread out to the shoulders), or simply *flat ruffs*, minus the old starch and wireworks, that stream down over the chest.

Women persevere in wearing ruffs a little longer, but soon also abandon them for whisks—sometimes worn three at a time—or for high, pleated *corona collars* radiating behind their heads like halos. The style with the most chic is the *Medici collar*, a broad, wired model with squared-off edges framing the face, often made of lace.

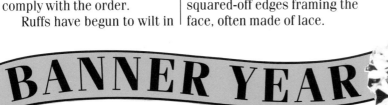

A BANNER YEAR

With ruffs out of the way, people's unburdened shoulders become a new possible site for decoration. So, early in the seventeenth century, the *military sash*, made out of silk embroidered with silver and gold, emerges as a favorite accessory. Born in Denmark, the sash is draped diagonally across the body like a Miss America streamer, stretching to the knees, and often tied in a pouf, like a pair of water wings, in the back.

By the 1630s or so, men begin to realize that the sash can do double duty—and so the *baldric*, a Middle Ages staple, comes back. Why clutter up the beautiful front of a doublet with a tawdry old sword belt when you can wear a lavishly embroidered baldric across your chest, dashingly supporting your sword over the left hip.

Opposite page: top left: Portrait of John Eliot, "the Apostle to the Indians," who translated the Bible into the language of the Algonquins in 1685; left: Louis XIV, at age fifteen, portraying "The Sun." This page: clockwise from top right: Laurie Lea Schaefer in her "Miss America" sash, 1972; Charles II of England (1600–1649); The collar-full Banquet of St. George's Archers (detail), Frans Hals (1582–1666).

BOUND FOR GLORY

Although the farthingale's deflation gives her some relief, the seventeenth-century woman is still imprisoned in her corset. Bodices are gripping in the early decades, stretching down to a low, pointed waist, which by mid-century flounces out as a *peplum*. And as if boned or iron foundations aren't bad enough, a *stomacher* completely flattens her breasts and belly. The stomacher is adorned with embroidery, jewels, or a row of ribbon bows called an *eschelle*—to console her for being unable to bend or breathe. This ironing-board effect is so prized that in Spain—the country that, after all, gave us the Inquisition—girls' breasts are bound from early childhood to prevent them from developing.

OFF THE CUFF: Shirts were glimpsed during the Renaissance through the slashes of stylish doublets. But when the slashing fad dies down, men still want to flash their fancy underwear and so begin to decorate their shirts.

Seventeenth-century shirts are lavishly cut and decked out with latticework and ribbons. The pièce de resistance of these shirts is their cuffs—deep, floppy layers of ruffles or broad lacy or embroidered bands turned back over the sleeves, reaching almost to the elbow. Over the course of the century, cuffs grow so elaborate that they take on a life of their own—as separate decorations attached to the sleeves with buttons. And, of course, jewelers (and children stuck for ideas for Father's Day presents) welcome the new fad, because it promises the invention of yet another new fashion accessory—where there's a cuff, can a cufflink be far behind?

DRESSED TO THRILL

A princess of the Algonquin tribe, the dark-haired Pocahontas (meaning Playful One) catches the eye of Jamestown colonists when she saves Captain John Smith from death after he's captured by her tribe in 1607. She becomes an instant celebrity by flinging her doeskin-dressed body down on the earth next to him. In 1613, Pocahontas is kidnapped by colonists and held hostage for English prisoners. The following year, she becomes a Christian, changes her name to Rebecca, and sports a wide-collared ruff, embroidered sleeves, a man's hat (with obligatory feather), and a fan. In 1614, she marries Englishman John Rolfe and is received as a princess by the king and queen of England.

*Top, left to right: Embroidered stomacher, Italian; two frameworks for corsets, 17th c.; stomacher, 17th c. **Center right:** Pocahontas in western dress.*

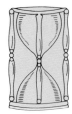

HAZARDOUS TO
WARNING
YOUR HEALTH

ONLY SKIN DEEP: Promise him anything but let him kiss your Aqua Toffana if you're not planning on coming through. The makeup made of liquid arsenic created by Signora Toffana in 1625 is said to be responsible for the deaths of over six hundred husbands.

Less dangerous, but still daunting, is *sulama*, the herb Greek women of the 1600s use on their faces to give them a red glow. One man reports that breathing on a su-lama-faced seductress after you've eaten cloves turns her skin yellow.

Above: Stolen Kiss, Fragonard, ca. 1788. **Below, left to right:** A couple of mask masters: a print from La Noblesse, by Jacques Calbot, and Winter from the series Great London Seasons, Hollar, ca. 1640.

MASK TRANSIT

Afraid of the bad effects polluted air can have on the skin, the 1620s woman dons a black velvet mask for a stroll down the avenue. Nice touch. Of course she's still more likely to croak from her own hand than from allegedly poisonous fumes. The mask is worn over a face which she has heavily made up with our old favorite, powdered white lead.

ARMED: As cuffs come to the fore, sleeves sadly lose their glamor. For men, they begin to take on a natural outline, fitted to the arm, with only caps at the shoulders to hint at their old glory. But soon they suffer an even worse indignity— shrinking to elbow length to let the billowing, ruffled sleeves of the undershirt carry the day. It is not until the 1680s that they're able to fight back, creeping down to the wrist and subduing the undersleeves to a mere modest frill.

Women are more reluctant to part with their massive sleeves. They wear vast *leg-of-mutton* styles, filled out with pads, up until the teens. Then, as for men, more natural cuts predominate, though long, streaming false sleeves still flank the genuine article. By the 1630s and 1640s, the paneled sleeves of the Renaissance are back, now gathered at the elbow with bows to form huge puffs. Enormous lacy cuffs, of course, lend drama. And by the 1650s, for the first time in hundreds of years, sleeves shrink to allow the forearm to emerge. The lacy sleeves of the chemise, spilling out from shortened sleeves, help bridge the gap for a while, until the end of the century, when rows of ruffles from the elbow down—so-called *pagoda sleeves*—help restore feminine modesty.

DIAMOND FINDS

Long before Annette Funicello in *Beach Blanket Bingo* fought off her boyfriend's advances with the infamous line, "Not until there's a ring on this finger!" diamonds are a symbol of true love. They are also the subject of superstition, generosity, pettiness, and the object of ostrich hunts.

In 800 B.C., the Dravidians of India first find diamonds. Because they grow in the ground like so many turnips, to weigh them the Dravidians balance the diamonds on their scales against the seeds of the carob, or "carat," tree.

The diamond is the hardest substance known. In 16 A.D. the Roman poet Manilius borrows the Greek word *adamas* (invincible) to name it.

While up until the Renaissance, most other gems are believed to be beneficial, despite its beauty the diamond is not thought to possess the virtues ascribed to other stones. In Persia, it is considered a source of sin and sorrow. One sixteenth-century writer explains that a diamond "makes the wearer unhappy because its brilliance irritates the soul as an excess of sun irritates the eye." Around this same time in history it is believed that "a good diamond could lose its virtue through the sin of the owner." And you had to be careful about resale value as well: The spirit of the diamond, common knowledge held, resented being sold. Diamonds must only be given away, in love or friendship.

Among the Hindus, poor diamonds are believed to cause jaundice, leprosy, and lameness. In medieval Europe, however, the diamond is thought to be protection against just such illnesses, as well as plague and pestilence. (It obviously doesn't work so well.)

A seventeenth-century authority on gems, De Boot, concedes that diamonds can repel poison, witchcraft, and even madness. But he disproves the popular belief that the diamond can identify an adulteress when he places a diamond under his wife's pillow and she fails to be thrown violently out of bed.

Alexander the Great gets his diamonds from India, the chief source of the world's diamonds until 1725, when they are discovered in Brazil. Then in 1867, diamonds are found in South Africa, where ostriches are hunted down because, like goats, they'll eat anything. More than fifty diamonds are once found in an ostrich's "living diamond mine"—his stomach.

In the mid-fifteenth century, the first diamond necklace in history adorns the neck of courtesan Agnes Sorel. She is the first commoner in history to wear diamonds, but she complains that the necklace is heavy and that the points of the stones scratch her neck.

Louis XIV pays 337,500 francs for just twenty-one diamonds—which he uses as buttons on his justaucorps.

Russia's Peter the Great gives his first mistress, Anna Mons, his portrait—executed in diamonds. When she falls out of favor in 1703, he demands it back.

Larger-than-life nineteenth-century financier Jim Brady has a different set of jewelry for every day of the month—diamonds for one day, emeralds the next—thirty-one sets in all. He owns twenty thousand diamonds, sometimes wearing $250,000 worth of them in one day—earning him the nickname "Diamond Jim."

In 1477, for his marriage to Mary of Burgundy, Maximilian of Germany orders a diamond engagement ring. This diamond, he says, represents "lifelong devotion." Unfortunately, Mary dies a scant few years later. The diamond engagement ring, however, lives on. By the 1900s, the large solitaire has become the traditional engagement gift.

During the 1750s, Vincent Peruzzi invents the "brilliant cut," and, for the first time, diamonds show off to their best advantage and truly dazzle. Everyone wants them, but the real things are too expensive. So to meet the demands of working girls in need of a best friend, inventor Josef Strasser comes up with imitation, glass-like paste diamonds. These so-called *rhinestones*, made of potassium and lead mixed with borax, alumina, and white arsenic are so well crafted and designed that soon the likes of Marie Antoinette and Madame du Barry are wearing them (partly to deter highwaymen who are more likely to pounce if they're decked out in real gems). But why aren't the gems called "Strasserstones" after their inventor? They take their name from Strasser's home territory, along the Rhine River.

1632 TWO GREAT PHILOSOPHERS ARE BORN: ENGLISH JOHN LOCKE AND DUTCH BARUCH SPINOZA.

1635 HARVARD COLLEGE IS FOUNDED IN NEWE TOWNE, CAMBRIDGE, MASSACHUSETTS.

"Goodness, what lovely diamonds!"
"Goodness had nothing to do with it."
—Mae West in conversation in
Night after Night

DIAMONDS ARE FOREVER

Jewelry is fairly modest in the seventeenth century—after all, how can it compete with all that baroque frippery? Still, even if Elsa Peretti's diamonds by the yard are still centuries away, diamonds *in* the yard (or anywhere else, for that matter) are always in vogue.

The Duke of Buckingham has a string of diamonds loosely sewn to his clothes so he can break the thread and scatter the gems wherever he goes. Needless to say, the Duke attracts scads of loyal followers.

". . . the first yellow beam of the sun struck though the innumerable prisms of an immense and exquisitely chiselled diamond—and a white radiance was kindled."
—F. Scott Fitzgerald,
"The Diamond as Big as the Ritz"

Opposite page: *Diamond fringe necklace, Russian, 18th c.* **Far left:** *Mae West is a gem in She Done Him Wrong, 1933.* **Center:** *Ostrich munching on a diamond pendant, French, 17th c.* **Above right:** *The Cullinan III and IV diamonds, originally set in the crown of Queen Mary in 1911.*

189

PEEK TIMES: After a century of confinement in high collars and stiff ruffs, women have a lot to get off their chests. So, as early as the 1620s, necklines begin to plunge. The most daring clotheshorses wear the deepest decolletages, often in the popular square and V shapes (though nipples now stay under wraps). The more modest (or married) fill in with *partlets*—jeweled or embroidered sheer fabrics or strips of precious lace. Sometimes, trying to cover all the bases, a fashion victim will wear a low decolletage, a V-necked sheer partlet and a high lacy collar framed by a huge corona, all at the same time. Real prudes keep their collars high, and as an extra sop to virtue, swathe their necks and shoulders with lace-trimmed kerchiefs.

By the 1650s, an admirer's eye will wander left and right as wide, off-the-shoulder necklines replace low decolletages. Of course, for a hint of secret delights, there is often a glimpse of lacy underwear to be seen peeking forth from underneath.

"All women, of whatever age, rank, profession or degree, whether virgins, maids or widows, who impose upon, seduce, or betray into matrimony any of his Majesty's subjects by virtue of scents, cosmetics, washes, paints, artificial teeth, false hair or high-heeled shoes, shall incur the penalty of the law now in force against witchcraft."

— Seventeenth-century New Jersey law

(Just proving that you can't get a man with a gun, your Avon representative, or your Maud Frizons.)

Top left: Dorothy Percy, Countess of Leicester, *engraving by H. T. Ryall, 1659.* **Below:** *Elizabeth Arden's Venetian line of cosmetics, ca. 1925.*

BEAUTY REFORMS

Still plagued with pimples, despite your mask? Try this recipe from the 1633 revised *Gerard's Herbal*:

- Eat a dish of cucumbers for three weeks, mixed with oatmeal and mutton.

- Also, during the three weeks, wash face with a combination of:
  one pint vinegar, powder ireos or orrice roots, half an ounce of brimstone, 2 dragmes of champhore mixed with 2 almonds, 4 apples (sans core), juice of 4 lemons

How to keep your lips kissable? To soothe chapping and cracking, try this inexpensive, fast seventeenth-century recipe:

1. With finger, wipe sweat from behind the ears.

2. Without washing, rub finger on cracked lips.

For all-over softness, try to avoid bathing. But if you must wash, try this fragrant bath concoction:

- Take musk, amber, myrrh, aloes, cedar leaves, and lavender and mix together in tub of warm water. Jump in, avoiding leaves.

PROGRESS

The early 1600s knock the stuffing out of menswear. Now bulging peascod bellies give way to sleeker lines, offset by long, pointed fronts. By the 1640s these new stream-lined *doublets* take on natural waistlines, and fasten with dozens of tiny buttons. Soon dandies crop them off for a snappy bolero look and leave them open to reveal a new seventeenth-century craze—the shirt.

Next thing you know, we'll be seeing hairy chests and gold chains.

Left: *17th-century cartoon.* **Right:** *English doublet, 17th c.* **Below:** *Demurely clad dancing girls, early 1900s.*

ESSENCE BARE

Attention is centered on the neck and bosom, but no woman worth her petticoat would *ever* expose her calves. The female leg is so completely disguised that courtiers spend hours gossiping about whether or not a certain lady is wearing shoes, because no one's ever seen them. Inventors even devise a collapsible carriage curtain to successfully hide the feet of dismounting women.

A shoe unseen is, naturally, invested with mystical powers. So it's not surprising, in 1644, when sorcerer Patrick Malcolm is accused of trying to persuade a woman to give him her left shoe. Had the rake succeeded, superstition has it, he would have had her in his power, and she would have been forced to follow him.

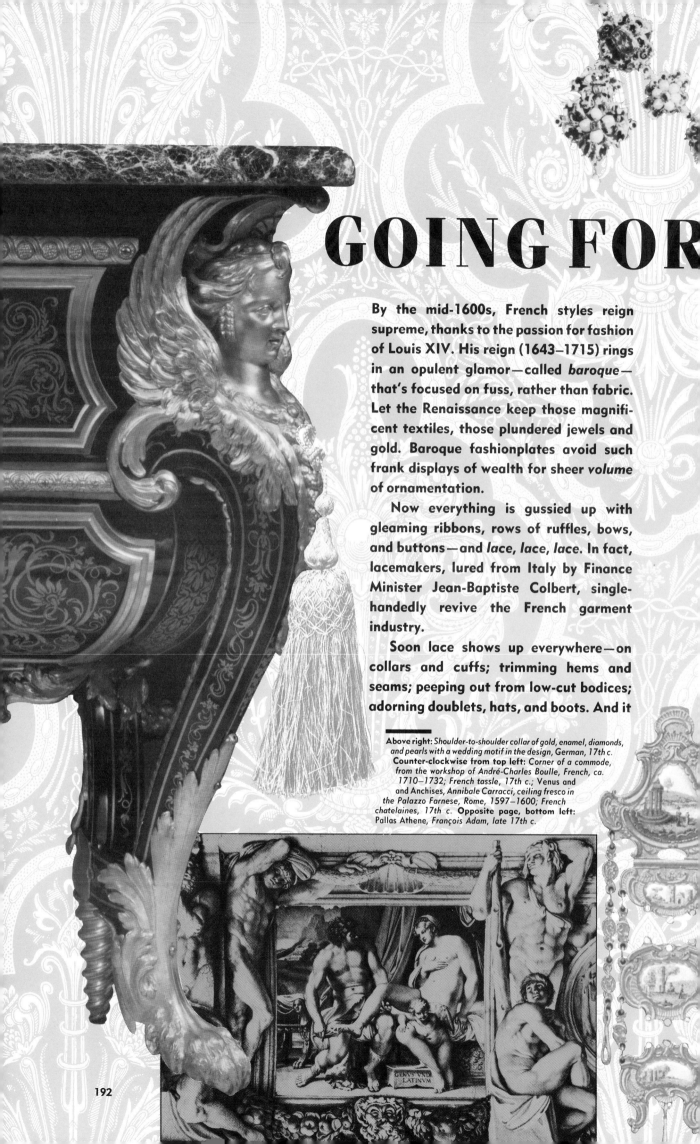

GOING FOR

By the mid-1600s, French styles reign supreme, thanks to the passion for fashion of Louis XIV. His reign (1643–1715) rings in an opulent glamor—called *baroque*—that's focused on fuss, rather than fabric. Let the Renaissance keep those magnificent textiles, those plundered jewels and gold. Baroque fashionplates avoid such frank displays of wealth for sheer *volume* of ornamentation.

Now everything is gussied up with gleaming ribbons, rows of ruffles, bows, and buttons—and *lace, lace, lace*. In fact, lacemakers, lured from Italy by Finance Minister Jean-Baptiste Colbert, single-handedly revive the French garment industry.

Soon lace shows up everywhere—on collars and cuffs; trimming hems and seams; peeping out from low-cut bodices; adorning doublets, hats, and boots. And it

Above right: *Shoulder-to-shoulder collar of gold, enamel, diamonds, and pearls with a wedding motif in the design, German, 17th c.* **Counter-clockwise from top left:** *Corner of a commode, from the workshop of André-Charles Boulle, French, ca. 1710–1732; French tassle, 17th c.; Venus and and Anchises, Annibale Carracci, ceiling fresco in the Palazzo Farnese, Rome, 1597–1600; French chatelaines, 17th c.* **Opposite page, bottom left:** *Pallas Athene, François Adam, late 17th c.*

BAROQUE

soon worms its way into chic French homes as well, where even the bathtub may be draped with lace.

Any space not trimmed with lace is embellished with *embroidery*. Now designs grow highly sophisticated, often derived from the paintings of contemporary artists such as Rubens and Van Dyck. Favorite styles include *stumpwork*, with stitches etching patterns in padded white satin, and *Richelieu work*, named for the French cardinal, with cutout designs connected with embroidered bars.

The stitching craze gets so extreme that, in 1656, French Cardinal Mazarin tries to curb excesses with a decree banning the use of gold and silver thread. However, an outraged public bent on beauty threatens to storm the palace of Louis XIV—and so the edict is quickly rescinded.

Clockwise from top right: *Swedish crystal candelabra from the early 18th c. atop a French candlestick from 1710; the "Grenville Jewel," English, ca. 1635–40, a gold enamelled locket decorated with gems; detail from the wall-hanging Air, portraying Louis XIV as a sunburst, French, ca. 1684.*

193

SETTLING SCORES

In the mid-1600s, England is distracted from the French fashion fever by a brewing civil war. The conflict is religious, but equally intense is the opponents' clash of styles. Here's a quiz to help you find out which side you're on: the straitlaced Puritans' or the swashbuckling Cavaliers'.

1. **ARE YOUR HATS:**
   a. Like your counterparts' in Germany: tall, dark, steeple-brimmed?
   b. Dashing, low-crowned, floppy toppers trimmed with ostrich plumes, cocked at a jaunty angle?

2. **IS YOUR COLLAR:**
   a. Plain white and starched, drooping modestly over your chest?
   b. A wide, unstarched falling band with a deep edging of lace?

3. **UNDER YOUR DOUBLET, DO YOU WEAR:**
   a. A heavy leather vest, with hook-and-eye closings to protest expensive gold or silver buttons?
   b. A billowing shirt, of fine fabric, with massive lacy cuffs draped over your hands?

4. **ARE YOUR BREECHES:**
   a. Black and baggy, fitted about the knee, and fastened with simple buttons?
   b. Gaily colored, decorated with braid, and cuffed at the knee, where they're trimmed with ribbons or lace?

5. **ARE YOUR HOSE AND BOOTS:**
   a. Made of rough wool and leather, respectively, in utilitarian designs?
   b. Made of fine silk or linen, worn with high-heeled bucket-top boots trimmed with lace or ruffled boot hose?

6. **DO YOU ACCESSORIZE WITH:**
   a. A bible, a staff and a turkey, or an apron, if you're female?
   b. A cane, or sword hung from a bright sash, and a single, pearl earring (until your model, Charles I, removes his on the occasion of his beheading)?

7. **IS YOUR HAIR:**
   a. Short and uncurled if you're male or, if you're a woman, concealed in a serviceable white cap?
   b. Long and worn in gleaming ringlets, with a lovelock—an extra-long tress—arranged cunningly at one side?

8. **ARE YOUR FAVORITE COLORS:**
   a. Black, mauve, brown, and gray, offset by purest white?
   b. The flashier the better?

9. **IS YOUR CAPE:**
   a. Scarlet or black, designed for warmth?
   b. A splash of color, worn over one shoulder for an air of drama and mystery?

10. **ARE YOUR CLOTHES TRIMMED WITH:**
    a. Nothing—lace is a "temptation of Satan"; at most you'll risk a little embroidery, but only Biblical quotations?
    b. The sky's the limit?

BONUS QUESTION: IS YOUR WORST FEAR:
    a. That someone will remark on your appearance?
    b. That no one will notice you?

SCORING:

If you chose *a* in most cases, you are a Puritan. You won't have fun, but your costume will be immortalized by the sculptor Saint-Gaudens. And in two hundred years, it will be ranked the forty-eighth most popular costume for Halloween by *People* magazine.

If most of your answers were *b*, beware: Cromwell's victory in 1653 will make you an endangered species.

Above, left to right: *A difference in style: An engraving of a cavalier Dutchman by Knilling, 17th c., and his austere contemporary, The Puritan, a bronze by Augustus Saint-Gaudens, 1887.*

1661 THERE'S A FAMINE RAGING IN INDIA, WHERE THERE'S BEEN NO RAIN SINCE 1659.

Above: The Merry Company, Franz Hals (1582–1666). **Below:** French waiters and English guests wear the same justacorps, French engraving, 17th c.

TO "RESTORE" YOUR LOOKS: With the monarchy back in the saddle, frivolous court life can resume. Here's what every seventeenth-century beauty needs to keep on hand for emergency ballroom touchups:
• Ceruse—a liquid makeup base of lead in vinegar, available in stark white or pale pink. Thick enough to fill in wrinkle lines, it also leaves a heavy makeup line around the face and chin (and eventually poisons you).
• Red enamel—for cheeks; or, for a softer look, try pale rose matte powder; both can be applied in clown-like circles on each cheek.
• Red lipstick and blue eyeshadow—both made from natural vegetable dyes.
• Plenty of perfume (since you probably still don't bathe!).
• Coal or green eyeshadow—to tint lids black or green (appropriate for *either* milady or milord).
• And for your man, a light base of white, and some extra red for his cheeks.

IMITATION IS THE SINCEREST FORM OF PARODY: Once Cromwell is deposed and the British monarchy "restored," one of the first things Charles II wants to do is to challenge French control of fashion. So, in 1660, he instructs his designers to develop a "totally English" look for noblemen. Their concept: a long overcoat, which Louis XIV derides as "Persian." Worse, to ridicule Charles, he appropriates the style as a uniform for his lackeys.

BROADSIDE: The new dignity of the French court affects men too, completely derailing the sexy short doublet. Now the *justaucorps* is born, a boon to all men with less-than-perfect derrieres. It starts as a slender, knee-length coat with short sleeves to offset the elaborate cuffs of shirts and doublets. But by the end of the century, when it acquires a nipped-in waist, full-length sleeves, and massive cuffs of its own, it becomes the foundation of everyday menswear.

Dandies adorn their justaucorps with embroidery, straps, braids, and the hottest new feature—slash pockets. These horizontal pockets are placed just out of reach, near the hem of the coat; and as if to offset their inconvenience, they are decorated with buttons topped by a neat row of totally useless buttonholes.

195

1664 THE BRITISH CAPTURE NEW AMSTER-DAM AND RENAME IT NEW YORK.

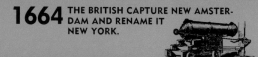

1665 THE GREAT PLAGUE OF LONDON BEGINS IN JULY, AND BY ITS END IN OCTOBER WILL HAVE KILLED 68,596 PEOPLE.

WHEN IT REIGNS, IT POURS

The umbrella is introduced to England in the 1660s by Charles II's bride, Catherine of Braganza, who brings it as part of her trousseau from her native Portugal (where, in fact, it is used as protection from the sun). It soon joins the noble lady's wardrobe of essential accessories—her masks, patches, gloves, and fan.

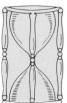

THE SHAPE OF THINGS TO COME: Women begin the 1600s trapped in cagelike skirts, fattened with padded "life preserver" rolls around their hips. But as midcentury approaches, with the spirit of the Renaissance dimmed, enormous farthingales go the way of the ruff. Only in Spain, as a last vestige of glory, do skirts balloon to outlandish proportions.

In the rest of Europe, though skirts are still hooped, they fall more naturally from the waist. Now they're tucked up at the sides to reveal silk or satin petticoats adorned with a riot of trimmings—fringes, flounces, tassels, and golden lace and braid.

By the close of the century, to display more of their glamorous petticoats, women start bunching up their overskirts in back. And now the fullness of the farthingale migrates to the derriere—and the bustle gets a boost.

PATCH IT UP: **X marks the spot . . . and in France in the 1660s so do hearts, diamonds, circles, and clubs. Those little black patches made from taffeta or thin leather are all the rage and are more than mere blemish coverups. An engaged woman wears a patch on her left cheek, switching it to her right after marriage; a patch near a woman's lip is a "come-hither" signal; a Whig lady wears a patch to the left, a Tory to the right, and if you want a gal who'll vote for political coalition, look for patches on both cheeks. As a whimsical touch, noble ladies patch their noses and even their chins; and sexy sirens carry a small patch box with them wherever they go so they can replace any patches that fall off during a hot waltz around the palace ballroom. By no means solely the prerogative of highbrow ladies, patches are seen on the jowls of dandies as well. It is recorded that one amorous marquis arrived at a ball wearing sixteen patches on his face—including one in the shape of a tree with two lovebirds kissing. Not only do they wear their hearts on their face, as it were, but ladies and gents sometimes wear family albums—profile patches of family and friends are also a popular fad.**

Above: *Queen Marie-Therese, engraved by Nicholas Bazin, 1682, after a portrait by Jean-Baptiste Martin.* **Right:** *Sixteenth- and early seventeenth-century women patch one on to face the nation.*

196

1666 LONDON IS NOT HAVING A GREAT COUPLE OF YEARS: THE GREAT FIRE RAGES FOR FIVE DAYS AND VIRTUALLY DESTROYS THE CITY.

1667 MILTON PENS THE IMMORTAL *PARADISE LOST.*

BEDROOM THIGHS

As women's skirts begin to slim down, men, thrilled at the chance to get close to their dates, start trimming back their breeches, too. Indeed, even by the early decades, most breeches gain their girth from stiff interfacings, rather than from sawdust and bran. Very soon, the pumpkin breeches craze is completely squashed.

Now men opt for full, longer *cloak-bag breeches*, narrowing at the knee, where they are tied with a fringed sash or a fillip edged with lace. By the 1630s, breeches grow longer still and end in loops of ribbons, often with the bottoms left open to flop gamely about the legs.

Then, in the 1650s, pants gain a new boudoir allure as *rhinegraves* or *petticoat breeches*. Their legs are so wide—each might be more than five feet around—that they look like divided skirts. Ruffles, lace, and embroidery trimmings on these bloomers enhance their lingerie appeal. Sorry, ladies; men only.

But toward the end of the 1600s, possibly out of embarrassment for all these excesses, breeches all but disappear from view. Streamlined to become the knee breeches of the eighteenth century, they barely peep out from beneath men's long slim coats and waistcoats to cover the tops of knee-high hose.

WELL-HEELED: We don't know what the Mad Hatter would have said, but smart seventeenth century hosiers say "Socks with *clocks*!" as fancy patterns decorate dandies' colorful thigh- or knee-high hose. At the beginning of the century, the well-gammed man wears them with blunt-toed pumps, often adorned with a splashy *shoe rose*, a bright pompom of ribbons that may be so large that is nearly hides his foot.

Over time, however, party shoes lose ground to more dashing boots, which start out slim and then sprout—you guessed it— enormous, floppy cuffs. Boot cuffs give men a whole new area to decorate, and so *boot hose* step in to fill the gap. Lavishly ruffled, scalloped, or lace-trimmed liners that spill out from the leather, they give their wearers all the cachet of a messy lingerie drawer.

These frills and furbelows need a more masculine counterpoint, so spurs become *the* essential shoe accessory. Every well-dressed man sports a glamorous pair—even if he never dreams of setting foot in stirrups. Shoes eventually make a comeback around the 1660s, however, when Louis XIV (who wants to show off his good gams and appear taller) makes stockings and high heels a must. Red is a favorite color, restricted to members of Louis' court, and shoes are now trimmed with bows or, later, buckles rather than elaborate rosettes. Men will not be able to cool their heels until Louis kicks off, half a century later.

A leggy Louis XIV by Hyacinthe Rigaud, 1701.

ABOUT LACE

Lace isn't warm—it's so hole-y that it can't offer any real protection against a strong wind. The only practical reason for wearing lace is to let other people know you can afford it. And, it's pretty. Lace is always one color, and can only be produced in limited widths. Fragments of fabric that are ornamented openwork have been found in ancient Egyptian tombs, but lace is called "the child of the Renaissance," because the art of lace making was developed in fifteenth-century Europe in either Flanders or in Italy. Lace, which is elegant yet simple (or at least simpler than ornate gold embroideries), comes into vogue during the Renaissance, when form is celebrated over color and unadorned raw materials are the ticket (marble statues are selling better than painted wooden ones.) By 1600, lace is a great luxury, an item of commerce, and large quantities are worn by both men and women. Puritans give up lace believing it to be a "temptation of Satan." By the eighteenth century it is only seen worn demurely around the wrist and throat, and on better armchairs and tables of grandmothers throughout the world.

PICTURE THIS: Holland's favorite embroidery design is the tulip (it's so popular that it's even declared the national flower). It's stitched onto doilies, stenciled onto furniture, and woven into textile designs. And if this isn't enough, conservatively dressed women are often seen sporting little hats shaped like tulips.

Background: *Point à la Rose lace pattern.* **Left:** Margaret Bromsen, M. Hiert, 1641. **Above right:** *Dutch tiles, 17th c.*

Clockwise from top: *Portrait of a woman* by Voet Ferdinand; *Girl with a Red Hat, Jan Vermeer, ca. 1666–1669; Duchess of Fontagnes, Pierre Mignard (1612–1695).*

COINAGE

By the second half of the seventeenth century, most of Europe has adopted the mercantile system. This new coin-based economy challenges old-fashioned bartering, shaking the power of the guilds, and lets nations hoard their gold and silver, rather than use them as currency. But whose face do you put on a metal coin? In 1666, one Frances Stewart is chosen as the model for "Britannia."

What does Frances Stewart look like? Does she deserve such an honor? Here are two eyewitness accounts:

According to diarist Samuel Pepys: "Methought she was the beautifullest creature that ever I saw in my life, more than ever I thought so . . . She wears a cocked hat with a red plume, and has a sweet eye, little Roman nose and excellent taille."

The Count de Grammont recalls in his *Memoirs:* "It is impossible for a woman to have more beauty . . . or less wit."

Well, no one ever said they were offering her the penny for her *thoughts*.

Above: *Frances Stuart, mistress of England's Charles II, ca. 1670.*

HOME IS WHERE THE HAIR IS: Like the ruffs of the Renaissance, the high collars of the 1600s create a field day for hairdressers and a nightmare for hatters. Early in the century, women's hair is worn upswept, sometimes anchored over foundations for extra height, and trimmed with jewels.

But by midcentury, as necklines simplify, hairstyles do too. Most women wear their hair in buns, often bejeweled, with bangs and *love-locks*—curls allowed to droop teasingly over the ears, often much longer on the left. These calculatedly stray locks are soon enhanced by frizzing to create a halo around the face, sometimes with the help of wire frames. In the 1670s and 1680s, buns are eschewed altogether for an overall mass of curls, a coif known as the *hurly-burly*. These styles finally make it possible for women to adopt a variety of hats—beautifully embroidered *snoods* stretched over buns, hoods for protection from the elements, and best of all, glamorous wide-brimmed picture hats.

But in the last decade of the century, hair gets hemmed in again, when, on a hunt with Louis XIV, the coquettish Madame de Fontanges loses her hat and provocatively pulls back her curls with a lace-edged garter, thus creating "the Fontange." The *fontange* is a white cap with curls cascading from the front, often as not made of false hair. It soon gains so many rows of ruffles and ribbons that it needs a wire superstructure for support.

The new hairstyle takes hours to create, and women don't dare touch their hair for at least three weeks after these long hairdressing sessions; they even sleep (or try to) with their heads suspended on a wooden neck rest. Their efforts are appreciated, if not always rewarded—fawning men praise the towering creations, while crabs and lice settle comfortably into new homes.

1670 ITALIAN SCIENTIST GIOVANNI BORELLI ATTEMPTS TO USE ARTIFICIAL WINGS FOR FLYING.

1671 THE PARIS OPERA OPENS WITH A PRODUCTION OF ROBERT CAMBERT'S *POMONE*.

TRIVIAL HI

The seventeenth century is tress-obsessed, from the time the close-cropped Roundheads square off against the Cavaliers to the end, when the wig makes the man. But throughout history, social and political lines have often been determined by a hair.

As William Hogarth observed and Veronica Lake demonstrated, "One lock of hair falling across the temples has an effect too alluring to be strictly decent"; hair is sexy. While we're pretty much stuck with our physical attributes, hair offers hope. It is constantly changing and growing, and can be manipulated to transform our appearance and identity.

Hair has been used as a sign of commitment. Turkish potentates swore by "the beard of the prophet," the medieval family friend who gave a child his first haircut automatically became the child's godparent, and in modern times young McCarthy supporters went "Clean for Gene."

Medieval people were warned to bury their hair cuttings so they couldn't be found by birds and used for nests—if they were, the haircuttee would be cursed with continual headaches. And a group of old women who lived in Ireland probably carried out the most literal interpretation of any superstition associated with hair. "The hairs on our heads are numbered," they read in the Scriptures; it is recorded that they stored each and every strand of their cut hair in the belief that they would be called upon to account for them on the Day of Judgment.

The longest preserved male beard, housed with other treasures in the venerable Smithsonian Institution, is seventeen and a half feet. The longest recorded female beard, which nobody bothered to save, was fourteen inches.

Three hundred years before the Beatles, a one hundred-page attack on "The Loathsomeness of Hair" was issued by an Anglican pastor. But it was a century too late to help Hans Steininger, the Chief Magistrate of Branau, Austria, who tripped over his eight-foot-nine-inch beard, fell down a flight of steps, and killed himself in 1567.

There is the art of hairdressing—the world record was set by Louis Sanft in 1976 for a marathon two-hundred-hour session of cutting, combing, primping, and perming. And there is hair as art. Jewelry, portrait paintings, and cross-stitch textiles have all been executed in human hair. The wreath hanging over the marble mantle in a sedate Victorian parlor was likely to have been woven from family members' hair, and though in light of today's postal service it's hard to imagine they arrived intact, postcards with figures capped off with real hair were popular in the early twentieth century.

And lest you think hair has escaped the watchful eye of psychiatrists, note the theories that people playing with their hair have a hidden sexual agenda, that scalping represents the castration of the enemy as well as possession

1672 CZAR-TO-BE PETER THE GREAT IS BORN.

1673 EXPLORERS MARQUETTE AND JOLIET REACH THE HEADWATERS OF THE MISSISSIPPI, AND DESCEND TO ARKANSAS.

RSUTE

of another person, and that the most primitive and universal expression of rage is to "tear out your hair."

On March 21, 1633, Bessie Skobister's long tresses got her into trouble. She was convicted of "taking off her kerchief, shaking her hair loose and causing vehement and continual pain to Margaret Mudie." In ancient Scotland "shaking the hair loose" was considered the act of a person casting a spell. Similarly, it was believed that hairy chests were a sign of strength, that people with hair on their arms and hands would be wealthy, that if hair grew on the forehead and retreated up the head above the temples it was a sign of long life, and that red-haired people couldn't make good butter.

And finally, less eloquent than Hogarth, but full circle and to the point, the letter from one of Napoleon's generals: "Don't shave it, don't wash it," he wrote to his wife, "I'll be home in two weeks."

Counter-clockwise, from opposite top: Enamel, ivory, and shell hair-comb, Henri Lalique, French, ca. 1900; hairdresser's tool, wrought iron and chased steel, 17th c.; the late Bob Marley, reggae artist, ca. 1970's; Lady Kinnaird, William Owen (1769–1825); Don King, flashy fight promoter; The Haircutting, Nikolaus Gysis (1842–1901); illustration of the proper way to oil the the scalp, from the Encyclopedia of Health, 1937; laundress' bonnet-crimping iron, wrought iron, 17th c.

HOME OF THE BRAVE: What would *you* pack for a twelve-week journey across the Atlantic Ocean to the New World? The settlers bring whatever keepsakes they can, tools, and of course, clothes.

The clothes that they bring are worn only to church and on special occasions, and are naturally à la mode of each of their home-lands, creating a unique set of styles in the different colonies: the wealthy burghers of New Amsterdam follow the latest fashions of Amsterdam and Paris; the Spaniards, who colonize Florida and California, sport dramatic capes; the English, in Virginia, Delaware, and the Carolinas, import Cavalier-style clothes from home right up until the Revolution.

Everyday wear, however, is another matter. Velvet capes and lacy collars and cuffs will not do for churning butter or raising roofs. The settlers turn to the Native Americans, who share their knowledge of growing and weaving flax, hemp, cotton, and wool into simple, durable cloth. The Native Americans also teach the settlers how to tan an animal hide of deer or buckskin into the finest chamois. In general, the Native Americans themselves wear clothing made out of these softly tanned skins: the men preferring a breechclout of two small leather aprons (one in the front, the other in the back), hanging from a narrow belt; the women donning a fringed skin tied apron-fashion around the waist. The Native Americans copy the settlers' bandolier (adding distinctive quills and beadwork), and the priests who succeed in converting them to the Christian faith congratulate themselves on the questionable accomplishment of inducing the young men to wear short breeches. But the Native Americans' contributions to the colonists' dress is more long lasting: the soft-soled moccasin; silver and turquoise jewelry; the headband, which keeps the wearer's hair out of his face; and the first Snugli—a three-piece wooden "baby frame" that makes it easy for young mothers to carry their babies on their backs.

An Indian woman carrying baby in the world's first Snugli.

MUFF-INS

The other classic accessory of the seventeenth century is the *muff*. It's worn by both men and women, not only for warmth, but also as a pocket. A man's fur muff (made from beaver, otter, or even panther) hangs from his belt, and as it is the custom to comb one's hair in public, you can count on a comb being tucked inside.

That little French coquette the Marquise de Montespan uses her muff like a fan, to conceal the expression in her eyes when embarrassed, to flirt, or playfully to put it up to her face in delicate moments.

By the 1700s, cloth muffs, festooned with ribbons, are worn throughout Europe. But in the middle of the century, in an effort to give his business a boost, a Parisian furrier whips up a velvet muff and presents it to the local hangman. No one is allowed to wear what the hangman wears so cloth muffs are instantly taboo—now everyone flocks to their furriers to buy muffs. In the 1770s muffs take a beating in Frederick the Great's German court. Finding a large muff belonging to his enemy, Herr von Kameke, Freddy flings it in the fire—thus damping the fashion for muffs in Germany.

In the 1900s Pioret gives the muff a comeback, and smartly dressed women are seen carrying muffs that match their fur stoles, providing an elegant look for promenading and prettily posed Currier & Ives ice skating prints. But over time, as the agile-fingered glove wins out, the fashion is eventually muffed.

THRILL
DRESSED TO

Top left: *Engraving of a gentleman in winter dress, 17th c.* **Below:** *Nell Gwyn (1650–1687), earthy mistress of Charles II of England.*

Courtesans consolidate their influence in the seventeenth century. In England, actress Nell Gwynn becomes the mistress of Charles II and chooses to go "natural," wearing her hair in a mass of curls parted down the middle for a demure look that becomes all the rage in England.

Across the Channel, following in the celebrated footsteps of Agnes Sorel, Madame de Montespan becomes the confidante of Louis XIV, as well as a trendsetter of the royal court. It is she who first wears loose, flowing gowns (to conceal her numerous pregnancies) and introduces the art of muff flirtation. She loves "busy dresses"—the look of bows, ribbons, and lace; patterns; parasols; shoes that are brocaded and festooned with buckles and bows, pointy toes, and high curvy heels. She likes full, pleated sleeves, too.

But the mistress the widowed Louis eventually marries, Madame de Maintenon, deplores such feminine frills and furbelows. Too shrewd to give her rivals any quarter, she promotes subdued styles in sober hues, especially black. The reform never really takes hold, but she does succeed in banning low decolletages. And as a final precaution, she converts the frivolous court to a deep Catholic piety—and so manages to keep the promiscuous king from straying.

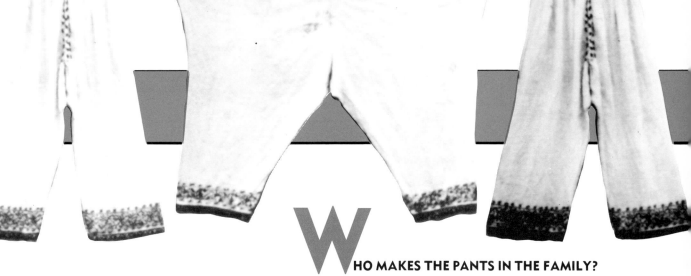

WHO MAKES THE PANTS IN THE FAMILY?

During most of the seventeenth century, the dressmakers and tailors are male. Then, in 1675 Louis XIV receives a petition asking that women be allowed to make petticoats, skirts, and various accessories. The king agrees, and as women set up shop, the dressmakers' guild is formed. By the end of the century, the two most famous tailors, Monsieur Regnauly and Monsieur Gautier, are replaced by two women, Madame Charpentier and Madame Villeneuve.

The original petitioners get their is by claiming it is immodest for men to make women's underclothes. But that doesn't mean that they are planning to hide their handiwork. Instead, they bring the petticoat right out in the open, sweeping overskirts all the way back into the new bustles. And then they encrust the exposed underwear with flounces, lace, ribbons, fringes, tassels, and braid to draw attention to them.

COLORS OF THE DAY

Blue is the color of the heavens, so people hope it will protect their infant sons from the Devil. What about their little girls? Oh, girls are so unimportant . . . the Devil won't even be interested in them. When a special color is chosen for girls, people think pink because of an old European fairy tale which charmingly claims that baby girls spring forth from pink roses.

Top of page: *Undergarments from a nobleman's trousseau, linen embroidered with colored silk and gold and silver thread, 17th c.*

Left: *Detail from a song slide shown at movie-houses during sing-alongs, early 20th c.*

203

WIGGED-OUT

Doctor, lawyer, Indian chief? Just check out his wig. In the seventeenth century, that's how you can tell a man's profession. Custom dictates that ordinary folks wear little wigs, so anyone with a *big wig* is easily recognizable as a man of prominence.

Men and women both wear false hair in the early seventeenth century to add a little pizzazz to their hairstyles. Then Louis XIII of France sows the seeds of a fad when he puts on a *peruke* (in English, *periwig*, later shortened to just plain *wig*) to cover his bald pate. By the 1660s, fashionable Frenchmen are cropping their own hair to make way for long, curly wigs, which have become an indispensable accessory. And now the nightcap is invented—the kind worn on the head—to keep drafts off defenseless, shorn scalps.

The finest wigs are made of human locks, while the less well-tressed get by with horsehair or wool. But Charles II of England, who brings the style across the Channel when he goes prematurely gray, boasts the ultimate wig—it is made from the pubic hair of his many mistresses.

By the 1680s, wig fever is full-blown. Now wigs grow enormous and are parted in the middle, with towering peaks of ringlets, tumbling down the back nearly to the waist. These giant confections—called *full-bottomed* wigs—are so costly that the government holds lotteries which Frenchmen enter in the hopes of winning a wig. Louis XIV loves the style so much that he has ten personal wigmakers. And a new breed of criminal is born—the dreaded wigsnatcher.

You would think that the full-bottomed wig would prove an impossible challenge for hatmakers. Not true—European dandies love elaborate hats and buy them by the dozens. But when wigs get huge, savvy swashbucklers resort to drastic measures—rather than actually *wearing* their hats, they carry them around under their arms.

HAZARDOUS TO
WARNING
YOUR HEALTH

Dutch women dare to wear the *houftijsertgen,* an iron cap with metal clips that wraps around the head. It's used to keep their popular white linen crownlike caps in place, far back on their heads. The tight metal clip winds around the back of the head, and ends at the cheeks. (Where, due to the extreme pressure caused by the clip, it is doubtful that you will see a smile.) And this in the days before Advil, no less.

DIARY OF A WIG PICKER: Seventeenth-century diarist Samuel Pepys loves to kvetch and worry. He reports that, one grim day, a dog attacked his garters. Another disaster: When strolling in St. James Park, he passes the Duke of York and, as etiquette demands, uncovers his head. Unsatisfied, he worries: "I might not have walked far enough with my hat off." So, hat in hand, he pens an apology.

The periwig craze provides new grist for the mill. For a full three months, Pepys worries about buying one. Will the fad last? Should he waste his money? Finally, he decides to take the plunge. Before long, he has a new string of complaints: His wig is infested with lice. What can he possibly wear while it's out being cleaned? Why should he invest good money in another? Finally, happily, he finds something great to carp about, a truly worthy obsession—the rumors that wigs are made from the infectious hair of plague victims.

Top right: *Ivory portrait medallion of Samuel Pepys, David Le Marchand, late 17th c.* **Top left:** *Illustration of the wigs available to dandies in the 17th c.* **Left:** *Dutch linen cap and head iron trimmed with "krullers," brass corkscrews attached at the cheeks.*

HOUSE OF THE RISING SUN KING: Perhaps it's the new, sober dullness of the court that accounts for the popularity of the king's *levee*, Louis XIV's morning ablutions. Unlike his ancestor Henry IV—who smelled so bad on his wedding night that Marie de Médici had to douse herself with perfume to mask *his* odor—Louis likes to wash, especially in the presence of toadying courtiers. The fun begins when Louis wakes and then bathes as he is shaved (every two days), groomed, and daubed with water and wine (plain water is considered too abrasive for the royal body). Nobles who miss out on the levee vie for the privilege of seeing the *couche*, the ritual of putting the king to bed in the evening.

But lest anyone think Louis selfishly hoards such pleasures, in 1675 he opens the first beauty parlors, to accommodate dignitaries traveling through France. Visitors are encouraged to rest and relax, to partake in depilatory baths (eggshells ground into paste are rubbed onto their bodies), and since a house is not a home, they can also meet lovers there.

Other services include hair care and expert advice on dress; virility potions; and, in a pinch, abortions.

DRESSED TO KILL

COLLARITY: What happened to collars underneath those huge wigs? They fade away around midcentury, until Louis XIV's Croatian mercenaries introduce their traditional linen scarves to Europe. The scarves, called *cravats*, are wrapped and tied into such tight bows that soldiers sometimes faint during maneuvers. But since it is believed that the cravats protect a soldier's heart in battle, a swoon or two seems a small price to pay. In a short time, the cravats become popular all across the continent—perhaps in the hopes they'll provide the same heartfelt protection in the battle of the sexes.

Then, in 1684, when French soldiers are surprised by a dawn attack at Steinkirk, they quickly knot their cravats, twist the ends, and thrust them through the buttonholes of their coats. Soon men and women alike are sporting the new style, patriotically named the *steinkirk*, trimmed with lace and edged with pearls.

WOULDN'T YOU RATHER LOOK LIKE ERROL FLYNN?

Once the justaucorps gets gussied up and comes indoors, men need other ways to elude the elements. Many choose the *topcoat*, a long, practical garment made of wool trimmed with braid or embroidery; or for soldiers, made of leather. Over time, the topcoat comes to be known as the *brandenburg*, after the German province where its fasteners originate—braided strips with their tips formed into buttonholes.

More swashbuckling fashionplates still cling to their capes, which allow for sweeping dramatic entrances and exits. And since enormous coat sleeves have made elaborate gloves redundant, a cavalier who can't bear the more stripped-down models might opt for a large furry muff.

Top left: *The Persian ambassador to France bathes in the nude, an innovation for his time.* **Bottom right:** *Errol Flynn in The New Adventures of Don Juan, 1948.*

THE EIGHTEENTH CENTURY

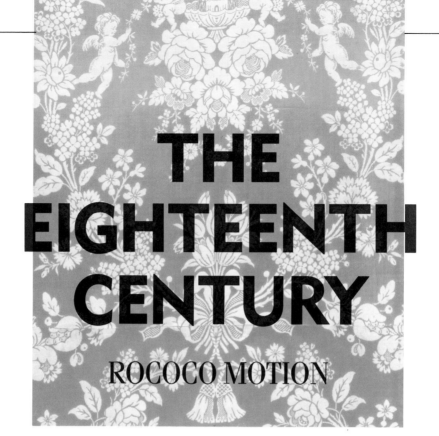

THE EIGHTEENTH CENTURY

ROCOCO MOTION

I t is the Age of Enlightenment. Hume, Kant, Voltaire, and Rousseau philosophize that the nature of man can be discovered through the use of rational thought. It is an age of humane and rational legislation. The Age of Reason: politically, socially, and fashionably. Well, at least for a while. Gone are the high heels of Louis XIV, the impossible wigs, the frilly ribbons, and fussy bows. Ben Franklin charms the French court with his "backwoods" look. Lord Chesterfield advises his son that it is best "to dress so as not to draw attention to yourself." And when fashion (and expenditures) *do* become *un*reasonable in the hands of Marie "Let Them Eat Clothes" Antoinette—it spells the downfall of the entire French court and the beginning of the end for the monarchy.

The old order is giving way to the new: The American colonies win their freedom; Russia, under Peter the Great, begins its ascent as a world power; the first encyclopedias appear; and the invention of the flying shuttle and the spinning jenny, along with the development of waterproof dyes and new methods of printing, put Europe on the brink of the Industrial Revolution. Mass-produced textiles are more affordable

Overleaf: *Design from gilt and color printed leatherwork, 18th c.* **Above:** *Patterned silk, French, late 18th c.* **Right:** *La Marseillaise (detail), engraving, ca. 1789.* **Opposite page:** *Engraving of the massacre at Fort Saint-Jean, Marseilles, 1795.*

to the masses and the profits they spur ensure the rapid growth of an affluent middle class. The breakdown of class distinctions that began in the Middle Ages continues—in an unprecedented move, Louis XV invites untitled guests to a great ball at Versailles celebrating the marriage of the Dauphin and the Infanta of Spain.

By the early 1700s, a new softness and prettiness is introduced into women's clothes as, for the first time, they cease to be made by tailors and instead are cut and styled by ladies' dressmakers. The easy grace of the *Rococo style* of interior decoration, which combines a seashell motif with flowers, feathers, curlicues, and all forms of curves, is reflected in clothes. (Although too much of a good rococo thing does result in all of these embellishments being piled on top of each other.) A loose sack gown, named after the painter Watteau, is made from about twenty yards of fabric which fall in loose folds from the neck to the hemline. As styles change, the gown is remodeled in the 1770s into the *polonaise*, a short dress which grazes the ankles, worn over hoops; and

later, into the high-waisted *empire gown* of the early 1800s.

Not content to leave well enough alone, however, in the 1730s basket-like *panniers* find their way under skirts: they make the circumference around the hips so wide that women can no longer relax their arms by their sides, and so the best designers equip them with padded elbow rests.

As for men, they wear coats, vests, and breeches—the forerunner of the three-piece suit. Except that these coats are tight-waisted and flare out at the hips, and are made of plush vermilion velvets and azure brocades and worn with frilly shirts and ruffled sleeves. In the 1760s we see a move towards even simpler dressing, as everyone, including Voltaire, seems to be tending a garden; emphasis switches from French court clothes to an English country mode. This is the style of gentlemen farmers who know how to hunt—not dissimilar in spirit to Ralph Lauren's country style, c. 1989.

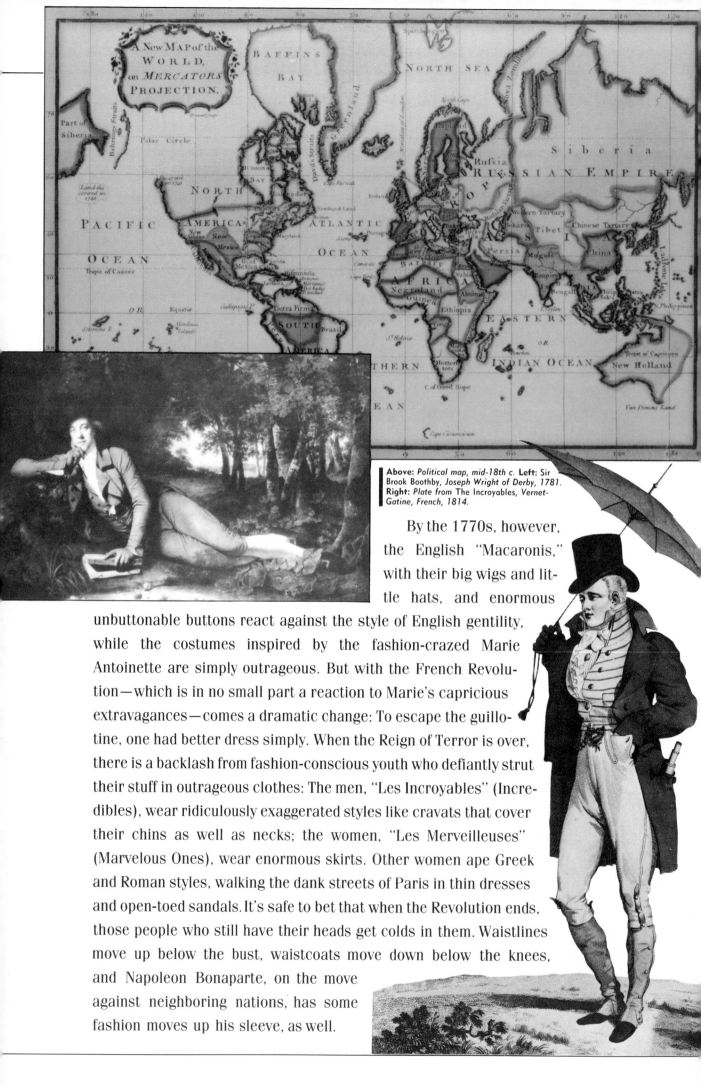

Above: *Political map, mid-18th c.* Left: Sir Brook Boothby, *Joseph Wright of Derby, 1781.* Right: *Plate from* The Incroyables, *Vernet-Gatine, French, 1814.*

By the 1770s, however, the English "Macaronis," with their big wigs and little hats, and enormous unbuttonable buttons react against the style of English gentility, while the costumes inspired by the fashion-crazed Marie Antoinette are simply outrageous. But with the French Revolution—which is in no small part a reaction to Marie's capricious extravagances—comes a dramatic change: To escape the guillotine, one had better dress simply. When the Reign of Terror is over, there is a backlash from fashion-conscious youth who defiantly strut their stuff in outrageous clothes: The men, "Les Incroyables" (Incredibles), wear ridiculously exaggerated styles like cravats that cover their chins as well as necks; the women, "Les Merveilleuses" (Marvelous Ones), wear enormous skirts. Other women ape Greek and Roman styles, walking the dank streets of Paris in thin dresses and open-toed sandals. It's safe to bet that when the Revolution ends, those people who still have their heads get colds in them. Waistlines move up below the bust, waistcoats move down below the knees, and Napoleon Bonaparte, on the move against neighboring nations, has some fashion moves up his sleeve, as well.

I'M GONNA GIVE YOU MORE . . . : The baroque glamor of the seventeenth century is a hard act to follow. How can you possibly outdo a style that covered everything—even bathtubs—with lace? The answer is *rococo* (a lighter touch, but with more fuss), which dominates Europe through 1789. Lace stays in the limelight, but it's now paired with flowers—fabrics printed with floral sprigs; lavish garlands trimming a neckline, a hem, or a sleeve; and small bouquets adorning an enormous skirt swag. Fresh flowers are so popular that bodices are often fitted with tiny "vase" pockets, to hold small bottles of water so fragile blossoms won't wilt.

Other trimmings called *garnitures*—fringes, tassels, and *plastiques* (thin stuffed tubes of fabric stitched onto skirts)—embellish every leftover inch to save the eighteenth-century beauty from the unspeakable horror of unadorned space.

❙ Portrait of Madame de Pompadour, *Boucher (1703–1770).*

CAGE-Y

Freed from her farthin-
gales, what does the eighteenth-century lady do? Fly
right into the *hooped skirt*.
The trend starts out innocently enough as the sim-
ple bustle carried over
from the 1600s. Then, taking a cue from English
styles, French skirts begin
to swell into a gentle bell
shape. Around 1730, leg-
end has it, two obese ladies
have their hips fitted with
hoops so they can air their
thighs on summer strolls
in the Tuileries. These *panniers* create a sensation—
soon the only dimension
you need to wear them
is wealth.

And what were the first
panniers, from which
these hoops get their
name? The wicker baskets
slung from the hips of
mules and donkeys.

With no more sense
than donkeys, women now
adopt skirts that fall flat in
front and back but spread
out on the sides to a width
of eight feet or more. In
1742, at the first public
performance of Handel's
Messiah in Dublin, ladies
are requested to dress
without hoops and their
escorts to leave their
swords at home so the
theater can seat seven
hundred instead of six
hundred people. Special
chairs must be fashioned
to let wearers sit down,
and doorways across Eu-
rope are widened. But
since these strategies are
less than practical, necessity proves the mother of
invention: a collapsible
pannier develops, so
women can fold up their
skirts to enter rooms and
negotiate tight spaces.

In the 1760s and
1770s, though these broad
styles remain in vogue, a
new hoop configuration
muscles its way in. The
popular *polonaise*, which
looks like a decorated
cake, requires the support
of at least three small panniers to bulge out the hips
and derriere. Then, by pull-
ing and tying a variety of
hidden cords, the wearer
can bunch up her skirts to
form large poufs and
swags. Despite the deadly
complexity of its construction, the polonaise is supposed to evoke the tucked-
up skirts of a dairymaid.
Go figure it.

Below: *Les Adieux, Jean-Michel Moreau Le Jeune, 1760's.* **Opposite page:** *Contemporary cartoon of a pious Russian nobleman reluctantly having a barber shave his beard during the reign of Peter the Great (1683–1725).*

Above: *French "country style," illustration by Le Clerc, 1778.*

1719 DANIEL DEFOE PENS *ROBINSON CRUSOE.*

1720 HANDEL AND BACH ARE COMPOSING, GEORG TELEMANN IS APPOINTED DIRECTOR OF MUSIC IN HAMBURG, AND MUSICAL COMEDIES CALLED *VAUDEVILLES* APPEAR IN PARIS.

UN-HOLEY ALLIANCE: Like women, men begin the eighteenth century in an expansive mood. Though they're still wearing their standard uniform of coat, waistcoat, and breeches—a combo that comes to be called *l'habit française*—early on the coat looks like a goblet upside down: slim and straight to the waist, where it flares into pleated skirts. And they haven't forgotten that century-old trick to make the skirt stand out from the hip—it's reinforced with canvas and horsehair.

As the century progresses, silhouettes slim down, and coats lose their pleats for a more streamlined effect. By the 1780s, however, things get out of hand—coats finally get too narrow even to close over a manly chest and belly. Since no one even dreams of fastening them anymore, their buttonholes are usually fake.

HEAVENLY HAIR: As befits any six-foot-seven-inch-tall monarch, Russia's Peter the Great is a man with large ideas. He wants nothing less than to create a "modern" Russia, and to costume the transformation, he looks to the west.

Before Peter's early eighteenth-century reign, women are kept in a kind of purdah—seen only in their homes by family and friends. Peter introduces balls and masquerades to which young girls as well as married women are invited. Women wear western-inspired petticoats, skirts, and shoes. In place of the traditional costume of wide breeches, loose, embroidered shirt, colorful floppy boots and a long caftan, men wear shorter robes, with smaller, more tailored sleeves. Peter's troops wear breeches and waistcoats in the French style. Peter's efforts to westernize the Russian masses goes along relatively smoothly, until he messes with their beards. Sporting a beard has a long and religious tradition in Russia. The Orthodox Church believes it is a mortal sin to go without one: "God did not create men beardless; only cats and dogs." Those who can, flee. Others try to find a way around Peter's decree: They comply, but secretly hide the beards they've shaved off so they can be buried with them and avoid standing barefaced at Heaven's gate.

SACQUE IT TO ME: The death of Louis XIV in 1715 ends an era of incredible extravagance—the French nobility has nearly gone broke trying to uphold his standards of style. But if they're expecting relief, they're in for a shock. For the next sixty years, Louis XV will try to beat the record of his predecessor.

His ambitions start out modestly. In the Regency period, running till 1723, a new comfort reigns in fashion. Now women adopt the flowing *sacque*—a long, draped gown with loose elbow-length sleeves—and wear their hair short, in natural-looking curls, topped by a simple lace cap. Regency style is perfect for the frumpy French queen, Marie Leszczyńska, who's soon abandoned along with it, when Louis XV catches the fever for glamor.

CHILD'S PLAY

Before the eighteenth century, child's play wasn't exactly child's play: children were pinned, hooped, codpieced, and corseted in adult fashions—the only concession to their youth the miniaturization of sizes. But the eighteenth century is, after all, the Age of Reason, and it is philosopher Jean-Jacques Rousseau who puts forth a new view of childhood as a separate state, and calls for a change, not only in the education of children but in their dress: "The limbs of the growing child should be free to move easily; there should be nothing tight, nothing fitting closely to the body, no belts of any kind. The French style of dress, uncomfortable and unhealthy for a man, is especially bad for children. The best plan is to keep children in frocks for as long as possible, and then to provide them with loose clothing, without trying to design the shape, which is only another way of deforming it. Their defects of body and mind may all be traced to the same source, the desire to make men of them before their time."

The emancipation of childhood ushers in frocks to frolic in, and simple trousers for traipsing about. But, of course, who can ever leave well enough alone? By the twentieth century, adults are accused of wanting to look like children, and kids, who can't wait to grow up, co-opt adult styles.

Above: Prince Baltasar Carlos, *Velasquez*, 1634–1635. Left: Infanta Margarita, *Velasquez*, 1653. These royal children were born too early to enjoy being kids. Far left: Benneton kids, 1989.

1727 THE FIRST "PERSONAL" AD APPEARS IN A MANCHESTER NEWSPAPER.

1728 DUTCH EXPLORER VITUS BEHRING DISCOVERS THE BEHRING STRAIT.

Above: Wigmaker's warehouse in Vienna, ca. 1780. **Left:** Self Portrait, Maurice de La Tour, 1751.

COVER UP: By the early eighteenth century, men bored with their full-bottom wigs (or tired of trying to keep hair out of their eyes) spur a ponytail craze. Ponytail wigs come in a wide range of styles: a bunch of loose curls caught up in a band; a tasteful braid; or a smart pigtail ending in one curl (for majors), two (for brigadiers), or a knot called a *catogan*, formed by tucking the end of the tail into the band. For extra dash, the ponytail might be covered with a bag or dressed up with a large bow that might be accessorized with a matching small bowtie, called a *solitaire*, fastened to the wig in back.

Soon even these wigs grow tiresome, but no self-respecting man would ever bare his head. So, for a quiet evening at home, he covers his locks with a lavishly embroidered cap edged with fur.

LANGUAGE LESSONS

A gown that is fitted in front, but falls in straight pleats from the neck down in back is called the *robe à la française*.

A dress that is fitted at the waist all the way around is called the *robe à l'anglaise*.

A dress that falls straight down in back, or sometimes in front, with no pleats, is simply called the *sacque*.

Above: *French costume, 1775.*
Below: *Dustin Hoffman in* The Graduate, *1967.*

Above: L' Enseigne de Gersaint *(detail), Antoine Watteau, 1720. Sacque gowns were so often worn by Watteau's subjects that the style also became known as the "Watteau" gown.*

THERE'S ONE BORN EVERY MINUTE

The Persian *shir o shakkar* literally means "milk and sugar." Indian manufacturers translate it freely into "a striped linen garment" and during the mid-eighteenth century sell the thin, crepey material to eager Americans as *seersucker*. By the turn of the century this light, cool, and cheap material is used to produce the still-popular seersucker suit. Author Damon Runyon, who was always someone to give a sucker an even break, made the seersucker suit his trademark in the 1940s.

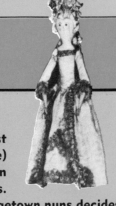

ALL DOLLED UP

How to know what's in vogue before the first issue of *Vogue* (or any other fashion magazine) is out? French designers issue dolls dressed in miniature versions of their latest creations. When a group of seventeenth-century Georgetown nuns decides to form a convent they want every detail to be right—so they write to France for a description of what to wear. They are sent a doll, dressed in black robe, guimpe, cap, and veil. When the doll arrives in New York en route to Georgetown, customs officials place it in solitary—claiming it looks like the work of the devil. Fortunately for well-dressed nuns everywhere, the doll is released and sent on to the convent.

In eighteenth-century France fashion dolls dubbed "Big and Little Pandoras" are sent all over Europe, displaying the exact clothing to wear at formal functions (Big P) and at more informal gatherings (Little P). The dolls are exact replicas of fashionable French ladies, down to the hair style, jewelry, and makeup. So popular are the Pandoras that, during Napoleon's blockade, safe passage is given them to London, Rome, and the rest of western Europe.

Left and above: School for Scandal *dolls, complete with leather gloves, early 18th c.* **Below:** *English woodcut,* The Housewife and the Hunter *(detail), early 18th c.*

SPINNING THEIR WHEELS: In 1745 the Boston Society for Promoting Industry and Frugality's annual event attracts three hundred young women to the Boston Common, where yarn spinning is the major activity of the weekend. Spinning, however, is traditionally a lonely activity—a woman who sits in front of a loom all day and spins is, appropriately enough, called a spinster. Use of the spinning wheel declines markedly in the nineteenth century, when the automatic loom is introduced. Paradoxically, the number of spinsters is reported on the rise.

HEN-SOME IS AS HEN-SOME DOES

To restore their aging hands, mid-eighteenth-century ladies don chicken-skin gloves every night. They also tie on linen-lined headbands and masks to prevent wrinkles and crow's feet. Are their husbands too, er, chicken to enter the boudoir? It is not recorded.

"It was at her mouth that she commenced to lose her beauty. She had early acquired the habit of biting her lips to hide her emotions. At thirty her mouth had lost its brilliant tones. It had to be repaired after a meal and each kiss."

— André Houssage

ELIZABETH ARDEN, EAT YOUR HEART OUT

The New World cosmetic industry is launched in New York by a Mrs. Edwards, who advertises "An Admirable Beautifying Wash For Hands, Face and Neck, It Makes The Skin Soft, Smooth and Plump. It Likewise Takes Away Redness, Freckles, Sun-Burning or Pimples . . . All Sold Very Cheap."

This page, center left: *Cosmetics advertisements, 19th c.;* bottom left: *Elizabeth Arden's line of anti-aging cream, 1980s.* Opposite page: *Folly Embellishing Decrepitude with the Adornments of Youth, an engraving after a painting by Charles Coypel, ca. 1740;* Inset: *Kitty Fisher, courtesan and famous model of Joshua Reynolds', 1770s.*

AND ON EVERY BEAUTY TABLE

- Rice powder
- Eyebrow pencils
- Rouge in dry and liquid form, available in ten different colors. (Shop toward the end of the century if you want mauve.)
- Patches: stars, crescents, circles, squares, hearts, animal- and people-shaped
- Ivory teeth, false
- Amber to scent wigs
- Tuberose, jasmine, and other essences to scent a wig or buttonhole
- Beauty creams for everything from rough, red skin, to pimples and wrinkles
- Powder puffs
- Lip salves
- Lemon peel for breath
- Small gold boxes for storing patches and rouge, some with mirrors inside and some with small makeup brushes
- Curling irons and false curls
- Snuff
- Almond paste for smooth, white hands
- Rose water, water of the Queen of Hungary, and lemon water for delicate faces; some scented with lavender, strawberry, or violet
- Soaps of lemon and amber and Neapolitan soap from Italy

DRESSED TO THRILL In eighteenth-century France, a "painted lady" is just that—high-born ladies of the court wear thick white powder and paint their lips and cheeks a deep ruby red, while prostitutes go in for the well-scrubbed look. In England, it's just the opposite—only courtesans dare wear rouge or paint, sometimes with deadly results: The beautiful English courtesan Kitty Fisher dies at the height of her career from that perennial killer powder, white lead.

1752 LIGHTNING STRIKES AS BENJAMIN FRANKLIN INVENTS THE LIGHTNING ROD.

1754 THE FIRST-EVER FEMALE M.D. GRADUATES FROM THE UNIVERSITY OF HALLE, GERMANY.

MACHINE RAGE

The Industrial Revolution is in full swing by the nineteenth century but only because it started gearing up in the 1700s.

With the invention of the flying shuttle, the spinning jenny, mechanized weaving looms, and knitting machines, the textile industry is the first to be industrialized. The steam engine propels a prodigious production of cotton. Light-weight printed cottons, *indiennes*, are particularly popular. To meet production demands, mills are multiplying at a fantastic rate. Many of the machines are tended by children. And there are few, if any, experienced mechanics who know how to repair the new-fangled machines. So when things go haywire the standard explanation is one we now use to describe strange behavior of any kind: There must have been a screw loose.

1755 SAMUEL JOHNSON WRITES THE FIRST *DICTIONARY OF THE ENGLISH LANGUAGE.*

1757 WILLIAM BLAKE, ENGLISH MYSTIC, POET, AND ARTIST IS BORN.

CORSET-ERIA

The broad skirts of the mid-1700s need necklines to match, and the most popular style is wide and low, trimmed with a band of fine lace called the *tatez*-y ("touch here"). A bow at the neck is called *parfait contentment*, or "perfect contentment."

But clotheshorses who thirst for a little more decoration gussy up the fronts of the gowns, either by wearing wraparound bodices, with a teasing ruffled dickey peering out from the deep vee; or more commonly, by adding *robings*. These ornamental trimmings line the edges of the bodice, from the shoulders to the waist, where it meets the stomacher—still around and tormenting its wearers after two centuries. Since women often design their robings and stomachers themselves, bodices become a showcase for personal taste.

By the 1760s, many women abandon stomachers, but not to increase their circulation. Instead, they press their corsets into double duty—now covered with elegant fabrics and trimmed with metallic lace just begging for display.

Not only fashionplates wear corsets. In the eighteenth century, there are styles for every occasion—including pregnancy and horseback riding—and for everyone, including young boys.

Above: *An 18th-century textile factory.* **Above right:** *Portrait of a woman in the court of King Frederick the Great of Prussia (1712–1785).* **Below right:** *Crown of Catherine the Great (1729–1796).*

JEWEL OF A GIRL: Catherine the Great's 1762 coronation robe is a record seventy-five yards long and takes fifty-five men to carry it as she walks.

Emulating the styles of the west, Catherine wears lace ruffles on her sleeves, and pearl and diamond buttons on her gown. She wears an ermine-tail cape flung over her shoulders, and although her hair is naturally blonde, she dyes it black to offset her skin. Her crown has 2,564 diamonds and pearls—and one giant red ruby.

CITY SLICKERS
FASHIONABLE TOWNS

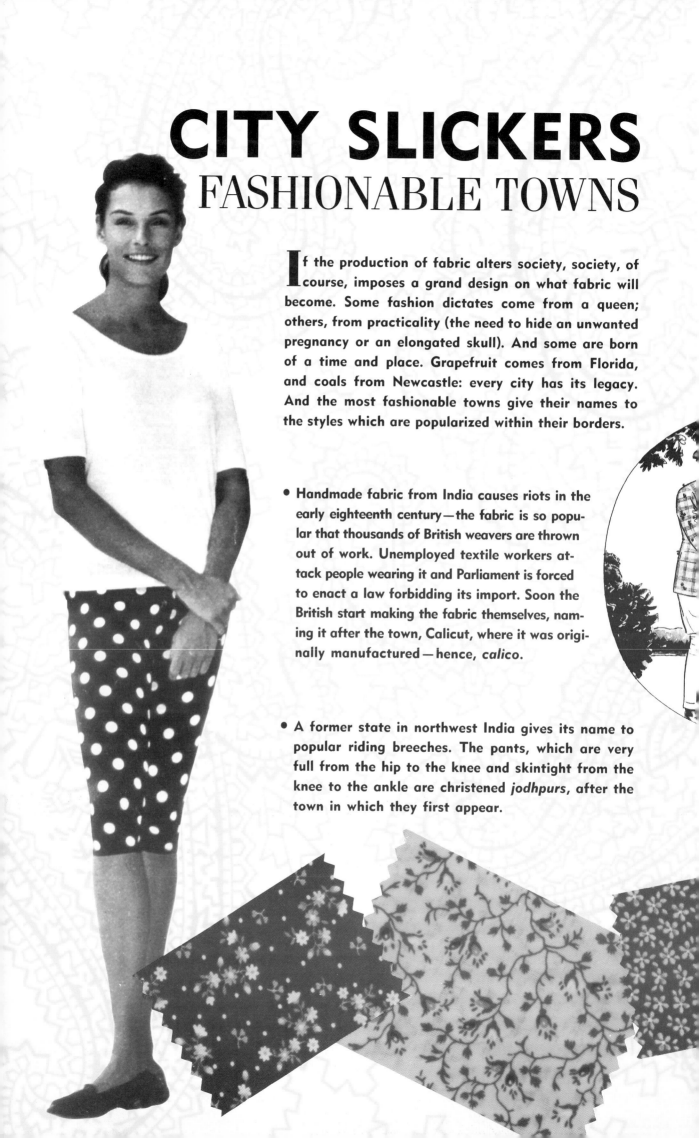

If the production of fabric alters society, society, of course, imposes a grand design on what fabric will become. Some fashion dictates come from a queen; others, from practicality (the need to hide an unwanted pregnancy or an elongated skull). And some are born of a time and place. Grapefruit comes from Florida, and coals from Newcastle: every city has its legacy. And the most fashionable towns give their names to the styles which are popularized within their borders.

- Handmade fabric from India causes riots in the early eighteenth century—the fabric is so popular that thousands of British weavers are thrown out of work. Unemployed textile workers attack people wearing it and Parliament is forced to enact a law forbidding its import. Soon the British start making the fabric themselves, naming it after the town, Calicut, where it was originally manufactured—hence, *calico*.

- A former state in northwest India gives its name to popular riding breeches. The pants, which are very full from the hip to the knee and skintight from the knee to the ankle are christened *jodhpurs*, after the town in which they first appear.

- India once again provides inspiration, this time with the production of cashmere shawls which in the nineteenth century bear amoeba-like motifs. But the design eventually takes its name from the Scottish town in which weavers adapt and popularize the pattern—*paisley*.

- Inspired by a lovely young thing while on vacation in 1950, Italian designer Emilio Pucci creates a line of beachwear for her, including skintight pants. Where did they meet? *Capri*.

- During the 1940s, local laws in this popular holiday resort forbid women to reveal their legs. So, taking a tip from policemen on the island who wear knee-length shorts, tourists beat the heat and create a new fashion—*Bermudas*.

- During the late nineteenth and early twentieth centuries a double-breasted coat of rough woolen material with a high-button collar and half belt originates in the Irish province of *Ulster*.

- And a white-belted leisure suit worn with white shoes tells anyone you're a *full Cleveland*.

Opposite page: *J. Crew capri leggings, 1989.* **Above left:** *A riding party, 1928.* **Right:** *Men's Bermuda walking shorts, 1954.*

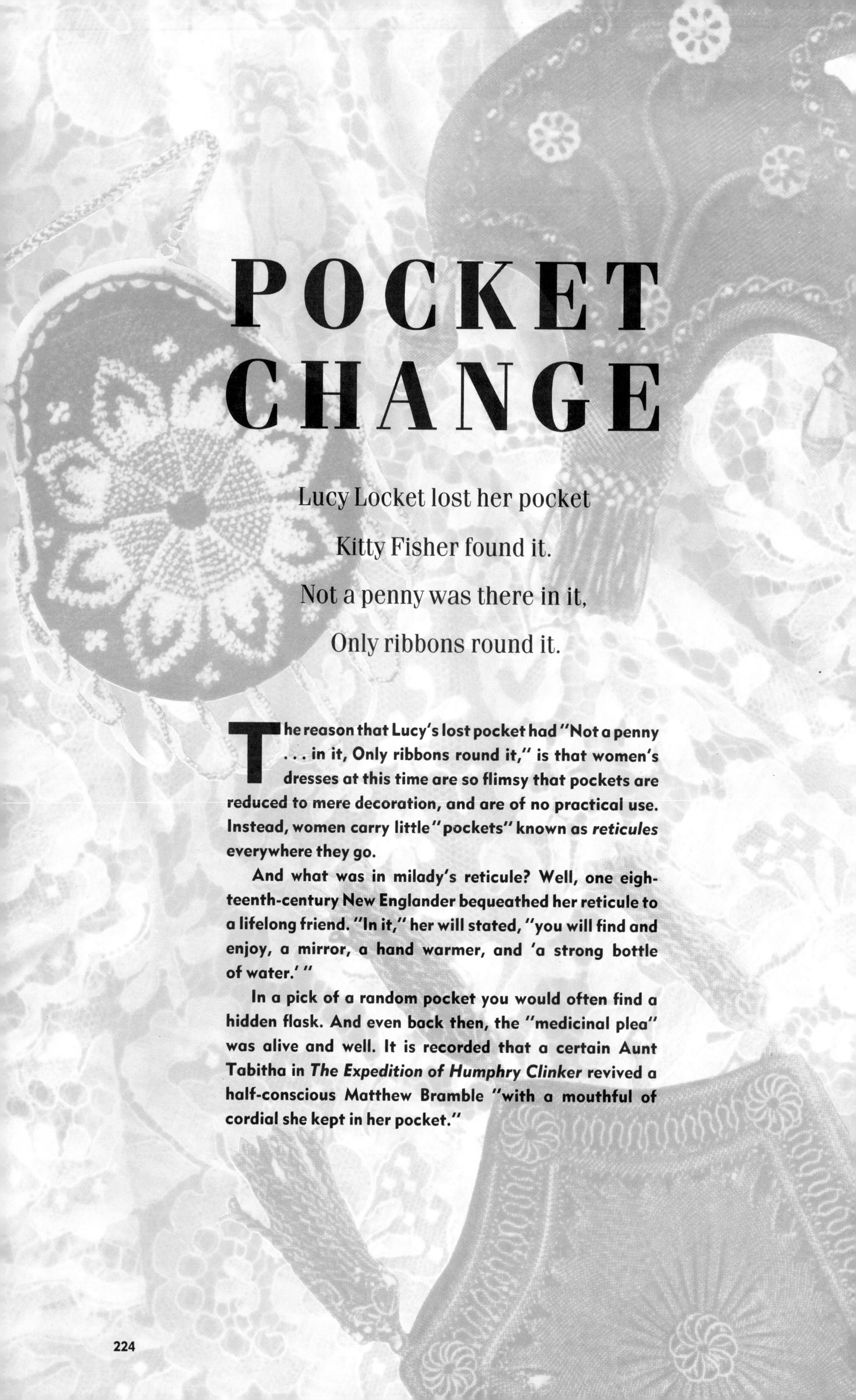

POCKET CHANGE

Lucy Locket lost her pocket

Kitty Fisher found it.

Not a penny was there in it,

Only ribbons round it.

The reason that Lucy's lost pocket had "Not a penny . . . in it, Only ribbons round it," is that women's dresses at this time are so flimsy that pockets are reduced to mere decoration, and are of no practical use. Instead, women carry little "pockets" known as *reticules* everywhere they go.

And what was in milady's reticule? Well, one eighteenth-century New Englander bequeathed her reticule to a lifelong friend. "In it," her will stated, "you will find and enjoy, a mirror, a hand warmer, and 'a strong bottle of water.'"

In a pick of a random pocket you would often find a hidden flask. And even back then, the "medicinal plea" was alive and well. It is recorded that a certain Aunt Tabitha in *The Expedition of Humphry Clinker* revived a half-conscious Matthew Bramble "with a mouthful of cordial she kept in her pocket."

1760 JOSIAH WEDGEWOOD FOUNDS A POTTERY WORKS IN STAFFORDSHIRE, ENGLAND.

1759 IN THE BEST OF ALL POSSIBLE WORLDS, VOLTAIRE WRITES *CANDIDE*.

COLD CAUSE

From the time of Louis XIV, the French court is a magnet and a model for nobles from all over Europe and even as far away as Russia. In fact, Elizabeth Petrovna, Empress of Russia from 1741 to 1762, imports all her clothes from France, shunning the homegrown finery. Her court soon follows suit, and from mid-century on, grows immersed in French language and culture, as well as dress. Her successor, Catherine II, disgusted with the extravagance of French dress, attempts to turn the tide—but to no avail.

Other European rulers pass similar edicts to curb yearnings of their glamor-hungry subjects. The most successful is King Gustav III of Sweden, who designs a national dress and decrees that nobles must wear it, instead of lavish French style. He wins out only because the climate is on his side. Vast panniers, garlanded silks, and fine leather shoes cannot withstand the snowbound Swedish winters.

Opposite page: *Reticules of iron, silk, and glass, late 18th c.* **Above:** Empress Elizabeth at Age Seven, *Louis Caravaque, 1716.* **Below:** Empress Elizabeth in Coronation Dress, *J. E. Nilson, 1785.*

1764 AN EIGHT-YEAR-OLD MOZART WRITES HIS FIRST SYMPHONY.

1766 THE MASON-DIXON LINE IS DRAWN BETWEEN PENNSYLVANIA AND MARYLAND.

PANT-ASIA

After their abashed withdrawal at the end of the seventeenth century, breeches now creep back into view. Slowly at first—just six inches or so peeping from beneath a long waistcoat—but over the decades they reclaim a substantial expanse of thigh. They gain a new slim silhouette in 1759, when, in an attempt to raise revenues, the French Minister of Finance imposes taxes on fabric. Now pockets become an unwarranted luxury, and hands come out of hiding.

By the 1780s, breeches are cut skin tight, often of leather—the only fabric that can take the pressure. With pants so snug, it's impossible to sit down, so men have to order suits with two pairs of pants—one to wear for stylish, standup receptions, and another, looser pair to walk around in.

1770 THE FIRST PUBLIC RESTAURANT OPENS IN PARIS.

1772 DANIEL RUTHERFORD AND JOSEPH PRIESTLEY EACH INDEPENDENTLY DISCOVER NITROGEN.

SUZI'S SCANDALS

What king was hiding under a fir tree at the ball last night to celebrate the **Dauphin's** marriage to the **Infanta of Spain?** It was, of course, none other than our **Louis XV,** dressed as a tree, entering the forest of brocaded, embroidered, and perfumed celebrants in search of Diana the huntress, who, of course, was none other than our very own **Madame de Pompadour,** as ever, blonde, blue-eyed, and very, very charming.

Cinderellas *do* have a chance in the splendiferous mid-eighteenth-century court of Versailles, and Madame de Pompadour is a case in point. Having received the notice of the king, she has gone on to become his mistress, an accomplished artist, and an influential member of the court—and all this from the bourgeoise daughter of a weaver, no less. She brings fashion à la française to new heights of glamor—with the square-necked stomacher, ending in a V, with touches of lace on its border, and usually accompanied by a tier of bows down the front. She dances and plays cards until three in the morning, only to wake up to go to Mass, fully dressed, at eight.

The king himself had grown tired of his wife, **Marie Leszczyńska,** and who could blame him, considering Pompadour's aura? She is witty and elegant (setting the styles for the twenty years of her unofficial reign, until her death in 1764), and the real power behind Louis' throne. As for Louis, you can see him hunting and playing cards in rich waistcoats of brocade and embroidery, his hair always powdered gray. But his court, believe me, is a place where boredom begins with a capital B, where fifteen hundred people work in stables, where five hundred people work in the Department of the Mouth to prepare delicacies for the king and his retinue, and where Louis' wardrobe requires over one hundred servants to wash, tailor, and tend to our French emperor's new clothes. In a court where fashion is all and immorality is in with a capital I, he is a bit too stodgy for our tastes. . . .

But **Giovanni Casanova,** simply called Casanova by his friends (and believe me, there are many), is another story. An Italian by birth, this rogue charmingly made his way into Louis XV's court, earning his keep through excellent card-playing and irresistible charisma.

At the party in Lyons in 1758 the other night, he was seen dapperly turned out in an ash-gray cut velvet coat, embroidered with silver and gold; an outfit, we understand, that cost him in the neighborhood of 150,000 francs. Pretty good card playing, Mr. Casanova. And pretty astute observations about those heavy court gowns, with those wide, stiff panniers which force the ladies to move in a painfully slow, stately glide. According to Mr. C., when the femmes want to dash, they lift their hoops to their chins, bend their knees, and "hop along like kangaroos."

Until tomorrow, this is Suzi, signing off Rococoly Yours—Au Revoir!

YOU'RE SO VAIN

With a priest at her bedside to recite the last sacraments, a dying Madame de Pompadour summons her last bit of strength—and pauses. "Wait a second," she says to God, and proceeds to apply two dabs of rouge.

Opposite page: Unknown Gentleman with Two Children, *Henry Eldridge, 1799.* **Far left:** *Madame de Pompadour (1721–1764).* **Left:** Portrait of Casanova, *Anton Raphael Mengs, (1728–1779).*

227

1773 BOSTON THROWS THE WORLD'S MOST FAMOUS TEA PARTY.

1774 LOOK INTO HIS EYES: AN AUSTRIAN PHYSICIAN NAMED MESMER TREATS HIS PATIENTS WITH HYPNOSIS.

DRESSED TO KILL

General Patton said, "A soldier in shoes is only a soldier; but in boots, he becomes a warrior." Just look what happened to Benedict Arnold, whose thigh-high boot is immortalized as a monument in Saratoga, New York, where he marched on British troops.

Arnold's scarlet-coated major-general's uniform—after he changed sides and went over to fight for the British—was studded with gold epaulettes and tassels; he wore a high-pointed hat, sword belt and knout, and dark pants with gaiters (leather leg coverings) tucked into the boots. But strip away the uniform and boots and what lurks beneath? The first American traitor.

As for General George Washington's Continental Army, well, they were a little more ragtag. Ideally, officers wore blue or black square-bottomed coats over single-breasted waistcoats, cocked hats with plumes, half-gaiters, epaulettes, a gilded sword. In a 1775 memo, Washington ordered that each member of the army should have: two linen hunting shirts, two pairs of stockings, two pairs of shoes, two pairs of overalls, one woolen jacket, one pair of breeches, and one leather cap. Mid-war, with supplies scarce, these ideals couldn't always be met. But one sartorial standard that Washington did demand was that his men "Shave, have clean hands, and a general air of neatness."

Top: Benedict Arnold, engraving, H. B. Hall, 1865. **Below left:** Illustration of the capture of Major John Andre on his return from visiting Arnold. **Below right:** Platoon of American recruits.

Top left: *Elizabeth Griscom Ross (1752–1836), portrait by Gustav Liebscher.* **Below:** *Betsy Ross and friends sew the first Stars and Stripes.*

COLONIAL WEAR

An American flag isn't the only thing Betsy Ross has up her sleeve. What does she sew when she's not stitching stars and stripes? Probably delicate lace caps with ribbons and bows, quilted petticoats in bright colors to peek out from under long-bodiced silk and brocade hoop dresses, lace collars to tickle her throat, and drawstring reticules to store her sewing materials and spectacles. After she's dressed, Betsy, like other ladies of her day, probably finishes off her ensemble with a dusting of powder on her high, rolled-up hair, puts on a pair of pointed, heeled shoes, a strand of long pearls, and to stave off a colonial chill, a warm cape or mantle.

Dressed as she is, Betsy could hop on a boat, travel to Paris, and feel perfectly in style. Americans are thinking independence, but not in terms of fashion; the major American contribution to what people wear comes from the frontiersmen who create a rage for American beaver and raccoon hats with a tail hanging at one side.

But colonial ladies and gents still look to Europe for designs of the times. Of course the French and American revolutions have a quieting effect on what people in Europe as well as the colonies wear. In Paris, trend-setters adopt the simple silhouette of the ancient Roman republic; the English, with their love of country life, opt for informal soft chintzes and light silks. In the colonies, jewelry and ostentatious ornamentation are discarded for the time being, as are foreign goods. In 1789 President George Washington is dressed for his inauguration in dark brown broadcloth, the first made in the United States. He also wears white silk stockings, silver-buckled shoes, and a dress sword.

THAT'S JUST DANDY: When Yankee Doodle "stuck a feather in his cap and called it Macaroni," he wasn't just noodling around—he was emulating the young English dandies who affect Continental mannerisms and wear exaggerated pompadours topped by tiny hats. Like their French counterparts "Les Incroyables" and "Les Merveilleuses," the Macaronis are rebellious children of revolutionaries. The Macaronis (and the Americans who ape them) wear tiny shoes decorated with elaborate ribbon rosettes, two buttons on their overcoats, and affect two watches—one for telling the wearer what time it is, and the other for telling him what time it isn't.

THE FRANKLIN CLOTHES:

While Benjamin Franklin is often celebrated as a diplomat, publisher, scientist, inventor of the Franklin stove and the lightning rod, and framer of the Declaration of Independence and the U.S. Constitution, these worthy achievements shouldn't overshadow his contributions to the world of fashion.

Franklin begins every day in his bedchamber—reading and writing stark naked—to enjoy what he calls the refreshing benefits of a cold air bath. Perhaps it is on one of these occasions—while he is sitting in the pink waiting for a bolt from the blue—that he invents suspenders, or "gallowkes," as they were then called. Although today suspenders give an investment banker something to hold on to, back in 1736 they are the only official part of an otherwise improvised uniform worn by the nation's first team of volunteer firemen, stationed in Philadelphia.

When traveling, the bespectacled Franklin wishes to be able to look up and enjoy the scenery, so in the 1760s, he begins experimenting with bifocal glasses.

But perhaps most impressive of all is the fashion reception Franklin manages to receive from the haughty French court. In 1778, while dressing for an all-important dinner, Franklin discovers that the wig and formal clothes he has brought with him especially for the occasion are too small. Undaunted, he goes to dinner in his everyday "Republican" dress—unadorned waistcoat and breeches, sans wig or affectation. Ben's outfit is hailed by the chic French for its naturalness, and his "backwoods homeboy look" has all the girls looking his way.

Opposite page: *Caricature of a "Macaroni," drawn by Philip Dawe, 1773.*
Bottom left: *Contemporary drawing of a fop dressed in the "macaroni" style.*
Right: *"Back-home boy" Ben Franklin at the French court, painting by Baron Jolly, 1778.* **This page, left:** *Philadelphia firefighter still wears suspenders a century later.*

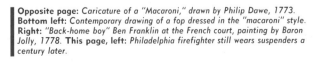

1779 NO KIDDING: AN ITALIAN SCIENTIST PROVES THAT SEMEN IS REQUIRED FOR FERTILIZATION.

1781 IMMANUEL KANT WRITES *THE CRITIQUE OF PURE REASON,* A FUNDAMENTAL WORK OF MODERN PHILOSOPHY.

DOWNPOUR: There is no singing in the rain when one of the locals appears with the first umbrella the residents of Windsor, Connecticut, have ever seen. They form a "bucket brigade," carrying improvised umbrellas of broomsticks and pails, and mockingly parade after him down the street.

Clockwise from top: Battle of the Umbrellas, 1784; George Washington, *Gilbert Stuart (1755–1828);* Washington Crossing the Delaware, *Emanuel Gottlieb Leutze, ca. 1840;* Woman with an umbrella, 17th c.

Dental prosthesis from Le Chirurgien Dentiste, 1728.

TUSK, TUSK: That disapproving scowl on George Washington's face as he crosses the Delaware doesn't just come from the teeth-chattering cold. It's that his own chattering teeth are decaying and cracking, giving him a swollen-lipped, down-turned mouth. Washington is finally fitted with a set of false teeth carved from the tusks of a hippopotamus. But his new set of ivories proves only slightly more satisfactory—they never fit properly and the large quantities of port wine he consumes are forever turning them black.

OFF THE CUFF: After nearly a century of splendor, cuffs lose their edge in the eighteenth century. Over time, they get smaller and smaller until they all but vanish from menswear. One group that retains a little pizzazz at the wrist is the military, thanks to Frederick the Great. Disgusted by his soldiers' lack of couth, he orders that buttons be sewn on the sleeves of their uniforms so they'll stop using them as snot rags. "An officer," says Frederick prophetically, "is a gentleman."

As cuffs shrink, collars expand and take on a greater allure, now often made of velvet or satin and trimmed with embroidery. By the end of the century they've grown to reach the ears, and an especially high version is named for Robespierre—an ironically fitting trademark style for a revolutionary who died on the guillotine.

Above: Anonymous portrait of Maximilien Robespierre, the "Green Incorruptible," (1758–1794). Below: Marie Antionette losing her head.

IS SOMETHING UP HER SLEEVE?

While men's sleeves strip down over the eighteenth century, women's remain in full bloom. They're still elbow length—women are loath to surrender the hard-won forearm territory—but now they have explosive bursts of ruffles and lace. One of the most exuberant styles is the *engageants*—two or three stiff frills of exquisite lace emerging from a dress sleeve that is already ruffled and garnished with fringe, bows, or silky braid.

It's not until the 1780s that Marie Antoinette, renowned for her other excesses, rather surprisingly promotes the unadorned wrist and does away with extravagant sleeves in favor of slim models like those worn by the men.

THE BIG HAIR

In the 1770s, French fashion achieves its most ridiculous heights of caprice, nowhere more evident than in women's hairstyles. Now hair is stiffened with flour-and-water paste that whitens it and lets it be molded into an array of shocking constructions. These coifs begin with modest ambitions—supported by horsehair pads, the hair is heaped high on the head and arranged in towers of curls. Marie Antoinette tops her freshly built do with a spray of ostrich plumes. When she sends a painting to her mother, the alarmed Maria Theresa writes back: "There has no doubt been a mistake. I received the portrait of an actress, not a queen."

Unchastened, Marie Antoinette persists in encouraging still more bizarre creations. Headdresses combine lace, ribbons, pins, paste, and false hair, and when a woman is standing, her face and bedecked hairdo account for more than one-third of her entire height. Members of Marie's court lodge vases of real flowers in their coiffures, or entire stage sets featuring hunters, ducks, and a mill. Hairdos even commemorate the headlines of the day—with one of the most celebrated being a ship in full sail, to honor the American struggle for independence.

Such elaborate styles, of course, take hours to erect, so they are redone only once a month or so. Over time, unwashed, floured hair becomes an incubator for vermin rivaling even the hairshirts of medieval times. To give the ladies a little relief from predatory lice, slits are made in the stiff walls to let trapped insects escape.

Naturally, a special headdress evolves to protect these hairdos—the *therese*—which is literally a bag worn over the head. Women have to kneel to enter carriages; and in 1780, the doorway of St. Paul's cathedral is raised four feet to accommodate female worshippers sporting their own steeples of hair.

Ridiculous as these styles seem, we do owe them one debt of gratitude—thanks to the intricacy of their structures, the *hairpin* is invented. And thanks to the hairpin, twentieth-century baseball players can get base hits, or so they believe. Since hairpins bring good luck, players scour hotel rooms looking for pins before a big game.

TAKING A POWDER: The "flouring" of faddish hairstyles requires a room in each noble's mansion to be set aside as a separate "powder" room—behind a closed door flour is blown toward the ceiling and allowed to settle evenly on the wig.

In battle, with not enough barbers to go around, British officers have their hair powdered and plastered the day before a big battle and sleep face down so as not to disturb the elaborate coiffures.

Background: *Contemporary cartoon of a young lady in London.* Left: *Lucille Ball and Red Skelton in DuBarry was a Lady, 1943.*

WHALE, WHALE, WHALE

Who coined the expression, "A whale of a good time"? Certainly not women balancing teetering headdresses; men wearing pointed, foot-long shoes; or ladies in tightly cinched corsets. They're more likely to be wailing in pain—thanks to these fashions that depend on whalebone for support. But we knew that, didn't we?

Less well-known is the fact that ambergris—the smelly waxy-gray secretion of the sperm whale, is the only substance in the world that binds oil and perfume essences together.

HORSE CLOTHES

THE FIRST FASHION VICTIM: MARIE ANTOINETTE: It might have happened to you, too, if you had been married (not even in person, but by proxy) to that Louis XVI at the tender age of fifteen, a blond, blue-eyed, porcelain-faced child fresh from Austria.

Marie arrives in France, a little wary at first. But finally freed from the strict restraints of her mother Maria Theresa's austere court, she starts to have a good time. And who could blame her? Most agree that she is a good-natured girl; perhaps a little naive. Heady with freedom, Marie refuses to be restrained, not even by corsets; she gambles recklessly, and, well, she does run up enormous bills (the expense of her toilette alone is rumored to run as high as 258,000 livres in just one year). Indulged by her husband and aided by her newly appointed "Minister of Fashion," Rose Bertin (a one-time errand girl who has risen to become France's leading fashion designer), Marie quickly becomes the unquestionable arbiter of taste, albeit not always good.

You see, Rose never hears that less is more. Under her guidance, hoops spread; breasts are pushed up, necklines, down; and there's no such thing as too much tassle, fringe, ruffle, lace, plumes, or artificial flowers. The logical extensions of these excessive costumes are excessive hairstyles, and Marie's hair is brushed up over towers of wire and crinoline, slathered in a papier mâché mixture of pomade and flour, and festooned with all the leftover lace, flowers, and plumes that she didn't have room for on her dress. This creates a hornet's nest: not only for potential lice and vermin to nest in, but for the public at large. The economy is depressed; crops have failed; France is practically insolvent. People are struggling for something to eat. Maybe just a little flour for some bread, instead of pomade mixtures. But you know what Marie said to that, an unfortunate remark if ever there was one because, truly now, if they couldn't find bread, where would they get cake?

Marie was vain, and certainly lacked a social conscience. How could she ignore the starving masses in frivolous pursuit of a new dress, a new coiffure? But was Marie an insidious force in the collapsing French empire? Certainly her excesses represented all that was wrong with an indifferent government and inadequate state. But did she deserve to lose her head over a hairdo?

Top: Harpooning a Whale, engraving, 19th c. **Right:** Portrait of Marie Antoinette from 1777.

1787 THE IMPERIAL RUSSIAN DICTIONARY IS ISSUED, WITH 285 WORDS IN 200 LANGUAGES.

1788 GEORGE III SUFFERS HIS FIRST ATTACK OF MENTAL ILLNESS AND PRECIPITATES A REGENCY CRISIS IN ENGLAND.

ESSENCE BARE

You are dressed in the height of eighteenth-century fashion if you show off your breasts and shoulders, so there should be nothing unmentionable (but there is) about the fact that during a royal performance, a French prima ballerina named Nina pirouettes in the air and shows off the drawers underneath her petticoat. Such a brouhaha ensues, in fact, that the next night the headstrong Nina performs her pirouette again—this time without *any* underwear. Which is how multi-petticoated girls arrive for a Sunday afternoon "swing" with their gentlemen friends. Though genteel girls tie their hooped skirts around their ankles with their beau's hatband, there's always the chance that the band will come undone as she swings higher, and higher, and . . .

HAZARDOUS TO WARNING YOUR HEALTH

Women wearing hooped skirts can't walk through doorways, and they must kneel on the floors of carriages. In 1737, Madame de Bussy trips over her hooped skirt and dies.

The six-inch-high heels women favor scrunch their toes and thrust their entire foot forward, making for bad posture and bone formation. To walk at all in the shoes, they develop an inelegant, semi-crouching stance.

Top: *Delft good luck shoe, Dutch, early 18th c.* **Center:** The Swing, *Fragonard, 1766.* **Bottom:** Mlle. de Clermont in her Bath, *Jean Marc Nattier, 1733.*

DOUBLE EXPOSURE

A popular spot for receiving visitors is milady's bath, where friends, lovers, hairdressers, and other relations come to talk and exchange gossip while the lady of the house, further surrounded by a maid, cats, and toys, takes a long soak.

After hours of pampering and fussing, it seems only fair that high-born ladies let the servants of the house see the results of their handiwork. So every afternoon fashion plates sit on display while maids and butlers come from all over town to gaze at them.

As if all this attention isn't enough, in the afternoon, milady often takes a long stroll along the promenade to feast the eyes of admiring onlookers. This exercise is such an institution that parks and gardens reserve special days and hours for the ritual.

LEG O' MY HEART

Scientists report that our lower limbs represent one third of our body weight. (We'll have to take their word for it—this *is* a bit difficult to check out.) Easy to verify throughout history, however, is rampant leg appeal.

• The Wife of Bath admits that it is his handsome legs, seen as he walks behind the bier of her fourth husband, that makes her choose her fifth.

• Sixteenth-century men are very aware of their leggy charms—so prideful of owning a terrific pair of legs they often give preference to one over the other and put their "best foot forward."

• Interestingly enough, while men's legs remain in view until the eighteenth century, throughout most of history, women's are kept under wraps.

• Not only are female legs unseen, the word "legs" is unheard. In the eighteenth century an ambassador bringing silk stockings to the royal bride is rebuked for the indecent implications of his intended gift by the statement, "The Queen of Spain has no legs." If they had to, genteel nineteenth-century ladies and gentlemen spoke of "limbs" (which probably explains why everybody wants to be out on one). In England, as a sign of modesty, even the legs of chairs, tables, and pianos are covered with lacy pantaloons.

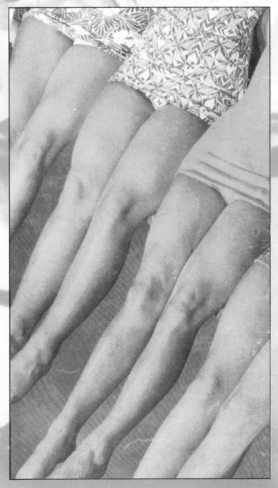

Background: *Can-can dancer's leg.* Above: *Legs of champion American swimmers, 1942.*

• By the twentieth century the female leg comes out of hiding. First there is the 1920s "flapper" style, which bares the calves. Famed showman Flo Ziegfeld, who glorifies the American female, claims he never even glances at the faces of potential chorus girls—he just sizes up their gams.

• In the 1960s, legs get their day in the sun when the *miniskirt*—and its even skimpier sister, the *micromini*—are born. These thigh-revealing styles not only thrill leg watchers, they impose new rules of propriety (no bending over to pick up quarters). Revived in the 1980s, the mini gets everyone out jogging, cycling, and climbing stairs, and even helps boost a new medical specialty—liposuction. Clearly, leg appeal is on the rise.

(FRENCH) REVOLUTIONARY MANIFESTO

In the wake of the storming of the Bastille by Paris mobs, the overthrow of the National Assembly, and the Reign of Terror that sends even suspected traitors to the guillotine, it is decreed that French fashion will change overnight.

It will no longer be safe to be seen in silk, velvet, or any other luxurious fabric that might cause you to be mistaken for a royal sympathizer. In the spirit of the revolution, all women must abandon extravagant panniers, wigs, and plumage in favor of simple, flimsy muslin gowns. To align yourself with the Jacobins, you must discard proper courtly manners, and to prove your loyalty to the revolutionary cause, affect uncouth and gruff behavior. Fellow revolutionaries, discard your powdered periwigs, your embroidered waistcoats, your ornate dress swords. Drop your breeches in favor of the wide, floppy trousers of the working class. The *carmagnole*, a short jacket with wide collars and lapel, is in, as is the red Phrygian cap of liberty.

We can assure you that during the turbulent years of the Republic (1792–95), revolutionary ideals will continue to be expressed through what you wear. The artist Jean Louis David will be commissioned to design a national costume that will celebrate the idealized Greek Republic. (You might think that David is an unlikely choice, as he *was* the protégé of Louis XVI; but after all, he is an adroit politician, and he did vote for the king's death.) David will try to get men into togas, but you'll probably be more comfortable wearing those old reliables, a coat, waistcoat, and breeches.

If you are a woman in 1795 when the Directoire has assumed power, you will most likely shiver in the sheerest of muslin (sheerer than any self-respecting Greek would have worn), in a clingy *robe en chemise*. This licentious, nouveau-

Opposite page: top left: Taking the Bastille, July 14, 1789, John Wells (1792–1809); **center:** On the cutting edge: French physician Joseph Guillotin's machine for beheading; **right:** Charlotte Corday (1768–1793), engraving by Julian Story, 1889. **This page: left:** Madame Tullien, Circle of Jacques-Louis David, ca. 1810–20; **below right:** Marie-Madeline Guimard, Dancer, Fragonard, 1769.

IT'S MY PARTY AND I'LL WEAR WHAT I WANT TO

Female guests at Empress Josephine's Bal à la Victime are told to have their hair piled high on their heads and to wear blood-red scarlet ribbons tied around their necks to commemorate those who died on the guillotine.

riche society of the Directoire is a little weak in the virtue department, but then too, a little more liberal in matters of attire. If you want to be part of the lunatic fringe, rebel against your parents, and show a certain longing for the royalist regime, you can join "Les Incroyables," who achieve overemphasis by wearing coats and jackets that are either much too large or much too tight. Wear collars that reach to your earlobes; waistcoats that trail on the ground. Your helpmate, one of "Les Merveilleuses," can teeter about in enormous skirts. Both of you must dishevel your hair.

You may note that this is where the Revolution came in. And when Napoleon provides France with a court again, he will be named emperor in a ceremony of unparalleled magnificence. Josephine will wear a bee-strewn silver brocade dress, a crimson velvet, bejeweled ermine-lined robe, golden brooches, bracelets and necklace, and a pearl tiara entwined with diamond leaves. The emperor-to-be will don a blood-red velvet doublet, a short satin-lined

cloak, white velvet breeches, silk stockings, a ruff, a sword and sash, and a diamond clasp. The tailor Leroy will outfit the empire, once Josephine decrees him her favorite designer. Under his hand the *empire cut* will be established, completely waistless, marked beneath the bosom by a thin ribbon; deep square necklines, tight-fitting sleeves that cover the back of the hand and puff at the shoulder. Women will wear crepe, satin, taffeta, cashmere, and velvet. Napoleon will decree that no woman at court can wear the same dress twice, and if all of this sounds familiar, it will at least revive a flagging economy by employing the out-of-work shoemakers, tailors, and hairdressers to whom the sandal-wearing, au naturel look of the Revolution was the kiss of death.

When the kiss of death comes to Napoleon's empire after the 1815 debacle at Waterloo, he will be shipped off to St. Helena, and such strict codification of styles, and these French manifestos of fashion (both revolutionary and post-revolutionary), will cease to exist.

FAN-SEE TALKING

Sally Rand's "Fan Language" isn't too hard to understand, but the vocabulary of the eighteenth-century coquette is a little more subtle. Clutching a fan to her heart tells a young man that Cupid has struck, tapping a closed fan to her chin signals, "Kiss me," and if he hits the jackpot, a gay blade will be counting the number of struts fanned out in a partially opened fan to find out the time of the trysting hour.

• A fan may not be opened in the presence of the queen in Versailles, except if used as a tray to hand something to her. When the Baroness Oberkirch leans over to show Marie Antoinette her bracelet (Marie is nearsighted), she accidentally opens her fan. She has committed a real faux pas.

• In 1774, fans are said to be evil. They can be like sharp knives, the medical journals report; it is also supposed to be bad to cool parts of the body so hastily.

• Eighteenth-century fans come in tortoise shell, ivory, embroidered silk, or might even be painted by one of the great artists of the day, like Watteau, Boucher, or Lancret.

• Fans can hide faces at inopportune times. Some of them have tiny windows made of magnifying glass so a woman can peek out and see someone's reaction to her coquetries.

• There are puzzle fans, fans with watches, fans that bend in half, and Chinese fans.

• During the Reign of Terror, fans are made that look harmless enough, but when opened a certain amount show a weeping willow or a basket of white flowers—the symbol of the French royalty. It's a way of showing secret loyalty to the king and queen.

• In 1795, there is a telegraph fan. The owner spells out words, using an alphabet printed on one side of the fan and a metal pointer. Robert Clarke of London, a successful fan dealer, actually takes out a patent on this "fan language," believing it will become popular.

1791 LOUIS XVI, TRYING TO ESCAPE FRANCE WITH HIS FAMILY, IS CAPTURED AT VARENNES AND RETURNED TO PARIS.

1792 MARY WOLLSTONECRAFT WRITES *VINDICATION OF THE RIGHTS OF WOMEN.*

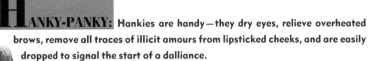

HANKY-PANKY: Hankies are handy—they dry eyes, relieve overheated brows, remove all traces of illicit amours from lipsticked cheeks, and are easily dropped to signal the start of a dalliance.

During the fifteenth century, explorers return from China with the first handkerchiefs—large linen cloths that are so costly they are often bequeathed in wills.

Adorned with lace and considered a fashion accessory in the sixteenth century, by the eighteenth century, they have a more utilitarian purpose: snuff-takers find it a necessity to keep a hanky in one's hand.

By the late eighteenth century, hankies are so large that Marie Antoinette has hubby Louis XVI sign an edict regulating their size: On June 2, 1785, it is decreed that their length cannot exceed their width. Handkerchiefs at this time are tucked into sleeves or belts, because it is considered unhygienic to keep one in your pocket.

In 1859 Empress Eugénie sends the sales of handkerchiefs soaring when at a performance of *Cinderella* she weeps so copiously that all the women of Paris immediately recognize the necessity of weeping in order that they too might display their luxurious hankies.

One hundred and twenty years later, handkerchiefs once again make an appearance on stage—Luciano Pavarotti's. The famed tenor uses them as a sort of security blanket because, he says, "I didn't know what to do with my hands when I began to sing."

It makes sense. In fact, everything about handkerchiefs makes sense, including their name, once you realize its origin. It comes from the word "couvrechef" or head-covering: which is what their original inventors, the Chinese, used them for as they worked in the fields.

Opposite page: **background:** *Sally Rand, née Helen Gould Beck, (1904–1979);* **Top:** *Regency-style painted fan, French or Italian, 1700–1750;* **Center:** *Carved ivory fan, English, early 18th c.* **This page: left:** *Regency-era fan mounted on mother of pearl, with gilt figures, painted on vellum from the School of Lancret;* **Top left:** *Luciano Pavarotti with security blanket, from "Pavarotti at Madison Square Garden," PBS special, 1986;* **Center right, left to right:** *Louis XV chased gold and strawberry enamel snuff box, P. M. Colas, Vienna, ca. 1765; Gold snuff box with paintings by Hamelin on enamel, Jean Ducrollay, Paris, 1759; Portrait of Louis XV by Welper (1730–1789) on a gold snuff box, Paris, 1771.*

STRONG SNUFF

One of the most cherished accessories of the eighteenth-century gentleman is his snuff box, often ornately carved and wondrously bejeweled. Popular shapes include grapes, vases, baskets, fruits, animals such as dogs and lions—and even skulls. Dandies carry several boxes around at once, sometimes using them for money—this personal currency has the donor's face stamped on its lid.

Possibly jealous of their men's lovely baubles—not to mention their drug consumption—women start taking snuff, too. Madame de Pompadour carries hers in a box shaped like a swan. Women enjoy the boxes so much that, before long, they help themselves to other men's accoutrements as well: dangling watch fobs and seals, and status-symbol tasseled canes.

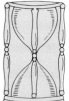

VEST-ED INTEREST: Child of the seventeenth century, the waistcoat gains a new fashion momentum in the eighteenth, shifting its hemline every few decades or so. It starts out at the knee and is worn buttoned tightly up to the neck, with a few lower buttons left undone to permit the wearer to walk.

By mid-century it rises to thigh height, and from the 1780s on, hits barely below the belt. And its embellishments grow simpler as time goes on, its fabulous embroideries and brocades giving way to stripes, dots, and small pattern prints.

As some minor compensation for its diminished status, it achieves more prominent display as coats keep getting trimmed back to reveal an expanse of beautifully embroidered and brocaded stomach.

THE CHILDREN'S HOUR

No bones about it, the *skeleton suit* has a menacing name—but this short, soft suit worn with the trousers buttoned to the jacket is a relief to young boys who have been stuffed into corsets, stiff breeches, high-collared shirts, and tight-waisted coats. Around the end of the eighteenth century, girls, too, begin to shed their crushing stays and smothering petticoats for simple, ankle-length, high-waisted dresses, encircled with a sash.

Right: Boy with a Dog, A. W. Evis, late 18th c. **Below:** *Illustration of a Parisian salon during the Directoire period, François Bosio (1769–1845).*

COLD COMFORT: As they approach the turn of the century, women show abandon by abandoning bustles, panniers, and even corsets. Their *robes en chemise* are high-waisted, made of muslin or calico and look more like undergarments, but they do achieve their goal of giving women that Greek goddess statue look. Not only are the lightweight dresses often flimsy and see-through, they are also damp: Before they leave for a night on the town, French trend-setters moisten them with a wet cloth, to achieve maximum sexiness. Maybe only a wet blanket would wear a dry dress in gay Paree, but more often than not the result of wet dressing is dry dock in bed for two weeks with a bad cold.

1796 GEORGE WASHINGTON REFUSES A THIRD TERM AS PRESIDENT AND DELIVERS HIS FAREWELL ADDRESS.

CAPE-ABLE

Since late-eighteenth-century men can't button their coats, they need some way to keep warm. Capes remain a popular choice, of course—both sweeping, circular, ankle-length styles and the collared, tentlike *roquelaure*. But *the* coat of the century is the *redingote*, a triple-collared topper with huge lapels, trimly tailored and often double-breasted.

Surprisingly enough, women soon take to the redingote too— its heavy wool contrasting sharply with the lavish silk gowns they wear underneath. And at the close of the century, women appropriate yet another men's style—the *spencer*, a short, boxy jacket named for a lord who had his coattails sheared off in a nasty fall from a horse.

Still, pelisses or capes trimmed with expensive furs—lynx, ermine, and fox— never go out of style. In the late 1790s, the favorite French fur is chinchilla, which must remain a passion, rather than a trend. The reason: pelts are so rare and costly that only four or five women in Paris can afford them.

One of the strangest toppers of the century is the *caraco*, an innovation of the extremist 1790s. A ruffled jacket, it fits smoothly to the waist and then bells out to sit like a bowling ball cover over the vast behind of the polonaise.

Redingote, fashioned after clerics' long frock coats, with a three-tiered collar, Bavarian lapelled vest, and a coal miner's hat, 1786.

1797 COLERIDGE WRITES *KUBLA KHAN.*

WASH AND WEAR

After 1797, they'll have to do something else besides the wash down by the riverside…

NATHANIEL BRIGGS PATENTS A WASHING MACHINE.

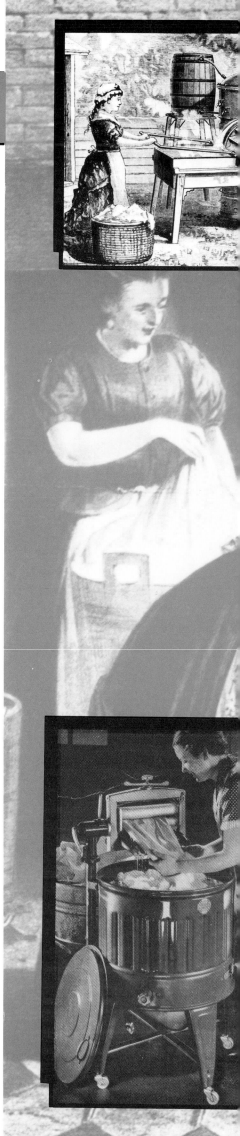

Top left: *Bleaching laundry in the 1600s;* **Above:** *"Laundress" engraving by G. Volpato, after Maiotto, ca. 1780.* **Right, background:** *Woman, ca. 1870 enjoying her home washing machine.* **Clockwise from upper left:** *Engraving of the new, improved washing machine by Thomas Merony, ca. 1880; GE washing machine, ca. 1940; Sears Roebuck washing machine ad, ca. 1930s; The "Lessiveuse" wash boiler, ca. 1880; Montgomery Ward washing machine ad, ca. 1935.*

244

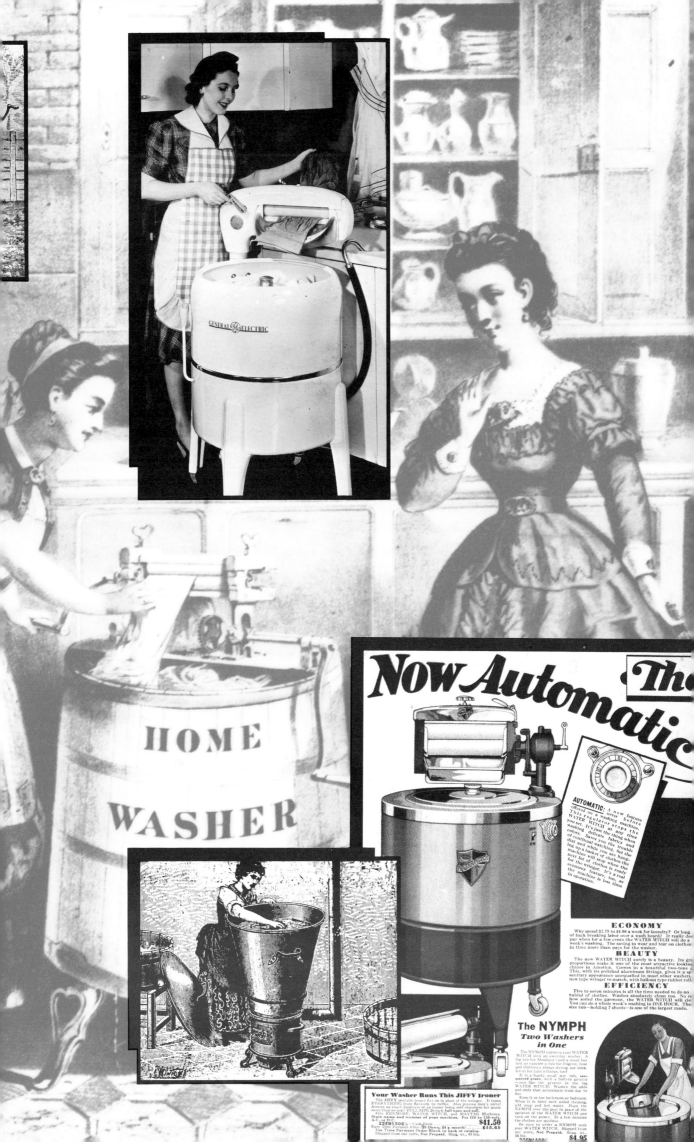

HOME WASHER

GENERAL ELECTRIC

STRAW-NG STYLE: In 1798, twelve-year-old Betsey Metcalf plaits strands of straw into braids and fashions them into a bonnet lined with pink satin—the first *straw hat.* Once the needle in the haystack is found, every last straw is used to make hats—fourteen thousand people in England alone make their living from the straw hat industry. Round, sailor, and soft felt-like shapes are popular. Like other "rustic" eighteenth century fashions, people who wear straw hats—and shoes and even bands of straw decorations on their silk dresses—are neither countryfolk nor poor. By 1846, when Zachary Taylor leads an army of men into the throes of the war with Mexico, he wouldn't dream of wearing anything else— Taylor dons a hickory shirt and a straw hat.

Above: *Cartoon attesting to the popularity of the straw hat, 18th c.* **Right:** *1915 cover illustration by Milo Winter for Robert Louis Stevenson's* Treasure Island. **Below:** James Cook, Nathaniel Deuce, 1776.

SPOT CHECK

After a long, lonely winter at sea, any woman would look good, but those who greet Captain Cook's crew in New Zealand in 1796 leave a really lasting impression—their faces are swathed in red ocher and olive oil that stains the sailors' faces when they embrace. After they return to the ship, the sailors' faces aren't the only things that are "spotted." Outraged by his men's amorous cheekiness, Cook puts each and every one of the sailors on report—the first time in naval history that a blemished complexion leads to a blemished record.

"He came to the inn one day, a tall, heavy nut-brown man; his tarry pigtail falling over the shoulders of his soiled blue coat; his hands ragged and scarred with black, broken nails; and the sabre-cut across one cheek, a dirty livid white . . . a cock on his hat hanging down and his coat full of patches at the end . . . and he said, 'Beware the pirate with only one leg and a crutch.' "

—Robert Louis Stevenson, *Treasure Island*

WOULD YOU *PLEASE* MAKE UP YOUR MIND?

A GUIDE TO THE EIGHTEENTH-CENTURY BODY

"At the beginning of this century it seems to have been the prevailing opinion that nature had made the female waist greatly too large; to remedy which, the stiffest stays were laced in the tightest manner, lest young ladies should become clumsy, or grow crooked. Towards the middle of the century, it began to be discovered that, besides the uneasiness of such a situation, it frequently produced the very effect it was intended to prevent; physicians and philosophers now declaimed the stays.... We discovered that our mothers had been all wrong, and that Nature had not made the female waist nearly so large as it ought to have been; but the ladies supplemented this defect so well with clothes that about the years 1759 and 1760 every woman, young and old, had the appearance of being big with child. In ten or twelve years the fashion began to take the opposite direction again, and small waists are now esteemed so great a beauty, that, in endeavoring to procure them, women have outdone all the efforts of their grandmothers in the beginning of the century.

"About the beginning of the century it was highly indecent to be naked two inches below the neck; about the middle of it, she was dressed in the highest taste who showed the greatest part of her breast and shoulders; some years afterwards, every female of whatever condition was muffled up to the chin; at present, the mode is discarded, and naked breasts and shoulders begin again to appear."

— Notes from the 18th-century physician, William Alexandra

Top: A Little Tighter, *Rowlandson (after Libron), 1791.* Left: The Corset Fitting, *P. A. Wille, 1780s.*

THE NINETEENTH CENTURY

THE NINETEENTH CENTURY
INDUSTRIAL STRENGTH

The nineteenth century discovers history: spiritual history (Hegel); biological history (Darwin); economic history (Marx); and personal history (Freud). In the nineteenth century, France's government is in shambles, the sun never sets on the (ever-growing) British Empire, and America's "Manifest Destiny" leads toward the Louisiana Purchase and expansion out west.

Dub it "The Steel Age": Thanks to Henry Bessemer's converters the new material is readily available. Steel makes it possible to build the Eiffel Tower—proving how high (984 feet) and how memorable a monument nineteenth-century man can now create. Steel also makes its way into fashion—in the ubiquitous corsets and crinoline cages of the era. And it is the strength of steel that provides a metaphor for the times.

The invention of the sewing machine and the principle of the assembly line leads to mass production, standardization of sizes and ready-to-wear clothing sold in department stores.

But perhaps most notably, the nineteenth century is a time when hard work can win you a place once earned only by birthright: a person can go from rags to riches, or from a log cabin to the White House. Legal reforms, particularly in England and America, alter the lives of slaves,

Overleaf: *Advertisement for the Amoskeag Manufacturing Co., ca. 1840.*
This page: top: *Montgomery Ward's High Arm Sewing Machine, which sold for $19.50 in 1895;* **Right:** *Engraving of Charles Darwin from the magazine* Every Saturday, *April 15, 1871.* **Opposite page: Left:** *Eiffel Tower, designed by Alexandre Gustave Eiffel, 1839;* **Center left:** *Karl Marx (1818–1883);* **Bottom center:** *Georg Wilhelm Friedrich Hegel (1770–1831);* **Top right:** *Fess Parker in Daniel Boone, NBC, 1964;* **Center right:** *Trade card for Austin Baldwin & Co., general agents, 1885.*

women, and criminals. It is a century whose feminine heroes range from Empress Josephine to Queen Victoria to the independent-minded Gibson Girl. The middle class, whose influence is first felt in the mid-eighteenth century, is increasing in number and wealth. And wealth is the one common language of the century.

As the century opens, Daniel Boone is popularizing fringed frontier wear in the American West, and Josephine is making a name for herself and the Empire look. When Napoleon is exiled, the rage for the Empire look has an understandably low ebb, and everyone's (fashion) attention turns to England, where the Industrial Revolution is in full swing. Seeking an escape from a banal (and soon to be automated) world, men are surging with Romanticism—they cloak themselves in mystery and velvet capes. They don heavy corseting which—due to the constriction—makes their manly breasts swell with pride and their hearts beat a little faster, too—not a bad touch. They are artistes—ill-shaven and slightly dissolute-looking, with windblown locks and piercing gazes. The ladies loved by these romantic dandies are fluttery and helpless, at least partly because they are once again swathed in layers of clothing. Gone is the freedom of the Empire dress—they wear full-skirted gowns with full leg o'mutton sleeves and have (thanks to corsets) teeny, tiny waists.

By mid-century, plumbing comes indoors, gas lighting is installed in the finest houses; ocean liners cross the vast Atlantic in a mere fifteen days and steam engines chug along at thirty miles per hour. The pace of life quickens. It is the Age of Expansion, and women's fashions follow suit—once again ladies widen their hips and scrunch through doorways, this time wearing voluminous petticoats and *crinolines*. The crinoline, so beloved by Queen Victoria, stays around for more than twenty years, and even little children are forced to wear them. The courageous Amelia Bloomer tries to get women into trousers, but most prefer crinolines to comfort. Women practice getting the vapors (which isn't difficult as corsets are cinched tighter and tighter) and conversations are peppered with sighs. The sewing machine enables seamstresses to complete in just a few hours jobs that once took them days by hand. Men's pants grow up and come down, as they finally reach ankle length. Gone from men's closets forever are embroidered silk waistcoats, red damask coats, plumed hats, and jewelled robes. To face the brave new world, men (perhaps sadly) decide that in dress, discretion is the better part of valor.

By the end of the century, Impressionist paintings are dotting the landscape. Couture houses (the first founded in 1858 by Charles Worth) are in; crinolines are out; the bustle is back. Lillie Langtry, the statuesque 5'8" one-time mistress of the Duke of Wales, is christened "England's most beautiful woman," despite her size and Greek profile. Wealthy women have outfits for morning, noon, and night as it becomes de rigueur to wear special clothes for special occasions—riding, formal dinners, afternoon teas, even walking. With the growing interest in sports, it is necessary to wear more comfortable clothes. Renoir celebrates light, Toulouse-Lautrec celebrates the night, and everyone is hustling off to department stores (for ready-to-wear) and Savile Row (for custom tailoring) in search of Edwardian chic.

Left: *Photograph of Abraham Lincoln from Doc Aubrey's Recollections of a Newsboy in the Army of the Potomac, 1861–65.* **Top right:** *The downside of a crinoline cage, ca. 1862.*

PROFILES IN BEAUTY

JOSEPHINE
Famous through marriage, Napoleon's appreciation of Josephine's beauty thrusts her into the limelight.

LILLIE LANGTRY
English actress "the Jersey Lily" Langtry is noted for her voluptuous charms as well as her affair with King Edward VII.

MRS. CHARLES DANA GIBSON
After marrying the famous creator of "The Gibson Girl," socialite Irene Langerhorn remakes herself to fit Gibson's idealized image.

BYRON
Good looks, lameness, and a flamboyant lifestyle all contribute to the Romantic Byronic legend.

By the turn of the century, a succession of revolutionary governments have left France in ruin. Even after Napoleon begins to restore political order, fashion remains in disarray.

During the revolution, prudent men adopt the long pants of the working class. But Napoleon (whom the Brits nickname "Little Corporal") tries to promote extravagant dress, both to stimulate the economy and to promote his court's prestige. Traditional knee breeches do make a comeback under Napoleon, and remain in vogue for another thirty years. But the Napoleonic Wars wreak such economic devastation that for financial reasons alone, the bourgeois can't keep up with the luxurious fashions being worn at Versailles. And

Left: *French costume, 1880s.* **Below left:** Portrait of an Irish Girl, *Adam Buck, ca. 1820.* **Below right:** *German man and woman, 1810.*

English tailoring, which had made an impact on French fashion before the revolution, continues to be influential.

Napoleon decrees that the flimsy *robe en chemise* "lacks dignity," and the simple sheath is now made from heavier silks, with long, narrow sleeves and a puff at the shoulders, decorated à la conquering heroes with frogging, epaulettes, and braid. Military braiding may be all right for intimidating an enemy (one of its intended purposes), but it does nothing to scare away an ill wind, so women wear fur-lined garments with sleeves and a hood—the first overcoat of the sort you might see in Saks today. Ankle-length dresses are worn with soft, heelless slippers. Although women's dresses become more colorful, you have to be careful about drinking red wine: White is still a favorite color.

Below: First Awarding of the Cross of the Legion of Honor *(detail), Jean-Baptiste Debret (1768–1848).* **Right:** *French costume: 1815.* **Far right:** A Reception at the Tuileries, *Baron Myrbach, ca. 1885.*

BE PREPARED: Why does Napoleon hide one hand in his coat? Certainly not because he's embarrassed about his gloves. The self-proclaimed emperor acquires two hundred and forty pairs early in his reign and then, in 1806, he orders an additional forty, lined with ermine, for good measure.

Amazingly, he had the chance to wear them—gloves will remain a must, indoors and out, throughout most of the nineteenth century.

Women prove equally susceptible to the craze. Early on, they wear elbow-length styles by day, colored to match their shoes, and full-length gloves for evening. And when sleeves begin to muscle out longer styles, gloves fight by growing fancy. By midcentury, they're made of lace or silk net, often worked with gold, and worn constantly—as one ladies' journal advises: "Gloves are always graceful for a lady in the house, except for meals."

How to be well-bred while pushing those peas? Simple. High-born ladies place their gloves—or black silk mittens for parties—discreetly next to the napkin ring.

Right: Lady with a Glove, *Charles Carolus-Duran, 1869.*

Left: Her Weight in Gold, 1771, *J. L. G. Ferris, 1921.*

SIZING UP THE SITUATION

You *are* worth your weight in gold—until the dawn of the nineteenth century, anyway. Shoes and clothing are priced by the inch, and it pays you, if not the merchant, to stay slim and short. But the system is confusing and merchants opt for standardization—naturally going with the fattest prices.

A MOVING STORY

The Battle of Waterloo in 1815 is waged in high style. Soldiers wearing fashionable skin-tight white trousers attempt to ride horseback and unsheath swords without splitting their pants. They are unsuccessful. Fortunately, the pants are so stylish that both the French and English wear them, and suffer the same handicap.

Not surprisingly, European men soon begin to question the value of such pants, however sexy, and soon a looser style is born. The new trousers of the teens and twenties come with stirrups, like modern stretch pants, worn over boots to maintain the essential slim line. The tops are eased with pleats so that wearers can sit down, but men still can't bend over; they wear tight corsets underneath.

Above left: *French cartoon, ca. 1830.* **Left:** *English caricature of a Frenchman crying for mercy (because of his tight pants?), by Thomas Rowlandson, 1813.* **Right:** *Moet & Chandon advertisement, 1950.* **Below Left:** *A drawing of Napoleon's hat, Charles Bouvier after Carl von Steuben, 1840.*

HEADY: When Napoleon surrenders at Waterloo, he loses the French crown jewels, which he has had set in his famous *tricorne* for safekeeping. France soon recovers the jewels, but the hat remains at large for a century, when it surfaces at an auction. It sells for $29,471, the highest price ever paid for a chapeau. (The buyer? Who else but a champagne magnate—the owner of Moet et Chandon.)

OF CORSET MATTERS

As Napoleon begins to consolidate his might, he grows preoccupied with building a dynasty. To do so, he'll need a male heir to assure his throne and lots of male infants to swell the future armies. So, in 1800, he issues a denunciation of corsets—they interfere with pregnancy, he declares. Of "corset," the dictum falls on deaf ears; fashion-conscious Frenchwomen, including his two wives, continue to wear them.

Corsets give pain a new meaning in the nineteenth century as women lace up whalebone garments to achieve an ideal eighteen-inch waist. Anna Pavlova wears a pink corset to dance her "dying swan"; Sarah Bernhardt wears hers in the bath; and even in the heat of darkest Africa, missionary Mary Livingston wouldn't dream of discarding her corset.

The word comes from the French *corps*, or "body." Some sort of corset or lacing to make the body appear slimmer is worn as far back as the Golden Age, when Greek lovelies strap leather bands around their breasts and hips under their chitons. The modern corset, which shapes the bosom and hips while accentuating the waist, evolves during the fourteenth and fifteenth centuries; and while this is far from the time of equality between the sexes, they do share similar vanities: the corset is worn by men as well as women.

The shape of corsets changes continually with the changing ideal of what the body silhouette should look like. Sometimes women wear corsets which accentuate or raise their bosoms; sometimes corsets diminish or emphasize the hips.

In the sixteenth century the corset, stiffened with stays of metal, wood, or whalebone, forms a sort of armor around a woman's body. Her hips are enlarged and supported with the farthingale; her décolleté emphasized. Short-waisted in the seventeenth century, corsets become longer, more pointed, and cone-shaped in the eighteenth. The nineteenth-century vogue for Scarlett O'Hara-like waists means that women have trouble breathing as corsets are more and more tightly laced.

In fact, corsets are so tightly laced by the mid-1800s that they restrict breathing, cause ribs to overlap, and are a general pain in whatever they happen to be constricting. Doctors, philosophers, and reformers rail against the confounded contraptions. But fashion is fashion, and no matter how uncomfortable, women aren't willing to throw them out until styles change. That happens around the turn of the century, when designer Paul Poiret creates the corsetless chemise. Finally, women can breathe easier for a while—at least, that is, until the invention of the girdle.

1813 THE WALTZ SWOOPS INTO THE BALL-ROOMS OF EUROPE.

1816 NOW HEAR THIS: R. T. LAËNNEC INVENTS THE STETHOSCOPE.

CON ARTIST

> " **B**eware of all enterprises that require new clothes."
> —Henry David Thoreau, *Walden*

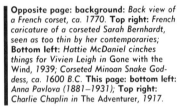

Opposite page: background: *Back view of a French corset, ca. 1770.* **Top right:** *French caricature of a corseted Sarah Bernhardt, seen as too thin by her contemporaries;* **Bottom left:** *Hattie McDaniel cinches things for Vivien Leigh in* Gone with the Wind, *1939; Corseted Minoan Snake Goddess, ca. 1600 B.C.* **This page: bottom left:** *Anna Pavlova (1881–1931);* **Top right:** *Charlie Chaplin in* The Adventurer, *1917.*

The trend toward uniformity in menswear reaches every element of society. In 1816, inmates of Auburn State Prison in upstate New York are issued custom-designed clothing. These first con clothes, dubbed "lock, step and striped suits," are cheap, highly visible, difficult to camouflage, and, in keeping with their function, take as their design motif strong black bars.

Con men have always taken a keen interest in clothing, and according to the author of *The Handbook of Swindling*, published in 1839, they need more than a good fence to make it in the business. "I have never yet known the instance of a swindler in a shabby coat," he writes. "Read the police reports, how, nineteen out of twenty times they commence, 'A young man dressed in the highest style of fashion. . . .' Hence, the tailor is indispensable to the swindler."

ISN'T IT

The direct challenger of bourgeois values and social conformity is the Romantic hero of the early nineteenth century. Think of Laurence Olivier as Heathcliff in *Wuthering Heights*—locks of windblown hair; two-days' growth of beard that bespeaks his moral abandon. (Do not think Don Johnson in *Miami Vice*—he's just a bad, soulless boy in need of a shave.) The Romantics are all attitude, swooping about in capes or fine velvet jackets to proclaim their bohemian sensitivities. Their loose trousers, harking back to the French Revolution, suggest a wistful, democratic idealism—but also give them a raffish, exotic flair. Their waistcoats are vibrant,

ROMANTIC

their shirts flowing, their necks swathed in elegant cravats. The Romantics yearn for simple, nobler, times when troubadors sang of chivalry and hopeless love.

By the second decade of the nineteenth century, women have tired of skimpy muslin gowns—or maybe they're getting too old to show so much skin. Still, they're reluctant to abandon their winsome classical charms, and so the romantic fad is born. Just as her mother aped the Greeks, the early Romantic beauty looks to the Middle Ages and the Renaissance for inspiration and comes in with a neo-Lady Guinevere look. She wears long, full sleeves, bound with cords spiraling down the arm, a skirt that gradually begins to expand in circumference, and even the *betsy*—a modified ruff. And though she bathes far more often than her medieval counter-part, she shuns cosmetics to affect the delicate pallor brought on by drafty castles and poor food.

And what to do if your complexion is ruddy? Take lead or drink vinegar to blanch your skin for a sickly, genuine Romanticism.

Opposite page: **left:** *French costume, 1812;* **Center:** *Mens' Costume, 1820s;* **Right:** *Humphry Davy, Henry Howard, ca. 1845.*
This page: left: *Laurence Olivier and Merle Oberon in* Wuthering Heights, *1939;* **Center:** *A Viennese design, 1816;* **Right:** *illustration of an Arthurian castle.*

1818 A BIG YEAR FOR PUBLISHING: KEATS WRITES *ENDYMION*, WHILE BYRON WORKS ON *DON JUAN*, JANE AUSTEN PENS *NORTHANGER ABBEY*, AND MARY SHELLEY DELIVERS *FRANKENSTEIN*.

1819 BEETHOVEN LOSES HIS HEARING, BUT GOES ON TO COMPOSE SOME OF HIS LOVELIEST WORKS.

BEAU BRUMMEL'S TRIVIAL PURSUIT

The nineteenth century sees a sea change in menswear, from the wigs and brocades of the eighteenth century to the tailored suits that are the basic male uniform today. In the upheaval, not surprisingly, men need some strong fashion leadership, and so the century gives birth to a series of great dandies. The first of these famous fops is George Bryan Brummel, the English clotheshorse who reigns until 1816. He earns the nickname "beau" for his sartorial conservatism (he wears his favorite color, blue, nearly every day) and for his insistence on fastidious grooming. His life is spent in such trivial pursuits as concocting original ways to shine his shoes and correcting the cut of his coat. Since one trivial pursuit leads to another, how many questions about Beau can you answer?

1. How does Beau Brummel take a bath?

2. What does Beau Brummel wear to go to his club for lunch?

3. How long does it take Beau Brummel to get his cravat creased and fastened just right, and give his chin the proper haughty tilt?

4. How many cravats does Beau Brummel go through to get the perfect fit?

5. How do Beau Brummel's new suits acquire the proper casual, comfortable look?

6. How many hairdressers does Beau Brummel have?

7. How many glovemakers does Beau Brummel have?

8. How many tailors does Beau Brummel have?

9. How often does Beau Brummel change his clothes?

10. What is Beau Brummel's most memorable quote?

11. What does Beau Brummel always take with him when visiting friends in the country?

12. How does Beau Brummel arrive at a party?

13. How does Beau Brummel polish his boots?

14. What are Beau Brummel's two favorite pastimes (besides buying new clothes)?

ANSWERS

1. Very slowly—in 15 quarts of warm water and 2 quarts of warm milk. 2. Skin-tight doeskin breeches, yellow waistcoat, starched and cleaned white shirt and, of course, his trademark cravat. 3. Three hours. 4. Approximately fifty—plus one or two valets. 5. He has a valet whose job consists of little else besides wearing a new suit until it becomes "broken in." 6. Three—one to cut the back, one to cut the right, and one to cut the left side of his luscious locks. 7. Four—including one "palm" man, and another who's a thumb specialist. 8. Three—one for his dark blue or black coats, one for his trousers, and one just for his waistcoats. 9. With each meal—three times a day. 10. "The less a gentleman is noticeable, the more he is elegant." 11. His chamber pot—in a traveling case of mahogany and brass. 12. In his white satin quilted sedan chair—which picks him up in his dressing room and deposits him in his host's drawing room so he never has to go outside and get dirty. 13. He pours champagne over them to give them just the right shine. Ever since the days of Beau Brummel, well-polished boots have been the sign of a well-dressed man. 14. Gambling and insulting people.

DOUBLE YOUR FUN

As their clothes fade into businesslike conformity, male fashionplates cling desperately to their waistcoats. After 1815, the classic high-necked white waistcoat gives way to a sportier, colorful shawl-collared style. This proves so popular that during the 1820s and 1830s, men take to wearing them two at a time—a nice solid velvet paired with, let's say, a smart plaid or striped satin or silk brocade.

BOOT-Y: Beau Brummel isn't the only shoe lover in the early nineteenth century. In 1800 Lieutenant Colonel Kelly of, appropriately enough, the First Foot Guard actually dies while trying to rescue his boots from a fire. Because his boots are renowned for their extraordinary patina, his funeral is a hotbed of activity—the dandies vie to sign up the services of his valet, so the secret of Kelly's boot polish formula will "shine on."

Why all this footwear fever? By the dawn of the nineteenth century, boots have become a staple in every fashionable man's armoire. Favorite styles are the *jockey boot*, made of smooth dark leather with a cuff that turns down to reveal a lighter-colored lining; the *Hessian*, a hardier boot adorned with tassels; and the *Wellington*, also called the *Napoleon*, depending on your loyalties. High in front and cut away in back to let you bend your knee on horseback, the Wellington survives today to commemorate the "Iron Duke"— now all the more invincible for being waterproof.

Opposite page: bottom left: "Beau" Brummel (1778–1840), engraving by James Cook; Right: Beau Brummel, as seen in a modern advertisement. This page: top left: Mr. Joseph Woodhead, pencil on paper, Ingres, 1816; Top right: Drawing of Count Alfred D'Orsay in the New York Times Sunday Magazine, 1820s, captioned, "Great fashion leader of early Victorian days in London"; Bottom left: Engraving of a nineteenth-century boot fancier.

263

HAZARDOUS TO

WARNING

YOUR HEALTH

Bella Donna might mean "beautiful lady," but it's also deadly—especially when Romantic beauties put a few drops in their eyes to make them luminescent. Extracts from plants from the *Atropa belladona* (or deadly nightshade) family *do* dilate the eyes' pupils; but belladonna is also a potent toxin which has been used since ancient times as a poison and as a drug which produces hallucinogenic effects.

•

Leave it to Beau Brummel to introduce collars that are so high and so stiffly starched that many an ear is cut, the result of a too-quickly turning head.

•

In the eternal quest for youthful lily-white skin, Victorian ladies sometimes get more than they bargain for. The prescribed treatment, daily sips of arsenic, sometimes stops the clock rather than turning it back.

Background: *Dangerous* Atropa belladona *plant.* **Opposite page: top right:** *Lord Byron (1788–1824);* **Bottom left:** *Lady Noel Byron, née Annabella Milbanke, engraving after a portrait by W. H. Newton, ca. 1830.*

264

LORD BYRON'S APPOINTMENT BOOK

Byron's fame as a romantic figure eclipses his place as a Romantic poet, although it is his poetry, good looks, lameness, and flamboyant lifestyle that contribute to the Byronic Legend.

Byron washes his hair in cold water every morning and it dries into tight curls; thousands of women follow his example. Byron's interest in well-kept hands has everyone running to a manicurist. And as he diets (in constant combat with a lifelong weight problem) the world diets, following his acidic advice to dine only on vinegar and water. How does he pass his days? Perhaps . . .

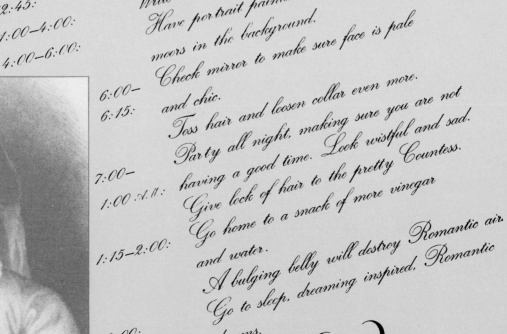

March 2, 1820

11:00 A.M.:	Lie in bed and dream Romantic dreams
11:30:	Wake up and call for valet.
11:45:	Rip strangling cravat from throat of a full-sleeved shirt and create a news easier style with loose, unbuttoned collar and cravat askew.
12:00 P.M.:	Don velvet jacket and loose trousers to hide game leg
12:15:	Dine on vinegar and water to lose weight.
12:30:	Yell at wife, Annabella Milbanke, for eating food. Tell her it's vulgar.
12:45:	Toss long, chestnut hair for disheveled Romantic look.
1:00–4:00:	Write Romantic poetry about children and flowers.
4:00–6:00:	Have portrait painted with lightning and moors in the background.
6:00– 6:15:	Check mirror to make sure face is pale and chic.
7:00–	Toss hair and loosen collar even more.
1:00 A.M.:	Party all night, making sure you are not having a good time. Look wistful and sad. Give lock of hair to the pretty Countess.
1:15–2:00:	Go home to a snack of more vinegar and water.
2:00:	A bulging belly will destroy Romantic air. Go to sleep, dreaming inspired, Romantic dreams.

DIRTY LAUNDRY LEADS TO CUTAWAY

DATELINE: Troy, New York, 1827

Housewife Hannah Lord Montague was composed as she described the events leading up to the amputation. "I was tired, just bone tired," she said, a result of having to wash hundreds of her husband's otherwise clean shirts just because they had ring around the collar. "Before I knew what I was doing," she went on, "I was standing there with scissors, ripping the collars away."

Celebrated rather than condemned, Hannah will be forever remembered as the woman who invented the detachable shirt collar.

PUPPY LOVE

After the wigs and wild coiffures of the eighteenth century, both men and women are eager for simpler hairstyles. Men keep their hair short for most of the 1800s, while they concentrate on their curls, whiskers, and beards. The fop of the 1830s opts for a bunch of curls at each temple, which merge with the newest hair trend—sideburns. And as the century progresses, elaborate mustaches grow popular, with their ends smartly waxed and curled.

Women allow themselves a little more pizzazz, especially in the 1820s and 1830s. Now the simple "classical" chignon gives way to whimsical sausage curls—a mixture of innocence and artifice—that can be wired up into a variety of exotic styles for evening. But by the late 1830s, an ingenuous mood produces one of the most unflattering styles ever developed—two braids clumped in front of the ears à la Elizabeth Barrett Browning or Princess Leia. Perhaps because they make all women seem like dogs, these dos are dubbed "spaniel's ears."

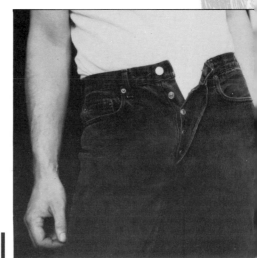

UP FRONT: The 1830s bring on an innovation that spells relief—that's when men's trousers button down the front for the first time (The silk band that runs down the sides of tuxedo pants recalls the old tradition of side buttoning.) One of the few opposed to the new style is Mormon leader Brigham Young. Appalled, he dubs them "fornication pants."

Left: Carrie Fisher as "Star Wars"
Princess Leia wears retro spaniel's ears.
Right: Button-fly Levi's 501s, 1990.

THE SHOW MUST GO ON: In 1828, Nelson Howard's role as "bareback rider" in the Buckley and Wicks Circus takes on new meaning when his costume fails to arrive on time. Undaunted, he strips down to his long johns, which—dubbed "circus tights"—have been the preferred costume for circus performers ever since.

Another nineteenth century performer's choice of costume is more calculated. What to wear if you're the most famous French circus aerialist, heart-throb, and body beautiful to boot? Between somersaults, the performer gives a lot of thought—and his name—to the answer: a *leotard*. "If you want to be adored," Jules Léotard advises, "put on a more natural garb which does not hide your best features."

"Muscle" may conjure up a picture of a virile Charles Atlas *after* his body-building program, but in Latin, it means "little mouse." Huh? The description was probably chosen because rippling biceps look like there's a little mouse running up and down underneath the skin.

Above right: *Jules Léotard, ca. 1865.*
Below: *Caricature from Modern Oddities by P. Pry, 1820.*

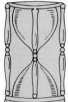

IN ARMS WAY:
Hurry to get your new *leg o' mutton* or *gigot* sleeves. In 1830, sleeves balloon-shaped from the elbow to the shoulder, fitted from the elbow to the wrist, replace demure, classical puffs. If you'd rather not be a fashion sheep, try an *elephant* sleeve—tight at the top, voluminous at the elbow, and gathered tightly at the cuff. And if you're foolish enough to follow every fad, you'll want the *embicile* style, very full but tamed with bands.

During the 1830s, sleeves reach their most ridiculous dimensions—padded or boned to form enormous puffs and wings—but complex styles dominate the whole century. Shoulders virtually disappear until 1840, as huge, flat collars slope from women's necklines down to the fullest points of their giant sleeves. By the 1850s, the *pagoda sleeve* is revived—a full, open, three-quarter-length style gussied up with a lacy or ruffled undersleeve. There's only one brief stretch in the 1870s and 1880s when common sense rules and arms shrink down to normal size. Then it's back to vast melons, balloons, and legs o' mutton until the turn of the century.

G Y M   "S

Except in a few progressive nations, like Crete and Persia, exercise was something you caught on the run — playing baseball or hunting down wild boar. But thanks to the nineteenth-century revolution in exercise, a special room equipped for sports — the gymnasium — becomes popular. Here's a brief rundown on the fore-runners to the New York Health and Racquet Club:

• The ancient Cretans create the first gym in 3,000 B.C. to help boys develop the physical strength needed in combat.

• In 500 B.C., Persian boys are taken from their families when they turn six and sent off to the gym to learn to be good soldiers. The Greeks and the Romans, on the other hand, turn their gymnasia into social clubs, where they can get a massage, meet a dancing girl, or plan the overthrow of a government.

• By the Middle Ages, exercise — swimming, wrestling, horsemanship — is an important part of the preparation for knighthood. It is a serious business, but even would-be sirs get to "jostle" with each other once in a while.

• In 1811, the Berlin Turnverein, a school devoted to gymnastics and exercise, opens in Germany. Not to be outdone, West Point opens its first gym in 1817. Harvard becomes the first university to introduce gymnastic courses in 1826, pressing a German professor into service as its instructor. Taking the "tiger" by the tail, Princeton follows suit and builds the first separate gym building on a college campus. Inside are parallel bars, flying rings, Indian clubs, a running track, and a pool. The locker room continues the classic tradition of gym as social forum, but instead of meeting dancing girls here, as the ancient Greeks and Romans did, students just talk about them.

• Amherst creates the first inter-collegiate gym department in 1869, where basketball, volleyball, handball, track and field, and crew are offered.

• As for girls, the prevailing view that women are the weaker sex keeps them pretty much

Background: *The gymnasium at West Point, ca. 1892.* Upper left: *Greek athletes practicing on an ancient amphora.* Below left: *Amherst College track team, 1888.*

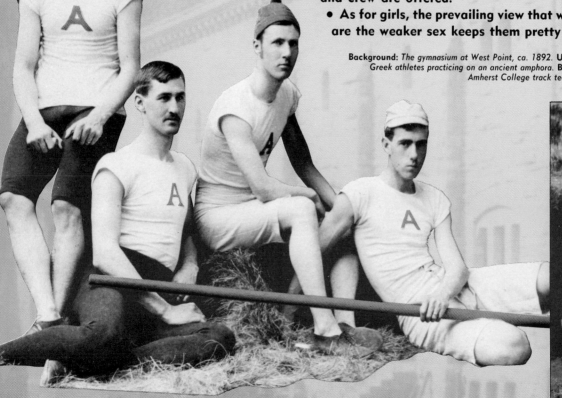

H O R T S"

out of the action for centuries. But in the 1800s there is a growing movement to encourage women to exercise. Calisthenics—using wands and dumbbells—is devised around mid-century as a "safe" form of physical exertion, although *Godey's Lady's Book* still rates housework as the best exercise.

● By 1871, however, a French actor has women everywhere "Doing Delsarte" as he introduces a popular form of exercise, marketed under his name, which includes mime and dance and stresses repetition as a path to spiritual as well as physical well-being. And in 1885 a Swedish teacher, Mrs. Bergman Osterberg, introduces the first women's gym uniform—a sleeveless, knee-length tunic worn over a blouse and bloomers. Until then women had been exercising in steel corsets.

Engraving of women doing calisthenics, 19th c.

● By 1925 the battle of the bulge is fought over the airwaves as the world's biggest gym class is broadcast for ninety minutes to two and a half million New York radio listeners.

● And in 1936 there is Jack Lalanne. After a warm-up in his family's Berkeley backyard, where he charges people five dollars to try lifting his cement-filled paint cans on their biceps, he opens the first Jack Lalanne Health spa (with more sophisticated equipment) in downtown Oakland, California.

● It is in the back room of a YMCA in Tulsa, Oklahoma, in 1948 that former jack-of-all-trades Arthur Jones first starts attracting customers to his Nautilus Time Machines. His conviction that the American public needs something more than barbells leads him to produce the machinery that concentrates on specific muscle areas—machinery whose sales grow into a twenty million dollar business by 1978.

● Today, of course, everyone is fonda' those exercises by the California actress, which has worked out well for her, too—staying in shape has helped her create a million dollar empire.

Below left: Lycra spandex bicycle shorts got hot in the late 1980s.
Below: The first public women's basketball game, Smith College, 1893. Right: An aerobicized Jane Fonda, 1987.

DON'T TIE ME DOWN

There are fifty ways to leave your lover, and at least one of them is in a bind over tying the knot. As the century progresses, the *cravat* Beau Brummel popularized evolves into a myriad of styles. In the 1820s, it's still stiff and high, with a simple bow in front; but over the next two decades, it balloons to cover its wearer's entire chest. Black is the favorite color for day, with elegant white for night, but the most fashion-forward gentlemen favor wilder patterns—polka dots, stripes, even flowers.

It's not easy to stabilize these huge, slippery cravats—until the Tie School is founded, that is. Opened in Paris by an Italian businessman, it offers lessons, which last a trying six hours, at 54 francs each. Books with elaborately illustrated instructions are included in the price—one showing over twenty cravat styles, including the Orientals and à la Byron. And, not surprisingly, the hottest new accessory is the pearl-headed tie pin.

By the 1850s, with the Industrial Revolution booming, gentlemen are too busy to fuss with their clothes; the flowing cravat is trimmed back to a modest, narrow bowtie. But, as men's clothing styles grow more austere, the necktie becomes one of the last spots for a fashionplate to flaunt his individuality. There's a brief flurry of favor for stocks and scarves during the 1860s, until a compromise is reached—the simpler, knotted, four-in-hand tie that school boys and Wall Street financiers wear today.

Above, background: *Illustrations from* The Art of Knotting a Tie in Sixteen Lessons, *Italian, 1827;* Inset: *A trio of Frenchmen, 1830.*

LET'S KISS AND MAKE UP

By the 1840s every good New York drugstore employs a full-time cosmetician. To apply a lady's makeup? Sometimes. But primarily they are on call to repair male customers' black eyes.

In 1867, the department store B. Altman's introduces a "making up" department where fashionable ladies learn to apply rouge, powder, and eyebrow pencil. The job of makeup at this time is to enhance naturalness: the rouge is discreetly applied, and there's lots of cheek pinching and lip biting for color. Less proper ladies, however, opt for pearl and violet powders, rouge, and a drop or two of belladonna in their eyes for that "dreamy" look. There are also "falsies"— for ears! Women can buy better- shaped ears than God gave them, with—if they want—earrings attached.

Right: *Prize-fighter Al McCoy, after losing to Joe Louis, December 16, 1940.* Far right: *A Paramount starlet, 1934.*

270

HAT TRICKS

Children scream and women faint as James Heathrington dons a *top hat* for his 1797 afternoon stroll through the streets of London. Heathrington is convicted on charges of "wearing a tall structure to frighten timid people." The top hat is originally designed in 1730 to be worn on fox hunts— if a rider falls from a horse, the stiff "topper" cushions his collision. But initial resistance to wearing the top hat for social occasions is overcome when, in the 1850s, that old reliable trendsetter Prince Albert dons a top hat; men everywhere follow suit, wearing them day and night. Short men take a fancy to the tallest and straightest of all—the *stovepipe*, the hat that becomes the trademark of one Abraham Lincoln (who is anything but short, but there you have it). In fact for a night at the opera, the top hat dominates, so to speak, until the end of the century, but with a new twist. Called the *gibus*, after the man who invented it in the 1840s, the contraption is made with an internal spring so it can be conveniently collapsed and carried. (After all, not everyone can afford to follow the lead of financier J. P. Morgan who builds a limo with an especially high roof so he can ride around without taking off his hat.) In the twentieth century, Fred Astaire jauntily dances through at least a dozen movies wearing the top hat, but, as early as 1814, Frenchman Louis Conte has found another use for it: He is the first magician to pull a white rabbit out of a top hat.

• For a few years after 1810 large *beaver hats* allow the French aristocracy to "high hat" it over common people.

• In the 1840s the Earl of Derby dons a melon-shaped hard felt hat to wear to the races. Americans call the hat a *derby* in honor of the peer who popularizes it—the British sportingly call it a *bowler* after the hat's creator.

• It's not until mid-century that another great hat revolution occurs, fueled once again by Prince Albert of England. He introduces a low, wide-brimmed hat made of felt for winter and of straw for summer—and the *boater* is born.

Above: Prince Albert and his bowler, engraving by D. J. Pound from a J. J. E. Mayall photograph, ca. 1860. Counterclockwise from above left: Tony Curtis as "Houdini" pulls a rabbit out of his hat; a bobby's hat conveniently covers a streaker; and Laurel and Hardy sport trademark derbies in Sons of the Desert, 1934.

271

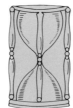

FRONT LINES: The 1800s grant men's shirts one last burst of glamor before they fade to the drab uniforms of today. As the century opens they sport collars so high that they all but cover a man's befuddled grin. By the 1840s, men get some relief as their stiff collar points are turned down to form wings—a style known as "gates ajar." And in the 1860s, their spouses breathe easier, too, when disposable collars are born. Made of linen glued to paper, these throwaways are even printed with fake stitching.

For the first half of the century, the fashionable men's chest is bedecked with rows of pleated ruffles; and here, too, in the 1840s and '50s, fakery prevails. The ruffles are attached to false fronts—starched, biblike plackets—held on by ties at the shoulders and waist.

Gentlemen go in for a little pizzazz in the 1840s, wearing shirts that are striped or floral; in the evening, they're often embroidered. The fronts of these shirts often boast studs, instead of buttons, with matching sets at the wrists. It is considered ostentatious for gentlemen to wear too many studs. (How much stud a gentleman is allowed to show, however, is ultimately left to his discretion.)

Clockwise from above left: *Shepperd Strudwick in Belle Star, 1941; Albert G. Gilman, A. Ellis, 1831; Portrait of a Youth, Johann Scheffer von Leonhartshoff, early 19th c.*

LEADING THE MID-CENTURY BESTSELLER LIST

"The Toilette of Health, Beauty, and Fashion; Embracing the Economy of the Beard, Breath, Complexion, Ears, Eyes, Eye-Brows, Eye-Lashes, Feet, Forehead, Gums, Hair, Head, Hands, Lips, Mouth, Mustachios, Nails of the Toes, Nails of the Fingers, Nose, Skin, Teeth, Tongue, Etc., Etc., Including the Comforts of Dress and the Decorations of the Neck; also the Treatment of the Discolorations of the Skin, Corns—Eruptions—Spots—Pimples, Scorbutic or Spongy Gums, Tainted Breath—Tooth Ache—Carious or Decayed Teeth—Warts—Whitlows, Prevention of Baldness, Grey Hair, etc., with Directions for the Use of Most Safe and Salutary Cosmetics—Perfumes—Essences—Simple Waters—Depilatories, and other Preparations to Remove Superfluous Hair, Tan, Excrescenses, etc., and a Variety of Select Recipes for the Dressing Room of Both Sexes."

To save room on the title page, the author's name is mercifully given as "Anonymous."

PIN MONEY

On the nose, but not on the money, or, would there have been punk without Hunt? That's Walter Hunt—who invented the safety pin in 1849 but sold the rights for a measly $100.

Left: *Advertisement for safety pins in a turn-of-the-century program from Barnum and Bailey's circus.*

1842 EDGAR ALLEN POE TERRI-FIES THE WORLD WITH *THE MASQUE OF THE RED DEATH.*

1845 THE KNICKERBOCKER BASEBALL CLUB CODIFIES THE RULES OF THE GAME.

WHICH CAME FIRST, THE CHICKEN OR THE EGG?

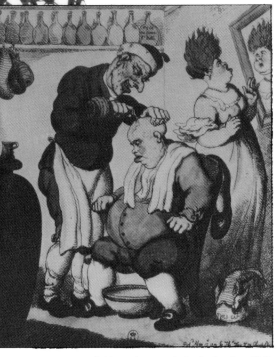

Sales of crocheted doilies soar around 1850 as macassar oil, which men use to slick back their hair, becomes popular. The doilies protect upholstered furniture from the hair oil and so become known as antimacassars.

Above: *A cartoon by Rowlandson from 1840 captioned, "Macassar Oil: an oily puff for soft heads."* **Bottom left:** *Cigarette advertisement, 1947.* **Bottom right:** *Cuffed pants by Brooks Brothers, 1969.*

CUFF LUCK: One rainy day around 1850, an unnamed Englishman on his way to a wedding in New York turns up the bottoms of his trouser legs so they won't be splattered. He arrives late, neglects to turn them down, and so trouser cuffs are born.

273

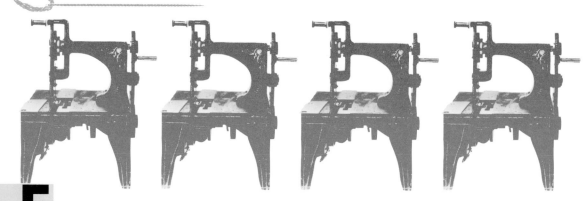

SEW IT GOES

For forty thousand years, when you wanted to whip up a new party dress or mend a hem, you did it by hand. Which is more incredible: that the eyed-needle — made from ivory, bone or walrus tusks — was used by the caveman, or that no one invented anything better until the nineteenth century?

The "better" is a sewing machine invented by French tailor Barthélemy Thimmonier in 1830. By hand, an experienced tailor could make about thirty stitches a minute: Thimmonier's sewing machine makes two hundred. The French government gives Thimmonier a contract to turn out military uniforms, and he puts eighty machines into operation. But his colleagues, fearful that the newfangled invention will drive them out of business, enter his shop, break his machines, and run Thimmonier out of Paris.

It is another twenty years before the name that is to become synonymous with sewing machines is affixed to patent number 4050683. But I.M. Singer doesn't think up the sewing machine — he refines a much cruder model he's seen only eleven short days before. Elias Howe, the inventor of the original machine, is less than thrilled. Howe sues, and finally settles out of court — and Singer pays him license fees for making machines. But Singer still sews up a fortune. Shortly after the court battle he moves to England and buys a palatial homestead, which he quaintly nicknames "The Wigwam."

Singer's machine has a straight needle that moves up and down. At first it is used for shoemaking, but by the late 1850s, even the great French couturiers are using it, and by the 1860s it has revolutionized the clothing industry: almost all clothing is now machine made.

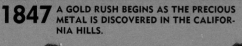

Opposite page: **top:** *Isaac Merrit Singer (1811–1875);* **Center:** *The 1851 patent model of Singer's first sewing machine;* **Bottom:** *Women and children do "piece work" at home.* **This page: above:** *James Tissot's Too Early shows a lot of ruffles and flounces, ca. 1885;* **Bottom inset right:** *First Work in America, Lewis Hine, 1910;* **Bottom inset right:** *Sweatshops were commonplace by 1910.*

(In 1867 over two hundred thousand sewing machines are manufactured in the United States alone.) By the 1870s most sewing machines can sew seven thousand stitches a minute—some models zip along at 8,000.

The effect of the sewing machine on clothing design is immediate: Designers add more flounces, frills, and otherwise time-consuming stitchery to dresses. Previously, hand finishing a custom-made gown took days; now, it takes hours. Also, clothes can now be mass produced.

Mass production of ready-made clothing requires mass distribution, a boon to department stores. The sewing machine makes clothing more affordable, and it also heralds the opening of factories. Before the sewing machine, an individual tailor, possibly working with an apprentice, makes a dress, or a suit, or a coat. After the sewing machine, rooms full of workers are gathered together to mass-produce clothing, by piece—one worker might be responsible for attaching the sleeves of a garment to the bodice, for example, over and over again. In many factories, workers own their machines and lug them from factory to factory. By the turn of the century, this piece-work is farmed out to workers in their homes and "bundle brigades"—men, women, and children trudging through the streets of lower New York, with bundles of finished garments—are a common sight.

Most apparel factories are crowded, poorly lit, and airless and the term "sweatshop" is coined to describe them. And it is an unpleasant reality that the sewing machine—which has proved a boon and a blessing to so many—creates such a burden for others.

ts architecture—for example, the Crystal Palace—and fashions—notably the crinoline—make the early Victorian era seem big, bustling, and embellished in ways reminiscent of the Rococo period.

Late Victorian fashions are by all lights "prudish"—this is, after all, an era named for a queen who is in mourning for sixteen years, and a time when it is improper to mention the word "legs" let alone spy them beneath a lady's demure attire. But there is an expansiveness to the era, typified by the width below the waist of women's costumes, and a richness of materials. Trade and commerce flourish, despite the upheaval of wars, while steamships and railways make it possible for Europeans to shop the world. Opulent silks, satins, and fine worsteds are commonly used for daytime outfits; cottons and luxurious cashmere shawls are prized possessions brought back from the East.

Left: *German costume, 1850.* **Below:** Victoria Greeted as Queen, *H. T. Wells;* **Bottom right:** Queen Victoria Receiving the Holy Sacrament at her Coronation in Westminister Abbey, June 28, 1838, *Charles Robert Leslie, 1839.*

EVOLUTION

The Industrial Revolution has decidedly different effects on men's and women's clothing. Men's clothing becomes plain and practical—floor-length capes or even complicated neckties just aren't appropriate for the office. The Victorian male's sober costume approaches the form it is to keep right up until today. Conversely, women's costume flourishes, becoming more colorful and complicated—thanks to the sewing machine and aniline dyes.

▌**Below:** *French costume, 1840's.* **Right:** *Italian costume, 19th ca.*

CRINOLINE CONVERSATION STOPPERS

In French *crin* means horsehair; *linum*, thread. Put them together and you get a *crinoline*. Sew in flexible, steel-hooped cages, and it's ever so much lighter. Empress Eugénie is the queen of the crinoline; she wears a gray one with black lace and pink bows under her gown when she's presented to Queen Victoria. Soon everyone who is anyone is wearing them: shop girls, peasants in the fields. The inventor of the crinoline earns a million francs in the first month it's on the market. Voilà! A new trend; a new fashion phenomenon; and something new to talk about. So the next time you're at a Victorian cocktail party wearing your new crinoline and feeling like a bull in a china shop because your skirt's in full swing, pause, take a

deep breath, regain your composure, and wow other guests with your fashionable conversation. Drop little tidbits like . . . Did you know that, sociologically speaking, the crinoline has redefined our sense of personal space, since only three women wearing crinolines can possibly stand in an average-sized room at once. And how about the way the crinoline has changed relations between the sexes, ask your listeners, who by now are paying rapt attention: Explain that a man can no longer bend over to kiss a lady—her crinoline is just too wide. Why, he can't even hold her hand. Talk of social humiliation: Women in crinolines have to kneel in a carriage or sit on the floor. Decry the discrimination of the New York Omnibus Company which raised fares for "ladies with hoops" from 7 to 12 cents. Applaud the efforts of the American Medical Association which, for the first time in history, issues dressmaking instructions, in an effort to minimize the crinoline's discomfort. Finally, play fashion-know-it-all, predicting that although the crinoline will finally go the way of the bum roll, it will make a minor comeback a century later in the 1950s, with wide-skirted, strapless gowns.

Top: *Design for a crinoline, American, 1860's.* Left center: *Women in hooped skirts, English, 1863.* Right: *A dress in a revived eighteenth-century style.*

1849 IT WAS THE BEST OF TIMES, IT WAS THE WORST OF TIMES: CHARLES DICKENS WRITES *DAVID COPPERFIELD*, WHILE DOSTOEVSKY IS EXILED TO SIBERIA.

1850 THE POPULATION OF THE UNITED STATES IS 23 MILLION, OF WHOM 3.2 MILLION ARE SLAVES.

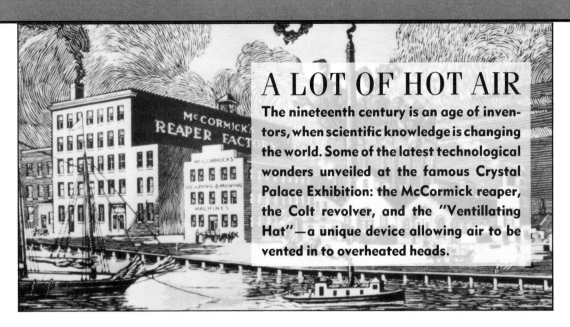

A LOT OF HOT AIR

The nineteenth century is an age of inventors, when scientific knowledge is changing the world. Some of the latest technological wonders unveiled at the famous Crystal Palace Exhibition: the McCormick reaper, the Colt revolver, and the "Ventillating Hat"—a unique device allowing air to be vented in to overheated heads.

McCormick Reaper Factory on the banks of the Chicago River, before it was destroyed by the Great Fire of 1871.

DRESSED TO THRILL

In the past, famous courtesans to kings —Agnes Sorel, Madame de Pompadour—dictated the fashions at court. But nowadays, a bourgeois class is emerging from the shadows, and ladies in fine drawing rooms are oft presiding over high tea and dinner parties garbed in fashion ideas plucked from street corners in the seedier part of town.

• In the 1850s prostitutes rush off to San Francisco to do their bit for the Gold Rush. Since American society frowns on prostitution, these ladies of the night take daytime jobs at local saloons or, better yet, pretend to be dressmakers. Do they really dress like Amanda Blake on *Gunsmoke* in rustling bustled gowns of velvet and taffeta with deep décolleté? Probably. But since fashion magazines take a year or two to make it out west, assume that whatever they're wearing is one or two years behind the times.

• In 1855 the smash French play *Le Demi Monde*, by Alexander Dumas, the son, re-creates the immoral world of the French Second Empire, and coins a new word, *demimonde*, for the world of the prostitute. By the end of the century, Charles Worth is producing a line of racy ankle-length dresses that reveal sexy, laced-up boots, a tart comment on the clothing worn by these women of easy virtue. The dresses are a runaway success with Worth's regular clientele, and better-heeled courtesans rush off to Worth as well.

• In 1867 Whistler's mistress (not his mother) brings the notorious cancan to England. Finette dances up a storm in Leicester Square—but so as not to create *too* big a scandal, she wears male clothes.

Amanda Blake and Milburn Stone in *Gunsmoke*, CBS, 1955.

1853 FINALLY! AFTER QUEEN VICTORIA ACCEPTS CHLOROFORM DURING CHILDBIRTH, ANESTHETICS COME INTO GENERAL USE.

1854 COMMODORE M. C. PERRY NEGOTIATES THE FIRST AMERICAN-JAPANESE TRADE AGREEMENT, FOREVER CHANGING THE FACE OF JAPAN.

DEPARTURES: The democratic movements of the late eighteenth century give the middle class more power than ever before. Naturally, they need clothes that suit their new station, but work keeps them from spending endless hours on tailors' fittings. So ready-to-wear debuts around 1800, as tailors whip up leftover cloth into over-the-counter fashions. In America, especially, the trend takes hold and gives birth to a new industry: the department store.

The flagship American department store, Brooks Brothers, opens in New York in 1818. Over time its influence swells—not only will it pioneer ready-to-wear clothes for men, it will sell Abraham Lincoln the suit in which he is assassinated, introduce button-down shirts in 1900, and later virtually invent that archetype of the 1950s, the "Man in the Gray Flannel Suit." When Samuel Lord and George Washington Taylor open splashy new digs at Broadway and Grand Street in lower Manhattan in 1859, awed customers come to the new Lord & Taylor as much to admire the new Tiffany chandeliers and steam elevators as to shop.

Department stores get a tremendous boost with the coming of mass production around the mid-nineteenth century. Sadly, progress requires sacrifices—design, individual taste, and personal fittings fall by the wayside; and factory-created construction often yields shoddy merchandise. But the customers don't care—department stores are an idea whose time has come.

• The first great European department stores, the Galeries du Commerce et Industrie and the Palais Bonne-Nouvelle, emerge by the second third of the nineteenth century. Close on their heels come Ville de France (1844), Grandes Halles (1853), and Bon Marché (1876)—all in Paris; and Liberty of London soon follows. These early department stores are less like Macy's than like today's suburban malls. They're loose affiliations of merchants offering everything from clothes to accessories, shoes, and hats.

• Some department stores, such as Sears and Montgomery Ward, emerge from mail-order operations. These outfits offer everything from farm implements and food to fashion for their far-flung clientele. In 1875, an ad for the Montgomery Ward catalogue promises, "Give us your age and description of your general build, and in nine cases out of ten, we'll give you a fit." The first mail-order clothes are sized by trial and error—some customers find it helpful to include their astrological sign.

• Unlikely as it seems, Brigham Young, the Mormon leader, becomes a merchandising pioneer. In 1868, he establishes the very first Salt Lake City department store, the Zion's Co-operative Mercantile Institution. Why does Young take time out from saving souls to sell clothes? The polygamous patriarch is desperate to control his many wives' spending.

YLOR,

Retail Dealers in

DS.

LEVI STRAUSS & CO.
SAN FRANCISCO CAL.
ORIGINAL RIVETED
QUALITY CLOTHING. XX
TRADE MARK
PATENTED IN U.S. MAY 20 1873 WPL 423
100% Cotton Made in U.S.A
CARE INSTRUCTION INSIDE GARMENT
501 W32 L32

Opposite page: inset: *The first Lord &*
Taylor store at Catherine Street Slip, New
York City, 1826–1853; Far left: *Lord &*
Taylor took out this full-page ad in the
1854 Illustrated American Biography, an
annual catalogue of stores and resorts.
Above, left and right: *Levi's 501 jeans.*
Above center: *A cowboy working in his*
jeans in 1960. Left: *The famous Levi's "Two*
Horse Brand" leather patch, introduced in
1886, is still affixed, though no longer in
leather, to every pair of Levi's. Bottom left:
A little cowgirl from Sedalia, Missouri, in
1950.

JEAN-ESIS

In the 1850s, 21-year-old Levi Strauss comes
to America seeking his fortune. But who
could imagine that a remark made by a miner
would lead to what has been called America's most important contribution to fashion? As Strauss is trying to sell him canvas
tents, the miner bellows, "You should
have brought pants." Strauss listens. The
originals get their name when miners come
around looking for "those pants of Levi's."
Later Strauss switches from canvas to
denim. Jeans? The Americanization of the
French "Genes," for Genoa, the town which
produced denim pants in Italy. The blue?
When Strauss adds indigo dye, he puts the
blue in blue jeans.

eet, cor. Chrystie, N.

281

Left: *This gentleman hunts in a Norfolk jacket.* Center left: *Woman's golfing costume.* Below: *Bloomer costume, N. Currier, 1851.*

THIS SPORTIN' LIFE

When sports first come into play in a big way, in the middle of the nineteenth century, people—especially women—face a fashion problem: the lack of suitable sports clothing.

Men loosen up a little, wearing a hip-length tweed jacket with patches, belt, and box pleats, known as the Norfolk jacket, with loose-fitting knee breeches and gaiters. This outfit gets them through any number of rounds at shooting matches and, for cricket, they inexplicably (but invariably) don the same garb, with a more brightly colored shirt.

Women up until this time have very little experience with sports. So once it becomes respectable for a girl to engage in a game of golf, lawn tennis, or roller-skating, it's only natural that she would look to her male counterpart, and don men's hats and stiff white collars. The participation in sports represents a great emancipation for women—but you'd never know it from these first fashions, which are heavy, made of homespuns and tweeds, and usually dark. This style, however, does affect everyday wear, and for daytime, there is a new vogue for the tailored suit consisting of a jacket, skirt, and "shirtwaister," a female version of a male shirt which becomes a runaway bestseller by the Gay Nineties.

For cricket, women wear a hip-length blouse tied at the waist with a sash; a game of golf calls for a serge coat, skirt, and a sporty *tam o'shanter;* undeterred by their long skirts, women even throw themselves into tennis.

But it is the bicycle craze that ushers in not only a genuine sense of mobility, but new attitudes about comfort in women's dress.

In 1850 when feminist Amelia Bloomer suggests that women abandon their horsehair crinolines and voluminous long skirts in favor of more practical, loose knee-length trousers, she is ridiculed. But the outfit becomes a cause célèbre, and forty years later, with women tearing around the countryside on bicycles, Mrs. Bloomer's fashion views are vindicated. It finally becomes practically obligatory to throw out long skirts that get caught in the cogs and chains of a bicycle, and women embrace the free-wheeling "bloomers." Not only do bloomers become the ideal riding attire, they also challenge the long tradition of Who Wears the Pants in the Family.

Sports, which tone up the body, not only affect how women look in clothes. They become a totally new influence on the style of clothes as well.

Above left: *British cavalry camp during the Crimean War.* Above right: *Robert Preston, Ray Milland, and Gary Cooper in Beau Geste, 1939.*

PLEASE RELEASE ME, I SURRENDER: In 1854, the British Army arrives to do battle in Turkey wearing stiff, starched uniforms, gold braid epaulettes, and bearskin sashes. As a modest concession to the extreme heat, soldiers are permitted to hang white handkerchiefs from their towering headdresses, presumably to shield them from the sun. However, they could also be used as white flags—to let sweltering soldiers surrender and get out of those ridiculous uniforms as quickly as possible.

FIT TO BE TIED

In 1854, when Florence Nightingale organizes thirty-eight nurses to leave for the Crimean War front, she insists that they be provided with homogenous dress. Her demand for "grey tweed wrappers," worsted jackets, caps, and brown scarfs with "Scutari Hospital" emblazoned in red is, remarkably, met in only four days—and the result is the first uniforms for women. The catch is, they don't fit. There is simply no time to measure the nurses individually so a variety of sizes are made and randomly handed out to the women.

Above: *"Lady with the Lamp": Florence Nightingale pictured in the Illustrated London News on February 24, 1855.* Above right: *A pencil drawing of Florence Nightingale's carriage done by a reporter during the Crimean War.*

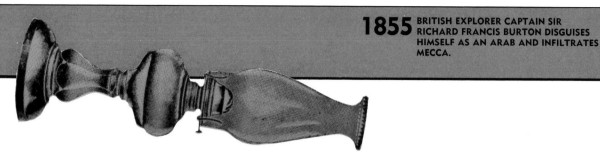

OILY TO RINSE: On a chilly night in Paris in 1855 Jean Baptiste Jolly accidentally upsets an unlit oil lamp. He wants to continue working, so he quickly removes the soiled tablecloth and doesn't get back to it for several hours. When he does, he is surprised to see the spill gone; in fact, the oiled part of the cloth is actually cleaner than the rest. Thus, the first commercial dry cleaner is in business. But it is a laborious method. Each garment must be dipped in a pan of turpentine and brushed clean, then the smell of the spirit must be dried off.

WOOLY TALES

Besides telling you how to order the perfect striped bass from room service, the author of *The Art of Travel,* scrupulously tabulates the number of his fellow travelers who die during his journeys, reporting that most of those who dropped dead weren't wearing woolen undies. This he claims conclusively confirms the teachings of the fanatical Dr. Gustav Jaeger, who believed that human beings could only be healthy if clad, at all times, in wool. (Think about *that* the next time you pop into Jaeger's to pick up a cashmere sweater and balk at the price.) Among the good doctor's later devoted disciples, who would have followed him to Tahiti in their long johns? Rudyard Kipling and George Bernard Shaw.

Below, left to right: *Everyone from stooges to sages wore Jaeger underwear: Rudyard Kipling, Moe Howard, and George Bernard Shaw.*

1856 SIGMUND FREUD IS BORN IN AUSTRIA. HOW DO YOU FEEL ABOUT THAT?

1856 THE WORLD'S LONGEST BARE-KNUCKLE BOXING MATCH TAKES PLACE IN AUSTRALIA. IT LASTS SIX HOURS AND FIFTEEN MINUTES.

HOW TO READ A BEARD

Ⓐ   Ⓑ   Ⓒ   Ⓓ   Ⓔ

Ⓐ **Long whiskers and a mustache become known as the *Franz Josef* in honor of the Austrian Emperor.**

Ⓑ **Luxurious sidewhiskers are known as *mutton chops* or *Piccadilly weepers*. In the U.S. they're called *sideburns* after Civil War General Ambrose Burnside.**

Ⓒ **_Dundrearys_ are named after a whiskered character in the play *An American Cousin*.**

Ⓓ **The *imperial*, a pointed tuft of whiskers on the chin, is named in honor of Napoleon III.**

Ⓔ **In the British Army it's the *walrus* mustache that's popular; in the U.S., the *handlebar*, which curls upward.**

BELLY-UP: Like the managers of early baseball teams, in the 1850s umpires wear business suits so they can sit calmly on stools between first base and home plate and prove they mean business when overseeing a game. Dressing for success proves dangerous after several umps are hit by foul balls—so they take to wearing uniforms with padded chests and wire masks.

| **Above:** *Engraving by Du Maurier in an 1878 issue of Punch, captioned, "No accounting for tastes." **Right:** Batter and ump from* The Home Baseball Game, *1905.*

CHIN-CHIN: For all the attention to their sideburns, men always shave their chins—until 1855, that is. Liking their newly sprouted whiskers, British soldiers return home from the war burly-faced. But the start of the so-called "Beard Movement" is prickly. Women hate it, pastors protest, newspapers editorialize, and one particularly proper English law firm is forced to lay down the law. "Young men in our employ," reads a somewhat befuddled memo, "may not wear their beards during working hours."

1857 THE FIRST SAFETY ELEVATOR IS DEMONSTRATED BY CIVIL ENGINEER E. C. OTIS.

1857 THE FIRST TRANSATLANTIC CABLE IS LAID. WHEN IT IS FINISHED IN 1866, IT WILL PROVIDE INSTANTANEOUS COMMUNICATION BETWEEN THE UNITED STATES AND BRITAIN.

H C L O O R T S H E E S

HAIL, VICTORIA!

Princess Di can be excused her occasional black sheep sweater or Italian jeans—she, after all, was a commoner who married a prince (and these are the 1990s). But Queen Victoria, who came to the throne in 1837 at the age of eighteen, had been brought up from birth to be queen of England. Her influence is so great that the period of her sixty-four-year reign is dubbed the "Victorian" era. And everything she does (or wears) is imbued with the utmost sense of propriety.

The Victorian era is a time of respectable dress, bone-waisted rigidity, and rules: Ladies' fashion magazines spell out correct etiquette for each and every occasion. The short and plump Victoria isn't as interested in making the fashion pages as she is in spurring the economy. But to spur the economy, she is willing to make the fashion pages. Using the trend-setting clout that comes along with the title of queen, she always wears clothes manufactured in Britain. Her silk coronation robes and cream-colored satin wedding dress are specially woven in London; the lace for her wedding gown is handmade in Honiton (rather than imported from Brussels), in a deliberate attempt to assist a declining industry. Victoria presides over three fancy-dress balls each year: Textile workers, dressmakers, and caterers are kept busy for months preparing for each. Victoria enjoys the nineteenth-century passion for shawls, but hers decidedly do not come from the looms of France, and as a result of Victoria's patronage, the world takes note of the Norwich shawl.

Fashionable children of the Victorian era are dressed as miniature versions of their parents (little girls even wear crinolines and bustles). And when Victoria has a tiny sailor suit made for one of her sons to wear on the royal yacht, she starts a trend that will continue well into the twentieth century.

But perhaps Victoria's greatest influence is in the area of mourning dress. When her beloved husband Prince Albert dies in 1861, she is completely bereft. For the rest of her life Victoria only wears black—becoming the archetypal widow. During this period Victoria means to forgo fashion, but she can't help starting a vogue: To keep up appearances, other widows follow suit, and members of this cult of mourning swell through the second half of the nineteenth century.

Left, top: Queen Victoria with her great-grandchildren, King George, Princess Mary, Prince Edward, and baby Prince Henry, 1900. Left, bottom: Girl's ball gown. 1866.

1857 CZAR ALEXANDER II BEGINS THE EMANCIPATION OF RUSSIAN SERFS.

1858 LIONEL DE ROTHSCHILD BECOMES THE FIRST JEWISH MEMBER OF THE BRITISH PARLIAMENT.

DESIGNER LABELS

Paris, during the reign of Napoleon III with the grand Eugénie by his side, is indisputably the fashion capital of the world. But take a peek at the labels, and you'll see that the clothes on these fashionable French backs have been put there by two egomaniacal Englishmen—dressmaker Charles Frederick Worth and tailor Henry Poole.

Poole has impeccable manners, the wisdom to extend limitless credit, and an eye for detail. In the vanguard of tailors who move into Savile Row during the middle of the century (replacing the fashionable surgeons who had once populated the block), Poole quickly rises above the crowd. Today a bespoke suit from a Savile Row suitmaker is synonymous with elegance, and the name of Poole still reigns. To ask the difference between ready-to-wear and a handmade suit is to suggest you don't know a Chevy from a Rolls Royce. But how *can* you tell a Savile suit from a Robert Hall? Look for extra buttons at the jacket cuff, a ticket pocket, "flashy lapels," and trousers cut with a high waist. You won't have to peek at the label.

Left: *Queen Victoria paper cutout, 1890;* **Inset:** *Souvenir pin from Victoria's fiftieth Jubilee celebration.*
Above: *The Worth label.*

DYE STUFFS: Can you imagine a world without chartreuse? Now you don't have to, because in 1856 William Henry Perkin invents synthetic aniline dyes. They are cheaper than natural dyes, and available in a whole range of colors. The subdued shades of bygone eras are now replaced with pre-fluorescent hues. Chemically made dyes give color a bizarre intensity, and the result is garish pinks and blinding greens. The effect on fashion makes clothes look something like patchwork quilts: Because dying cloth is now inexpensive, the bodice of a dress is likely to be one color; the trimming another; and the skirt itself, a third. Invented names for the colors result in the whimsical: nile-water; mignonette seed; amorous toad; spider meditating crime; and one name that couldn't be applied to anyone bold enough to wear these colors—frightened mouse.

1858 THE NEW YORK SYMPHONY ORCHESTRA GIVES ITS FIRST PUBLIC CONCERT.

1859 CHARLES DARWIN SHOCKS HUMANITY WHEN HE PUBLISHES HIS VERSION OF ITS FAMILY TREE, *ON THE ORIGIN OF SPECIES BY NATURAL SELECTION.*

FOR WHAT IT'S WORTH

The story of Charles Worth, creator of French haute couture, is a true rags-to-riches fable. He begins working at age thirteen in the drapery department of a rundown London department store, and arrives in Paris eight years later, to seek his fortune, with barely five pounds in his pocket. Undaunted, Worth promptly lands a job with a classy ready-to-wear tailor, Maison Gagelin, marries a pretty shopgirl, and parlays this into the start of a brilliant career. He sends his wife, all decked out in dresses he's designed, to call on the tailor's clients. "Where did you get that dress?" everyone wants to know. Worth's following grows quickly, and a Swedish merchant bankrolls him so he can start his own business. Worth's big break comes when Princess Metternich, captivated by his designs (and his prices—half off for royalty), wears a Worth gown to a ball given by the Empress Eugénie. "Where did you get that dress?" asks the empress; with the answer to that magical question, Worth's future is set.

To Charles Worth, whose grand ego once leads him to compare himself to Delacroix, Napoleon, and God— all in one quote—this is a natural turn of events. Certainly there have been fashion designers before Worth: one need only remember Rose Bertin's sway over the raiments of Marie Antoinette. But before Worth, most so-called fashion designers have been of the "little dressmaker" variety—comparatively humble, visiting ladies in their homes. Throughout his reign, Worth—an Englishman, no less!—dictates what fashionable Parisian women will wear. And except for the occasional princess, his clients come to him and line up patiently in his salon, hoping the great designer will allow them to buy something. He also influences the designs of great jewelers, according to his son-in-law Louis Cartier, who credits Worth with "helping me visualize jewels as ornaments."

The boy has moxie. Surely in today's culture, which so richly rewards its greats in ways Worth never dreamed of, Charles Worth would have wangled himself an American Express commercial and a glossy Dewar's ad on the back of a prominent magazine.

Above: Yachting costume by Worth, Harper's Bazaar cover, 1894. **Right:** *Worth evening dress, 1894, worn by Mrs. Stanford White, with a concealed maternity panel.* **Far right:** *Charles Fredrick Worth, 1864.*

288

CHARLES WORTH

JOB: Creating the haute couture

MOST NOTABLE ACCOMPLISHMENTS: Prepared collections in advance to show to his clients. For the first time, women can *see* the dresses they're ordering. • Hired mannequins to model clothes. Called "doubles," they are not chosen for their beauty, but, cannily, for their likenesses to Worth's best clients (which recalls his third most notable accomplishment—the subtle lighting of his salon). • Made satin popular again. • Got rid of all the ruffles, embroidery, ribbons, lace, and other geegaws that women up until this time gussied up their dresses with. • Got women to throw away their crinolines by designing a crinolineless dress that was gathered in the back. • Made the tailored suit, with a skirt and jacket in the same color, popular.

LATEST ACHIEVEMENT: Creates a sensation with a skirt called a *polonaise* that covers a petticoat, but is draped so as to show off the petticoat. (Did he simply borrow an idea from the previous century? Certainly not! The inspiration for this gown, says the master, was Worth's washerwoman, who tucked up her skirt at the waist to avoid dirtying it.)

LAST BOOK READ: *Who's Who in Royalty*

MOST MEMORABLE QUOTE: "I am an artist. I have the color sense of Delacroix and I create. A dress is equal to a painting. In every artist there is a Napoleon. Art is God; the bourgeois are made to take our orders."

And, since egotists are allowed *two* quotes: "I dethrone the crinoline."

HEART ATTACK: Sent in 1859 to woo Napoleon III's support in Italy's battle against Austria, Countess Castiglione appears at a masquerade ball in a black satin dress of extreme decolletage with a jeweled heart perilously placed between her breasts. "Madame, your heart is too low," the jealous Empress Eugénie remarks. But Napoleon disagrees, and aids in the Italian triumph—proving conclusively that Castiglione's heart is in just the right place.

Left: *Countess Castiglione, holding a frame as a mask, photograph by Mayer & Pierson, ca. 1860.*

DESIGNING WOMAN? In 1859 the first paper patterns for clothing are sold. Their male American creator cashes in on the snob appeal of all things French by calling them "Mme. Demoreset's Mirror of Fashions." It works. Patterns for cloaks (37 cents), infants' clothes (12 cents), and "fancy dresses" ($1.00), are snapped up by American women.

Before patterns, clothes are cut to size in one of two ways: a new garment is made either by copying an old one or tailor made-to-measure by basting a rough shape of the garment cut from muslin on the wearer, and reworking it until the seamstress gets the fit right.

Paper patterns, made in standard sizes, make this whole process so much easier and more economical that they are immediately popular. And chic, too. Queen Victoria sends to America for Butterick patterns to have suits made for her sons.

Above, left to right: *Demorest pattern illustration for a misses' costume, 1881; boy's suit shown in Harper's Bazar, 1859; little girls' formal dress, Demorest's Magazine, 1866.* Opposite page: top left: *The Source, Gustave Courbet, 1868;* right: *Illustration of a carriage dress, 1873.*

ANATOMY OF A VICTORIAN

What modern, twentieth-century, liquid-dieting woman hasn't dreamt of returning to the Victorian era—when, even if women had fewer accomplishments, they were well rounded? We're talking about statuesque women like Jennie Churchill and Lillie Langtry. These were the days when mothers chased after scrawny daughters crying, "Essen, mine kind"; when girth was a gift; when corpulent was admiringly equated with "opulent."

But as the old saying goes (probably never more appropriately applied), "There's no such thing as a free lunch." The Victorian woman needs this extra weight to help support the burden of her costume. "A properly dressed woman," reads an etiquette book of the day, "must be dressed in a minimum of seven pounds of clothing." But with up to ten petticoats; a hoop skirt or crinoline; a long, boned dress adorned with hundreds of beads; and a hat decorated with flowers, ribbons, veiling, *and* feathers, her excess baggage is a lot closer to thirty pounds. Her neck is encased in a high collar (which hides her double chins), and her hands are tucked into a fur muff. Because she's not supposed to have any legs she also develops a peculiar gait.

HOW TO WALK LIKE A VICTORIAN LADY

1. Use mincing steps.
2. Put your right foot in front of your left, your left foot in front of your right.
3. Repeat as often as necessary.
4. In case of emergency, don't run—faint.

1861 THE AMERICAN CIVIL WAR ERUPTS WHEN THE CONFEDERATE ARMY TAKES FORT SUMTER IN SOUTH CAROLINA.

1861 RAIN TODAY, SHOWERS TONIGHT, POSSIBILITY OF SHOWERS TOMORROW: DAILY WEATHER FORECASTS ARE BEGUN IN BRITAIN.

SUIT-ABLE

Any trendsetter tracking the "vogue mode" of the Cavaliers should have seen it coming. After all, that fashionably elongated silhouette—those long breeches and sleek doublet—could only lead to one thing: the *suit*. By the eighteenth century the doublet has been shortened and evolves into a jacket-like coat, and a waistcoat or vest is added. When post-French Revolution radical chic makes it politically incorrect to be seen in rich attire, knee breeches, a symbol of the aristocracy, disappear, and by 1800, trousers are ankle-length.

By modern definition, a suit consists of a matching jacket and trousers, and occasionally a vest. But these first "suits" are made from a mix of materials: Striped brown trousers, a bottle-green silk jacket, a flowered waistcoat, perhaps. And while today a suit is most likely seen in an office,

these first suits aren't worn as business attire—as you can tell by their name: lounge suits. The cut is loose, bordering on baggy, and they are intended for country wear. Because country lounge suits are also worn for horseback riding, tailors often slit the jacket up the back—a feature that remains today. The suit's lapel hole has practical virtues as well—truly a buttonhole, a man can turn up his collar against the wind on cold days.

By midcentury it becomes fashionable to have all parts of the suit made out of one fabric. And by the end of the century, the matching suit has become standard male attire.

What happened to the peacocks of yore? Why did men surrender their

floppy lace collars, their luxurious purple silk tunics, their satiny blue pantaloons, for a jacket, a vest, and a pair of pants? Blame the same Industrial Revolution which makes suits affordable for the fading away of flamboyant clothing. Solidarity and sobriety are the order of the day in an office, not gay colors.

So while men enjoy some variation in the waist, length, and width of a pair of pants, the suit trouser becomes an unchanging male staple. And the waistcoat just becomes smaller and smaller as the century wears on. There is one glimmer of hope, though—the jacket—which becomes a place where a nineteenth century man can truly express himself:

• Cut straight across the front with knee-length tails at the back, the *tail coat*, available in bottle green, navy, and tobacco brown has large lapels, a

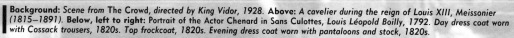

Background: *Scene from The Crowd, directed by King Vidor, 1928.* Above: *A cavelier during the reign of Louis XIII, Meissonier (1815–1891).* Below, left to right: *Portrait of the Actor Chenard in Sans Culottes, Louis Léopold Boilly, 1792. Day dress coat worn with Cossack trousers, 1820s. Top frockcoat, 1820s. Evening dress coat worn with pantaloons and stock, 1820s.*

Far left: *Formal wool dress coat with a velvet collar, c. 1845.* **Left:** *French men's fashions, 1836.*

trousers. It is single-breasted, with a small, high-buttoned collar, and being somewhat shapeless, it is dubbed the *sack coat.* You'll recognize it because it is like the better suit jackets still worn today. Black and gray are popular colors during the Industrial Revolution, since there is lots of soot around.

Jackets become more colorful in the twentieth century (see *The Official Preppy Handbook* from this publisher, for the truly remarkable dress of a native American tribe) and, occasionally, the suit takes on an exaggerated form (see ZOOT—pg 362). But for the most part, a suit is a suit.

high collar, and fitted sleeves. By mid-century it is most often seen at the best parties, in black velvet.

• By the 1820s and '30s, as women's upper bodies swell with gigantic padded sleeves, men feel compelled to keep pace. Now their chests balloon out, pinched from below by tight corsets, and their biceps get a boost from leg-of-mutton sleeves that narrow to knuckle-grazing cuffs. These *frock coats* reach the knee in front—more flattering to manly torsos—and they soon, well, defrock the tail coat as daytime apparel. They also have a vented back, making them more suitable for sports activities. For trips to town, or to Sunday church, it's caddish to wear anything but your frock or morning coat.

• The *cutaway* is another coat with tails, but it is single-breasted, high-cut in front and dropping back to shorter, more rounded tails. More formal than the frock coat, less formal than the tail coat, it is available in black or gray.

• The *morning coat*, single-breasted, with three or four buttons and an outside pocket, is "dressy without being formal, stylish without being stiff,"

according to an 1897 edition of *Tailor and Cutter.* It sits between the popular lounge and the dressier frock. It probably is also what your cousin Morris wore to his wedding last summer.

• In the 1850s a short black coat is worn with plaid, striped, or checkered

Right: *The Earl of Dalhousie, John Singer Sargent, 1900;* **Inset:** *Hart, Schaffner & Marx advertisement, 1897.*

1862 POPULATION: RUSSIA, 76 MILLION; ITALY, 25 MILLION.

1862 SHE WAS DIVINE: SARAH BERNHARDT MAKES HER DEBUT AT THE COMÉDIE FRANÇAISE.

PRINTS OF

While the industrial revolution heralds progress to some, others see it as the forebear, literally, of bleak times. In contrast to the ugliness of the machine world, these "Pre-Raphaelites," as they become known, urge a spiritual return to medieval ideals of beauty: pride in craftsmanship, and a recognition that the decorative arts are as important as painting and sculpture, the so-called "fine arts."

Englishman William Morris is renowned for so many talents—as a poet, artist, designer, social reformer, printer—that it almost seems appropriate to dub him a "Renaissance Man." But his heart is in the Middle Ages, and as a leading Pre-Raphaelite, in 1861 he founds Morris and Company, creating carvings, stained glass, tapestries, carpets, chintzes, furniture, and wallpaper. Morris's romantic floral designs are so popular that they are still being produced in the twentieth century, perhaps beloved more than ever in the post-modern age for their pre-industrial motifs.

1863 LONDON DIGS IN TO CREATE ITS UNDER-GROUND TRANSIT SYSTEM.

1863 EDDIE CUTHBERT OF THE PHILADELPHIA KEYSTONES STEALS THE FIRST BASE IN BASEBALL AGAINST THE BROOKLYN ATLANTICS. HE DOES NOT GIVE IT BACK.

THE CITY

GATOR AIDE

The year is 1863. The Civil War rages, and supplies of everything are scarce. The last cows have been slaughtered and eaten; there is no more beef, and no more cowhide. Stalwart Confederate president, Jefferson Davis, devises a plan. He dispatches a special brigade of troops to the muddy Mississippi swamps. They wrest their bounty and complete the mission, returning with batches of alligator skins. The southern cavalry can now be outfitted with stirrups, bridles, belts, and shoes made from the exotic leather.

Egyptian princes draped alligator skins around their bodies as talismans and Marco Polo heard the best of alligator-skin drums when he visited China. Alligator is the most durable leather in the world—like the tortoise's shell, the alligator's undulating skin armors him, never shedding or wearing out. And if at last the Confederacy doesn't have a leg to stand on, Confederate soldiers do—they each walk away with a solid pair of shoes.

DRESSED TO KILL

THE CIVIL WAR: At first, Civil War uniforms are helter-skelter, because everyone assumes the war will be over soon. So, any kind of coat, shirt, pantaloons, and cap or straw hat will do for either side. But as time goes on, sentiments (and garments) change.

The New Orleans regiment dons pale blue braided jackets, pants with light gray and red stripes, and red caps. The Union Army wears flannel shirts and pants with a visored hat. But soldiers in the Union's First Battalion of Rifles wear dark green jackets and trousers with light green trim, while the 14th Brooklyn New York State Militia wear blue jackets with red pantaloons. All Union soldiers do get together on one thing, though: they wear a *kepi*—a sort of squashed cap—a leather belt, and epaulets on their jackets.

An 1862 patent for sewing uppers to soles helps hasten the supply of boots to the army. The need for uniforms during the Civil War coincides with the availability of new methods of factory production, and they become the first mass-produced clothes produced in volume. And now that the clothes are not hand-measured and tailored, the need for thousands and thousands of mass-produced uniforms makes manufacturers realize the need for—and makes them develop—standard sizes in men's and women's clothing. Before sizes are standardized, unless a dress or a suit is made-to-measure, a prospective buyer just looks at a rack of clothes and chooses two or three garments that look "about right" and tries them on.

Top left: *Alligator bag in Montgomery Ward's 1884 catalogue, priced at $8.00.* **Center:** *New York's Seventh Regiment parades in Washington Square, 1851.* **Above:** *Private Francis E. Brownell, 11th New York Infantry, known as the Fire Zouaves.*

Above: *Elizabeth Taylor in* National Velvet, *1944.* **Background:** *The Water Jump, J. Charlton, Harper's Weekly, 1881.*

YOU'RE GETTING TO BE A HABIT WITH ME

From the American cowboy to the twelve-year-old heroine of *National Velvet,* anyone who can master a horse seems master of his own fate. The ability to ride a horse—especially in the days before the automobile—has always been associated with freedom and independence.

So it's not surprising that women who rebel against the prudish dictates of the Victorian era express their rebellion through a passion for horsemanship. "La Lionne" or the "Amazon Woman" (named after the legendary warlike race of Greek women) can ride like a Lancer and handle a whip. And her riding costume becomes a symbol of her independent spirit.

Correct female riding attire consists of a man's top hat with veil, a man's tie and collar, a man's coat (wasp-waisted and minus the tails), masculine trousers worn under a very long skirt, and boots. Women ride only sidesaddle until the early twentieth century and, rebellious or not, they dare not wear breeches sans skirt until after World War I.

Of course if "La Lionne" actually goes riding, the skirt undercuts her bid for independence, as it makes it almost impossible to dismount the horse without help from a groom. But if, like the famous woman writer George Sand, "La Lionne" merely dons the habit, her bold stance can strike fear in the heart of any man.

TAKE ME TO THE CASHMERE

On the high plateaus of inner Asia lives a band of temperamental mountain goats that produce the softest, warmest, strongest, lightest, costliest, and most luxurious wool: cashmere. These kashmir goats refuse to thrive anywhere else—take away the bad climate and the impossible terrain and give them a nice place to live and they produce lackluster wool. Once a year, only in the spring, nomadic tribesmen come to remove the goats' soft undercoats with primitive combs.

In the 1860s genuine cashmere shawls become all the rage (probably because, fashionwise, they complement and add a little warmth to the neo-Grecian gowns with their short sleeves and low necks that are in vogue). How popular are these shawls? Well, in 1883 *Le Journal des Dames and des Modes* reports the feat of a young man who dives into the Seine to save a drowning woman, deposits her on the shore, and then swims back to the middle of the river to rescue her cashmere shawl. And, at a royal cost of $8,000 in today's dollars, Empress Eugénie reigns supreme in majestic shawls so finely woven they could pass through the width of a wedding band.

Top left: *Print from a cashmere dress that Prince Albert had made for Victoria from the wool of her favorite goat.*

CELLULOID DREAMS

Plastic, the material and the pejorative for our century, is actually a Victorian invention. Introduced around 1850, vulcanite, or hard rubber, is used for tires, imitation jet jewelry and, despite the fact that it is usually black, to make false teeth.

In the 1860s, when a shortage of elephant tusks sends billiard-ball makers on a quest for a substitute material, New Yorker John Wesley Hyatt dreams up Celluloid. The would-be billiard balls unfortunately break on impact, but the tough, pliable, semi-synthetic plastic made from wood pulp and shellac is soon being used for buckles, combs, brushes and gemstone-inlaid jewelry. Celluloid collars and cuffs are especially practical (if a little awkward to wear) because they can be wiped clean. But celluloid is highly flammable and celluloid dentures soften in hot water. Still, celluloid ushers in the age of modern plastics—by the turn of the century, Bakelite, a less-flammable synthetic plastic (usually associated these days with old fashioned black telephones), will be on the market. Bakelite is used for everything from Fred Astaire's slick dance floor to chic Chanel bracelets. Later there will be plexiglass and nylon. And because Celluloid can be dyed to look like marble, coral, ivory, or even perfect imitation mother-of-pearl and tortoiseshell, from their earliest inception, plastics have been associated with inexpensive, practical alternatives to natural substances.

Left: *"Spider" celluloid comb, French, late 19th c.* **Above, clockwise from left:** *Plastic sunglasses, 1950s; plastic clock, early 1940s; Lady's hat in cellulose acetate, 1938; plastic-handled flatware, 1930s.*

SHOWING SUPPORT

It didn't take man long to think up the first umbrella, but it was to shield him from the sun, not the rain. Thirty-four hundred years ago a Mesopotamian slave would carry one over his master's head. (The word umbrella is derived from the Latin *umbra*, or shade.)

By Victorian times, a pretty parasol has a new use—as an ornament or, sometimes, a walking stick. If every cloud has a silver lining, so do these Victorian umbrellas: To cheer up Madame on a rainy day, her parasol is lined with frilly bows, lace, and ribbons. But of course that's just one in her wardrobe of parasols, because it is also de rigueur to carry one regardless of the weather. One Victorian letter writer recalls packing for the weekend, listing the parasols she must remember to take along: A practical, solid, simple one; a brightly colored parasol; a good colored silk to go with her best street costume; an airy one; and one decorated to match her afternoon gown.

Empress Eugénie used a parasol/walking stick, but it is generally agreed that trendsetting Alexandra, Princess of Wales, started the fashion in 1867. A rheumatic illness left the lovely Alexandra with a slight limp, and she used her heavy parasol to support her as she walked. We've often seen how royalty sets the fashion. And in this case, not only was Alexandra's parasol adopted, so was the limp!

Left: *At the Louvre, Edgar Degas, ca. 1879.*
Right: *Nike of Samothrace, 200 B.C., wearing Nike's Air Challenge tennis shoes.*

RUBBER SOUL

Although a patent for "attaching India Rubber soles to boots and shoes" is awarded to Wait Webster in 1832, it isn't until 1868 that canvas uppers and laces are added and the first sneaker steps into fashion. Called a "croquet sandal," it costs six dollars and, at first, is worn only by the very rich. By 1873 a sneaker is called a sneaker, and by 1900, Sears is selling them for sixty cents.

In 1917, U.S. Rubber introduces Keds—with a name conjured up from a combination of "ped" (Latin for "foot") and "kids" (the audience they're aiming at). While hemlines rise and fall, your basic sneaker remains in vogue for about fifty years, until University of Oregon running coach Bill Bowerman is making breakfast one day. Hoping to find a surface that will provide better traction on a sneaker, Bowerman uses his waffle iron to heat up a piece of rubber. The result? The first modern running shoe sole. In addition, Bowerman's Nikes—named after the Greek goddess of victory—feature three other innovations: a wedged heel, a cushioned mid-sole, and nylon tops.

UNDERALL

Don't go looking for satiny, silky, frilly undergarments in the men's department. Your favorite fop might don colorful jackets and flowery silk vests, but down under, he craves standard issue (leaving the arena of erotic undergarments and their sexual allure wide open, shall we say, to women). A pair of drawers (which look like long boxer shorts or cotton leggings) and a lambswool or merino undershirt-like vest in the winter will do him fine, thank you. By the end of the century men begin to wear B.V.D.'s—the brand name of a loosely fitting knee-length underwear suit. This replaces drop-seated woolen underwear, and is mass-produced beginning in 1863, thanks to a knitting machine that shapes while it weaves. Hardly the stuff of poetry.

Milady, on the other hand, wears any number of undergarments. And although they are fetchingly bowed and bedecked, they also obscure her figure.

Top left: *Parisian underwear advertisement, 1913.* Left center: *Advertisement for Allen-A men's underwear.* Above left: *boxer shorts from the 1950s.* Right: *Advertisement for Piccadilly Athletic Underwear, 1921.*

Top right: *Scene from French CanCan, directed by Jean Renoir, 1955.* Above: *One-piece undergarment, 1875.*

First comes the chemise, a straight, unshaped linen shift that doubles as a nightshirt. Nothing more appealing? you may ask. Well, remember: This is B.B.C.—Before Birth Control—and an unalluring nightgown is perhaps a calculated discretion; women cling to plain, shapeless garments. (After the introduction of birth control in the 1880s, there is a trend toward more beguiling nightwear, and Empire-style gowns of soft silk trimmed with lace and ribbons are fashionable.)

But back to daytime. Over the chemise comes a petticoat. And then another petticoat. And another. Heavily starched or made of crinoline, these petticoats swell her skirts to great dimensions. Down-stuffed sleeve puffs worn on her arms support the enormous sleeves of her dress and make Joan Collins's shoulder pads look like kid stuff. And, like the sleeve puffs, the padded linen roll she is apt to tie on to fill out her rear, is likely to slip out of place. Her corset, now cut in many intricately shaped pieces, is heavily boned along each seam; perhaps padded at the bosom.

*Above: Chemise with Valenciennes lace and a chemise with plaston. **Left**: lithograph, Style of Louis-Philippe, ca. 1830. **Below**: "Studies in the Toilette," Henri de Montaut in "La Vie Parisienne," 1881.*

*Above center: The Corset, N. Maurien, French lithograph, early 19th c. **Insets, top to bottom**: corset; haircloth hip-pad and bustle; Ladies' drawers; Ladies' muslin under-skirt with linen lace.*

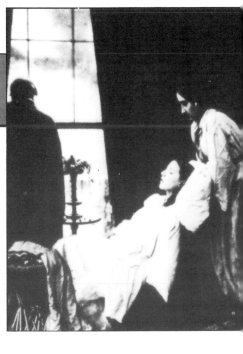

CONSPICUOUS CONSUMPTION

It should be no surprise to any of us who have suffered through pantie girdles, stiletto heels, or grapefruit diets that our great-great-grandmothers suffer from a similarly misguided ideal of beauty: In the nineteenth century, it is fashionable to appear ill.

Little Eva in *Uncle Tom's Cabin*, Beth in *Little Women* and Mimi in Puccini's *La Bohème* are all heroines who fade away gracefully. Women are taught to feign fatigue, which they equate with delicacy. Of course, since they are tightly corseted, rarely exercise, and eat improperly, their exhaustion might not be just an act.

❙ *Fading Away,* Henry Peach Robinson, 1858.

WAVE HELLO: In 1872 French hairdresser Marcel Grateau introduces a new wavy hairstyle. The "Marcel wave" is achieved by reversing curling tongs to produce a curl, rather than a crimp. The style remains in vogue until the permanent wave crimps *its* style in the 1920s and '30s.

Above: Advertisement for an automatic hair curler and waver, late 19th c. **Right:** Home hair dryer, 1940s. ❙

A BLAST FROM THE PAST: In the 1870s Alexander Godfrey invents the first hot-blast hair dryer. It'll be almost one hundred years before you whisk it off with you for a wonderful weekend in Watchitachi, though. Hardly portable, Godfrey's dryer weighs more than a full set of Louis Vuitton luggage, and is for commercial use only.

COWBOY CHIC

A STETSON: The high-crowned wide-brimmed felt hat, nicknamed "The Boss of the Plains," designed by Philadelphia hatmaker John B. Stetson. The Stetson will protect you from the blazing sun and the deep crevice in the hat's crown will keep you from being drenched during a downpour. It costs $20 (a lotta money for a dude only earning $30 a month), but it lasts a lifetime. Stetsons are available in black or white, so you can tell the good guys from the bad. We don't have to tell you which makes the best impression on a first date, do we? Save the white one for hoe-downs.

A BANDANA: folded and tied around the back of your neck with the triangle at the front. Nicknamed a "wipe," use it to soothe an overheated brow, to pull up over your nose on a long, dusty trail so you can breathe, as a disguise so you can play bandit, or to drop in front of a hot-looking honey so she can adoringly retrieve it.

A SHIRT WITH SNAPS: instead of buttons, so you can unfasten your shirt with only one hand while the other is firmly gripped around the horse's reins. Snaps are also handy when one hand is firmly gripped around a girl.

CHAPS: leather hides worn on top of your Levi's which will protect your thighs, and add a touch of animal magnetism to your outfit.

A METAL BELT BUCKLE: to strike a match and light up that obligatory cigarette, afterwards.

LEVI'S (see page 281).

A HORSE: Make sure you get one that complements your height. If you're 4'8" and you want to look "tall in the saddle," consider getting a pony. Also, pick a horse you're sure won't throw you. Getting thrown off your horse in front of a girl makes you look dumb.

In 1848 the U.S. acquires Nevada, Arizona, New Mexico, and California via a treaty with Mexico. In the same year, the California gold rush attracts thousands and thousands of fortune-seeking men. By the last quarter of the century the American West is rough and ready and *the* place for action. Enter the American cowboy—who rounds up herds of cattle, protects them from wild animals and thieves, and becomes a picturesque legend in his own time. Do you long for more rough and tumble times? Do you want to win the heart of a plains-clothed girl? It's easy with *cowboy chic.* Here's what you'll need:

BOOTS: with heels to hold your foot in the stirrup so you can stay astride.

Background: Bronco Buster, William H. Dunton (1878–1936). Right: Suburban cowpoke, 1961.

1880 THOMAS EDISON AND J. W. SWAN INDEPENDENTLY INVENT THE FIRST WORKABLE ELECTRIC LIGHTS.

(SOME OF) THESE SHOES ARE MADE FOR WALKING

In keeping with the classical simplicity of their dress, early nineteenth-century beauties favor dainty pumps or laced slippers usually with sexy, pointed toes. The styles may be simple, but the colors are bold, with turquoise and red vying with "classical" white and ivory for popularity. These shoes, however, are extremely delicate: In 1800, Josephine, Napoleon's empress, complains that hers developed a hole after only one wearing. "Ah, I see your problem," her shoemaker replies. "Madame, you have walked in them."

• At midcentury, decency requires that women's feet be heard and not seen. The endearment "My little angel" takes on new meaning when photographers erase women's shod feet from negatives—making them look, literally, like they are floating on air.

• For the first time, in 1865, "straights" are replaced by shoes designed to fit either the right or left foot, but not both. Machine made, they are also a lot more practical.

• A pair of front-laced polished shoes with patent leather tops wins the silver medal at the Grand Industrial Exposition of Manufacturers in 1872. The shoes, made by Stribley and Co. of Cincinnati, are sewn together with a record 287,816 stitches. They're finished within hours of the competition—perhaps inspiring the expression "A stitch in time."

Above: *Empress Josephine's coronation slippers, white taffeta embroidered in gold with popular bee motif, 1804.*

UNSUITABLE: In 1882 Oscar Wilde tours America wearing the "Little Lord Fauntleroy," a look that becomes popular with mothers of young boys—a black velvet jacket, knickers, white blouse with a Vandyke collar, colored sash, silk stockings, pumps, oversized beret, and curls. Much to the relief of children across the nation (who'd rather have worn Levi's, if they'd only known about them), after Wilde is jailed in 1895 the popularity of the suit dies down.

Far left: *Velveteen Lord Fauntleroy suit with a linen blouse, ca. 1885.* **Left:** *Illustration by Reginald Birch for* Little Lord Fauntleroy, *written by Frances Hodgson Burnett, 1886.*

DRESSED TO KILL

SITTING BULL is no sitting duck, as Custer's regiments can tell you after Little Big Horn. A Sioux with clout, he stands up to the white man's "bull" wearing a long white shirt, two white feathers fastened to a band wrapped around his head, long beaded braids, dark baggy pants, and white slippers.

The nicest-looking bank robber you ever want to see, **JESSE JAMES** is the quintessential milk-fed boy, with blond, smooth-cut hair, clear blue eyes, and small white hands. When he's not dressing up like a Ku Klux Klan member to rob a train, he dons a shirt, a cravat, and a nattily trimmed waistcoat; or, when working on his mom's Missouri farm, he can be seen in loose shirt and pants.

Dark haired, athletic, and romantically handsome, **JOHN WILKES BOOTH** causes many a lady to swoon—especially when he's emoting as Romeo to her Juliet. Dressed to the nines with gloves, a handkerchief in his breast pocket, patterned tie, and trim jacket, he always looks distinguished. But he really stands out in the crowd this fateful night in April, when, sporting a derringer, he jumps into President Abraham Lincoln's theater box and kills him.

On an oppressive, foggy night in November, **JACK THE RIPPER** slithers out to claim yet another victim. How is he dressed? In semi-genteel fashion, in dark waistcoat and pants, with his treacherous knife hidden perhaps in his pocket, or carefully tucked under his voluminous cravat.

SCALED-DOWN

An enterprising Egyptian invents the first scale in 5000 B.C.—a balance beam with equal arms. However, the Egyptians use the new device only to weigh material goods like lapis lazuli rings and gold collars, not people. Apparently no one was worth his weight in gold. Or lapis, or wheat or . . .

Many centuries later, in 1772, John Clais of London invents the dial weighing machine. The very first public weighing machine, based on his creation, is opened in Bath in 1799. In 1831 Vermonter Thaddeus Fairbank contributes the platform scale and Percy Everlitt weighs in with the first coin-operated scale on December 13, 1884. It is such a huge success that the scale finally takes its rightful place next to the fortune teller's booth at the circus. Today, the scale can be found in doctors' offices, posh health club locker rooms, and under bathroom sinks, collecting dust.

TIPS ON USING THE SCALE:

1. *Never wait on line to weigh in. It is a well-known fact that scales do not work when someone is looking over your shoulder at the dial.*

2. *Never get on a scale if you are in earshot of its last user—she just might be babbling, in a confused but delighted manner, "Gee, I thought I weighed more than that." Scales are like slot machines— every once in ten thousand times they make someone happy just to keep us coming back for more.*

3. *Always weigh yourself in the nude. Remove earrings and nail polish, and shave off all your body hair.*

4. *Weigh yourself while standing on tiptoe. Maybe that way you can avoid foot weight.*

The thinnest man in the world was Edward C. Hagner. Nicknamed the Skeleton Dude, he stood 5'7" and weighed only 48 pounds. The thinnest woman was a Mexican dwarf, Lucia Zarate. At the time of her seventeenth birthday she weighed only 4.7 pounds. She "fattened up" for her twentieth, with a chunky 13 pounds on her 18-inch frame.

The fattest man is a taxicab driver from Bainbridge Island, Washington, who once weighed in at 1,400 pounds. After a two-year 1,200-calorie diet he trimmed down to a svelte 476. But within seven days of stopping his diet, he gained back 200 pounds.

1943 advertisement for Vita-Kaps, a dieter's vitamin supplement.

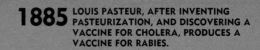

BAH, HOMBURG: Crazy as a loon, you can understand. But mad as a hatter? The expression refers to the insanity suffered by nineteenth-century hatters exposed to the mercury used in pressing felt. Employers try to keep this outrageous situation under *their* hats, but workers "put a bee in the bonnet" of public opinion. The first worker safety laws, in aid of hatters, are passed in 1885.

Above left: *Sir John Tenniel's illustration of the Mad Hatter from the 1865 edition of Alice's Adventures in Wonderland.* **Below:** *Jim Broadbent and his patient Katherine Helmond in* Brazil, *1985.* **Inset:** *Boris Karloff in* The Mummy, *1932.*

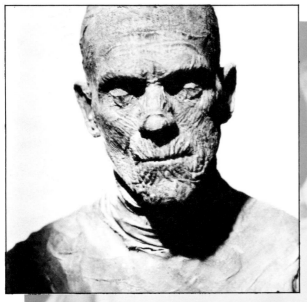

ABOUT FACE

If your face appeal seems to be sagging, by 1886 you can have a face *peel:* beauty parlor operators will apply acid and electric currents to remove the outer layer of skin. You can have paraffin injected under your eyes or to round out your cheeks. Can plastic surgery—or lawsuits—be far behind?

HOME DELIVERY: The first Avon lady is a man—David McConnell, a door-to-door book salesman who, in 1886, with the aid of a local pharmacist, mixes up a batch of perfume to be given away as a free introductory gift for allowing him to make his sales pitch. McConnell soon realizes that the books still aren't selling, but that women clamor for the perfume. He names the company Avon because his hometown of Suffern, New York reminds him of Shakespeare's Stratford-upon-Avon. He enlists the aid of Mrs. E. F. E. Albee, a New Hampshire widow, who becomes the first official female Avon lady.

▌ Above: Mrs. P. F. E. Albee, the first Avon lady, 1886.

HOW YA GONNA KEEP 'EM DOWN ON THE FARM?

Neither rain nor sleet will keep the postman . . . and now the fact that you live in Tuscaloosa is no excuse for not having the latest fashions. In the 1880s, Richard Warren Sears starts the Sears Watch Company. In 1887 he hires Alvah Roebuck, a watch assembler and repairman, and later that year, the first Sears Roebuck catalogue is born. Unlike the Sears of today, which sells Cheryl Tiegs's togs and washing machines, the first catalogue features what these toney gents know best: watches, diamonds, and other precious jewelry. Soon, however, it expands to include home supplies, equipment, and fashion. And by 1905 over two million readers eagerly await their copies of the Sears Roebuck catalog, which brings the big city to the country.

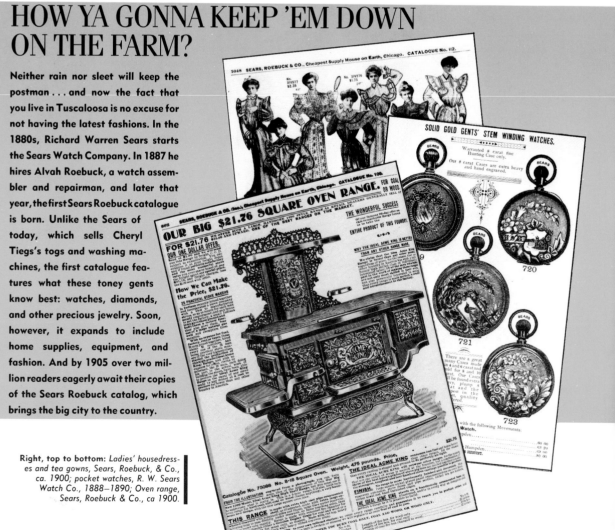

Right, top to bottom: Ladies' housedresses and tea gowns, Sears, Roebuck, & Co., ca. 1900; pocket watches, R. W. Sears Watch Co., 1888–1890; Oven range, Sears, Roebuck & Co., ca 1900.

WHERE THERE'S SMOKE . . .

Smoking Jackets: Think plush silk or velvet, double-breasted, shawl collar, sash belt. Getting it mixed up with the tuxedo? Let's add to the confusion. Nobody can quite figure out where the smoking jacket comes from (the silk jackets worn in Chinese opium dens?), but it does serve as the inspiration for the tuxedo. Hoping to escape from the stiffly formal tailed coat and white tie, back in the 1880s, the trendsetting Duke of Wales asks London tailor Henry Poole to modify a black smoking jacket into comfortable evening wear. When tobacco heir Griswold Lorillard wears this jacket to a posh party at the Tuxedo Park Country Club, the garment gets its name; although the French continue to call the tuxedo *un smoking*. Never mind. It's just that the tuxedo (which was meant to be less formal than a tie and tails) is the formal version of the smoking jacket, and now, for women, the smoking jacket is turning up at formal affairs.

Top right: *An original sketch for Yves Saint Laurent's woman's tuxedo, 1966.* **Above:** *A gentleman of leisure in a comfortable smoking robe and hat chats with a buttoned-up friend, 1830s.* **Left:** *Cary Grant, an unlucky producer promoting a dancing caterpiller, feigns success in a silk robe in Once Upon a Time, 1944.*

309

L a Belle Epoque is Russian dukes, dinner at Maxim's, madcap automobile races, lawn croquet, elegance, flirtation, champagne sipped from slippers, and a magnificent stage for the last gasp of the European aristocracy.

The Edwardian grande dame has servants to sew and launder her clothes, dress her, and to help pile her hair over "rat pads" to give it height. She changes her clothes at the drop of a hat (and at every change of activity) and must visit Paris at least twice a year for her fittings.

By the end of the century, the bustle is back and sleeves are voluminous and echo the flowing lines of Art Nouveau. Our grande dame is wearing draped and pleated satin, striped, or checkered linen by day. Her evening gowns, predominantly white, are cut daringly low at the bosom. Large hats, kid gloves, ornate necklaces with matching earrings that sometimes reach the shoulders, and parasols (for fashionable skin is always shielded from the sun) complete an outfit.

The Pre-Raphaelites, the Rational Dress Society, and probably even her husband wish she weren't so corseted and cosseted in clothes. Alas, she is waiting for Paris (or a turn in world events) to set her free.

Opposite page: left: *Nineteenth-century fashionplate of a garden-party frock;* **Center:** *Advertisement, 1890.* **Right:** *Royal Hunt Cup Day at Ascot, Hal Hurst, ca. 1900.* **This page: left:** *fashion photograph, ca. 1900.* **Below:** *sketch of designs by Mrs. Ralston, ca. 1900.*

BUSTLING OFF TO . . .

BOA-TING

In the 1890s, when huge Victorian sleeves make coats impractical, and deep decolletages expose ladies to a chill, some consider the latest fad to be simply a necessity. Still, members of the Society for the Protection of Birds are in a flap over the new narrow scarves, four or five feet long, made from hundreds of ostrich feathers each. These "boas" grimly recall the constrictor snake that winds itself around a victim's neck.

Just because Worth "dethrones" the crinoline, don't get the idea that women get to sit down easily. In comes the *bustle*. Fashion sense and sensibility now requires the wearing of a wire or whalebone cage which sweeps the fullness of a dress up toward the back. The first modified versions of the bustles are worn by French peasants in 1793—called *conforts*, no one confuses them with comfort. Bustles are at their largest in the 1880s; they get smaller by the 1890s, but stick around on more matronly figures until the first World War. At the height, so to speak, of their popularity, Lillie Langtry designs her own bustle: When you sit down its metal bands pivot up, and when you rise from your chair, the bands spring back into place.

Top: Officers and Ladies on Board H.M.S. Calcutta, *Tissot (1836–1902);* **Inset:** *advertisement for a bustle named after Lillie Langtry, 1877.*

On the average:
In 1890, the American female measures 36–22–40.

Above: *Advertisement for shirtwaists in the Montgomery Ward & Co. catalogue, 1895.*
Right: *The Judson slide fastener from 1891.*

SHIRTING THE ISSUE: By 1891, New York City's 472 clothing manufacturers are busy turning out *shirtwaists*—the single hottest selling item of American dress. Often having no mannequins on which to display them, these manufacturers stuff shirtwaists with paper and prop them up in store windows. They look sturdy, but they're actually as flimsy as the opinions of a pompous man—which is why he's called a *stuffed shirt.*

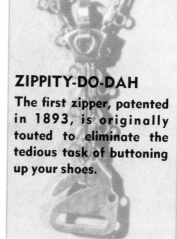

ZIPPITY-DO-DAH

The first zipper, patented in 1893, is originally touted to eliminate the tedious task of buttoning up your shoes.

TRAIL BLAZING

What late-nineteenth-century gentleman's sporting jacket is sported by women who dress for success eighty-five years later? The *blazer.* Made of flannel, loose fitting, and lightweight, the blazer is originally the preserve of English gentlemen who don it to compete in cricket and tennis matches and boating races. In fact, the term "blazer" is said to have originated back when Cambridge boat clubs tried to outdo each other in sartorial splendor. According to the story, members of the St. John's College boat team were triumphant in their sprightly red jackets—so much so that someone from a rival club remarked "Did you see that chap's jacket? Bit of a blazer, isn't it?"

The classic English blazer, which grazes the top of the thigh, has a bold or thin regimental stripe which proclaims a man's membership in a particular school or club. Around 1915, on this side of the ocean, men can buy a dark blue, single-breasted version of the jacket. During the 1920s, women appropriate the blazer, wearing it with pleated skirts and ties. And in the '70s, it becomes practically the required uniform for climbing the ladder of corporate success.

Right: *A nautical look, Polo by Ralph Lauren, 1980s;* Inset: *Brooks Brothers blazers, c. 1927.*

1887 SIR ARTHUR CONAN DOYLE WRITES *A STUDY IN SCARLET*, THE FIRST SHERLOCK HOLMES STORY.

1888 GEORGE EASTMAN PERFECTS THE KODAK BOX CAMERA.

THEY GAVE

• Long before Norma Kamali came along, actress Lillie Langtry, "The *Jersey* Lily," pours her voluptuous body into stretchy, skin-tight dresses, popularizing the material known ever since as "jersey." The dresses inspire a popular 1880s ditty: "She wore a jersey fitting/Like an eel skin all complete/With a skirt so tight that sitting/Was an agonizing feat." And they may have inspired a mini-marriage-boom as well, either as a result of their allure or of the fact that they are made without fasteners, and require the help of at least one other person to get into and out of them.

• Breech Birth: In the mid-nineteenth century, wide pants gathered just above the ankle bring her ridicule, but at the same time they immortalize the name of suffragette Amelia *Bloomer*. "Bloomers," which free

David Johansen, a.k.a. Buster Poindexter, affects a pompadour, c. 1989.

Above: Peter Stuyvesant's Army Entering New Amsterdam, *an illustration for Washington Irving's* History of New York, *1809.* **Left:** *Orson Welles wears a chesterfield coat in* Jane Eyre, *1943; and a Chesterfield cigarette package, 1951.* **Below:** *Bing Crosby in a Stetson hat.*

women from tight corsets and yards of petticoats, become a sign of women's liberation—ironic, when you consider that the first breeches were worn in 1,000 B.C. by Greek slaves, so they could be told apart from their chiton-clad landlords.

• In the eighteenth century the mistress of Louis XV, the Marquise de *Pompadour*, gives her name to a hairstyle.

• The Scottish clan of *Argyll* gives its name to multi-colored diamond-patterned socks based on their tartan.

• The seventeenth-century Flemish painter *Van Dyck* gives his name to a trim, pointed beard.

• The Duke of *Wellington*, victorious general of the battle of Waterloo, gives his name to a boot and to beef in pastry.

1888 THE FIRST MODERN BEAUTY CONTEST IS HELD IN SPA, BELGIUM.

1889 HITLER IS BORN.

THEIR NAMES

BEWARE OF IMITATIONS
BAKER HORSE BLANKET

Left: *Advertisement, ca. 1870.*

• And the *Chesterfield* family (pre-licensing agreements!) really spread around, giving their name to a couch, a double-breasted overcoat with a velvet collar, and a cigarette. The distinctive velvet collar is first worn by princes and noblemen who, fleeing France during the Revolution, sew black velvet strips onto their collars as an expression of mourning for Louis XVI.

• The high-crowned, wide-brimmed felt hat worn by cowboys, Marlboro men, and J.R. Ewing is designed by Philadelphia hat-maker John B. *Stetson* in the late 1800s.

• The first woven wool cover comes off the fourteenth-century loom of the enterprising Thomas *Blanket*.

• The light-colored scarlet coat worn by gentlemen members of a hunt is named after the nineteenth-century London tailor, *Pinkie*.

• Characters in Washington Irving's *A His-tory of New York*, published in 1809, are dressed in baggy breeches nicknamed after the pseudonym he uses for the book, *Knick-erbocker*.

• *Pantaloon* is the name of the foolish old man who wore these baggy trousers in the Italian commedia dell'arte which flourished from the sixteenth to the eighteenth centuries.

• A collar, popular in the 1920s, is named after *Peter Pan*, the James Barrie character who "won't grow up."

• And in the late eighteenth century, Scotsman Robert Burns becomes the only poet to have a hat named after the hero of his poem—one *Tam O'Shanter*.

Below: *Tam O'Shanter and the Witches, illustration by John Faed, ca. 1880.* Right: *A tam o'shanter.*

GIBSON GIRLS

In 1895 American illustrator Charles Dana Gibson creates a sensation—the tall, commanding Gibson Girl, who is a luscious babe with upswept hair, small mouth, snub nose, and large bosom and hips. The Gibson Gibson Girl is a "new woman": she looks strong and self-confident; her dress reflects feminist reforms; and if she is never pictured working, at least she participates in sports.

Confronted with such graphic proof of her fiancé's fantasies, it's no wonder svelte socialite Irene Langerhorn feels a little underendowed; so before slipping on her wedding gown for her marriage to Gibson, she pads her hips.

The model for Gibson's dream girl is said to be his sister, Josephine Gibson Knowlton. Clothes, and even dances are named "The Gibson." Barbie has Ken: Does the Gibson Girl have a Gibson Boy? Yes. But he never matches her in popularity.

Below: *The original Peacock Alley at the Old Waldorf-Astoria.*

A ROOM OF ONE'S OWN: By 1897 George Boldt, manager of the Waldorf-Astoria, has had it up to his boutonniere with clucking fashion plates who strut around dining rooms and up and down hotel corridors. In a bold move he gives them a room of their own—"Peacock Alley"—a special hallway where they can promenade to their hearts' content. (Today it is a bar.)

Clockwise from top left: *An Edwardian lady; Milady, C.D. Gibson, 1900; Charles Dana Gibson at his easel, 1902.*

LALIQUE CHIC

In response to the ever-increasing depersonalization of the Industrial Age, William Morris, Louis Tiffany, and other Pre-Raphaelites call for a return to the now-romanticized Middle Ages and Art Nouveau is born.

Art Nouveau jewelry—most notably from the workshops of René Lalique—is curved and romantic: flowing pins, necklaces, and bracelets are based on natural forms, often featuring butterflies, waving fronds, and nude figures. Denouncing ostentatious mid-Victorian jewelry, Lalique and his followers use milky opals and moonstones rather than diamonds and emeralds. But what about cashing in the jewels? The market for Art Nouveau jewelry zooms, and even today, it proves a wise investment.

Left: *Enamelled gold and glass anemone pendant by Lalique.* **Above:** *Dragonfly pin by Lalique, 1898.* **Right:** *Design for a cameo by Mayer & Pleuer, German, 1870.*

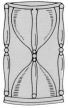

A JEWELRY BOX: In Napoleon III's France, women wear a *ferronniere*—a ribbon around the forehead, with a jewel in the middle of the ribbon. Matching jewelry also begins in the Empire period, when sets might include necklace, tiara, pin, bracelets, and earrings.

Jewelry throughout this century imitates ancient work—except for corals and cameos—in necklaces, pins, and earrings using motifs of flowers or animals or tiny people. Cameos also appear on bracelets—worn over gloves. There is lots of frou-frou jewelry: necklaces, bracelets, rings, brooches, in gold and enamel and jewels.

THE MILKY WAY: Why are armies of milkmen trooping up to actress Anna Held's New York hotel suite? In 1896 Held's husband, flamboyant showman Florenz Ziegfeld, calls in the press for a show-and-tell answer. Reporters find Held seductively immersed in a tubful of milk, claiming these daily soaks are the secret of her beauty—and anticipating Hollywood's teasing bubble bath scenes.

Sentimental jewelry is popular, made of the human hair of someone you love. Marie Louise, Douchess of Parma has a blond hair-bracelet made from a lock of her son's hair.

Men wear jeweled tie-pins. Their big cuffs in the eighteenth century make cufflinks popular, too, in gold with diamonds or silver or ivory. Men also wear trinkets and charms on watch chains.

WHEN THE THEATRE WAS FRAUGHT WITH ROMANCE
ANNA HELD'S MILK BATH
ENGRAVED BY JOHN HELD JR WHO IS NO RELATION

Left: *John Held, Jr., considered the leading graphic chronicler of the Jazz Age—he probably invented "The Flapper"—immortalized turn-of-the-century French starlet Anna Held in this 1930 scratchboard for* The New Yorker.

317

WEDDING BELLES

The nineteenth century is so obsessed with propriety that special clothes are designed for every occasion. Weddings are no exception, and it is now that the bridal gown we know today—a long white dress with a flowing veil—is born. Early nineteenth century gowns have sweeping trains, and by mid-century, they acquire high, prim necklines and long sleeves—symbols of virginity.

♥ For royal weddings, velvet and ermine remain the rage, but Queen Victoria, always an upstart, shuns them when she marries Prince Albert in 1840. Outraged observers deplore the "casualness of her dress," even though its lace alone costs more than one hundred pounds—eighty times the average English worker's yearly salary.

♥ For her marriage to Napoleon III in 1853 the Countess Eugénie comes up with a tall order: Incorporate the Imperial crown, a veil and a wreath of orange blossoms into her coiffure, she tells her hairdresser, Felix. He does, thus inaugurating the tradition of wearing orange blossoms (which are associated with fertility) to the altar.

♥ The wedding veil, long customary in Jewish weddings, becomes part of standard bridal wear around 1800. Early on, brides opt for simple, "classically" influenced veils that shrink to lacy, shoulder-length head coverings or bonnets by the 1850s. Around the 1870s, the bridal veils we know today—long and streaming, made of transparent net, lace, or tulle—finally become a fixture.

♥ In our own time, marriage has gone in and out of style, but the tradition of white weddings remains. In the 1960s, to comment on its endurance, Yves St. Laurent designs a decidedly unconventional wedding ensemble. In 1966, he creates a bride *as* bouquet—her torso is wrapped in white organdy adorned with flowers, while her legs serve as the stalks. His pop art bride wears a lily appliqued on her dress, with a light bulb blooming just below her chin.

Not every culture is willing to settle for white, of course:

♥ In northern India, brides wear red and yellow to ward off demons. They personally prepare their grooms' clothes—making sure to pleat the lower central portion of the robe which covers the genitals, to ward off evil spirits.

♥ Tunisian girls squeeze into whatever they can—they're fattened up before the wedding.

♥ Malayan brides are so heavily decked out in gold and silver jewelry that they can't walk (or run away).

♥ A nineteenth-century Japanese bride *does* wear white. But instead of a thin white veil, she wears a thick cover made of floss silk, hiding her face, which has been smothered in rice bran and painted white. Her lips are red and—very important—her teeth are black. Why? To offset the paleness of her face, or, more likely, to diminish her beauty so she can never leave her husband.

♥ In many eastern nations, a man and woman who wished to be married simply went before the patriarch of the community. After he gave his blessing, he would take the edges of their sleeves or two corners of their robes, and then *tie the knot*.

Opposite page: bottom left: *Queen Victoria's wedding on February 10, 1840, engraving after a painting by Sir George Hayter;* Bottom right: *1950s bride and groom.* This page: top left: *Elvis and Priscilla Presley, May 1, 1967;* Top center: *1922 wedding announcement photo;* Top right: *Illustration of Miss Haversham by F. W. Pailthorpe for an early edition of Charles Dickens's Great Expectations;* Bottom left: *Post-Valentine's Day bride Marian Rosenthal Edelman, 1948;* Bottom center: *The Marriage Feast (detail), Marc Chagall, 1973;* Bottom right: *Japanese woodblock print, c. 1800.*

THE
TWENTIETH
CENTURY

THE TWENTIETH CENTURY

BACK TO THE FUTURE

It's a brave new world. In one century we go from riding down cobblestoned streets in horse-drawn carriages to flying across the Atlantic in supersonic jets; from writing with crow-quill pens to communicating through fax lines; from shouting to neighbors across a picket fence to talking to Japan from the back seat of a car. No other century has seen so many innovations, so much change, or enjoyed as much freedom as the one we live in now.

Sears, Roebuck and Co. Chicago

Victoria is dead, and with her, Victorian repression. The world is young; everything seems fast and new. The upstart American nation is in its second century—a mere babe in the woods—but as European empires decline and America gains ascendency, a youthful American spirit pervades science, technology, and eventually, for the first time in history, even fashion. The motor car, ocean liner, prêt-à-porter, and Sears Roebuck and Co. all bring people closer to fashion. It is the century in which zippers and pantyhose will be invented; we will get bras, and later, burn them.

At the beginning of the century, the matronly Edwardian Grande Dame still reigns, but she—and her archaic S-shaped figure—are soon supplanted by a youthful post-World War I slenderness. Renowned architect Frank Lloyd Wright designs houses with clean lines and by 1910 women's clothes assume the basic shape they will maintain for the rest of the era—a clean, straight vertical.

Paul Poiret creates this linear silhouette, as he frees women from the corset (even if he does have them "hobbling" around in skirts which virtually bind their ankles). Colors are brilliant and inspiration is everywhere—Chinese, Oriental, and Russian motifs abound. There are telephones, electricity, and anything

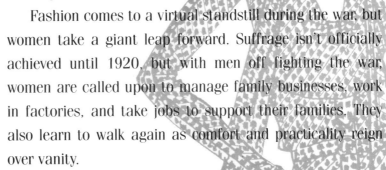

seems possible. Until the First World War.

Fashion comes to a virtual standstill during the war, but women take a giant leap forward. Suffrage isn't officially achieved until 1920, but with men off fighting the war, women are called upon to manage family businesses, work in factories, and take jobs to support their families. They also learn to walk again as comfort and practicality reign over vanity.

When the war is over, everyone wants to forget. Jazz babies celebrate the Roaring Twenties with short skirts, lots of leg, bobbed hair, and bound breasts. Fashions are youth-oriented—older matrons try to imitate their flapper daughters who have rouged knees and raccoon-coated boyfriends. (This is a trend that will be repeated in the '60s when "Never-Trust-Anyone-Under-30" Baby Boomers set the trends.)

Then suddenly the Great Depression hits with a crash and the good times are gone. It's *The Grapes of Wrath* rather than a chicken in every pot; *An American Tragedy* replaces the American Dream. Muckrakers expose big

business scandals; painters paint realistic pictures. As if in eerie anticipation of the market's fall, skirt lengths go down just before the crash. Among the hoi polloi, hand-me-downs become fashionable, and if there's any new trend at all, it's towards classic skirts and dresses meant to last. It's the age of Chanel and classic, comfortable lines. Mainbocher and Molyneux celebrate the simple in extravagant execution; Schiaparelli and her surrealistic hats and clothes and glittery Hollywood costumes offer escape. But then a world war comes for the second time, and wartime austerity demands restrictions—hems can be only two inches deep; only one

Page 132: *Chrysler Building, New York City.* **Opposite page: top:** City Activities with Dance Hall, *Thomas Hart Benton, 1930;* **bottom left:** cover illustration of the Spring/Summer 1927 Sears & Roebuck catalog by Norman Rockwell. **This page: top left:** *Suffragette marching in a protest, 1917;* **right:** design by Molyneux, 1920s; **above:** coffin of Queen Victoria, 1901; **left:** 1930s Packard.

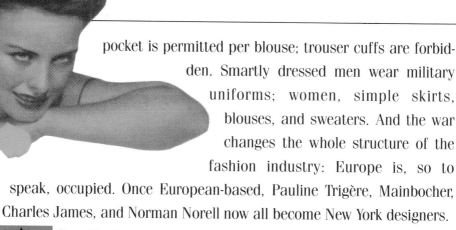

pocket is permitted per blouse; trouser cuffs are forbidden. Smartly dressed men wear military uniforms; women, simple skirts, blouses, and sweaters. And the war changes the whole structure of the fashion industry: Europe is, so to speak, occupied. Once European-based, Pauline Trigère, Mainbocher, Charles James, and Norman Norell now all become New York designers.

After World War II Dior creates a revolution by unleashing his "New Look"—dresses which use yards and yards of material—a voluptuous response to the years of war-forced restrictions. In America it's an age of innocence: Eisenhower is president. It's the era of bobby soxers and poodle skirts; true love is found with "the girl next door," and "The Man In The Grey Flannel Suit" works in your office. Claire McCardell makes clean-lined comfort a national pastime.

The '60s see another fashion revolution, but very different than the one imposed by Dior. The effects of World War II on fashion are still reverberating as the Baby Boomers—now the largest segment of the population—come of age. This time, it is the people who dictate fashion. And, the majority of the people being young, fashions are mini, hip, and psychedelic: Gypsy princesses, hippies, and Dr. Zhivago "Lara" look-alikes make the decade look like one big costume party. The First Lady of the

Clockwise from top left: *A woman with her favorite twentieth century invention, the telephone, in a 1943 advertisement; the simple lines of a Frank Lloyd Wright prairie house, here the Frederick C. Robie House, Oak Park, Illinois, 1906-1909; a depression-era cabin in Jackson, Mississippi; American women are an integral part of the war effort, here a uniformed member of the Women's Voluntary Service, 1942.*

United States is only thirty-four, and even "conservative" fashions are kicky.

The '70s witness a continuation by designers like Yves St. Laurent of '60s fantasy fashion; the pantsuit; and a schizophrenic split between punks, preppies, and disco fever. The '80s get down to business, body consciousness, and the Japanese: By 1982, no fewer than twelve Tokyo designers are making names for themselves in Paris. Wren-like fashions from Romeo Gigli, "pouf" couture from Christian Lacroix, and ethnic à la Alaïa fashions from designer of the moment Rifat Ozbek all have their impact on the mid to later part of the decade. As we enter the nineties, a new ease and comfort is finally taking hold. Still, when all is said and done, it's just as hard as ever to decide what to wear every morning.

Top right: *Genevieve Waite in Move, 1970.* **Right:** *Suit by Louis Dell'Olio for Anne Klein & Co., 1990.* **Below:** *Jacqueline and John F. Kennedy, October 1963.*

1900 A TRADITION IS BORN AS WILLIAM MULDOON IS NAMED THE FIRST PROFESSIONAL WRESTLING CHAMPION.

IF THE SUIT FITS

The century opens to the strains of Offenbach and La Belle Epoque. Society women are still traveling with eighteen trunks, changing their clothes innumerable times a day, and parading down the Bois de Boulogne. But while diehard fashion victims are swathed in feather boas, corseted into hourglass figures, and capped off with hats toppling over with false fruit and stuffed birds, by the early 1900s more and more women begin to earn their livings as governesses, typists, and shop assistants. The "tailor-made," a coat and skirt worn with a blouse, popularized in the 1880s by the English tailor Redfern, becomes fashionable, worn even by non-working women when they travel, or are in the country. Correct accessories are doeskin or suede gloves and plain boots with heels of moderate height. French bonnets look too fussy: one tops off the outfit with a fedora, or, in the summer, a straw boater.

Men are suitably attired in a vest, high-collared starched shirt, ankle-length pants, knee socks held up by suspenders, overcoat, and hat. Boring, but get used to it.

A BLOUSE BY ANY OTHER NAME: Much to the chagrin of dressmakers, the blouse becomes more and more popular. Some are elaborate confections with fluted muslin collars and delicate trimmings; gone are the "balloon" sleeves of the 1890s, replaced by a simpler, more elegant sleeve that is tight at the wrist. Expensive imported French blouses become all the rage in America. In 1910, one enterprising entrepreneur buys thousands of discarded Parisian labels: The woman on a budget can simply sew one into her Sears special.

Top left: *Ladies promenading in Newport, Rhode Island, ca. 1905;* Top right: *Suit by Redfern, 1893.* Left: *Shirtwaist in Scotch madras, designed by John Forsythe, 1909.*

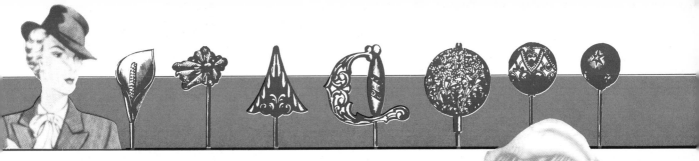

HATS OFF

In 1903 the *Hatter's Gazette* reports that the custom of touching the brims of their hats (bowlers, wide-brimmed felt hats, boaters, and panamas) as a sign of respect is "fast falling into disuse between gentlemen." While it has never been the custom for women to remove their hats, in 1907 when Sarah Bernhardt buys her own theater, one of her first acts is to ban hats because they obstruct the theatergoer's view of the stage—and of the actress upon it.

Hat wearing is all right on the other side of the footlights, though. When Bernhardt stars in a drama by Parisian Victorien Sardow in 1882 she wears a felt hat with a center crease that takes on the name of the play—*Fedora*. Bernhardt wears it offstage as well, and in America the name sticks to the homburg, a hat popular throughout the century for men.

The picture hats of the late nineteenth century are echoed in the extravagant cartwheels of the time, which are crowned with plumes, flowers, and yards and yards of ribbons. Also popular are "leghorn" hats made of straw, imported from Livorno (Leghorn), Italy, which are held in place by long hatpins that also serve another purpose—combatting muggers.

Top left: *1926 fedora.* **Top center:** *Hatpins of silver plate, sterling, gold plate, and tinted moonstone.* **Top right:** *Leghorn, 1907.*

GIVE THEM THE SLIP

At the turn of the century extravagant lingerie is a staple of a well-dressed woman's wardrobe. Madam spends one-fifth of her clothing allowance on lace-trimmed petticoats of satin, brocade, or silk in blue, pink, yellow, and even black. By 1902 it is considered vulgar for petticoats (even if they are *seen*) to be heard, and although some still prefer the rustling sound of a stiff silk or taffeta slip, silent petticoats of softer material are considered chic. In 1904 the Floradora sextette translates these fashions to the stage. Their dresses of lavender silk are lined with ruffles so they can teasingly lift them during their frou-frou number. It is reported that all six Floradoras marry millionaires.

In the 1920s, when Belle Epoque proportions yield to boyishly flapper fashions, Theodore Baer invents the "teddy." It follows the camisole in form, but not function. While the camisole was worn between a corset and dress as a sort of protective layer, the teddy stands alone.

Left: *Advertisement for ladies' slips, in the May 1919 issue of Ladies Home Journal.* **Right:** *Promotional picture for Busby Berkeley's spectacular, Gold Diggers of 1933.*

1901 IT'S THE END OF AN ERA: QUEEN VICTORIA DIES THIS YEAR.

1902 BEATRIX POTTER WRITES THE FIRST OF HER BELOVED PETER RABBIT STORIES.

IN THE SWIM

Although the idea was there for the taking to anyone who bothered to look at a fourth-century Roman mosaic, the two-piece bathing suit isn't introduced until fifteen hundred years later. Then, in 1954, when Paris designer Louis Reard comes up with the idea, he is stumped by what to call his new creation. Inspiration (and a good publicity idea) strike, however, on July 31st of the same year, when the United States drops an atom bomb in the Pacific Ocean. Reard immediately names his explosive swimsuit for the site of the bomb blast: Bikini Atoll.

Bikinis today are a common sight, and they show up (and off) in such scanty styles that in Brazil and Portugal, where the bikini's bottom half may be no wider than a strand of dental floss, that's what they're nicknamed. But even if designers had resurrected the bikini sooner, would-be bathing suit manufacturers of *any* styles would have gone broke: Prior to the early 1800s, almost no one ever goes swimming.

By the turn of the nineteenth century, however, "taking the waters" becomes a popular cure-all for whatever ails you, and suddenly thousands are bathing in costumes that look like street clothes: dresses with fitted bodices, high necks and elbow-length sleeves, stockings and low canvas shoes. (A man's costume is somewhat less cumbersome, but not much.)

By the late 1800s bathers switch to simpler (though still concealing) long tunics and knickers. But they are made from heavy wool or serge, and like the bathing dresses, they are still more likely to waterlog their wearer than help her stay afloat.

Finally, in 1907, competitive swimmer Annette Kellerman appears in a sleek-for-the-times one-piece bathing suit. (Kellerman herself is less than sleek: 5'4", 140 pounds) Onlookers are shocked, but the

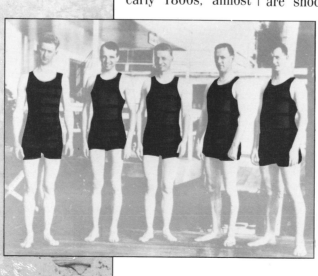

Counter-clockwise from top left: *Example of proper exercise attire for a woman, Encyclopedia of Health, 1931; swimsuit designed by Rose Marie Reid, 1953; founders of Jantzen, 1915 (Carl C. Jantzen is second from right); Annette Kellerman models "suitable tights for professional swimming and exhibition diving," 1918.*

suit swims. Of course, knowing that Edward VII will be in the audience watching her seventeen mile swim down the Thames, daring as she is, Kellerman knows she *can't* appear before His Majesty with bare legs. So she sews black tights to her swimsuit. Known as the "Annette Kellerman," the style is an immediate success—in Europe. But in the U.S., Kellerman is arrested in Massachusetts for indecent exposure. In 1909 when Adeline Trapp becomes the first woman to swim across New York's East River, the U.S. Volunteer Life Saving Corporation, which designs the suit she wears, hopes that Trapp's big splash will encourage other women to take the plunge. Women *do* take to the attractive form-fitting suits like ducks to water, but for many, ironically, they are just another costume—worn most nota-

bly by dry bathing beauties in swimsuit competitions. Further improvements in swimwear are made just before World War I, when knitting mill owner Carl Jantzen produces a skin-tight, rib-knit stretch suit which is immediately popular with athletes, as well as the general public. And finally, bathing suits actually get into the swim.

Counter-clockwise from left: *A sizzling Brazilian string bikini; tank bathing suit by Esprit, 1986; Annette Funicello, well-known mouseketeer turned "Beach" movie star, noted for two-piece bathing suits that covered her belly-button, here with Frankie Avalon in Beach Blanket Bingo, 1965; the original Barbie, 1959.*

329

TIME-LY CREATIONS

In 1904 Cartier makes a wristwatch for Brazilian aviator Alberto Santos-Dumont. It's about time: the new sports jackets simply don't have pockets for pocketwatches, and the name of the house of Cartier adds the seal of approval to the sporty new accessory.

SUNDAYS WITH JOHN

Bohemians of the nineteenth century are dead, but their spirit lives on. Sunday painters can thank Augustus John for their outfit. An academic painter of the early 1900s, John was the first to don a smock, full tie, and an oversized beret.

MOTOR TRENDS

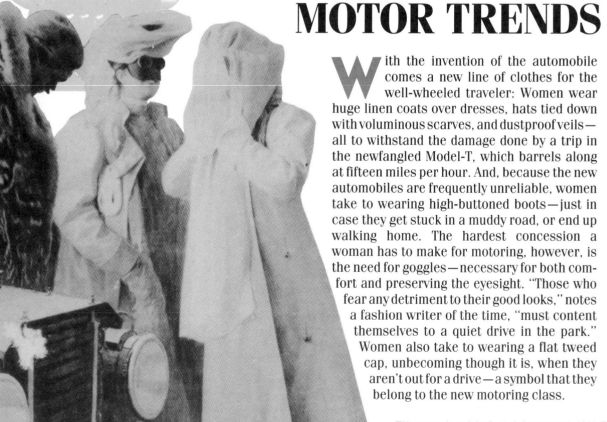

With the invention of the automobile comes a new line of clothes for the well-wheeled traveler: Women wear huge linen coats over dresses, hats tied down with voluminous scarves, and dustproof veils— all to withstand the damage done by a trip in the newfangled Model-T, which barrels along at fifteen miles per hour. And, because the new automobiles are frequently unreliable, women take to wearing high-buttoned boots—just in case they get stuck in a muddy road, or end up walking home. The hardest concession a woman has to make for motoring, however, is the need for goggles—necessary for both comfort and preserving the eyesight. "Those who fear any detriment to their good looks," notes a fashion writer of the time, "must content themselves to a quiet drive in the park." Women also take to wearing a flat tweed cap, unbecoming though it is, when they aren't out for a drive—a symbol that they belong to the new motoring class.

This page: above left: *Cartier's Santos watch, 1919;* above: *painter Augustus John (1878–1961) and Tallulah Bankhead in front of his portrait of her, 1910;* left: *Society Life and the Auto: An Introduction,* L. Sabbateur, 1905. Opposite page: top right: *Portrait of a New York socialite, ca. 1910;* center left: *evening gown in velvet, silk, and lace, by Ethel Rose, 1910.*

NECKING

After years of confining tailored blouses women celebrate 1910 as the year of the neck—a plunging reaction to the previous decade's decorous necklines. The vixenish V is denounced by prudish preachers; doctors warn that the new low line will cause pneumonia. But women love the seductively low-cut bodices which flaunt bold shoulders, and go to great lengths to make sure their skin is smooth and creamy white. A favorite beauty treatment? To sit for hours with cloths soaked in lemon juice wrapped around their necks. in 1920, London surgeon Sir James Cantlie warns, "Insufficient clothing about the necks and throats of women is causing an increase in goiter." As a less dire consequence, "The underclothed," he asserts, "will develop 'puffy necks.'" And in 1921, Virginia passes a bill forbidding women from displaying more than three inches of their throats.

SAY PLEASE

Before cheese, there were peas . . . prunes, potatoes, papas, and prisms—puckering P words young women of 1910 silently muttered upon entering rooms to achieve the then-popular "bee-stung" mouth.

"A small scarlet bow of velvet ribbon at her throat, two small garnet earrings in her ears, a very trim and tight-fitting black dress, with a heavily flounced skirt, seemed to indicate that she was not opposed to showing her figure, and prized it, a mood which except for a demure and rather retiring poise which she affected would most certainly have excited comment in such a place as this."

—Theodore Dreiser

HIP, HIP, POIRET

Born in 1879 to the owner of a cloth shop, Paul Poiret already knows something about silks and satins when he goes to work as a junior assistant to renowned couturier Charles Worth at the turn of the century. Like many great designers, Poiret's muses and inspiration are the women in his life: his mother gives him the money to open his first shop, and his future wife, Denise, shows him the shape of things to come. Unlike the rounded beauties of the day, Denise is tall and gangly, with good cheekbones: Poiret decides to re-cast women in her image, and creates slim-hipped designs. Success comes early when the Countess Greffulhe wears one of his flamboyant sheaths to her daughter's wedding.

Ten things you *must* know about Paul Poiret to pass Fashion 101 are:

- He drops the waist to the hips
- Puts the bust back where it belongs
- Tells fifty million Frenchwomen to throw away their corsets—and they do
- Introduces the "bandeau," a swatch of material wrapped around the crown of the head, which he devises after Denise crops her hair
- Popularizes the tunic, a soft, flowing T-shaped garment worn over an ankle-length skirt. The tunics are decorated, often match the skirt, and are sometimes belted. If the style looks familiar, it's because we've seen it before—in the Middle Ages
- Gets women to wrap their heads in turbans, a headcovering which becomes the headdress of the era. His inspiration comes from the shopgirls who wear scarves to keep their hair out of their way while working
- Slashes skirts up the middle, tightens them around the ankle and puts women in "harem pants," which along with turbans, become part of the great Oriental look
- Uses chiffons, gauze, and crepe. Also heavier lamés, brocades, and damasks, and the palette of the Impressionists: reds, oranges, and lemony yellows—in contrast to other designers of the day who use pale colors
- After enlisting in the army, designs his own uniform: a blue suit, blue silk shirt, and a tie with a nude woman on it. The army doesn't want him to wear it, but they do encourage him to re-design the French uniform in a more practical manner
- Gives the most talked-about party of the year in June 1911: "1002 Arabian Nights." In a space decorated to look like Ali Baba's cave, the garden is paved with oriental rugs, and overrun with flamingoes, parrots, and monkeys who mingle among the guests. Flutists play and the air is scented with myrrh. "Slaves" dance in transparent gauze; there are gold and silver fireworks. Poiret wears a turban, ruby-red harem pants, and beads. Denise, a transparent gold "lampshade" dress: a short, hooped skirt over pantaloons. It is quite a launch for Poiret's new Orientally inspired clothes line.

▌ **Right:** *"Melodie" dress, Poiret, 1912.* **Below:** *designs from Poiret's 1911 collection.*

MATERNALLY YOURS

Babymaking comes into its own and motherhood is as American as apple pie when, in 1911, pregnancy makes the back pages of the New York *Herald.* For the first time in history, a newspaper is willing to accept an advertisement for maternity clothes. The ad, placed by Lane Bryant, assures the expectant mother that she can be well dressed in clothes that will help her to look "normal." The big seller? A tea gown with an accordian-pleated skirt attached to the bodice by an elastic band.

Comfortable and Stylish Maternity Dresses

31T7000 Satin $32.50

31T7005 Wool Mixed Panama $12.98

BEETS ME

In 1912 the *Ladies' Home Journal* reports the tragic tale of a pasty-faced young woman who goes to a doctor in search of a healthful glow. After he injects her face with a carmine fluid, she turns a very unattractive beet red. Her boyfriend, not one to see the world through rose-colored glasses, breaks their engagement.

Top right: Hope, Gustav Klimt, 1903. **Center:** Maternity dresses, Sears & Roebuck catalog, 1919. **Right:** Syringes, 1920s or 30s.

COMMON SCENTS

At the turn of the century, "nice" girls don't wear perfume. The most it's proper to do is splash on a little Eau de Cologne; anything else is considered fast. Poiret is the first clothing designer to create perfumes, and he works with chemists to concoct mysterious, Oriental scents. Before Poiret, cologne is likely to smell like lavender or rose. But he creates the "Poiret" woman with Le Fruit Defendu, Nuit de Chine, L'Etrange Fleur—even Borgia. Instead of sweet, lady-like scents, the Poiret woman is a vamp, a seductress; next thing you know, women will be clamoring for My Sin, Obsession, and, ultimately, Opium.

As for more natural allure, this is the era of the corsage. Not only does the lovely corsage a deb receives from her beau spruce up her dress, its flowery aroma hides a multitude of scents. When the first commercial deodorant, Odo-ro-no, comes on the market in 1920, the sale of corsages declines.

Clockwise from top left: *Detail from a 1929 fragrance advertisement; advertisement for designer Paul Iribe's scent, "Pres de Vous," perfume by Rigaud, 1912; Young lady with a corsage; advertisement for "Odo-Ro-No", with an offer of a leaflet on "complete underarm dryness," 1930s; advertisement, early 1940s.*

1911 IRVING BERLIN HAS A HIT WITH "ALEX-ANDER'S RAGTIME BAND."

1912 SHE WENT DOWN TO THE BOTTOM OF THE SEA: THE SS *TITANIC* COLLIDES WITH AN ICEBERG, 1,513 DROWN.

Illustration of the tango, in a 1913 issue of the French magazine *Femina*.

ALL TANGO-ED UP: When Empress Eugénie leaves Spain for France, she brings along a sleeveless, no-button, waist-length jacket—the *bolero* (oh, oh!). The jacket, worn with frilly, high-necked blouses and long skirts, is all the rage.

In 1910, Paul Poiret who has had women hobbling around in ultra-narrow ankle-length skirts takes matters into his own hands when he escorts a group of models wearing *hobble skirts* for a day at the races. Poiret rips the skirts up one side, creating sexy slits. These *tango skirts* are popular everywhere from Berlin to Milan and London, where the sultry South American dance is catching on.

BEAN BOOT

On September 29, 1912, L. L. Bean marches on the scene with the Maine hunting shoe—a sturdy leather boot sewed to rubber bottoms. Bean gets the idea for the boot on a hunting trip when he suffers sore, cold, wet feet. He sells a hundred pairs of boots in his original design, but ninety are immediately returned when the rubber bottoms wear away. He reworks the boot and advises customers to send in the rubber bottoms, which he rebuilds for them. Then the boot definitely gets "legs"—and it's as popular and fast-selling today as when it first came out.

Right: *L. L. Bean's Maine Hunting Shoe, relatively unchanged since its invention in 1912, in a 1989 catalog.*

335

NEWS BULLETIN FROM PARIS:

Ladies' clothing is fitted with pockets! "So," exclaims the reporter in the 1913 dispatch, "it is all over with men's superiority over the other sex!"

Above, far left: Silk-lined suit in heather tweed, English, 1916. Above center: Advertisement for suits made in St. Louis, 1919. Above right: Coat with fur trim, French, 1915. Background: Map of Paris. Below left: Two steel ships under construction. Below right: This corset will soon become a thing of the past.

LOOSE HIPS BUILD SHIPS:

In 1917 America enters World War I and women gratefully donate their steel corsets to the effort. The resulting 28,000 tons of steel are enough to build two battleships.

BONES,

BUSKS,

AND

SIDE

STEELS

protected

by

LEATHER

BROWN'
PATEN
"DERMATHIST
CORSET

1915 MARGARET SANGER IS JAILED FOR WRITING *FAMILY LIMITATION*, THE FIRST BOOK ON BIRTH CONTROL.

Canvassing around for textile designs, fashion designers discover what they've been looking for in the work of contemporary painters. When Serge Diaghilev brings the Ballet Russe to Paris in 1910, designers co-opt the brightly colored Oriental designs of Bakst, Golovine, and Benois, as seen in *Scheherazade* and *The Firebird*, for everyday wear. French Fauvist Raoul Dufy is better remembered for the vividly colored silks and brocades he creates in 1911 for Poiret than he is for his paintings. In the '20s, Sonia Terk-Delaunay's bold geometrics in contrasting colors influence Schiaparelli and Patou. Terk-Delaunay's designs take inspiration from Picasso's Cubism, an influence which not only sets the art world on its ear, but changes the shape of fashion. As a result of Cubism, there is a trend toward tall and thin, and in 1924 Patou imports six tall American girls to model his collection.

PATTERN PAINTING

1914 ROYAL THEATRE, DRURY LANE PRICE 2 6

Russian Opera and Ballet

Illustrated Souvenir-Programme

M. MICHEL FOKINE 'Chorograph's Director of the Russian Ballet and Mme VERA FOKINE dancing "Scheherazade."

Counter-clockwise from far left: *Claire McCardell shorts-set made from a fabric printed after a design by Raoul Dufy, 1955; gallery-owner Gracie Mansion wears a "Jackson Pollack" dress by artist Mike Bidlo, 1983; Michel and Vera Fokine dancing "Scheherazade" in costumes by Russian painter Leon Bakst (1866–1924), illustration by Valentine Gross for a souvenir program, 1914; Pucci panties, ca. 1966.*

337

THRILL
DRESSED TO
(AND KILL)

Mata Hari, the exotic spy, goes to Paul Poiret's Paris shop for dresses designed by Erte. Though she prefers masculine-styled dresses in somber colors for her private life, when she's finally caught and sentenced to die, she dons a dark *redingote* (a feminine, full-skirted dress with a tight bodice worn by ladies for fashionable "promenades"), a feather boa swirled around her shoulders, and a small, chic hat for facing the firing squad.

Above: Reconstructed newspaper photo of Mata Hari (1876–1917). Above right: Greta Garbo and Ramone Navaro in Mata Hari, 1932. Below left: Patou bathing suits, one with designer initials JP, ca. 1924. Below right: Josephine Baker wearing one of Patou's later fantasy dresses, ca. 1930.

INITIAL INITIALS

Jean Patou invents the first designer label with his pants pockets outlined with a "J" and a "P." French designer Patou joins his uncle's fur business in 1907. By 1912 he has his own design shop, and his 1914 collection is sold out entirely—to one American. The next year he goes off to fight in World War I; returning in 1919, he re-opens his shop and shows bell-skirted dresses, high-waisted shepherd-style dresses, and lots of Russian embroidery. But he is best remembered for his sportswear: tennis outfits with calf-length pleated skirts and sleeveless cardigans, bathing suits, and sweaters with Cubist designs.

CAUSING A FLAP

By the mid 1920s, with the growing flapper craze, bobbed hair sweeps the nation. In Paducah, Kentucky, five nurses are suspended from training school for cutting their hair. The chic Chicago department store, Marshall Field, refuses to employ women whose hair doesn't come up to their standards—shoulder length. Doctors warn young women of "flapper's rash" (scalp irritation). But nothing stops them—"bobbed" hair is in. It prompts the invention of the bobby pin and within two years (1922–24) the number of hair cutting salons increases from 5,000 to 23,000 just to keep up with the demand. Some say the craze started with ballroom dancer Irene Castle, who cut her hair so it would be easier to care for while she recuperated from an appendectomy; others say that when Coco Chanel was lighting a water heater in her bathroom at the Ritz it exploded, and her hair was sprayed with soot. In a hurry to get to the opera, Chanel chopped off her hair so she could shampoo it more quickly.

Our heroine, Louise, doesn't really care who cut their hair first. Her mother, the Gibson Girl, just can't understand: Her daughter's skirts are short, her hair is short, her waist is on her hips, and her bust has disappeared. Just where did forty million busts go, she wonders? Louise just really doesn't care about this. It's noon, and drowsily, she must begin her day. "Oh you kid!" she giggles, as she remembers last night's frenzy of Charlestons and gin fizzes. She reaches into her closet for a short, shimmering dress and a purple felt cloche. It's hard to tell the front from the back of the dress; both sides plunge into a big V. Oh well. Louise knows it doesn't really matter. She rouges her knees, turns down her stockings, and goes back to her closet one more time—for Johnny, the college boy with slicked-down hair and a raccoon coat no respectable flapper would be seen without. They tuck a hip flask into the top of his Russian boots, light a cigarette, and 23-skidoo!

Q: "Why do flappers wear their hair pulled down over their ears?"

A: "So they'll have something left to show their husbands after they're married."

Top left: *Dorothy Provine in the 1960s TV series, "The Roaring Twenties."* **Top right:** *Gay Northeasterners on Seventh Avenue, James Van Der Zee, 1927.* **Right:** *Louise Brooks, ca. 1929.* **Left:** *Slim dresses of 1929.*

TUT FOR TAT

In 1922 Howard Carter and Lord Carnarvon discover the ancient tomb of Tutankhamen. They bring home sacred artifacts and sarcophagi that bedazzle the world and help unravel the riddle of the Sphinx. Capitalizing on the worldwide sensation, fashion designers spur an Egyptian revival. Egyptian motifs, slavishly copied from the originals, are seen on jackets, evening dresses, and jewelry.

Left: Molyneux design inspired by the discovery of Tut's tomb, 1923. **Right:** Madison Avenue cashes in on the craze for Egyptology in an advertisement for Palmolive shampoo, "a perfect blend of the oils Cleopatra prized," 1920s.

YOU WEAR WHAT YOU DRINK

TEA GOWNS, introduced in the late 1800s, are the first at-home fashions. Worn to receive guests at home at tea time, they are simple, high-waisted, long-sleeved dresses that can be comfortably worn with corsets unlaced, or even removed. When Americans invent the cocktail party in the 1920s, the demure tea gown is replaced by the racier *cocktail dress*: a black knee-length sleeveless sheath.

Far left: Woman in a slightly modified cocktail dress, 1960s. **Left:** Women at Tea, 1911.

1922 MUSSOLINI FORMS A FASCIST GOVERNMENT IN ITALY.

AMERICAN BEAUTY

In 1921, years before Bert Parks even has his teeth capped, the very first Miss America contest takes place at Keith's Theater on the Garden Pier in Atlantic City. At the two-day September carnival, created to extend the summer season, it's a fifteen-year-old high school student, Margaret Gorman, Miss Washington, D.C., who catches the judge's eye. Miss Gorman is blond and blue-eyed, stands 5'1" tall, weighs 108 pounds, and measures a tiny 30–25–32—the winning combination. Is she truly the most beautiful woman in America? Hard to say—there are only seven other contestants in this first contest. It isn't until 1958 that Miss America is chosen from all (then) forty-eight states.

TAKING THE CREDIT

In 1922 a 3" × 5" plastic card revolutionizes the fashion industry, and introduces a new phrase into the American language: "Charge it." Filene's department store in Boston pioneers the original charge card.

GO PACK YOUR . . .

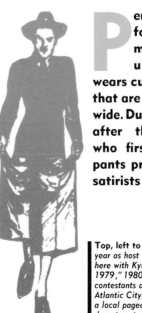

Perhaps to compensate for the skimpiness of milady's outfit, her unflappable date wears cuffed baggy trousers that are up to twenty inches wide. Dubbed "Oxford Bags" after the undergraduates who first sport them, the pants provide sharp-penned satirists with a new target.

Top, left to right: Bert Parks, in his 25th year as host of the Miss American Pageant, here with Kylene Barker, "Miss America 1979," 1980; parade of Miss America contestants and attendants on the beach in Atlantic City, 1920s; "Miss Johnstown" from a local pageant in 1924. **Far left:** Filene's department store and charge card. **Left:** Contemporary caricature of "Oxford bags," ca. 1925.

341

TENNIS, ANYONE?

In the 1880s women suffer a slight disadvantage while playing tennis—they have to hold up dragging skirts: the fashionable Chris Everts of the day sport bonnets, bustles, and heeled shoes for matched sets on the tennis court.

By and large, summer fashions double as tennis uniforms until the 1920s, when the short skirt finally gives women some freedom of movement. When skirt lengths drop again in the 1930s, women keep the ball in their court, refusing to wear long tennis dresses ever again. In 1929 a Mrs. Fearnley shows no fear at Wimbledon when she appears ready to play *sans* stockings. Two years later, Alice Marble of San Francisco comes onto the court in shorts.

"Tennis whites" make their appearance in the 1920s, borrowing the white knit shirts that have been de rigueur for polo players since the turn of the century. Tennis whites remain an inviolable tradition until July 5, 1972, when Rosie Casals creates a cause célèbre by appearing at Wimbledon in a dress decorated with purple scrolls. Rosie's dress, however, does nothing to dazzle her opponent—she loses the match to the demurely dressed Billie Jean King. Your serve.

Above left: *French tennis player Suzanne Lenglen in a tennis dress by Patou, ca. 1921.* **Above right:** *Unconventional tennis champ Andre Agassi, 1990.* **Below left:** *The Lacoste "alligator."* **Below right:** *Rene Lacoste himself, late 1920s.*

LA COSTA SUCCESS: In 1923, on an American tour with the French Davis Cup tennis team, the nineteen-year-old René Lacoste spots an alligator-skin suitcase in a store window. He boasts to teammates that he'll treat himself to the expensive bag if he wins his upcoming matches. Lacoste loses, doesn't buy the bag, and in jest (and perhaps with sly reference to his rather large nose) his teammates call him "Le Crocodile." Four years later, when Lacoste retires, he begins designing sports shirts, using his former nickname as a trademark. And although the garments today are popularly called "alligator shirts," the long-snouted animal stitched above the pocket is technically a crocodile.

342

HAZARDOUS TO
WARNING
YOUR HEALTH

A lady is asked by her doctor what she drinks at meals. "Don't be silly, Doctor," she replies. "I don't even *eat* at meals." Women are consumptive from obsessive dieting—they really weren't born with those reed-thin, boyish bodies, after all.

In the 1920s cigarettes become the latest accessory. Everybody's smoking. Women use long, thin cigarette holders, and vanity tables are built with a special place to hold them.

OUT, OUT, DAMNED SPOT: Why *are* people suddenly washing their hands more? In 1929 the U.S. government reports that the rise in expenditure on soap multiplies tenfold, from $790,000 in 1923 to over $7,000,000 six short (and dirty) years later.

Above: *Ivory Soap advertisement, 1927.*

Above: *Woman wearing a wizard's hat by Bernard Workman and confetti-dotted cotton jersey dress by Sportwhirl, 1955, sports an elegant 1920s style cigarette holder.*

ZIPPY

The Prince of Wales arrives in the United States and people are impressed by how quickly he can get into and out of his pants, which are equipped with a newfangled contraption—a *zipper.* Zipper sales zoom. Nine years later, a women's dress manufacturer out to spark business uses zippers as a gimmick—but it isn't until eminent designer Elsa Schiaparelli puts zippers on women's backs in 1936 that women can say, "Darling, help me with this, would you please?"

Left: *The Conmar Major, trademark, 1940.*

1927 LIZZIE BORDEN TOOK AN AX, AND, ACCORDING THE COURT, NEVER GAVE HER FATHER 40 WHACKS—SHE WAS EVENTUALLY ACQUITTED OF THE CRIME.

1927 BABE RUTH HITS 60 HOME RUNS FOR THE NEW YORK YANKEES.

UPLIFTING

The Greeks called them mastatedons, but in 1907 *Vogue* uses the French "brassiere," which, translated literally, means an infant's underbodice or a harness. Whatever you call them, they change the female silhouette forever.

In 1889 Frenchwoman Herminie Cardolle replaces the corset with a brassiere which enlarges the cup and counts on a new device—the shoulder strap. In 1914, with two hankies—French, of course—a piece of baby ribbon, and some help from her maid, America debutante Mary Phelps Jacobs (who changes her name to "Caresse Crosby" for marketing reasons) improvises the first boneless midriff-free bra.

344

1928 ALEXANDER FLEMING DISCOVERS PENICILLIN.

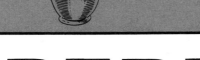

1928 THE FIRST MICKEY MOUSE FILMS ARE MADE BY WALT DISNEY.

EXPERIENCE

To shape a flapper's body, these first designs flatten the bust and push it downward. During the late '20s the Kestos Company comes up with a bra made of two triangular pieces of fabric secured to elastic that is pulled over the shoulders, crossed at the back, and buttoned at the front under darted cups. During the '20s and '30s manufacturers add bone and produce bras with different cup sizes. In the '40s you can buy a padded bra; in the '50s, you might feel that you had to, to fit the Mamie Van Doren/Jayne Mansfield fantasy of the "ideal" woman. By the late 1960s, however, bras become a burning issue, as feminists set them ablaze. And the bra—once a symbol of a girl's burgeoning womanhood, now becomes a symbol of a womanhood's burgeoning liberation.

Opposite page: top right: *Mamie Van Doren, c. 1955;* **center left:** *Kestos bra ad, Scottish, late 1920s;* **bottom left:** *Theda Bara, ca. 1917;* **Bottom right:** *brassiere ad, 1951;* **center right, left to right:** *Victoria Vetri in When Dinosaurs Ruled the Earth, 1970; sketch for a Jean-Paul Gaultier costume for Madonna's "Blond Ambition" tour, 1990; French bra and girdle advertisement, ca. 1966; advertisement, 1952.* **This page, left to right:** *Bra and girdle advertisement, 1948; in 1990 Betsey Johnson shows this design as bras come into their own as outerwear; advertisement, 1951; Jane Russell's cleavage baited censors in The Outlaw, 1943.*

1928 NICE TRY: THE KELLOGG-BRIAND PACT, OUTLAW-ING WAR, IS SIGNED IN PARIS BY 65 STATES.

1929 HITLER APPOINTS HIMMLER "REICHSFUHRER S.S."

THEY SAY THAT MAKING-UP IS HARD TO DO

As early as 1890 Sir Max Beerbohm predicts that "Cosmetics are not going to be a mere prosaic remedy for age or plainness, but all ladies and girls will come to love them." In 1915, lipstick sold in cylindrical metal containers is available in America for the first time, and at last you can get it on your collar, seal it with a kiss, or write billets-doux on mirrors. Before the 1920s, hardly any women are bold enough to openly wear makeup. On the well-equipped turn-of-the-century dressing table one might find a little purple book with powdered leaves (a *papier poudre*) for a touch of cheek color; rice powder for a pale base; perhaps some anti-chap cream for the hands. But the flapper throws caution to the wind: She paints her lips vermilion red, rouges her cheeks and earlobes, and enlarges her eyes with kohl. Vampy Theda Bara-like eyes become the focal point of the well-made-up face. In the Dark Ages before 1925, those daring enough to darken their eyebrows do so with burnt matches. After 1925, eyebrows are plucked and penciled into thin, thin lines. Makeup is here to stay. Empires begin to be built as Helena Rubenstein produces skin creams based on family recipes and Elizabeth Arden creates moisturizers, tonics, and eventually creamed rouge, eyeshadow, and lipstick. By the mid-'20s *Vogue* magazine has to admit that "Even the most conservative and prejudiced must now concede that a woman exquisitely made up yet may be, in spite of seeming frivolity, a faithful wife and devoted mother."

Top center: 24-foot-high "Lipstick Monument," 1969, Claes Oldenburg. Center: Elizabeth Arden advertisement, 1950. Bottom left and right: "Debutante" cosmetic line of the Fuller Brush Co., 1950s.

HEMLINERS

Take out your scissors, because:

• Skirts start out in the early 1920s at midcalf.

• By 1925, they skim the knee.

• And by 1926 they are the shortest ever, coming—gasp—right to the knee.

• By 1928 dress designers are tying to use more material; they show dresses that are longer in the back, almost touching the ankles—but the bee's knees stay exposed in front.

• By 1929, skirts come crashing back down to midcalf.

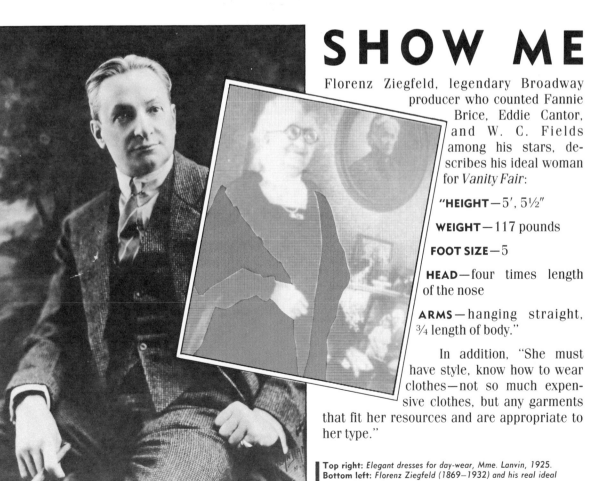

SHOW ME

Florenz Ziegfeld, legendary Broadway producer who counted Fannie Brice, Eddie Cantor, and W. C. Fields among his stars, describes his ideal woman for *Vanity Fair*:

"**HEIGHT**—5', 5½"

WEIGHT—117 pounds

FOOT SIZE—5

HEAD—four times length of the nose

ARMS—hanging straight, ¾ length of body."

In addition, "She must have style, know how to wear clothes—not so much expensive clothes, but any garments that fit her resources and are appropriate to her type."

Top right: Elegant dresses for day-wear, Mme. Lanvin, 1925.
Bottom left: Florenz Ziegfeld (1869–1932) and his real ideal woman, his mother.

THE REEL THING

During the Depression, life is going to the dogs, and everyone is going to the movies. In real life, fashion (and hemlines) comes crashing down, just like the stock market. Oh, there are some inventive "Idaho Potato"-stamped sack dresses and curtain-cut-on-the-bias gowns, but for the most part, even the rich think it is déclassé to be overly concerned with changing fashion. (And many of the formerly rich are no longer in a position to, anyway.) Cotton is used for evening dresses; haute couture loses its haute (and cheap, mass-produced clothing as well as *toiles*—patterns for making designer copies—come into their own); mail order catalogue sales are on the rise. Wearing hand-me-downs takes on a certain cachet, and when women *do* buy something new, it's the sensible, tailored suit.

But at the movies, Fred Astaire and Ginger Rogers are dancing cheek to cheek—he in a top hat and tails, she, in the most incredible gowns, like the one of shimmering ice-blue ostrich feathers which is said to have made Mr. Astaire sneeze; Jean Harlow is draped in slinky white satin and swathed in fur; scores of bugle-beaded Busby Berkeley "Gold-diggers" glide across the screen in opulent musical extravaganzas. (The movies make actors appear ten pounds heavier and the stars are always re-questing costumes with long, lean lines. Also, sequins and satin look great on camera. Hence, lots of bias-cut clothes that glitter.) *Gone with the Wind* re-creates the romantic costumes of the antebellum South; *The Wizard of Oz* leads us down the yellow brick road to the fantastic world of Munchkins, tin men, a fairy-tale beautiful good witch, and a pair of ruby red slippers.

In the early movies, the stars provide their own clothes. Sarah Bernhardt has Paul Poiret design the dresses she wears as Queen Elizabeth and she turns up wearing flattering, free flowing, high-waisted gowns, rather than the farthingales and severely fitted bodices worn by the real Virgin Queen.

But even if the movies don't always reflect what *was*, they sometimes inspire what will be. The sight of a sexy Dorothy Lamour wrapped in boldly patterned sarongs in 1935 sends thousands of women to department stores, clamoring for exotic beachwear (when Esther Williams dives into films twenty years later in form-fitting Helen Rose bathing

MOVIE EXTRAS: In 1932, Claudette Colbert as Nero's wife Poppea in Cecil B. De Mille's *The Sign of the Cross* languishes in a pool of asses' milk. Filming under heavy lights, the milk in Colbert's bath curdles. But all moviegoers see is a new symbol of luxury. Millions flock to their drugstores to buy bubble bath. And when Max Factor introduces a new cover-up in 1938, his pancake makeup (named for the "panchromatic" shades it comes in for film photography) is gobbled up by women everywhere.

suits, manufacturers immediately copy the tighter, lighter design); Garbo and Hepburn stride across the screen in pants, and suddenly the man-tailored look is in; a copy of the gown worn by Elizabeth Taylor in *Father of the Bride* (another Helen Rose design), becomes the 1950 top bestseller in New York bridal shops.

Marlon Brando (in *The Wild One*) makes the black motorcycle jacket a symbol of tough-guy rebellion; and a full thirty years before *Flashdance*, Brando scores again as a trendsetter with a ripped T-shirt in *A Streetcar Named Desire*. Diane Keaton (dressed by Ralph Lauren) as the waifish *Annie Hall* popularizes the layered look — women wear oversized men's jackets, droopy hats, vests, and floppy skirts; *Bonnie and Clyde* inspires a return to '30s-style calf-length skirts, fedoras for men, and a never before or since equaled interest in the beret; *Dr. Zhivago* in 1966 results in a romantic winter, as women don long, Russian-like coats, and fur hats.

Background: *Judy Garland as Dorothy starts down the yellow brick road, in The Wizard of Oz, 1939.* **Top:** *Fred Astaire and Ginger Rogers, née Virginia McMath, in a 1930s musical.* **Left:** *Dorothy Lamour in her sarong, ca. 1938.* **Counter-clockwise from below:** *Blonde sex goddess Jean Harlow (1911–1937), née Harlean Carpentier, in a bias-cut satin gown; Esther Williams wears a swimsuit she designed herself for Cole of California in Neptune's Daughter, 1949 — only fitting since in the movie she plays a bathing suit designer; Elizabeth Taylor and Spencer Tracy in Father of the Bride, 1950; Marlon Brando and T-shirt in A Streetcar Named Desire, 1951.*

In the 1930s, backs are bared on dresses, creating a new erogenous zone. In 1932 Hollywood designer Travis Barton dresses Tallulah Bankhead in a backless dress in the movie *Thunder Below*. Maybe dress backs just disappear as designers experiment with necklines—like the boat-neck, for instance—and just keep cutting more and more material away. Around about this time backless bathing

A LOOK BACK

suits are introduced as well; largely because bathing costumes are no longer just "beachwear"—they're used for actual swimming.

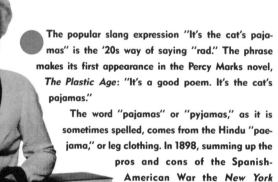

The popular slang expression "It's the cat's pajamas" is the '20s way of saying "rad." The phrase makes its first appearance in the Percy Marks novel, *The Plastic Age*: "It's a good poem. It's the cat's pajamas."

The word "pajamas" or "pyjamas," as it is sometimes spelled, comes from the Hindu "pae-jama," or leg clothing. In 1898, summing up the pros and cons of the Spanish-American War the *New York Times* reports that "One of the benefits of the war was accustoming the American soldier to the use of the pajama."

During World War I, wearing pajamas to bed rapidly rivals, if not overtakes, the nightdress. And just like the waistless flapper's dress, they emphasize a boyish figure. In the '30s, there are three types of pajamas: for sleeping in, for informal dinner dress, and resort wear. Made of shantung or crêpe de chine, widely flared trousers worn with loose short coats are seen at the best seaside hotels.

It would never have "Happened One Night" if Claudette Colbert and Clark Gable had shared a nightshirt. And in 1956 *baby doll pajamas* are made popular by the movie in which *Baby Doll* Carroll Baker wears short panties with ribbons, lace, and bows. By 1958 a machine that can press, fold, and package soft goods in one automatic cycle is put into operation at a pajama factory, where it is reported that an amazing 3,000 dozen pajamas are processed each day.

THE PAJAMA GAME

Top Right: *A 1930s advertisement shows lots of back.* **Center left:** *Judy Holliday in* Born Yesterday, *1950;* **Bottom left:** *Claudette Colbert and Clark Gable share a pair of PJ's—and more—in* It Happened One Night, *1934.* **Above:** *Odalisque, Auguste Renoir, 1870.*

STAYING POWER

Yards of Material Girl chains around the neck, waist, and wrists; quilted handbags; and fake gardenias pinned to the lapel of a suit jacket all have the look of "today"; yet they were conceived more than fifty years ago by Coco Chanel. Chanel, the fashion designer who seems so utterly timely, comes from an earlier century: She was born in 1883, the same year that work ended on the Brooklyn Bridge, that Czar Alexander and his Czarina (she wrapped in thirty-two kilos of fabric) were crowned Emperor and Empress of all Russia. Women were still wearing corsets.

Chanel's design solutions are born of practicality. When she borrows her beau's tweed jacket on a fishing trip, the blazer is born. When the insurance on her real jewels becomes too costly, she creates costume jewelry. And, history has it, when one of her legion of lovers is lost at sea, she vows to put the nation in mourning and invents the little black dress. In fact, from gamine SoHo street urchins in dark kohl eye makeup and boxy little black dresses to demure Connecticut matrons in shetland sweaters and pearls, Chanel has had a hand in today's most current fashions.

Left, top to bottom: Chanel beret, in a 1918 issue of Vogue; Jean Moreau in a little black dress and pearls from Chanel in Louis Malle's The Lovers, 1959; suited Coco Chanel, 1968. Right, top to bottom: Romy Schneider in a Chanel suit in Bocaccio '70, 1962; Chanel suit jacket, 1960s; Couture Chanel evening dress, mid-1960s.

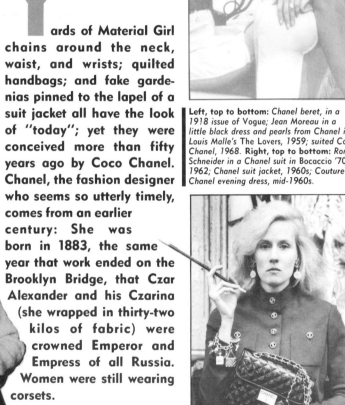

WEARING THE PANTS

In 1932 the Paris chief of police is outraged to see Marlene Dietrich walking along the Seine, clad in a man's jacket and pants—and he orders her to leave. It's long after Mrs. Bloomer daringly displays her cycling legs that women everywhere realize that "wearing the pants in the family" can be fun. Even though pantaloons are seen on ancient Persian sirens, pants don't make their mark in the West until Katharine Hepburn and Greta Garbo begin wearing loose trousers on the silver screen. But it is really the shortage of stockings during World War II that forces ladies to turn to trousers—to hide their stockingless legs. (And pants are more practical for working on the assembly line.)

In 1964, a New York socialite shows up for lunch at one of the city's most elegant bistros wearing a chic satin *pantsuit*. The maitre d' refuses to seat her because she is clad in slacks. Undaunted, she removes the pants and is seated wearing the jacket which, although it hardly covers her panties, *is* acceptable luncheon attire.

One of the very first pantsuits is a stiff, space-age costume designed by André Courrèges. Other designers soon follow, well, suit, and by 1972 pantsuit mania sweeps America—women can even wear pantsuits to lunch.

Above left: *Frances Gifford, lawyer turned leading lady, 1940s.* **Right:** *Employees of a Madison, Wisconsin, bank model pantsuits they are now allowed to wear, 1970.*

DOGGED: Thanks to Asta, the cute little terrier in the popular 1930s *Thin Man* series, tail-wagging canines become popular accessories in fashion layouts, nuzzling up to the most popular models of the day. Soon scotties are the latest motif on printed dresses, scarves, and shawls, as well as pins, which adorn suit and coat lapels.

Left: *Myrna Loy, Asta, and William Powell in* The Thin Man, *1934.*
Right: *Terriers are still in fashion: Scotty brooch by June Ponte, 1990.*

THE HAT PARADE

A TOQUE-EN OF ESTEEM: The *toque*, right, is a snug, brimless wool or jersey hat that is sometimes worn with a feather or jewel at its center, popular in the '20s and '30s.

CLOCHE CALL: From the toque comes a rounder and even closer-fitting hat, with a turned-back brim. The *cloche*, left, which is worn right over the eyebrows, is felt by day, gold lamé by night, often decorated with feathers.

Left: *Lady in a cloche,* Vogue, *1929.*
Above: *A toque keeps this shopper warm in a 1929 A&P ad.*

BUT CAN THEY YODEL?: The heroine of George du Maurier's novel *Trilby* gives her name to the soft felt hat with a dented crown, right, that is worn in the stage version of the book. The style, worn with a feather, becomes the perfect topper for the Tyrolean costumes—complete with lederhosen and dirndl skirts—that have inexplicably been adopted by both men and women.

IN THE PICTURE: Hollywood costume designer Adrian creates the *pillbox hat* (not pictured) for Greta Garbo to wear in the 1932 flick *As You Desire Me*. The small, oval hat with a flat top which sits neatly perched on top of the head is an immediate hit and enjoys a second run thirty years later when the pillbox becomes the much-imitated trademark of Jacqueline Kennedy.

Right: *Alpine beauties: Gloria Swanson, Marion Davies and Jean Harlow in Tyrolean costumes with Constance Bennett at a party at Davies' home, ca. 1934.*

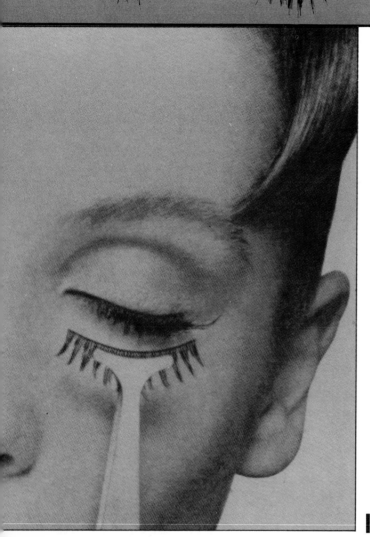

LASH BACK

False eyelashes come on the American scene in 1932, and by 1964 they've become big business—for eighty dollars a pair a woman can have hers custom-made in mink, sable, or human hair, or she can go to her local salon and have her lashes put on one by one for a look that lasts three weeks. By 1968 a false-eyelashed cutie can pick up a pair for a mere $4.98 in a multitude of styles like "standard spiky," or "medium shaggy"; she can even have lashes affixed with glitter or wear them three layers deep. And in 1970 she can even put them on in a flash when she oversleeps with Helena Rubenstein's "Minute Lash," boxed with its very own plastic applicator and glue. By the mid-seventies, as the vogue for the "natural look" intensifies, the sale of false lashes declines. By the late '80s, women are dying their natural lashes or using no-color mascara—to separate and lengthen their natural lashes, albeit discreetly. Will fashion lash back? Only time will tell.

*Top: Advertisement for false eyelashes made of real hair, **Left**: Lashes with applicator were essential for the look in 1970.*

THE EYES HAVE IT

Pencil-thin eyebrows and enormous saucer eyes help give flapper Clara Bow a fresh look that makes her everyone's favorite "it" girl in the '20s.

With overpowering arched eyebrows, heavily penciled in, and a steely-eyed look, Joan Crawford is the quintessential '40s career woman.

Elizabeth Taylor's fabled violet eyes receive even more notoriety when *a la* Cleopatra she bats them at co-star Richard Burton.

The heaviest thing about '60s model Twiggy are the triple rows of false eyelashes that complete her waif-like appearance.

Bushy eyebrows don't keep *Pretty Baby* Brooke Shields out of the public eye. In fact, she makes the natural-brow look fashionable in the late '70s.

Ex-televangelist Tammy Faye Bakker uses pencils, liquid liner, thick eyeshadow, and gobs of mascara to achieve her kewpie-doll-on-acid look.

THE SCRAP ON SCHAP

Who knows what line of thought she followed as a student of philosophy, but as a designer, Elsa Schiaparelli loves to amuse. A black sweater with a white "trompe l'oeil" bow puts her in business, and her company, Pour Le Sport, opens in Paris in 1928. She advances the broad shouldered "Pagoda sleeve," uses tweed for evening wear, puts (so-called) grown-up women in alpine Tyrolean peasant costumes. She dyes plastic zippers the same colors as her fabrics, and creates a need for husbands—it's impossible to zip up those back zippers by yourself. "Schap," as she is affectionately called, has zodiac designs embroidered on her clothes, creates a hat that is shaped like a shoe, and a handbag that plays a tune when you open it—perhaps the tune is "Anything Goes?"

Counter-clockwise from top left: *Schiaparelli from a 1933 advertisement; illustration by Christian Berard of an evening dress from Schiaparelli's 1938 Zodiac Collection; Schiaparelli and her friend Salvador Dali designed this "shoe" hat (notice the Dali-inspired lip-pockets on jacket), Fall 1937; advertisement for Schiaparelli's "Sleeping" perfume, 1948.*

KNIT PICKING

In 1935, sitting on a stool in Schwab's Drugstore wearing a sweater and sipping a soda (so legend has it), a voluptuous sixteen-year-old Lana Turner is spotted by a talent agent who snaps up the sexy starlet. Turner jiggles down the street in a tight blue sweater in the 1937 movie *They Won't Forget,* and she becomes an overnight sensation—pinups of Turner in the famous pullover are plastered all over the country. Not only do sweater sales soar, so do the sales of "falsies."

The term *sweater,* however, has a less romantic beginning. At the close of the nineteenth century, racing trainers use heavy blankets to make horses perspire during workouts. The blankets, logically enough, are dubbed "sweaters."

In the 1920s, "dandy" Gerald Murphy sports a striped knitted *jersey* worn by French sailors. Since the beginning of the century polo players have worn white jersey tops with loose collars and short sleeves, seen today in a variety of colors on people unable to tell one end of a horse from the other.

The famous *Fair Isle sweater* also comes into its own during the '20s when the Prince of Wales wears one to play golf. It's multicolored with geometric patterns, and named after the Shetland island it hails from.

In the 1930s designer Madelaine Vionnet, who cuts on the bias, creates clothes that curve with the body: It is she who is responsible for the *cowl neck* and the *halter*—translated into knits by designers everywhere. The *twinset*—a matching cardigan and sweater which becomes the basis of the English "Sloane Ranger's" uniform (with pearls, of course), is introduced in the same era by none other than the très French Madame Coco Chanel herself.

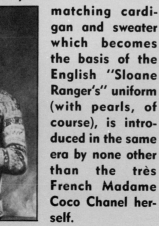

Top Left: *Woman inspecting a cashmere twin set, 1940.* Bottom, far left: *Lana Turner in* They Won't Forget, *1937.* Bottom left: *Edward, Prince of Wales, in a Fair Isle sweater, portrait by John St. Helier Lander, ca. 1922.* Left: *Dancer wears a French sailor's sweater, à la Gerald Murphy, in* Funny Face, *1957.* Clockwise from above: *Back-to-school clothes, 1959; Ann Baker in the early TV series "Meet Corliss Archer," 1954; Mini-skirted flower child, 1968; mod couple in* The Knack . . . and How To Get It, *1965; movie poster, 1946.*

THE AGE OF THE TEEN

In the '30s Andy Hardy hangs out at the soda fountain and Lindy-hops to tunes on the jukebox and we glimpse the beginning of a new cultural phenomenon—the teenager. There is no onslaught of Huns from the north, no anarchy or political referendum; all it takes is demographics and economic prosperity for the American teen to become a force to be reckoned with. By the mid-'40s the teen has his own fashionable fads, slang, and customs: ponytails; blue jeans rolled to the knee, worn with oversized men's shirts, and bobby sox; ankle bracelets, saddle shoes, felt poodle skirts.

In the '50s, the English "Teddy Boys" are neo-Edwardian teens who sport long overcoats, shoestring ties, stovepipe trousers, thick-soled "beetle-crusher," shoes and Byronic (or Elvis Presley-like) hairdos. How to recognize the Teddy Girls? They don a cap and carry a duffle bag. It's a passing fad, but it sweeps the nation—64 percent of all British youths claim membership in the Teddy Boy clan.

By the '60s, of course, the sheer numbers of adolescent Baby Boomers make the teenager more powerful than ever. The "flower child"; Carnaby Street's "mod" miniskirter; a nineteen-year-old model named Twiggy, and four mop-headed Beatles will not only set their own styles, they'll dictate what designers create for the haute couture. Fashion these days doesn't trickle down from some ivory tower. It goes from the street to the atelier and then to the stores where over-thirties buy clothes with designer labels.

9½ NEW and TERRIFIC!

...AUGHS AT ...ANDY HARDY

MICKEY ROONEY
LEWIS STONE

Welcome Back, Mickey Rooney!

SARA HADEN · LINA ROMAY · FAY HOLDEN
BONITA GRANVILLE · DOROTHY FORD

Screen Play by HARRY RUSKIN and WILLIAM LUDWIG · Original Story by HOWARD DIMSDALE
DIRECTED BY WILLIS GOLDBECK · PRODUCED BY ROBERT SISK

Above: *"Provocative Undressing,"* 1902.

BODY HEAT

Clothes have been growing lighter, skimpier, and freer since the days of the Gibson Girl. By 1938 it is reported that the average woman's summer costume weighs one pound, eleven ounces. It consists of: a dress, six and a half ounces; a slip, two ounces; shoes, eleven ounces; a girdle, three and a half ounces; a hat, three ounces; and stockings, one ounce. Although men's clothes are also lightening up, the male summer burden amounts to a hefty five pounds, nine ounces for: a suit, two pounds, eleven ounces; a shirt, eight ounces; drawers, three and a half ounces; shoes, one pound, ten ounces; a hat, three ounces; socks, two ounces; a belt, three and a half ounces; and necktie, one ounce.

These data make a strong case for weighing men in the nude. And, they lead the prestigious Harvard University School of Public Health to an unprecedented discovery: "Men," it announces in a widely attended press conference, "can't stand the heat because they are overdressed." Maybe that's why they got out of the kitchen.

Based on the facts, the Harvard experts conclude that newly invented air conditioners should be set at 72 degrees for men and 80 degrees for women.

CARMEN GEAR: Platform shoes elevate sultry songstress Carmen Miranda and she in turn elevates these chunky shoes to new heights of popularity. By 1939, when *Vogue* paradoxically declares that "Nothing is dowdier than a dainty foot," millions of women have jumped onto the clunky platform—and they stay there until the end of World War II. But, like old soldiers, the shoes refuse to die. They simply fade away until 1975, when platforms are back, bigger and thicker than ever.

Above: *Platform shoes from Saks Fifth Avenue, $100 in 1940.* **Right:** *Carmen Miranda, ca. 1945. The "Brazilian Bombshell" was actually Portuguese.*

1937 THE FIRST JET ENGINE IS BUILT BY FRANK WHITTLE.

1939 WAR IS DECLARED AGAINST GERMANY BY BRITAIN AND FRANCE.

COPPER TONES: When trend-setting fashion designer Coco Chanel is pictured in the press with tanned skin, black (at least for whites) becomes beautiful.

This is the first time in history that being tan is associated with leisure, sports, and the upper class, and not with laborers who have to work in the field.

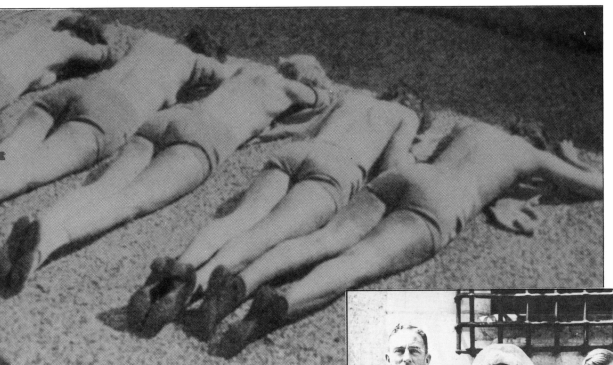

Above: *Members of an American women's athletic club sunbathing topless on a city rooftop, 1931.*

BUT FOR A SONG

If he hadn't lost his voice, Mainbocher might have become the successful singer he yearns to be. Instead, he turns to designing, in 1930 becoming the first American to open a successful haute couture house in Paris. His trouser suit of striped cotton imitates the suits of workmen. But he is best remembered for his evening wear. He designs the wedding gown Mrs. Wallis Simpson wears when she weds the Duke of Windsor and he creates the popular color "Wallis Blue."

Above: *Duke and Duchess of Windsor (center) immediately after their wedding ceremony in Monts, France, June 8, 1937.*

WAR-DROBE

Just as the World War I metal drives finally freed women from the corsets that had afflicted them for four hundred years, strictures and shortages during World War II also make their impact on fashion.

• English Board of Trade "Utility Clothes" restricts the amount of fabric manufacturers can use; limits firms to creating at most fifty styles each year; and issues consumers coupons—forty per person per year is the maximum clothing allowance—one suit alone takes eighteen coupons.

• The U.S. government decrees that to conserve fabrics, men's suits must be manufactured without cuffs, pleats, or patch pockets. Women's dresses have to be short, with hems only two inches deep, and ruffles are forbidden for the duration.

• The beret emerges as the favorite wartime hat, thanks to the shortage of elastic.

• The *wedgie shoe* comes into fashion, since its wooden platform sole helps conserve leather.

• The *shoulder bag* is invented so women have more room to store bandages, medicine, and cotton swabs for wartime emergencies.

• "Victory Fabrics"—"Flag Red" and "Victory Blue"—are introduced.

• One of the spinoffs of the war effort is the invention of aerosol—the key ingredient in Helene Curtis's Spray Net, without which the beehive hairdos of the 1950s could never have existed.

• The *Eisenhower jacket*—waist-length, belted, with a turned-down collar—named for the popular general, takes center stage.

• Dubbed a "wind cheater," the *windbreaker,* a waist-length jacket with a fitted waistline, made from wool, gabardine, or nylon and adapted from the British Royal Air Force jackets of the '40s, becomes popular.

• The *pencil skirt,* cut in one straight line from hips to hem, is invented as a result of clothing rations: it uses the least amount of material.

• The Betty Grable pinup boosts the boys' morale and makes women yearn for shapely legs and bottoms.

This page: background: *American bombers;* top right: *Dwight D. Eisenhower in his eponymous jacket;* bottom, left to right: *in her heyday, ca. 1942, before her career was sabotaged by a weight problem, actress Deanna Durbin models a pencil skirt; women's ensemble incorporating a shoulderbag and beret, 1943; bathing beauty and an aerosol can, ca. 1943.* Opposite page: top right: *Veronica Lake flirts behind a peek-a-boo bang, ca. 1939;* Center left: *World War II U.S. Army training film;* center right: *Wedgie with an ankle strap, 1943;* bottom: *demonstration of first aid under air-raid conditions, ca. 1941.*

A LAKELY STORY

Secretive, seductive, and luxurious—if wartime shortages limit other extravagances, there's no reason why you can't let your hair grow. The "Veronica Lake" look sweeps the nation.

I'M DREAMING OF A FIGHT CHRISTMAS

In 1939, war is rumbling across Europe, and as a precaution against gas attacks, thirty-eight million gas masks are distributed to civilians. For Christmas, a leading London retailer advertises "dainty cylinder gas mask cases in velvet or corded silk," and a combined bag and gas mask case in calf on a strong gilt frame. Both are available in a range of colors and patterns to match women's outfits.

ZUT ALORS

How could a suit with such a funny name cause riots? *Zoot suits,* baggy pants with tight cuffs and oversized jackets, worn with wide-brimmed hats and a long chain hanging from the belt, are popular with teenagers who call themselves "hepcats." In 1942, they spark protests in Los Angeles, New York, and a lot closer to home—wherever parents reside. The fad doesn't die out until the U.S. government steps in and bans the suits under wartime fabric conservation standards.

What is it about these suits that causes riots? Well, it's wartime. The men who have stayed home or haven't yet enlisted are the ones who don the zoot suit—in the same way that the Incroyables dressed up in Napoleon's bullish times. The suit exagger-

ates a man's shoulders, makes him look tall—he may not be off fighting for his country, but he's a man. The fight breaks out between civilians and servicemen who are probably feeling a little touchy. There's no female zoot suit—women aren't expected to go to war. But Elsa Schiaparelli's designs *are* considered outrageous in their own right—perhaps adding a little lightness to this somber, gray time.

Above left: *Zoot suit, 1943* Above right: *Movie extras in zoot suits, 1943.*

A FLESH START

Once upon a time stockings came in only two colors: black for the winter, white for the summer. But short skirts make stockings an important fashion accessory and in 1922 "flesh-colored" stockings are available—as long as your flesh is pinkish-beige. It will be another twenty-five years before brown and black-skinned legs are acknowledged.

Also in 1922, French count Chardonnet brings "artificial silk" to America. The new fabric, called *vicose,* is made by pushing nitro-cellulose through a machine-run jet. Vicose is cheaper than silk and sexier than cotton so the Flapper Girl can show off her Charleston legs without spending a fortune.

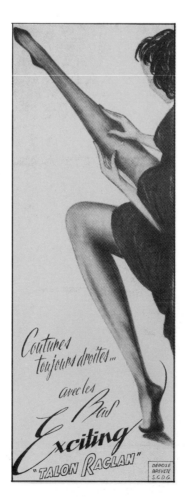

On February 16, 1937, Dr. Wallace Hume Carothers receives patent number 2,071,251 for a new miracle fabric called "nylon." Little could he suspect that on May 15, 1940, when the first nylon stockings (which are sheerer than silk) go on sale they prompt a veritable run on U.S. department stores. It is reported that 780,000 are sold on the first day alone. Alas, wartime shortages will soon force women to replace their precious nylons with leg makeup.

Far left: *Russian actress Alla Nazimova (1879–1945) in Madonna of the Streets, 1924.* **Left:** *Stocking advertisement, 1953.*

1945 THE FIRST ATOMIC BOMB IS DETONATED NEAR ALAMAGORDO, NEW MEXICO, ON JULY 16.

1946 THE FIRST COMPUTER, KNOWN AS AN "ELECTRONIC BRAIN," IS BUILT AT PENNSYLVANIA UNIVERSITY.

INDEPENDENTS

Curiously, World War II provides an opportunity for American designers (and designers working in America) to show their colors. With the Paris fashion world in limbo, Pauline Trigère flees Paris and opens a house in New York where she makes crisp, tailored, classic clothes and pioneers the wool evening dress. Norman Norell, who once designed movie costumes for Gloria Swanson, is hailed for the chemise, dolman sleeves, and glittery drop-dead all-sequined sheath dresses, still popular today. Englishman Charles James first comes to America in 1927, uses the States as his base from 1939–1947, and then alternates between the two continents. Best remembered for his lavish sculpted evening gowns, he also designs culottes for Lord & Taylor in 1932 that are still being sold in the '50s. And probably the most famous of all is Claire McCardell, the Parsons graduate who invents "American Sportswear."

Left: *Hooded dress of wool with rhinestones, Trigere, 1967.* **Below, left to right:** *Shirt and skirt, Trigere, 1955; gold sequined evening gown by Norman Norell, worn here by actress Lizabeth Scott, ca. 1950; Babe Paley in a gown by Charles James, 1963.*

THE AMERICAN SCHEME

Who invents the casual elegance of leotard dressing and takes the ballet slipper into the street? Not Donna Karan, but Claire McCardell, whose use of simple fabrics and clean lines creates what has been called "The American Look": a way of dressing characterized by comfort, freedom of movement, and high style.

Using denim, gingham, and new fabrics like wool jersey, McCardell creates easy-fitting, bias-cut dresses with an eye for detail: patch pockets, visible hooks, double stitching and deep armholes. Her "popover," a wrap-around denim dress (later resurrected by Diane von Furstenberg), is designed as something women can wear to do housework and still look smart. A bargain at the 1940s price of $6.95, 75,000 popovers are turned over in the first year of sales alone. On May 2, 1955, McCardell finds *Time* on her side as she is pictured on the cover of the prestigious magazine, which celebrates her as the innovator of casual, American separates. McCardell is the first fashion designer to be so honored. Only two others, Dior and Gernreich, have been pictured since.

*Claire McCardell

Above left: Cotton "Popover" wrap-and-tie dress by Claire McCardell, introduced in 1942; (inset) Claire McCardell (1905–1958). Top right: McCardell's "T-Square" shirt paired with short-shorts. Center right: This suburban dream house cost $6,000 in 1949. Bottom, left to right: Claire McCardell's Fuller Fashions, offered through the Fuller Brush catalog and available in stores, ca. 1955: "Princess" pants and wrap-and-tie top; striped cotton shorts and top; cotton "Princess" dress; kilt-length skirt and abbreviated shirt in crisp cotton.

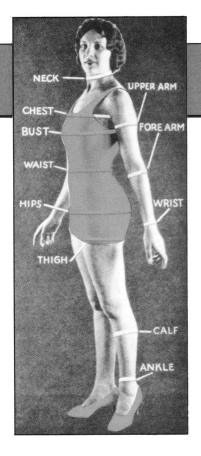

NECK —
UPPER ARM
CHEST —
BUST —
FORE ARM
WAIST —
WRIST
HIPS —
THIGH —
— CALF
ANKLE

Clockwise from left: *Irene Ahlberg, "Miss America 1929," judged as "typical of modern young womanhood"; L'Action Enchaînée, monument to Louis Auguste Blanqui (1805–1881), French revolutionary and radical thinker, by Aristide Maillol, 1906; Alberto Giacometti figure, 1967; Met Life Insurance weight tables from 1959 (left) and 1989 (right).*

YOUR "IDEAL" WEIGHT:

THE FIRST "IDEAL WEIGHT" charts were published by the Metropolitan Life Insurance Company in 1942 and they do not necessarily represent the opinion of this company (or anyone else) that this is the weight you should aim for if you want to look best in a skimpy bikini or a micro-mini. In fact, if Cheryl Tiegs had believed that, she might be slinging hash in a roadside diner in North Carolina instead of becoming a covergirl, as the weights on the chart are rather high for your haute couture look. Still, in an ever-changing world which offers too few standards, even if you can't be desirable, you can be "ideal." But at what weight? How come the current chart says that short women can be a full ten pounds heavier than they were allowed to be in 1959? And why can tall women only tack on three measly pounds more? What's "short" in a world of seven-foot basketball players? And, most confusing, whadda they mean: small, medium, or large frame? We know—your mother always said you had "big bones." But you never really believed her, did you, when she said that was why you needed a size 16½? So here, once and for all, we have the definitive answer (unadulterated) from Metropolitan Life itself:

WOMEN: 1959			
Height (with shoes on) 2-inch heels Feet / Inches	Small Frame	Medium Frame	Large Frame
4 10	92– 98	96–107	104–119
4 11	94–101	98–110	106–122
5 0	96–104	101–113	109–125
5 1	99–107	104–116	112–128
5 2	102–110	107–119	115–131
5 3	105–113	110–122	118–134
5 4	108–116	113–126	121–138
5 5	111–119	116–130	125–142
5 6	114–123	120–135	129–146
5 7	118–127	124–139	133–150
5 8	122–131	128–143	137–154
5 9	126–135	132–147	141–158
5 10	130–140	136–151	145–163
5 11	134–144	140–155	149–168
6 0	138–148	144–159	153–173

For girls between 18 and 25, subtract 1 pound for each year under 25.

WOMEN: 1989			
Height Feet / Inches	Small Frame	Medium Frame	Large Frame
4 10	102–111	109–121	118–131
4 11	103–113	111–123	120–134
5 0	104–115	113–126	122–137
5 1	106–118	115–129	125–140
5 2	108–121	118–132	128–143
5 3	111–124	121–135	131–147
5 4	114–127	124–138	134–151
5 5	117–130	127–141	137–155
5 6	120–133	130–144	140–159
5 7	123–136	133–147	143–163
5 8	126–139	136–150	146–167
5 9	129–142	139–153	149–170
5 10	132–145	142–156	152–173
5 11	135–148	145–159	155–176
6 0	138–151	148–162	158–179

DIOR-IOUS

When he is a young man, a fortune teller sees that Christian Dior will suffer poverty. "But," she predicts, "women are lucky for you, and through them you will achieve success. You will make a great deal of money out of them." And, the former art dealer certainly did.

Born in 1905, Dior runs an art gallery until 1935 and makes a living in Paris selling fashion sketches to newspapers. He apprentices with several designers—including Balmain—before cotton king Marcel Boussac gives him money to open his own house in 1947. He opens his new collection with the controversial "New Look." Dior makes variations of the *coolie hat*, to be worn with wide skirts with nipped-in waists; the "Princess line"—with small shoulders, short jackets, and high-belted backs—and in 1955 introduces the still popular **A** line. He is good with silhouettes, elegant lines, and sculpted looks. He loves black, navy blue, and white; pins at the neck, shoulder, and waist; ropes of pearls swung around the neck. Dior invents the "model walk," in which the mannequin is arched with her back tilted and her chin high, giving her stance a certain arrogance. He is also credited with re-establishing Paris as a fashion power base after World War II.

LEG APPEAL

In 1947, with restrictions on fabrics lifted, mannish wartime styles are out of fashion: Christian Dior's "New Look" is born. No more short skirts and padded square shoulders: The New Look has narrow sloping shoulders, a cinched-in waist, and a wide skirt which wantonly uses yards and yards of fabric and dips to midcalf. Women who have gotten used to showing off their gams angrily picket outside Dior's Paris showroom. But the New Look prevails, however, as most fall in love with the more feminine style.

1947 THOR HEYERDAHL SAILS FROM PERU TO POLYNESIA ON A RAFT TO PROVE PRE-HISTORIC IMMIGRATION.

1948 MAHATMA GANDHI IS ASSASSINATED.

HERE TO STAY

In the 1920s when a steam process is added to German hairdresser Charles Nestle's machine for waving women's hair, going straight is suddenly unfashionable. The "permanent" is here to stay: In 1936 beauty shops give thirty-five million permanent waves. And by the 1940s "home perms" offer an alternative solution.

Opposite page: top left: *Dior hat, 1947;* **bottom, far left:** *Dior "New Look" dress with a cinched waist and a skirt that reaches one inch above the ankle, 1947;* **bottom, near left:** *Dior "New Look" design, 1947;* **right:** *aloof model in an afternoon dress in Romaine crepe, 1952;* **right inset:** *woman's suit in the "New Look," 1947.* **This page: above:** *Advertisement for Toni home perms, late 1940s;* **below:** *a busdriver who always wears a tie: Jackie Gleason as Ralph Kramden in "The Honeymooners," 1955.*

TIE-LINE

What better time than Independence Day weekend to stage the Necktie Revolt? "Give me liberty," say the fourteen Union Bus Terminal ticket sellers when told that they can't continue working unless they tie one on. They refuse, and the knotty situation ties up business for the rest of the hectic 1944 holiday.

367

1950 SENATOR JOSEPH MCCARTHY ADVISES PRESIDENT TRUMAN THAT THE UNITED STATES STATE DEPARTMENT HAS BEEN INFILTRATED BY COMMUNISTS.

WILL THE REAL '50S MAN AND WOMAN PLEASE STAND UP

Everybody thinks "the Eisenhower years" and remembers one big snooze, right? How can that be? You have squeaky-clean Pat Boone squaring off against Elvis "The Pelvis" Presley. Sexpots Brigitte Bardot and Marilyn Monroe are reigning movie queens at the same time that everyone is in love with waiflike Audrey Hepburn. The two favorite colors of the decade are gray (flannel) and hot pink. Sounds like a little ego/id problem going on here. So once and for all, please: Will the *real* '50s man and woman please stand up?

"Funny Face" Audrey Hepburn exudes '50s innocence, while a racy Marilyn Monroe (née Norma Jean Baker) reminds us that "Some Like It Hot."

Elvis "The Pelvis" in tight pants with a greasy "duck tail" haircut croons, "Don't Step on My Blue Suede Shoes...."

Bucking Tradition: In 1957 Pat Boone sings "Love Letters in the Sand" and teenagers throughout America swoon over his clean-cut good looks. His trademark is his white bucks, a symbol of purity and innocence. Boone's bucks, size 10½, are made of rubber. The originals, first seen around 1870, were made from Brazilian or Chinese deer, and worn as tennis shoes.

Counter-clockwise from top left: *Dwight and Mamie Eisenhower on their 25th wedding anniversary, July 1, 1955; Audrey Hepburn, ca. 1952; Marilyn Monroe, ca. 1958; Pat Boone's white bucks, 1957; Pat Boone, 1958; Elvis Presley in his first national television appearance on "The Ed Sullivan Show," 1956.*

"The Man in the Gray Flannel Suit" wears a three-piece, narrow-shouldered sack suit, loose at the waist, with a long jacket. His white shirt has a (symbolically) buttoned down collar, and he wears a narrow (more symbolism here) tie. He plods through life in heavy Oxford shoes.

The wife of "The Man in the Gray Flannel Suit" wears a cashmere sweater set with a tweed skirt, or for a little variety, a "Peter Pan" collared blouse with a plaid tartan; either outfit spruced up with a strand of pearls or a gold circle pin.

Above: Gregory Peck in The Man in the Gray Flannel Suit, 1956. Far left: Brooks Brothers gray flannel suit, 1956. Left: The Washington Squares, credited with the beatnik revival, 1983.

The Beats wear black.

HABIT-ABLE

In 1952 Pope Pius XII decrees that nuns can modernize their habits. After all, the original idea was that they simply wear a modest adaptation of what everyone else has on. American designer Hattie Carnegie designs a simple black dress for the Society of Christ Our King Order that would be at home at any cocktail party. In 1960 Christian Dior designs nuns' outfits in France, and the fashionable New York department store Bergdorf Goodman offers a line of habits.

HAWAII FIVE-O:

In the 1950s, U.S. tourists wave "aloha" and come home from vacation lei-den down with Hawaiian shirts.

Top right: *Sisters of the Religious of the Sacred Heart of Mary, 1950, before dress deregulation.* **Below:** *70s hula girls eyed by tourist in a Hawaiian shirt.*

In 1952, in an effort to firm up a flabby industry, National Corset Week is declared in Britain. Over one thousand store windows are filled with mannequins wearing corsets.

WINDOWPAIN

Corset sales are constricted in the '20s by free-flowing flapper fashions. In 1947, Dior's "New Look" calls for a nipped-in waist, and the corset (in the form of a "guepiere") enjoys a brief resurgence as a waist-cincher. But by the '50s, most women have abandoned the corset for the pantie girdle, made of stretchable "lastex" with satin panels, although it is still less than perfect: the girdle rolls up if not held down by stockings attached to its suspender-like hooks.

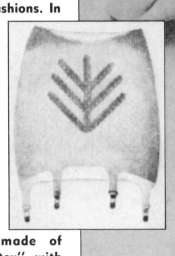

Counter-clockwise from right: *Dior bra and girdle set, 1956; the last of the modern-day corsets, 1954; Latex girdle with garters, mid-1950s.*

CARPET MAKERS OF THE WORLD, REVOLT

After the clunky wedgies of World War II, women crave more feminine shoes. In 1952, Italian designer Ferragamo introduces *stiletto heels*. The shoes have a steel spike inserted in the heel to give them sufficient strength to be raised to four- and five-inch heights. It is almost impossible to walk in them; the heels get caught in every tiny crack and crevice, and they ruin floors and carpets wherever they're worn. Naturally, stiletto heels are a huge success.

Above left: *Ferragamo stilletto, 1955.* Above right: *Satin stiletto pump, 1958.*

371

KING OF THE WILD FRONTIER

On December 14, 1954, forty million people tune in to watch the premiere of "Davy Crockett," starring twenty-nine-year-old Fess Parker. His coonskin cap, however, is the real star of the show: In one year, one hundred million dollars' worth of raccoon fur is sold to meet the demand for the cap, and prices rise to eight dollars a pound. Within a year of the show's premiere, the supply of raccoon tails in the United States runs out, and kids who want Davy Crockett hats must make do with rabbit and muskrat imitations. Raccoons should not feel put upon, however, since much the same thing happened to their cousin, the American beaver, when in the 1600s the rage for hats made of its skin became so great that the animal became nearly extinct.

IT'S NOT FAKE ANYTHING; IT'S *REAL* POLYESTER

In 1953, the Witty Brothers, a men's clothier, make the first polyester suit. To advertise their accomplishment, they have a model shower in it, swim in it, and wear it for sixty-seven days without pressing.

Polyester, which is made from large molecules of carbon, hydrogen, and oxygen, becomes the butt of many jokes, and enters the language as a pejorative for anything plastic or artificial. It suffers further offense when the Omaha Police Department bans polyester uniforms as "unprofessional" and filmmaker John Waters releases his raunchy *Polyester* in 1981.

The polyester controversy continues as some manufacturers applaud polyester's crease-resistant qualities and low price. But mainstream designers continue to eschew it. In 1984, responding to a question from *USA Today*, Ralph Lauren says haughtily, "I don't use polyester in my collections because I believe that natural fibers have more character. They fade, they wrinkle, and they become part of the person who wears (them)." Polyester *does* have a "personalizing" characteristic, however. In 1956 the U.S. Navy bars polyester uniforms because in a fire "the fabric melts and clings to the skin."

Background: Attack on an Emmigrant Train, C. Wimar, 1856; Clockwise from top left: Fess Parker as TV's Davey Crockett, 1954; boy following the coonskin cap fad, 1950s; Robert DeNiro in synthetic in King of Comedy, 1983; 1969 advertisement for a synthetic fabric; polyester-clad talk-show host Mike Douglas, 1976.

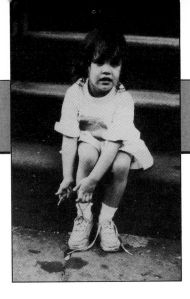

THE ZIPLESS STUCK

In 1955 when Swiss inventor George Demenstral watches two interlocked burrs blow down a hill, he shouts "Velcro!" He pioneers the first zipperless zipper, now seen on the very best sneakers, wallets, and waistbands. Children around the world no longer have to learn to tie their shoes.

SACK IT TO ME

As early as 1950 American designer Norman Norell introduces the *chemise*. But it isn't until seven years later, elegantly presented (if inelegantly re-christened the "sack") by Balenciaga and Dior that the shape takes hold. The *sack* is just what it sounds like and for the first time in over one hundred and fifty years, women don't have to watch their waistlines. Nevertheless, the style is controversial with the fashion press, unpopular with men, and a year later women themselves sack it.

Left: *Old-fashioned Cayley Barlowe tying her shoelaces.* **Background:** *The stinging nettle.* **Above left:** *Marilyn Monroe looks hot even in a potato sack.* **Above right:** *Tweed sack dress, Balenciaga, 1956.*

373

I CAN, CANOE?

In the late 1950s, the first men's cologne appears on American college campuses, when Dana imports four thousand bottles of Canoe from Paris—selling out their stock in 61 days.

CASTRO CONVERTIBLES

In 1959 charismatic revolutionary Fidel Castro liberates Cuba and popularizes army fatigues as de rigueur radical chic.

"She picked the black dress off the chair and smoothed it gratefully. It had done its work well. Other girls had floundered through the dance in wretched tulles and flounces and taffetas, like the dresses her mother had tried for two weeks to buy for the great occasion. But she had fought for this tube of curving black crepe silk, high-necked enough to seem demure, and had won; and she had captivated the son of a millionaire. That was how much her mother knew about clothes."
—Herman Wouk, *Marjorie Morningstar*

Top left: *Fidel Castro in fatigues, 1960.*
Top right: *"Canoe" advertisement, 1967.*
Right: *Natalie Wood and Gene Kelly in Marjorie Morningstar, 1958.*

374

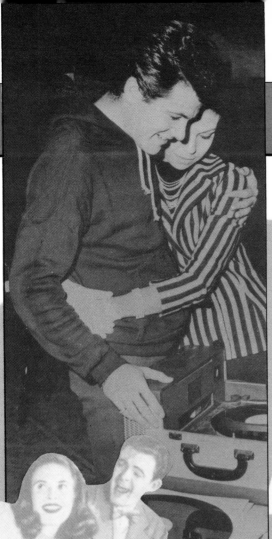

ROCK
AND
ROLL
CLOTHING

"Baubles, Bangles and Beads," The Kirby Stone Four, 1958

"Bell-Bottom Trousers," Louis Prima, 1945

"Black Denim Trousers," The Cheers, 1955; Vaughn Monroe, 1955

"Black Slacks," Joe Bennet & the Sparkletones, 1957

"Blue Suede Shoes," Boyd Bennett, 1956; Carl Perkins, 1956; Elvis Presley, 1956

"Blue Velvet," Tony Bennett, 1951; The Clovers, 1955; The Statues, 1960; Bobby Vinton, 1963

"Bobby Sox to Stockings," Frankie Avalon, 1959

"Brass Buttons," The String-a-Longs, 1961

"Cowboy Boots," Dave Dudley, 1963

"Dungaree Doll," Eddie Fisher, 1955

"Glad Rags," Tennessee Ernie Ford, 1959

"Golden Earrings," Peggy Lee, 1947

"High-Heel Sneakers," Jerry Lee Lewis, 1964

"Hip Hug-Her," Booker T & the MGs, 1967

"Hot Pants (She Got to Use What She Got to Get What She Wants)," James Brown, 1971

"I Got a Bag of My Own," James Brown, 1972

"I Got Ants in My Pants," James Brown, 1973

"I Said My Pajamas (And Put On My Prayers)," Doris Day, 1950

"Itsy Bitsy Teenie Weenie Yellow Polka Dot Bikini," Brian Hyland, 1960

"I've Got Sand In My Shoes," The Drifters, 1964

"Lipstick & Candy & Rubber Sole Shoes," Julius La Rosa, 1956

"Lipstick on Your Collar," Connie Francis, 1959

"Little Blue Riding Hood," Stan Freberg, 1953

"Mini-Skirt Minnie," Wilson Pickett, 1969

"My Bolero," Vic Damone, 1949

"No Shoes," John Lee Hooker, 1960

"Petticoats of Portugal," Dick Jacobs, 1956; Billy Vaughn, 1956

"Pink Pedal Pushers," Carl Perkins, 1958

"Pink Shoe Laces," Janet King, 1959

"Rockin' Shoes," The Ames Brothers, 1957

"Shoppin' for Clothes," The Coasters, 1960

"Short Shorts," The Royal Teens, 1958

"Silver Threads and Golden Needles," The Springfields, 1962

"Soul Dressing," Booker T & The MGs, 1967

"These Boots Were Made For Walking," Nancy Sinatra, 1964

"Venus in Blue Jeans," Jimmy Clanton, 1962

"Walk a Mile in My Shoes," Joe South, 1970

"Wear My Ring Around Your Neck," Elvis Presley, 1958

"White Sport Coat," Marty Robbins, 1957

Clockwise from right: *James Brown in Ski Party, 1965; teens dancing in an advertisement; Nancy Sinatra and Tommy Sands, 1960; couple dancing on "American Bandstand," late 1950s.*

FLUSHED

For those who aren't naturally shy, Revlon supplies the first powdered blush-on in 1963: a cake of pink powder applied with a stubby brush.

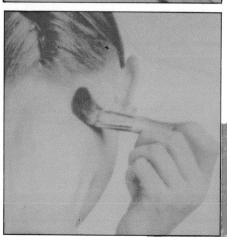

CAMELOT

Once upon a time in the olden days (before fashion magazines and television) the kingdom anxiously waited for news of what the queen was wearing to filter down. Now, after eight years of grandmotherly Mamie Eisenhower fashions, it's no wonder the public embraces the young, fresh styles of Jackie Kennedy. Her greatest contributions to the early '60s: the pillbox hat and the bouffant hairstyle.

Top right: *Jacqueline and John F. Kennedy, 1963.* **Left:** *Advertisement for Revlon's Blush-On, 1965.* **Right background:** *Illustration of Camelot, 1903.* **Right:** *Former First Lady Mamie Eisenhower and then-current White House occupant Jacqueline Kennedy, June 1962.*

376

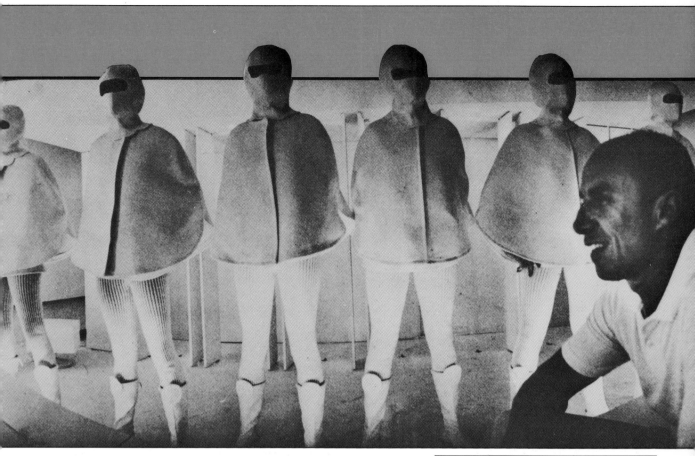

THE TAKE-OFF

HOW MANY MID-1960S DESIGNERS can be dubbed "space age"? At least two, Pierre Cardin and André Courrèges. Although neither collects a paycheck from Cape Canaveral, Courrèges creates uncluttered, futuristic fashions — stark cut-out dresses worn with helmet-shaped hats and the famous Courrèges square-toed, calf-length white boot, and knitted, long-sleeved one-piece *catsuits*, so-called because of their slinky fit. Cardin, who becomes the king of licensing, putting his name on everything from suits to toilet water to towels, first makes a name for himself with batwing jumpsuits, necklines that plunge to the navel, more helmets, thigh-high hemlines, and *bodystockings* — an idea that will propel Donna Karan into orbit twenty years later.

Top: *"Cosmonaut" suits, André Courrèges' 1968.* **Bottom left:** *Striped body stockings, Pierre Cardin, 1968.* **Right:** *Abbreviated jumpsuit, Courrèges, 1966.*

CLOTI... E ALWAYS CREATED AN ARTIFICIAL ATMOSPHERE AROUND THE BODY—but usually for the sake of glamor. Today, however, "the right stuff" for an astronaut has to protect him or her.

In 1933 stuntman Mark Ridge looks to the sea when he designs a space suit for balloonists, adapted from deep-sea diving suits. It never gets off the ground.

Aviation daredevil Wiley Post, who dreams of setting a high-altitude record in his monoplane, tries next, working with B.F. Goodrich in 1935 to develop the perfect pressurized suit. But when his plane crashes we lose Wiley and the suit, along with his passenger, famed humorist Will Rogers.

World War II aces wear pressurized suits that remain pretty much unchanged until NASA enters the space race in 1958. For Project Mercury, when an astronaut will stay inside the capsule while it orbits the earth, a suit is needed that will be comfortable during long hours of sitting. The final design is two suits in one. The inner suit is made of rubber, holding the oxygen that pressurizes the suit. Unrestrained, the rubber blows up like a balloon, however, so a second suit of heavy, canvas-like material is worn over the rubber. To get into the suit, our modern-day Captain Marvel steps into a zippered opening. A helmet and gloves then mechanically attach, and a hose connects him to the capsule's life-support systems. The Mercury suits create painful friction when the astronauts move

SPACE AGE FASHION

(FOR AN "OUT OF THIS WORLD" LOOK)

Counterclockwise from below: Jane Fonda in Barbarella, 1967; design for the Saturn C-5 rocket proposed for "Project Apollo," 1962; Wiley Post, who in 1933 was the first to fly solo around the world, wears the first full-pressure suit, precursor to the spacesuit, 1935; proposed excursion module and command unit for the U.S.'s first lunar landing, 1962.

around in them, and they are very hot and heavy. They also aren't the kind of thing you'd wear to meet

dignitaries from a foreign planet. But they do the job.

To take a giant step for mankind in 1969, physicists provide Buzz Aldrin with a white canvas outersuit that looks striking against the lunar landscape; beneath its canvas shell are layers and layers of thin plastic film that

Clockwise from above: First seven astronauts selected for "Project Mercury," which ran from 1961 to 1963; Robinsons and crew have no trouble with atmospheric pressure while "Lost in Space", 1965; Edward H. White III, pilot of Gemini IV, floating in space, 1965; Nichelle Nichols, George Takei, and William Shatner in "Star Trek," 1965.

have been sprayed with aluminum to protect him from extreme space temperatures. Unfortunately, this layered look not only insulates him from the climate, it raises his body heat to extreme levels. So a liquid cooling system—an inner layer of space suit filled with tubing that pumps water over the astronaut's skin—is developed. Another essential, obviously, is a diaper.

For hiking on the moon, our pioneers don backpacks that contain life-support systems along with apple juice and beef jerky. And although they weigh a hefty 130 pounds here on earth, the trip helps lighten their load—on the moon they weigh a mere 20 pounds.

Everything seems to be going along smoothly until 1970, when NASA allows women into the skylab program. Now, it's back to the drawing board for physicists who have to come up with designs suitable for the slighter, more compact female build. What they produce is a space suit in many different parts that come in standard sizes. The new suits have a fiberglass torso, where life-support systems are contained for easier movement. Now, instead of spending hours checking that all is A-OK, it takes a much shorter time to dress. And, depending on the needs of the mission, bits and pieces of the suit can be added or removed.

Now that they've worked out most of the kinks, will space fashion follow the way of all other dress? Can we expect designer space suits? Outré designs? Tune in a hundred years from now.

379

YOUTH FULL

In 1965 *Seventeen* magazine reports that teenage girls in America, who represent 11 percent of the population, purchase 20 percent of all apparel and 23 percent of all cosmetics sold in the country. They buy 72 million hosiery items, over 6 million pieces of costume jewelry, and 4 million belts. They also buy 3.5 million wallets—although we're not sure they have any money left to carry in them. No wonder there's a youth rebellion.

CHAIN, CHAIN, CHAIN

In 1965, Paco Rabanne creates a fad with his plastic dress—a mini made of linked plastic discs—and follows up with garments made of metal discs and chains. The concept may have scored big back in the Middle Ages when knights needed protection against dueling opponents. But in the laid-back Sixties, the last thing either side wanted in the Battle of the Sexes was women dressed in armor. Other Rabanne offerings included dresses of aluminum, and, for a softer look, toweling material held together with Scotch tape.

WASTE NOT, QUANT NOT:
THE LONDON STREET SCENE

In the 1950s on a walk through London's Hyde Park you'll see businessmen in Burberrys and bowlers; cockneys in caps and rumpled mufflers; Sikhs in turbans, their wives trailing in sarees; maybe even an Anglican bishop in gaitors. But by the 1960s one third of the population of England is under twenty and half the U.S. is under twenty-five—and it's no wonder there's a "Youth Revolution," and a demand for freer, spunkier, sexier clothing.

As usual, fashion is right there in the streets, waiting to be appropriated, at least in the working-class neighborhoods of Liverpool and Manchester where the Beatles and the Rolling Stones give the world a new sound, and designers like Mary Quant give the world a new sight.

Quant, who opens a shop with husband Alexander Plunket Green in Chelsea in the '50s, popularizes the infamous miniskirt, which brings her maxi profits. Credit for high boots, shoulder bags, and poor boy sweaters also goes to Quant. She opens a shop called "Bazaar" on King's Road, leading the way for other trendy London boutiques on the Road and Carnaby Street.

In France, it's older women who set the style; but in England it's the young—mods, punks, and rockers, and, yet to come, the trendsetting Princess Di.

ON THE MOVE

White boots and short dresses help girls go go.

Opposite page: center: dress constructed of gold and silver metallic plates, Paco Rabanne, 1968; bottom left: Seventeen cover, August 1965; bottom right: Rabanne's updated metal dress, 1990. This page: top left: Designs from one of the collections Mary Quant created for J. C. Penney from 1963 to 1968; top right: Mary Quant sketching, 1966; left: Nancy Sinatra, 1966; right: Courrèges hard hat and go-go boots.

Does she...or doesn't she?

DOES SHE OR

CREME
FORMULA
MISS CLAIROL
HAIR COLOR BATH

In 1909 French chemist Eugene Schueller develops the first safe commercial hair dye and founds the French Harmless Hair Dye Company. A year later he more glamorously re-christens his product L'Oreal; still most women resist the idea of coloring their hair. It is a kind of seven-percent solution, since by as late as 1950 that is the percentage of American women who dye their hair. By the late 1960s the figure jumps tenfold to seventy percent—what accounts for the change in attitude? A safer product? One-step-no-mess application? No. A New

DOESN'T SHE

York copywriter named Shirley Polykoff. For it is Polykoff who conceives of the now immortal lines "Does She or Doesn't She?" and "Only Her Hairdresser Knows for Sure," which help Clairol sales soar, and suggest to modern women that even respectable women are changing colors.

ESSENCE BARE The sexual revolution is on the way—heralded by fashions that will help popularize the birth control pill.

Women are wearing *hot pants*—and if that isn't enough to make Jerry Falwell take to his pulpit, braless see-through dresses, and the first topless bathing suit all make their appearance. Rudi Gernreich's 1964 *monokini* is considered scandalous, and banned in France; although the suit, which has straps going up the body from the waistband (rather than the shoulder) is meant more as a sign of the future than for actual sales. At the same time, nipples take on an attraction all their own in "skinny ribbed" pullovers, and some people just "let it all hang out." By the 1970s, we see (a lot) with the *string bikini*; and figure-conscious women are more interested in information on diets than support girdles. The cast of *Hair* bares all, and *Oh Calcutta* audiences rejoice at the nude revue. But on TV, Barbara Eden is ordered to cover her navel.

Counter-clockwise from top left: *Miss Clairol®* advertisement, 1960; Barbara Eden in *"I Dream of Jeannie,"* 1965; Rudi Gernreich's muse Peggy Moffit in his monokini, 1967; dress with large circular transparent windows in front and back, by Rety of Paris, 1966.

382

IT'S ONLY A PAPER MOON

But folks want something a little more substantial to tear off each other. Paper suits and underwear for men and women—the ultimate symbols of a disposable society—are marketed. It's the free-for-all '60s, but these cheap, throw-away clothes flop. Edible underwear, however, is here to stay.

Top left: *Paper dress made by the Scott Paper Co., 1966.* **Top center:** *Edible underwear, 1983.* **Above:** *Packaging for vintage "Paper-Delic" dress, sold in a New York City retro-boutique today.* **Right:** *Polyester Nehru jacket, ca. 1968.* **Far right:** *Jawaharlal Nehru, 1947.* **Below:** *Bob Hope admires two Nehru-jacketed hipsters in* How to Commit Marriage, *1969.*

Who was Nehru's tailor? We don't know. But the jacket he created sweeps the United States in the mid- to late-1960s, the first major variation on menswear for decades. The jacket is slim and reaches below the hips, with a short, standup collar.

COLLARED

383

Didn't live through it and don't want to read the book? Here are the 1960s in a nutshell:

CLIFF NOTES FOR THE '60S

To begin with, the term "hippie" does not mean that a large section of the population is walking around with fat bottoms. Hippie comes from "hip," a Jazz Age expression that means "with it." Thus the clothing worn is "cool." (In the '90s, however, it's "hot.")

Some examples of cool clothing include taste. Ideally, they should be well- for ten years, that's how cool must have bell-bottom legs (see ther discussion of bell-bottoms). adorned with studs, leather, ribbons, or patches that ex- inner conviction you need to at large. For instance, *Peace*, or *Boys*. Your bell-bottoms look dyed T-shirts. These shirts are color that form psychedelic pat- see behind your ping on LSD, and

jeans that express individual worn, as if you'd had them *you* are, and they "Moby Dick" for a fur- These jeans can be embroidered appliqué, press some deep share with the world *Draft Beer, Not really* cool with tie- dyed in splotches of terns, the kind you eyelids when you're trip- are worn both in the

country and the city, for formal and informal occasions. Sandals or moccasins are worn, or the feet are left bare. Hair is long and straight. For those hippies cursed with curly hair, "wrapping" comes into existence, a ritual in which hair is wrapped around orange juice cans and secured. (This should not be confused with "rapping," the hippie term for long exchanges of meaningful dialogue.)

You can't sleep with an orange juice can on your head, of course, but that's okay. You're on "speed" (amphetamines), and stay up all night rapping anyway.

Since this is the age of self-expression, there are several other hippie prototypes as well:

THE GRANNY LOOK

This fashion shows the high level of irony developed in the hippies' psyche. Sexual activity is at an all-time high—everyone is sleeping around and letting it all hang out. But the granny look is decidedly prim: long frilly flowered dresses, laced-up shoes, wire-rimmed glasses—whether needed or not—and hair worn in a bun.

THE FLOWER CHILD LOOK

This variation is simply a matter of accessories that enhance the jeans and T-shirt or the granny look. You simply add flowers to your hair, hitch a ride to California for some "California Dreamin'," and look sad, innocent, or vacant (drugs can give you the right expression and the right conversation—a long ramble on life, love, and childhood trauma). To complete the ensemble, string your neck with Indian bells and love beads—or pin on a button: *Power to the People; Turn On, Tune In, Drop Out;* and *Do You Grok?* are all suitable. The medium is the message.

Opposite page: center: *An attempt to straighten hair with orange-juice can curlers;* bottom left: *Levi's pushes bell-bottoms; members of a Seattle commune.* This page: clockwise from top left: *The granny-look; folk singers' stagewear is jeans; flower child in an advertisement for "Fleurs de Rocaille" perfume by Caron, 1963; Sonny and Cher; Michael York and Rita Tushingham in The Guru, 1969.*

THE ROMANTIC LOOK

This fashion evokes the Middle Ages or Middle Earth, depending on your orientation. To get this look, whether you're male or female, deck yourself out in velvet and frills. Let your hair grow long and luxuriant and leave your feet bare. A guitar or autoharp is a nice accessory, especially if you can play it.

THE AFRO LOOK

You don't have to be black to wear it, but this look works best if you are. Try it if you're ethnic, with curly hair, or get a permanent to mimic the full, tightly-curled look of the unstraightened "Afro" hairstyle. For clothing, choose loose-fitting dashiki with primitive designs, and accessorize with lots of beads, silver bangles, Indian bells, and large, dangling gold hoop earrings. Men, especially if they have read *Soul on Ice*, sometimes wear pure white caftans and shave their heads (this is a look which continues to be popular in some circles to this day). So do Hare Krishnas, though their costume, while similar, comes in saffron. The caftans are usually seen at rallies or at cocktail parties hosted by Leonard Bernstein.

Clockwise from top: Even an advertisement for pancake makeup takes on the natural look; bald is beautiful on Isaac Hayes; members of the Hare Krishna movement, begun in the U.S. in 1965; Jimi Hendrix, ca. 1968; Angela Davis at a rally in Los Angeles, 1970.

1968 RICHARD M. NIXON IS ELECTED PRESIDENT OF THE UNITED STATES.

1968 THERE ARE NOW 78 MILLION TV SETS IN THE U.S., 19 MILLION IN BRITAIN, AND 10 MILLION IN FRANCE.

OTHER 1960s groups also "do their own thing" in the liberated spirit of the age. Two popular prototypes are:

THE STRAIGHT LOOK

This style is usually seen on football players, cheerleaders, and other citizens not considered hippies. Men might wear cleanly pressed suits and shirts with polished shoes. Hair is clipped close to the skull and faces are clean-shaven. Women get manicures, wear shirtdresses, and practice saying, "Are you on that pot stuff?" A variant of the straight look taken to its ultimate is an ensemble made up of a blue uniform, a billy club, and a gas mask (riot helmet optional). In either case, both sexes must support Johnson, Nixon, and the Vietnam War, must refrain from listening to Beatles records, and must think Bobby Sherman is adorable.

THE RED-NECK LOOK

This is a regional interpretation of the straight look, commonly seen in dark Southern bars or in highway diners where the waitresses wear pink. Rednecks are always male. They are seen in white T-shirts and Levi jeans, though, unlike their hippie counterparts, their pants taper at the ankle rather than bell out. For footwear, construction boots are de rigeuer (you use them on the job), and a close-cropped crewcut is a must have. Biceps are often over-developed, and are bright red on the left side of the body from driving the pickup with one arm out the window. The right bicep and neck are often red as well, as a result of working long hours outdoors. The redneck look is often accessorized with tattoos, "gimme" caps, and beer cans.

Clockwise from top left: Donny and Marie Osmond don't have a drop of hippie in them in 1976; Mississippi's state flag; redneck still unchanged in 1990; Clarence Williams III, Peggy Lipton, and Michael Cole in "Mod Squad," 1968; beauty contestants from Smile, 1975.

TO FURTHER YOUR STUDIES OF THE '60S:

1. Read the complete works of Herman Hesse and Kahlil Gibran.

2. Take the Pill.

3. Get into herbal teas.

4. Practice saying, "Oh, wow, far out!"

5. Go to India.

6. Join a commune and raise organic corn and wild children.

AMERICA THE BEAUTIFUL

In 1968, Abbie Hoffman unfurls a flurry of consternation as he appears on Merv Griffin's TV show dressed in a shirt made from an American flag.

BIG

The late 1960s are expansive times—the economy is booming and men are spreading their fashion wings. Not since the last dandy gasp of nineteenth-century Romanticism have men dressed so, well, grandly: bell-bottomed pants with thick-soled platform shoes, wide-width ties, long hair, and mutton chop sideburns.

Clockwise from left: *The times they are a-changin' as 20 years later, flag-motif clothing (here, shirt designed by Mitch Chen for Camacia, 1989, photograph by Jim Malucci) are popular; Abbie Hoffman and his shirt for which he was charged with mutilation of the flag, 1968; ties, 1970; shoe boot, 1976; bargain hunters, 1990.*

WORN AGAIN

IN THE LATE '60S AND EARLY '70S a secondhand clothes revival has hordes of shoppers scouring consignment and thrift shops, flea markets, swap meets, tag sales, and even the Salvation Army. Reverse chic declares that old clothes are now "antique clothes." Why? There's a shortage of affordable clothes made from natural fibers and good workmanship is hard to come by at any price. Individuality is also key: Chances are nobody is going to see herself coming and going in a 1940s Swing Shift dress.

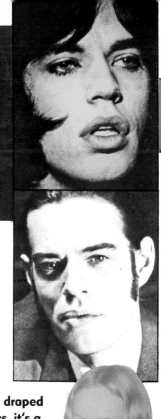

1969 ON JULY 21, NEIL ARMSTRONG TAKES A GIANT STEP FOR MANKIND ON THE SURFACE OF THE MOON.

SEXUAL DIFFUSION

Tarzan was unequivocably able to say, "Me Tarzan, You Jane."

But in the 1960s, when everyone is equal, it's sometimes hard to tell the girls from the boys... and vice versa. Lest parents despair, remember that through history there have been other moments of real confusion:

• In ancient Greece, males and females wear chitons draped the same way. But since women rarely venture outdoors, it's a safe bet that that lone figure on the Parthenon steps is a man.

• In the fifteenth century, despite clergymen's laments that they "can't distinguish the sexes," both men and women don the tight-fitting cotehardie, and take their chances.

• In the sixteenth century, there's a little reversal (which some see as a setback): Women wear doublets, while men, with their peascod bellies and bombast-filled jackets, look like pregnant ladies.

• Long before *La Cage aux Folles,* seventeenth-century men are using blue eye shadow and powdering their noses. They wear petticoat breeches with lots of lace and bows and periwigs, long, curly masses of hair. They use fans in the summer and muffs in the winter—and their heels are even higher than the ladies'.

• In the nineteenth century, the "La Lioness" set of Paris wear tight-fitting riding jackets, men's top hats, and sport pistols and whips.

• In 1926, the boyish figure is in; and flappers everywhere are borrowing their boyfriend's cufflinks, shirts, pajamas, sweaters, scarves, and hats to look sexy. Marlene Dietrich travels the streets of Paris in a man's suit and tie. And men, wanting to make their own fashion statement, take to "oxford bags," trousers so extremely roomy that they look like skirts.

• For the next thirty years or so, men get macho and women, buxom and leggy. And then along comes Twiggy. Soon women everywhere are starving themselves to look like her—that is, like a hipless, breastless adolescent boy.

• Thin is still in, and unisex fashions remain the vogue: From the long hair, jeans, and T-shirts that both men and women wear in the 1960s, to the cropped hair and baggy pants of the eighties. Both men and women wear sneakers, running shorts, and T-shirts; men as well as women dye their hair and wear earrings.

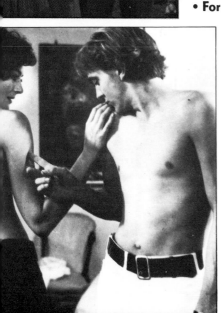

Clockwise from left: Vanessa Redgrave and David Hemmings in Blow Up, 1966; scene from Fellini Satyricon, 1970; Self Portrait, by Frida Kahlo, 1940; Dustin Hoffman in Tootsie, 1982; two faces of Mick Jagger in Performance, 1970; Twiggy, née Leslie Hornby, ca. 1970.

MILAN-AIRES

n the '50s, one-time Olympic ski team member Emilio Pucci catches the public's eye with *capri pants*, shorts, and swirling pastel-colored amoeba-like designs that are everywhere, from underwear to airline hostesses' outfits. But Italy is better known for frescoes and alfredoes until the Italian design industry steps up in the late 1960s and '70s. Worldwide customers clamor for slinky dresses and suits from Gianni Versace; Fendi furs; saddlemaker Gucci's leather goods and scaryes; Armani's perfectly proportioned suits; Missoni's fabulous knits; and in the '80s, kitschy clothes from Moschino, form-fitting layered looks from Dolce + Gabbana, and lady-like dresses and suits from Krizia.

Background: Wedding Procession of the Virgin Mary, Giotto, 1304–1306. **Clockwise from top center:** *Dolce and Gabbana design, 1991; coat-dress, Gianni Versace, 1990; Pucci outfit, 1967; alligator bag, Gucci, 1990; hooded fur stole, Fendi, 1990; man's suit, Armani, 1990; Moschino design, 1991; Missoni coat and blouse, 1990.*

UN-COVER GIRLS

Models like Verushka grow famous for the clothes they're *not* wearing in the 1970s, when everything is see-through. Barbra Streisand accepts the Academy Award for *Funny Girl* wearing a black, transparent sequinned pantsuit, and Cher shows off her curves on the cover of *Time* wearing a semi-transparent dress.

The extreme end of such revelations is "streaking"—making a naked run for it in public. Streakers make the scene at most major events in the '70s from the Olympic Games to the Academy Awards.

BY A HOSE

In 1970 distraught latex manufacturers spearhead an investigation to discover *what happened to the girdle.* Overwhelming evidence points to pantyhose, as well as to the let-it-all-hang-out ethos that makes it okay to jiggle when you walk. In 1974 football great and man-about-town Joe Namath makes history when he dons a pair of pantyhose for an ad for Hanes stockings.

Background: *American streakers in Paris, 1974.* Left: *Verushka in a cut-out body suit in* Blow Up, *1966.* Above: *Jantzen advertisement, 1948.* Above right: *Pantyhose advertisement.* Bottom right: *1950s leather-jacketed toughs in* Grease, *1977.*

ROCK AROUND THE CLOCK

The world is so fast-paced that in a mere twenty years there is a revival of '50s fashions. *The Last Picture Show*, *Grease*, and *American Graffiti* all contribute to the "new" popularity of black motorcycle jackets and circle skirts.

In response to the severe Courrèges lines of clothes in the '60s, in the early '70s there's an Edwardian revival, complete with lacy blouses, high, frilly necklines, and

REACTIONARY

cameos. Designer Laura Ashley, who makes loose, frilly, pretty clothes that look like they should be worn to a proper English pic- nic (and often dou- ble as wedding and maternity clothes), helps popularize the style. She uses 100 percent cotton and delicate nineteenth-century-looking floral patterns. The designs are so popular that not even a shrinking violet thinks twice about outfitting herself and her bed and even wallpapering her whole house in Ashley prints.

Background: Women in the Garden, Claude Monet, 1866–1867. **Top left:** "Arabella" print adapted from an 18th-century fabric, 1990. **Far left:** Straw hat with petersham trim, dress with a voile shawl collar, 1990. **Left:** Dress with a sweetheart neckline and a buttoned back, 1990. **Right:** Long dress with a tight ruffled bodice and a full skirt, 1983. **Below left:** Party-goer in hot pants from Dracula A.D. 1972. **Below center:** Ungaro print midi-dress, 1971. **Below right:** Striped hot pants on the set of "Hee Haw," ca. 1971.

EXTREMITIES

What can designers do to force women to revamp their mini wardrobes (and spend more money on fashion)? In 1970 they herald the Gibson Girl-length *midi* as the shape of things to come. Women (and the skirts, left hanging in department stores) remain unmoved. The fashion with legs the next season, however, is *hot pants*—thigh-high shorts, in satin, cotton, denim, and leather. Ironically, the fashion becomes hot in the winter, but dies down by the spring (when it might be more reasonable to wear them). By the late 1970s and early '80s both the mini and the midi re-emerge as popular styles. At first many women wonder about the "right" length. But it's only a knee-jerk reaction. Everyone soon realizes it's a matter of choice.

THE ALL MEN ARE CREATED EQUAL BUT SOME ARE MORE EQUAL THAN OTHERS DEPART-MENT

In 1973, Yves Saint Laurent "creates" the peasant look. Of course there have always been peasants, but in general, they've never had the time to be particularly fashion conscious. But as the forefather of that other great street stealer Ralph Lauren, Saint Laurent makes the peasant look "chic," in black velvet and swirling colored satin, like something women are willing to spend thousands of dollars on. The so-called "Gypsy" look becomes popular with the middle class too, who concoct their own versions from swirling chiffons, layered skirts, bangle bracelets, and big looped earrings.

The Algerian-born Saint Laurent scores his first hit in 1958, at twenty-two, with a little-girl-like "trapeze dress," that has narrow shoulders and a short, flaring skirt, which he designs for the House of Dior. In 1960, he looks around the streets of London, sees those American biker movies, and puts women into black leather jackets. He is drafted into the Algerian war; replaced at Dior by Marc Bohan; he opens his own house in 1962. Inspiration is everywhere: At the museum, he picks up Mondrian prints for his 1965 collection; the following year he puts men's smoking jackets on women; in 1968, more than seventeen years before they would be revived again by the *Out of Africa* craze, he introduces safari jackets; his 1969 pantsuits are a sensation.

Left: *Spanish gypsy, ca. 1941.* **Right, top to bottom:** *Yves Saint Laurent designs: "Russian Folklore" dress, 1976; "La Trapèze" dress, 1958; "Saharienne" safari jacket, 1968; "Momme" pant suit, 1969.* **Below left:** *Fashionable lady reading* Women's Wear Daily.

They walk around nameless until John Fairchild's *Women's Wear Daily* so ordains them. The paper, originally a trade publication, is filled with news on what's going on in the industry, fashion shows, parties, clothes, and best of all, gossip. Its sister publication, the splashy bi-weekly *W,* launched in 1973, has replaced the Gideon Bible bedside at all the best homes in the Hamptons.

THE BEAUTIFUL PEOPLE

PUNK FUNK

In 1974 Malcolm Mac Claren, co-owner (with designer Vivianne Westwood) of the London boutique "Too Fast to Live, Too Young to Die" (later shortened to "Sex"), meets Tom Verlaine and Richard Hell of the band "Television." Verlaine and Hell sport the first spike haircuts, which Mac Claren helps to popularize. The style is achieved by applying massive gobs of Vaseline to hold it in place, and then talcum-powdering down (à la eighteenth-century wigs) to relieve the wet look. The punk look is born.

Basic black—in turtlenecks, shirts, short leather skirts, and tight leather pants—is the mainstay of the punk uniform—accented by Mohawk haircuts in startling pink, fluorescent green, or purple. Of course, to avoid hair coloring decisions, some punkers simply shave their heads. Punks like to mix materials—they'll fling a squirrel fur over a chintz dress; stick feathers in their hair; women will don fuschia crochet golves. But their most important accessories come in metal—spikes and studs, heavy crosses, bracelets, belts, and safety pins—stuck lobe, chain, and several pairs of earrings worn in one through their noses. True punks slam dance and follow the beat of the Dead Kennedys. By 1980 the punk look has "crossed-over"—leopard skin slippers are seen in Bloomingdale's window, Tenax (to replace Vaseline) hawked by Vidal Sassoon and magenta hair highlights are worn by (some) ladies who lunch at La Cote Basque.

Clockwise from top right: Richard Hell, 1977; Patti Smith, 1977; Gary Oldman and Chloe Webb in Sid and Nancy, 1986; New York City artist with a mohawk, late 1970s; German rock singer Nina Hagen, 1981.

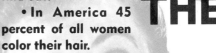

MAKE-UP MATH

Sixties makeup runs the gamut from layers of lashes and chalky lips to a nun-like abhorrence of artificial beauty. By the mid-1970s, to the industry's relief, the age-old impulse to "paint" is back. Here's how countries compare.

• Americans are complexion-conscious, with every other woman using makeup base and creams. But they dedicate 85 percent of their makeup dollars to perfumes, rouge, and blush-ons.

• The Swiss shun eye makeup and wear just a touch of lipstick, but 89 percent of their cosmetics budget goes to perfume.

• Canadians like to kiss and tell—90 percent of all women wear lipstick. Canadians also

wear twice as much eye shadow as Europeans, and 82 percent of all Canadian women wear perfume.

• Norway, with its dark winters, doesn't much go in for cosmetics: Only 40 percent of its ladies wear lipstick and only 11 percent use perfume.

• In France, chic mademoiselles spend only an average amount on cosmetics and, though long the center of the fragrance industry, only 58 percent of their francs on perfume.

Far right: *Farrah Fawcett, 1977.* **Right:** *Dorothy Hamill, ca. 1976.*
Above: *Lynn Redgrave in Smashing Time, 1967.*

THE HAIR FACTS

Blondes may or may not have more fun, but in 1975 a lot of women are eager to find out.

• In America 45 percent of all women color their hair.

• The Danes are close behind, with 42 percent—though they darken their hair, instead of lightening it.

• In France, only 10 percent color their hair, preferring the *au naturel* look.

• There are fewer dyed heads in Belgium than anywhere else in the world—a mere 4 percent of all women try to color away the gray.

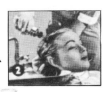

lovelier haircolor...

WHAT A DIFFERENCE A YEAR MAKES

Maybe you can't skate like Olympic medallist Dorothy Hamill, but in 1976 you can have your hair cut like hers. Your grandmother might think you've had your hair bobbed, but you can tell her the style is a "wedge." Of course, fame (and hairstyles) are fleeting, and a year later everyone wants to look like "Charlie's Angel" Farrah Fawcett. Now long, full hair with feathery wings is all the rage.

BORN IN THE

By the 1970s, American-based designers are really making their mark on fashion. The European press still isn't winging across the Atlantic for American ready-to-wear fashion shows, but they are taking notice of the young, clean, crisp American natural-fabric style represented by such names as sportswear designer Anne Klein; Calvin Klein, whose "designer" jeans are wildly popular; the textured tweeds, wools, and boxy jackets of Perry Ellis; Diane von Furstenberg, the princess who makes millions off of a perfectly-cut wrap-around dress; Ralph Lauren, with three-hundred-dollar denim skirts; Halston, Bill Blass, Oscar de la Renta, Adolfo, and Geoffrey Beene, who dress the ladies who lunch at Mortimer's.

U.S.A.

Top right: *Cape and hat, Anne Klein, 1990.*
Above: *Satin dress, Geoffrey Beene, 1971.*
Right: *Wool suit, Bill Blass, 1988.*

Center: *Merino wool knit ensemble, Perry Ellis, 1983.* **Clockwise from top:** *Diane Von Furstenberg in her trademark wraparound, 1978; wool pea coat over a sequin pantsuit, Marc Jacobs for Perry Ellis, 1990; "Harem-look," Halston, 1975; "Gypsy Dance," Oscar de la Renta, 1990; wool suit, Adolfo, 1978.*

Oscar

WHAT *WAS* IT ABOUT 1977?

The Birth of Venus, the Death of Reason: on January 23, 1977, a little-known designer named Serge Lapage unveils his latest creation—a diamond-studded

evening gown called "The Birth of Venus"—priced at $1,500,000.

On November 17, 1977, Miss United Kingdom appears at the Miss World Contest in a platinum bikini, valued at $9,500. She doesn't win the contest, but she does set a record—it is the world's most expensive bathing suit. (But given today's soaring precious metal prices it would cost a lot more, or would be a lot skimpier.)

In December of that same year, Emperor Field Marshall Jean-Bedel Bokassa of the Central African Empire commissions Guiselin of Paris to design a coronation robe. They come up with an enchanting little number, complete with a thirty-nine-foot long train encrusted with nearly 800,000 pearls, for a mere $144,500.

In 1978 Saturday night fever rages. The discotheques of the '60s and John Travolta in the '70s give rise to the look which, thanks to designers like Norma Kamali, Betsey Johnson, Stephen Sprouse, and Stephen Burrows, finally sees the light of day. The dance fever look, complete with shimmery spandex leotards, sequinned wrap-around skirts, glittery eye makeup, and disco bags—small bags that attach to a belt or are worn with a thin strap across the chest so that you can keep an eye on your pocketbag and boogey at the same time—are worn to the office.

DISCO KIDS

TO A "T"

By the late 1970s the short-sleeved cotton shirts worn by European men under their uniforms during World War I have become all the rage. T-shirts (named for their shape) sport political slogans, logos, jokes, and brand names. Like medieval tablons, they often express a wearer's convictions.

Clockwise from top left: *Emperor Jean-Bedel Bokassa, 1977; Bokassa in a red velvet cloak trimmed in ermine, 1977; T-shirt with a political slogan, 1990; Stephen Burrows disco ensemble, mid-1970s; Stephen Sprouse design, 1984.*

PREP

Do you wear a turtleneck, one or two cotton shirts, a crew-neck sweater, and a wool blazer all at the same time? Are your loafers tassled, your glasses horn-rimmed, and is there an alliga-

tor hibernating over your left breast? Do you favor Bermuda in shorts as well as vacations? Then you are a *prep-pie*. An upper-middle-class conservative dressed in retro '50s country-club style who, unless stopped, will grow up to be a *yuppie*. As a yuppie, you will sometimes revert to preppie dress on the weekends.

TALK

Clockwise from top left: Preppy posses-sions: double-breasted blazer, Brooks Brothers, 1968; tassle loafer with a beef-roll; penny loafer; buttoned-collar striped oxford shirt and tie, Brooks Brothers, 1979; young Republican in a Lacoste shirt; woman's madras wrap skirt and blouse, 1965; bride in Ralph Lauren flanked by attendants in Laura Ashley, 1985; worsted wool plaid jacket, 1960; trench coat, 1960; Shetland crew neck sweater, 1978. **Center:** Preppy Handbook, 1980.

T·H·E MALLING OF AMERICA

FROM ancient the Greek agora fairs where mereverything from to (authentic) it is just one bile ride to the markets like to medieval chants hawked silks and spices witches' brews, short automotwentieth century and the shopping mall, a Mecca for modern-day shoppers.

The word "mall" is Old English, and refers to a strip of green grass where a croquet-like game called pall-mall was played. After World War II, shopping malls, which are outdoor "strips" of shops featuring supermarkets, perhaps a shoe store or two, a local department store, and lots and lots of parking, spring up around the country. In 1956, architect Victor Gruen sets out to create a mall for a Minnesota locale where the weather is often extremely cold or extremely hot. His solution, an enclosed mall where the temperature is a constant comfortable 68 degrees, heralds the mall as we know it from the late '70s on. The modern mall is the new town square, where 50–60 percent of all of the nation's retail sales take place. Some 86 percent of us buy something to eat while we're there, and mingle with teenage "mall rats" (fifteen to nineteen years old), who spend an average of $25.96 each trip, a major contribution towards the three hundred billion dollars that the 25,000 malls across America take in each year.

Background: *Contemporary mall, 1990.*
Clockwise from left: *Layout for a mall near Philadelphia, 1953; teens from Valley Girl, 1983; Untitled, Barbara Kruger, 1987.*

TOKYO CLOTHES

Western design has been influenced by the Orient throughout the twentieth century, but usually indirectly, as French and English and American designers appropriate "Eastern" fabric patterns and silhouettes. But in the late 1970s and '80s, Japanese designers invade the West and revamp Western ideas about line, fabric, and even color. Many of the clothes introduced by the Japanese have the rectangular shapes of century-old kimonos, re-styled with boxy sleeves, hidden pockets, and an over-all, oversized, man-tailored look.

REI KAWAKUBO makes clothes that are sometimes torn or wrinkled, and often draped around the body. Kawakubo's early designs are extreme, and her company is aptly called "Comme des Garçons" (Like the Boys), because they ignore the female shape.

KENZO, one of the first on the scene, opening his sardonically named "Jungle Jap" in Paris in 1964, is known for his use of knits, Kabuki-colored tunics, wide-legged pants, and smocks, everything meant to be worn multi-patterned and layered.

The Hiroshima-born ISSEY MIYAKE worked for Guy Laroche, Givenchy, and Geoffrey Beene before striking out on his own with layered clothes.

YOHJI YAMATO makes unconstructed garments that envelop the body à la Comme des Garçons-style, accented with extraneous straps, pockets, and flaps.

Like a warrior in a Kurosawa epic, KANSAI's leopard-spotted fake fur football jackets and T-shirts (with his name boldly emblazoned in six-inch-high letters) accost all comers head on. Whoever dubbed the Japanese the "black pack" hadn't seen these lively creations.

Background: *Black wool geometric coat designed by Rei Kawakubo for Comme des Garçons, 1983.* **Top right:** *Off-the-shoulder dress and hat, Kenzo, 1990.* **Far right:** *Kansai T-shirt, 1982.* **Right:** *Dress by Yohji Yamamoto, 1990.* **Below left:** *Japanese dancers in kimonos with fans, 17th c.* **Top left:** *Japanese family crest, used to decorate garments, ca. A.D. 1000.*

1983 YOUNG AMERICA'S "TOP HERO" AC-
CORDING TO *THE WORLD ALMANAC*:
MICHAEL JACKSON.

1983 THE UNITED STATES INVADES THE
ISLAND OF GRENADA. THE UNITED
STATES WINS.

REF. NO.

ABCDEFGHIJKLMNOPQRSTUVWXYZ12345678901112123456791902O

DISK NO. 1

SUBJECT. MARKET PROJECTILE IMPACTION FORMULATION OF COMPUTER-
AGE DRESS WITH VARIANCE FACTORS A) STYLE, B) FINANCIAL STATUS,
C) AGE, D) SEX, IF ANY, E) WEIGHT, F) LOCALITY)

BEGINRUN:

A "DRESS FOR SUCCESS" PATTERN HAS BEEN NOTED IN LARGE METROPOL-
ITAN AREAS, SPECIFICALLY IN LARGE CORPORATE STRUCTURES. FEMALE
GENDER WEARS BLACK OR NAVY BLUE SUITS WITH SLIM SKIRTS ENDING
BELOW THE KNEE. BLOUSES ARE WHITE, NO FRILLS, THOUGH SUBJECTS
MAY WEAR PRIM BOWS AT NECK MADE FROM BLOUSE MATERIAL, USUALLY
SILK. LOW HEELS ACCOMPANY SUIT. MINIMUM MAKEUP. SHORT, NEAT
HAIR, OR SMOOTH, STRAIGHT HAIR TO SHOULDERS, NO LONGER. SEEN
HAILING TAXIS IN KHAKI TRENCHCOAT, HOLDING FLAT CORDOVAN AT-
TACHE CASE.

MALE GENDER LOOKS IDENTICAL EXCEPT SUIT BOTTOMS ARE TROUSERS.
HAIR IS SHORT AND CONSERVATIVE, ALTHOUGH APPARENTLY BLOW-DRIED
AND MOUSSED. SHOES ARE GOOD LEATHER, EITHER LACED OR LOAFER
STYLE, BUT ALWAYS ITALIAN. BRIEFCASE IS SLEEK AND FLAT, PREFERA-
BLY WITH GOLD TOUCH TO MATCH ROLEX WATCH.

BOTH GENDERS WEAR SNEAKERS TO WORK IN CASE THEY DON'T FIND A CAB.
FEMALES HAVE BEEN SEEN WEARING WHITE POMPOM SOCKS WITH SNEAK-
ERS. BOTH CARRY SQUASH RACQUETS AND THE WALL STREET JOURNAL.

FOUND IN OFFICE WITH LARGE PICTURE WINDOW AND SOFA, IN HEALTH
CLUB (SEE FONDA, JANE), OR SHOPPING FOR CD PLAYER. ALSO FOUND AT
NEIGHBORHOOD TAKE-OUT FOOD STORES WHEN NOT DINING AT CHIC RES-
TAURANT WITH LOTS OF NOISE AND BABY VEGETABLES. TASTES RUN FROM
SPICY CAJUN TO MASHED POTATOES AS LONG IS IT IS HIP. RECOGNIZ-
ABLE OUT OF UNIFORM BY VEHEMENT DENIAL AND DISCLAIMER OF YUP-
PIEDOM. LIKES THE GOOD LIFE AS PRESCRIBED BY SOMEONE ELSE.
NEVER LEAVES HOME WITHOUT THE GOLD CARD AND KNOWS MOST OF THE
WORDS TO OLD MOTOWN SONGS BY HEART.

▌**Opposite page:** *Photograph of a yuppie couple by Sheilah Scully, digitized by artist, Nancy Burson and David Kramlich, 1990.*

PRIESTLY GARB:

In January 1980 a most unusual name appears on the Best Dressed list alongside those of New York Mayor Ed Koch, actor Ted Knight, horse trainer Frank Wright, and Sheik Ahmed Zaki Yaman: Pope John Paul II.

Top left: *Fashion pundit Pope John Paul II.* Above: *Medal of John Paul II.* Below left: *Magazine illustration of "Custer's Last Ride," 1935.* Below right: *Polo by Ralph Lauren advertisement.*

PRAIRIE FLOWER

In 1981, Ralph Lauren introduces the retro/metro cowgirl look. All New York is flouncing around in layers of petticoats and denim skirts.

The fitness-conscious 1980s change not only our notions of femininity but also our physical shape—a 1983 study issued by the American Society of Podiatrists reports that one in every ten American women now wears a size ten shoe or larger, the result of increased participation in dancing, jogging, and aerobics.

BIG FOOT

D CHANEL UPDATE

esigner Karl Lagerfeld takes the helm at Chanel in 1983. His shorter skirts, re-designed versions of the classic jacket, baroque jewelry, and mix of T-shirt chic and couture keep the profit—and prophet— margins of the house on course. Madam would have approved.

S WISS SWITCH SWATCH

In 1983 time-honored Swiss watchmakers make Swatch the watch of the moment.

Top: *Plaid Chanel suits by Karl Lagerfeld.* **Right:** *Swatch advertisement, 1990.*

●In 1984 singing superstar Madonna markets her look. Would-be "Wanna-Bes" can buy lace tank tops, rolled tube tops, tight skirts, and black

LIKE A MERCHANT

elbow-length fingerless gloves from Madonna's teenage clothing line, or off lingerie racks, or from their favorite knock-off company around town. Accessorize with spiked heels, gobs of jewelry, and a waif-like look. But don't count on this as "investment dressing." Always wanting to keep everyone a little off guard, rock's prima donna leads a new trend in 1986: Back to the Fifties, à la her sleek blond-hair, red-lipped, tight-dress Marilyn Monroe look.

Clockwise from top center: *Madonna in Desperately Seeking Susan, 1985; Madonna's "Virgin Tour," 1986; Gaultier design for Madonna's "Blond Ambition Tour," 1990; Michael J. Fox in The Secret of My Success, 1987; Madonna at a press conference to promote Who's That Girl?, 1986; an original: Marilyn Monroe in Gentlemen Prefer Blondes, 1953.*

The public embraces the Monroe-comeback and blonde hair, Marilyn jeans, clothes, perfume, and towels, are all bestsellers, thanks to a push from Madonna and Monroe's enduring fascination.

SUSPENDER ANIMATION

By the mid-1980s, though Yuppies are still ascendant, corporate dressing has come to be a bore. Everyone wants some flash, but not at the risk of seeming too frivolous to make partner. The solution—*suspenders*, that time-honored Clarence Darrow look, snappy but still conservative. Rediscovered by British teens in 1985, suspenders sweep the United States the following year. At pricey Paul Stuart's, suspenders outsell belts by four to one—at $80 a pair. Purists still think that suspenders are meant to hold up your pants, but hipper wearers let them dangle from the waist.

Clockwise from left: Jean-Paul Gaultier, 1989; Gaultier's "Cut-out," 1989; stretch dress and fishnet gloves, Azzedine Alaïa, 1989, Alaïa T-shirt dress, 1990; a Claude Montana—selected drawing of a Claude Montana design, 1989; suit by Thierry Mugler, 1988.

LET'S FACE IT—a fuschia Thierry Mugler jacket with red "splotches," a tightly cinched flaring waist, and shoulders out to *here* might frighten a lot of people in Des Moines, or anyone living or traveling in more conservative communities. Some of this avant-garde designer's more outré

THE SHAPE OF THINGS TO COME

creations would be well-suited for a Wagnerian opera— and in fact, Mugler did design critically acclaimed fantastical costumes worn for the Comédie Française production of *Macbeth*. But along with designers like Claude Montana, Jean-Paul Gautier, and Azzedine Alaïa, Mugler and other Europeans are creating the shape of things to come. Body conscious and expensive, these clothes require a trust fund and a willingness to fast for a week before even trying them on.

407

1985 THE GOVERNMENT OF FRANCE ADMITS TO SABOTAGING AND SINKING THE GREENPEACE ANTI-NUCLEAR PROTEST SHIP, THE *RAINBOW WARRIOR*.

1985 NO ONE LISTENS TO E.F. HUTTON WHEN THE BROKERAGE FIRM TRIES TO EXPLAIN 2,000 FEDERAL CHARGES OF FRAUD.

EXCESS BAGGAGE

Contrary to popular opinion, deposed Philippine President's wife Imelda Marcos insists that she never had 3,000 pairs of shoes— only 1,060, including one pair that glowed in the dark (thanks to batteries). Unfortunately there were no magic slippers to whisk her away when she and Ferdinand beat a hasty retreat to Hawaii in 1985, nor room for her 508 ball gowns, 427 dresses, 888 pocketbooks, 464 scarves, 71 pairs of sunglasses, 65 parasols, 15 mink coats, or even one of her six silver fox stoles. The Marcoses did, however, manage to squeeze seven million dollars in cash and goods into the undoubtedly Louis Vuitton luggage, including 70 pairs of jeweled cufflinks, 75 watches, and two diamond-studded combs (valued at $135,000).

KARAN D'ART

The Claire McCardell legacy is carried on by designer Donna Karan whose "unitard" bodysuit dressing is an immediate success. Her sleek, modern, mobile collection is a result, she says, of asking herself, "What's missing from *my* wardrobe?" and then providing it.

ANKLES AWAY

In 1984 Don Johnson is elevated to TV star/sex symbol via his role in "Miami Vice," and the aid of his wardrobe woman: he wears pastel-colored loose linen jackets with T-shirts, gold watches, and loafers or sneakers sans socks.

Top left: *Imelda Marcos's shoes neatly stored in the basement of the presidential palace, Manila, 1986.* Top right: *Body suit by Donna Karan, 1985.* Left: *Claire McCardell's black jersey bathing suit, 1953.* Far left: *Stubbly Don Johnson, 1984.*

HORSE
CLOTHES

DI-MANIA

A frankly fashion-conscious Princess Diana provides a real shot in the arm for a flagging British fashion industry in the 1980s. Not since the 1960s era of Mary Quant and the miniskirt has British fashion enjoyed such popularity. No mere mortal can match the advantages of the 5'10", size 8 princess, which include two personal full-time dressers. But nothing can stop us from copying her style. Diana wears hats and hat sales soar; in 1983 Clarks, the footwear makers, report sales of 23,000 pairs a week of Di-style flats; her fake pearl earrings earn their designers several U.S. boutiques; and thousands of women follow her, well, like sheep, when she wears her now-famous black sheep sweater. She out-glitzes Joan Collins in gowns by Bruce Oldfield, and creates a minor sensation in a fishtail-backed, velvet-collared Belville-Sassoon suit. Everything she wears in public hails from Britannia, although in private she does enjoy slipping into Italian duds.

Marrying a prince has a way of calling attention to a girl, and when Prince Andrew slips a ruby and diamond engagement ring on Sarah Ferguson's finger in 1986, the sale of rubies takes off; and her quite conservative ivory silk wedding gown is, predictably, the season's most sought-after style. At first the size 14 Fergie is dubbed "frumpy" by the London press. But there's also something breezy and refreshing about Fergie's style—here's a lass who eats three squares a day and still landed Andy. Fergie loses some weight and goes to Saint Laurent for some stylish new clothes, but she's still no match for her sister-in-law. Diana lends Fergie a black and white dress for a much-publicized visit with Andrew on HMS *Brazen*, and then wears it herself a month later. On Fergie, unhappily, it looks like a let-out housecoat; on Diana, the old clothes look smashing.

Clockwise from left center: *Diana in a gown by Bruce Oldfield; Diana in a dress by Murray Arbeid with which she wore one red and one black glove, 1987; Diana in a series of hats; Sarah Ferguson, 1987; the Duchess of York, Christmas 1989; official engagement portrait of Prince Andrew and Sarah, 1986.*

409

SKINS AND NEEDLES

While tattoos are somewhat déclassé for men today, they're downright chic for women (witness Cher's derriere). The Egyptian word "tattu" means eternal — originally tattoos, which have been found on Egyptian mummies, may have been a way of preserving significant facts forever. Medieval Britons tattooed too, and in 1066, the body of Harold of Hastings bore the inscription "Edith" over his heart. Tattooing went out of fashion for a while, but in 1769, returning from a trip to Tahiti, Captain Cook repopularized the art. Accompanied by the "Great Omai," a decorated Polynesian, Cook toured London's finest drawing rooms. The Duke of York, Tsar Nicholas of Russia, and Lady Randolph Churchill all sported tattoos.

Today: ⋎ One in every ten Americans has a tattoo. ⋎ A man's tattoo is usually on his arm or chest. Look for a woman's on her thigh, shoulder, or buttocks. ⋎ Men are sentimental. They honor mother, sister, or lover by having her name elaborately etched across a heart or a bunch of flowers. Crucifixions are popular with men, too. The most popular motif for women is the much more flighty butterfly. ⋎ The most decorated man in the world was Vivian "Sailor Joe" Simmons, a Canadian tattoo artist with 4,831 designs on his body. ⋎ About one third of a tattooist's work involves "erasing" existing tattoos. ⋎ Truman Capote interviewed thousands of murderers for his bestselling *In Cold Blood*. The only thing they had in common, said Capote, was that every one of them had a tattoo.

In 1987 Christian Lacroix opens the first new Paris couture house in twenty years. Two years earlier as a designer for Patou,

POUF!

everyone wondered if his instant reputation, like his flitty, fluted bouffant dresses, was inflated. But Lacroix proves he's not a "pouf" in the pan.

A BUSH-EL AND A PECK

Women love Barbara Bush in 1988 and her three-strand fake pearl necklaces.

Counter-clockwise from left: *Barbara Bush surrounded by a genuine pearl choker, $140,000 in 1990; Pouf skirt by Christian Lacroix, 1987; Tattooed sailor, 1942; Maud Adams in Tattoo, 1980.*

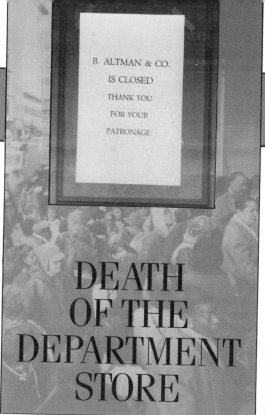

DEATH OF THE DEPARTMENT STORE

Greed and mismanagement spell doom for department stores in 1989, as B. Altman's closes and Bloomingdale's, Abraham and Strauss, Sterns, and Saks are sent into bankruptcy. Bonwit Teller bites the dust the following year.

PEDALING YOUR WEARS

Bicycle caps, day-glo Spandex bicycle shorts, and tied-around-the-waist bicycle messenger pouches ride onto the fashion scene in 1988. By 1989, these street-inspired fashions have made their way into Lacroix, Rykiel, and even Chanel's spring collections.

Top left: Crowd waiting for the doors to open on the first day of B. Altman's liquidation sale, November 24, 1989, and (inset) a sign now hanging in the vacant store's window. **Top right:** New York City bike messenger, 1990, and (inset) Chanel biker shorts, 1990. **Right:** Skin-tight striped dress by Sonia Rykiel, 1990. **Above:** By 1990, inspiration moves from land to sea as the wet-look Chanel suit by Karl Lagerfeld recalls the California surfer look (inset).

WESTWOOD HAUTE

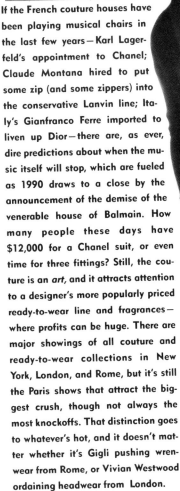

If the French couture houses have been playing musical chairs in the last few years—Karl Lagerfeld's appointment to Chanel; Claude Montana hired to put some zip (and some zippers) into the conservative Lanvin line; Italy's Gianfranco Ferre imported to liven up Dior—there are, as ever, dire predictions about when the music itself will stop, which are fueled as 1990 draws to a close by the announcement of the demise of the venerable house of Balmain. How many people these days have $12,000 for a Chanel suit, or even time for three fittings? Still, the couture is an *art,* and it attracts attention to a designer's more popularly priced ready-to-wear line and fragrances—where profits can be huge. There are major showings of all couture and ready-to-wear collections in New York, London, and Rome, but it's still the Paris shows that attract the biggest crush, though not always the most knockoffs. That distinction goes to whatever's hot, and it doesn't matter whether it's Gigli pushing wrenwear from Rome, or Vivian Westwood ordaining headwear from London.

A BLAST FROM THE PAST

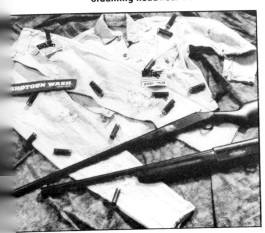

It seems you have to be quick on the trigger to get a leg up on the jeans business today. Taking aim on the market (with a twelve-gauge rifle), the Tennessee-mountain-based clothing company Jensen-Smith blasts denim jeans and jackets full of buckshot holes. The look is the latest... but is it new? Hardly. Cowboys in the Old West had a good chance of ending up with bullet-riddled duds—and they didn't have to pay $70 for the privilege, either.

THE DRY LOOK

Terry cloth comes out of the towel closet as designers show terry cloth jackets for spring. Just the thing for an April shower.

DOWN TO THE LAST DOLLAR

Optimistic 21-year-old designer Christian Francis Roth wraps up his spring '91 collection with greenbacks. Is this his idea of a money-back guarantee? Onlookers agree that this dollar looks strong.

Top left: *Vivienne Westwood headgear.* Center: *Romeo Gigli design, 1987.* Top right: *Basco's terry sports jacket, 1990.* Bottom left: *Jensen-Smith jeans, 1990.* Right: *Christian Francis Roth design, 1990.*

RE-REVIVAL OF THE FITTEST

In the fast-paced world of 1990, what goes around comes around—only more quickly. Now it doesn't take centuries for a style to make a comeback— just the next gen- eration, who obvi- ously ad- mire the fashions of the '60s.

Top left: *On the left designer Patricia Clyne uses lots of leg to update sportswear manufacturer Jack Windsor's 1964 basic fitted schoolgirl jumper.*

Top right: *A re-"vamped" Ivana Trump adopts Brigitte Bardot's 1967 sex-kitten-framed-by-beehive-hairdo look.*

Right: *Yves Saint Laurent's "Mondrian" dress, 1965; Adrienne Vittadini "Mondrian" sweater, 1990.*

Left: *In 1965, Paco Rabanne's plastic disc dress was considered racy. Twenty-five years later Michael Kor's "Tiddly-Wink" shift (inset) is cool and sophisticated.*

Above: Of the same bent: On the left, stretch clothes worn by New Wave actress Bernadette LaFont in Claude Chabrol's 1960 **Les Godelureaux**, and a contemporary model in Norma Kamali.

Right: The All American Jackie Kennedy look: **Above**, from Mary Quant, 1967; below, 1990-style, Byblos.

Which twin has the Toni? Or is wearing the "old" dress? On the **right**, a 1969 "glitter" dress; **far right**, Ronaldus Shamask's new silver mini.

Girls in swirls: Balenciaga evening wear from 1967 and (inset) Romeo Gigli's updated version.

Cut from the same cloth: **Above,** an off-the-rack knit print mini-dress, 1968; **below,** superstar designer Azzedine Alaia's knit print mini-dress.

Above left: Who could forget the sleek "Avenging" Diana Rigg? No one this year, as scores of designers show one-piece "cat-suits." **Inset,** Randolph Duke's version.

Top right: In "The Age of Aquarius," Pucci prints were the middle-class answer to the counter-culture's explosion of patterns and colors. After the staid 80s, Pucci prints seem wild themselves. **Far right:** (how much hipper can you get?) Lady Miss Kier Kirby of the pop group Deee-Lite.

Right: Now you see it . . . now you see it again: the plastic raincoat, 1966 style, on actress Jill St. John; and, **near right,** updated by Marc Jacobs for Perry Ellis.

PICTURE CREDITS

Photograph courtesy of Adolfo, Inc., p. 397.

Photographs by Thierry Chomel, courtesy of Alaïa New York, pp. 407, 414.

Photograph from the Amherst College Archives by permission of the Trustees of Amherst College, p. 268.

Photographs from AP/Wide World Photos, pp. viii, 2, 3, 4, 7, 94, 338, 341, 352, 354, 359, 362, 380, 382, 383, 384, 386, 388, 390–391, 397, 398, 408, 411.

Photographs courtesy of Elizabeth Arden, Inc., pp. 190, 218.

Photograph courtesy of Arista Records, p. 394.

Photograph courtesy of Giorgio Armani Fashion Corp., p. 390.

Painting by Marc Chagall and sculpture by Giacometti © 1991 ARS N.Y./ADAGP, pp. 319, 365.

Photographs courtesy of Laura Ashley, Inc., p. 392.

Photograph courtesy of Avon Products, Inc., p. 308.

Drawing and photographs courtesy of Balenciaga, Inc., pp. 323, 373, 414.

Photograph by Nick Anderson, courtesy of Pierre Balmain Paris, p. 5.

Photographs by Wayne Barlowe, p. 373.

Trade card from the collection of Kit Barry, p. 251.

Drawing courtesy of Lance Karesch for Basco, p. 412.

Photograph © Roberta Bayley, p. 394.

Photograph by Rona Beame, pp. 6, 15.

Photograph from the collection of Rona Beame, p. 191.

Photograph courtesy of L. L. Bean, p. 335.

Photograph courtesy of Becton Dickinson Consumer Products, p. 333.

Photograph courtesy of Geoffrey Beene, Inc., p. 396.

Photograph courtesy of Bellville-Sassoon Ltd., p. 409.

Photographs courtesy of Benetton, pp. 114–115, 214.

Illustrations and photographs from the Bettmann Archive, pp. 4, 7, 208, 229, 238, 240, 244, 244–245.

Photograph by Gideon Lewin © 1988, courtesy of Bill Blass Ltd., p. 396.

Photograph from a private collection, courtesy of the Mary Boone Gallery, p. 400.

Photograph courtesy of Brazil Tourism Office, p. 329.

Illustrations courtesy of Brooks Brothers, pp. 313, 369, 399.

Photograph from Camera Press, p. 6.

Photograph courtesy of Camicia, p. 388.

Photograph courtesy of Pierre Cardin, p. 377.

Photograph courtesy of Cartier, Inc., p. 330.

Photograph courtesy of the Leo Castelli Gallery, p. 346.

Photographs © 1961 Clairol®, p. 382.

Photograph by Bill Claxton/Globe Photos, p. 382.

Photograph by Rob Rich courtesy of Patricia Clyne, p. 413.

Photograph by Hans Feurer courtesy of Commes des Garçons Ltd., p. 401.

Photographs courtesy of Courrèges, p. 377.

Illustrations and photographs from Culver Pictures, Inc., pp. 3(tr), 65(tr), 110(cl), 157(bc), 218(cl), 245(br,tc), 267(tr), 316(l).

Illustration and photographs courtesy of Dana Perfumes Corp., pp. 165, 374.

Photograph by Arthur Elgort courtesy of Oscar de la Renta Ltd., p. 397.

Photograph courtesy of Christian Dior New York, p. 366.

Photograph by Dan Lecca courtesy of Randolph Duke™ Luke Industries, Inc., p. 414.

Photograph from the collection of Marion Rosenthal Edelman, p. 319.

Chanel clothes courtesy of Einstein's, New York City, p. 351.

Photographs from the Dwight D. Eisenhower Library, pp. 360, 368.

Photograph by Michael Halsband courtesy of Elektra Entertainment, p. 414.

Drawings and photograph courtesy of Perry Ellis International, pp. 397, 415.

Photograph courtesy of Esprit de Corps, p. 329.

Photographs © Fairchild Publications, Women's Wear Daily, pp. 351, 398, 401.

Photograph courtesy of Fendi®, p. 390.

Photograph courtesy of Ferragamo, p. 371.

Photograph courtesy of Filene's Boston, p. 340–341.

Photograph © Jane Fonda, p. 269.

Photograph by Robert Foster, p. 370.

Photographs by P. Villacampa and drawings courtesy of Jean-Paul Gaultier, pp. 344, 406, 407.

Photograph by Georgia Gebhardt, p. 399.

Photographs courtesy of Romeo Gigli, pp. 412, 414.

Illustrations courtesy of the Gillette Company, p. 367.

Photograph courtesy of the Goodyear Tire and Rubber Co., p. 157.

Photograph courtesy of Gucci America, Inc., p. 390.

Photograph by Adrian Boot courtesy of Island Records, Inc., p. 200.

Photographs courtesy of Izod Lacoste Menswear, pp. 342, 399.

Photograph courtesy of the Jantzen Archive, p. 328.

Photographs courtesy of J. C. Penney Company Archives, pp. 381, 414.

Photograph courtesy of J. Crew, p. 222.

Photograph courtesy of Jensen-Smith, p. 412.

Photograph from the collection of Mary Jewitt, p. 2.

Photograph courtesy of Betsey Johnson, p. 345.

Photograph courtesy of Norma Kamali, Inc., p. 414.

Special thanks to the Metropolitan Museum of Art for the following:

p. 25: {figurine} Harris Brisbane Dick Fund, 1949. (49.165)

p. 27: {chaplet} Excavations of the University of Pennsylvania and the British Museum, 1927–28; Dodge Fund, 1933. (33.35.347)

p. 31: {relief profile} Gift of John D. Rockefeller, Jr., 1933. (33.16.2)

p. 39: {cylinder} Purchase, funds from various donors, 1886. (86.11.1)

p. 42: {relief} Photograph courtesy of the museum.

p. 43: {netted birds} Photograph courtesy of the museum. (33.8.18); {coffin} Museum Excavations, 1930–1931; Rogers Fund, 1931. (31.3.102A)

p. 45: {bald gardener} Photograph courtesy of the museum; {jar lid} The Theodore M. Davis Collection, Bequest of Theodore M. Davis, 1915. (30.8.54); {kneeling figures} Photograph courtesy of the museum.

p. 47: {toilet box} Gift of Edward S. Harkness, 1926. (26.7.1438) Gift of Edward S. Harkness, 1927. (27.9.1) Gift of Miss Helen Miller Gould, 1910. (10.130.1269) Rogers Fund, 1910–11. (10.176.54); {face mirror} Fletcher Fund, 1920. (26.8.98); {toe guards} Fletcher Fund, 1922. (26.8.185–202)

p. 48: {linen} Rogers Fund, 1927. (27.3.105); {musicians} Photograph courtesy of the museum. (30.4.9)

p. 52: {statue} Rogers Fund, 1948. (48.111)

p. 53: {falcon necklace} Museum Excavations, 1906–1907, Rogers Fund, 1907. (07.227.12, 08.200.30); {vulture collar} Photography by Egyptian Expedition, MMA.

p. 55: {female head} Rogers Fund, 1919. (19.2.6)

p. 56: {Hatshepsut} Museum Excavations, 1922–1923; Rogers Fund, 1923. (23.3.2); {wall painting} Photograph courtesy of the museum.

p. 57: {game} The Carnarvon Collection, Gift of Edward S. Harkness, 1926. (26.7.1287)

p. 58: {sandals} Photography by Egyptian Expedition, MMA; {relief} Photograph courtesy of the museum.

p. 64: {vase} Bequest of Joseph H. Durkee, Gift of Darius Ogden Mills, and Gift of C. Ruxton Love, by exchange, 1972.

p. 68: {Amazon} Gift of John D. Rockefeller, Jr., 1932.

p. 70: {vase} Rogers Fund, 1906. (06.1021.189)

p. 72: {statuette} Rogers Fund, 1912. (12.229.19)

p. 74: {Nike} Rogers Fund, 1921. (21.88.62)

p. 78: {weavers} Fletcher Fund, 1931. (31.11.10)

p. 112: {shawl} Gift of Mrs. Russell Sage, 1916. (16.80.5)

p. 121: {tapestry} The Cloisters Collection, Gift of John D. Rockefeller, Jr., 1937. (37.80.3)

p. 126: {purse} The Cloisters Collection, 1952. (52.121.2); {man} Gift of J. Pierpont Morgan. (07.57.3).

p. 133: {sword} Purchase, The Lauder Foundation Gift. (1984.73).

p. 141: {veiled princess} Robert Lehman Collection, 1975. (1975.1.130)

p. 151: {goldsmith} Robert Lehman Collection, 1975. (1975.1.110)

p. 154: {helmet} Gift of J. Pierpont Morgan, 1917. (17.190.1720)

p. 161: {Bronzino} Bequest of Mrs. H. O. Havemeyer, 1929. The H. O. Havemeyer Collection. (29.100.16)

p. 166: {engraving} Gift of Georgiana W. Sargent in Memory of John Osborne Sargent, 1932. (32.37 Plate 40); {rings} Bequest of Emma A. Sheafer, 1974, The Lesley and Emma Sheafer Collection. (1974.356.649)

p. 183: {Poussin} Harris Brisbane Dick Fund, 1946. (46.160)

p. 192: {commode} The Jack and Belle Linsky Collection, 1982. (1982.60.82); {tassle} Rogers Fund, 1908. (08.103)

p. 193: {tapestry} Rogers Fund, 1946. (46.43.4); {candelabra} Gift of J. Pierpont Morgan, 1907, and purchase, Mrs. Charles Wrightsman Gift, 1989. (07.225.190ab, 1989.22.1-2)

p. 194: {Puritan} Bequest of Jacob Rubert.

p. 195: {Hals} Bequest of Benjamin Altman, 1913. (14.40.605)

p. 203: {underwear} Rogers Fund, 1910. (10.124.2-6)

p. 208: {textile} Rogers Fund, 1940. (40.134.15)

p. 210: {Incroyable} Harris Brisbane Dick Fund, 1924. (24.18)

p. 212–213: {Les Adieux} Purchase, 1934. (34.22.1)

p. 232: {Leutz} Gift of John S. Kennedy, 1897. (97.34)

p. 240: {French fan} Bequest of Mary Clark Thompson, 1924. (24.80.9); {English fan} Bequest of Mary Clark Thompson, 1924. (24.80.26)

p. 257: {tricorne} Gift of Georgiana W. Sargent in Memory of John Osborne Sargent, 1924. (24.63.737)

p. 290: {Castiglione} Gift of George Davis, 1948. (48.188)

We have made every effort to obtain the necessary permission to reprint the photographs and drawings in this volume, and to publish proper credit lines and copyright acknowledgements. We regret any error or oversight, and if informed of such, will make appropriate corrections in subsequent editions.